THE UNITY OF REALITY

*God, God-Experience and Meditation
in the Hindu-Christian Dialogue*

Michael von Brück

Translated by
James V. Zeitz

PAULIST PRESS
New York/Mahwah

A Note on Orthography

The problem of rendering non-Western systems of writing into Roman letters for English and other modern European languages is notoriously difficult. Joining many publishers who do not insert diacritical marks for words such as the Sanskrit *Śūnyatā*, this book also omits them.

Scholars and others who know languages such as Sanskrit, Pali, Arabic, or Japanese do not need the diacritical marks to identify words in their original written form. And persons who do not know these languages gain little from having the marks reproduced. We recognize that languages employing different orthographic systems have a richness and distinctiveness that are partially conveyed by the orthographics of diacritical marks. And while we do not wish to be part of flattening out the contours of our linguistically plural globe, the high cost of ensuring accuracy in using the diacritical remarks does not justify reproducing them here.

Copyright © 1986 Chr. Kaiser Verlag München. English translation copyright © 1991 by the Missionary Society of St. Paul the Apostle in the State of New York.

Library of Congress Cataloging-in-Publication Data

Brück, Michael von.
   [Einheit der Wirklichkeit. English]
   The unity of reality: God, God-experience and meditation in the Hindu-Christian dialogue/Michael von Brück; translated by James V. Zeitz.
     p. cm.
   Translation of: Einheit der Wirklichkeit.
   Includes bibliographical references and index.
   ISBN 0-8091-3214-1 (pbk.)
   1. Christianity and other religions—Hinduism. 2. Hinduism—Relations—Christianity. 3. Advaita. 4. Trinity. I. Title.
BR128.H5B7813   1990
231'.044—dc20   90-23584
                                          CIP

Published by Paulist Press
997 Macarthur Boulevard
Mahwah, New Jersey 07430

Printed and bound in the United States of America

Contents

Foreword

Many today are in agreement that an important—perhaps *the* important—theme of Christian theology is the encounter of world religions. We can only understand Christian faith and proclaim it intelligibly in the context of such an encounter, when we have become aware that Christianity is not alone, and that the truths of other religions cannot be met by superficial polemics. Christian reflections on God, for example, can no longer ignore Hindu ideas on *atman* and *brahman*, or Buddhist reflections on *dharma* or *sunyata.*

The author of the present book points to a similar convergence in the encounter and dialogue of religions; namely, how it involves a change in consciousness which has an effect on how global social problems may be solved. I am thinking of one of the theses of the ecumenical conferences of Chiang Mai in 1977 on interreligious diaglogue: "When world religions dialogue with one another they make a decisive contribution towards freedom and the humanistic, social quality of life in the future."

Interreligious encounter involves surprises. The theologian becomes aware that dialogue involves leaving behind preconceptions no longer able to handle experienced religious realities. For example, advaitic piety has been considered as monistic pantheism. That opinion is at best superficial. Its hidden prejudice is that a "monistic pantheism" excludes a personal face-to-face, an "I-thou" relationship. I have in mind such people as the Indian, Swami Ramdas (1884–1963), whose viewpoint is formally pantheistic (God in all things, all things in God), not theistic, while his spirituality and personal life of prayer are completely suffused with a personal trust in God, even a *providentia specialissima*, in all the details of his own life and the life of his neighbors. Our theological label, "monistic pantheism," becomes meaningless in this case.

A-dvaita—non-duality—should in no way be equated with monism. Advaita refers to what Christians call the sovereignty and

v

uniqueness of God, Nicolas of Cusa's *non aliud:* God is not simply an "other" to us and our world, which would limit us, but also be limited by us.

What is needed in interreligious discussion are particular studies, i.e., studies of particular instances of encounter or confrontation between individual concepts and manifestations such as Advaita and trinity, which analyze the structures of the two in all their similarities and differences so that they enlighten one other. Dialogue theology, a special need today, is theology which is not all-knowing in advance, but knows how to accept the adventure of a particular encounter. A general unified "theology of religions" brings us no further along our path. Nor can such a theology be an experiential basis for growth, since it is not grounded in an individual thinker.

By contrast, individual studies based on trustful experiences of encounter and dialogue bring us further, and their multifaceted results and insights can have heuristic meaning for future reflections and experiences.

The work of my friend Michael von Brück is an example of such a study, and I thank him for my first direct experience of the spirituality of Hinduism and for the insight that there is a widespread intellectualism in our Western Christian theology regarding the truth of lived faith (our intellectual style of pure distinctions, positions, counterpositions and erudite observations), and that we must develop new, more dialogical styles of reflection.

Heinrich Ott

Introduction

Western culture is determined more by reflection, Asiatic cultures by meditation. The meeting of the two is *the* important historical event of this present century.

Carl Friedrich von Weizsäcker[1]

I

The thesis on the rationality of the West and meditation in Asia needs interpreting. The relationship between rational thinking and meditative experience is not generally clear. This is the underlying theme of the present study. In Asia one finds, at least implicitly, all the themes which have determined human cultures in the last two thousand years. And in Europe, conversely, there is an experience of meditation.

The encounter of European and Oriental cultures takes place daily in many ways. There are many reasons for this exchange. Furthermore, this meeting continually affects the destiny of both partners. At the very least it leaves unmistakable traces; at best it can change the paradigms of our present worldview. What Thomas Kuhn,[2] examining the history of the scientific revolution, has called "paradigm shifts," can be applied to cultural movements. Paradigm shifts are basic changes in the way culture is determined. They are turning points. They alter the way people view truth, as well as their standards of behavior, their educational ideals and social relationships.

In the past the confrontation of different cultures and views of truth—such as the heliocentric and geocentric worldviews—has led to current paradigm shifts. Today, too, we are at a turning point in our history, and it is probable that the meeting between Europe and Asia will be an important factor, although not the only factor, in constructing a new paradigm of truth, behavior, political organization and religious thought. Unless, of course, today's nuclear

1

power struggle and mindless economic development terminate our history, this history will end up greatly strengthened by the encounter of peoples and religions.

The present paradigm shift is closely united with an awareness of the *unity of truth* which is gradually gaining strength. In the new paradigm, which recognizes life as a unity, we learn that rational, definable concepts run into difficulty. More often than not, rationality leads to fragmented truth. Fragmentation is the result of a viewpoint that cannot or will not coordinate the various aspects of truth. In order to confront fragmentation in all areas of life—at a time when the disastrous consequences of this worldview are becoming evident—a holistic method of viewing truth is needed, of the kind present in Eastern meditation techniques. However, were we to give up rationality, we would destroy the bases of our lives. The problem, then, becomes one of seeking out new avenues for the encounter of cultures, ways which allow both rationality and meditative consciousness to exist in polarity and thus open up a new field of knowledge that makes evident the unity of truth.

To understand this important question and find ways of solving it, we must turn to the past, for human reflection is dependent on its own past history. In the history of religions are there similar situations, symbols and ideas which would help us to find our way in the present? We are seeking models which help overcome fragmentary thinking. This search will necessarily be intercultural and it presupposes dialogue between religions. It will involve *dialogical theology.*

Christian theology will risk isolation if it does not take advantage of this situation as an occasion for deepening and renewing its own spiritual history. Exclusivity and denominationalism can neither proclaim evangelical freedom nor meet present needs, especially the need to find new symbols and models for the unity of humankind. Thus, encounter between religions is an important, perhaps *the* important theme of present Christian theology, not out of mere opportunism, but of inner necessity.

Dialogue as a human necessity was already made into an epistemological principle by Socrates. Today dialogue is a worldwide process. Only through dialogue are democracy, pluralism, justice and peace possible. Today's religious ecumenism grounded in dialogue has been gaining ground since the Second Vatican Council, as well as the dialogue program of the World Council of Churches. It now determines in a more decisive way the church's self-understanding. The Sixth General Assembly of the World Council of

Churches in Vancouver, 1983, described dialogue as a "mutual risk to give witness to one another and to the world in relationship to various conceptions of ultimate truth." In dialogue it expected a growth in knowledge "concerning God's work in the world" and hoped that the "insights and experiences which people of other faiths have of ultimate reality would be treasured for their own sakes."[3]

We cannot go here into the details concerning what has already been done or the as yet unsolved problems. A great part of the work is a matter of clarification. The dialogue partner is a mirror in which one's own weaknesses or strengths are reflected. Mutual mirroring leads to deepened self-understanding. The climax of dialogue occurs when the other becomes a source for my own self-understanding. When this happens people of different faiths experience interpersonal communion rather than struggle. In terms of our subject matter here, this implies that Advaita can become the source of the self-understanding of the trinity.

The fact that interreligious dialogue remains a marginal concern in German theology is largely owing to the power of majority rule.[4] The danger is that ecumenical development will bypass the German churches. This would be a shame for both parties: for the German churches, because they would become provincial, and for the ecumenical movement because it needs the rich historical and theological heritage of the churches of Germany.[5]

However, the situation is changing, and even for German theology there are three important reasons for entering into sincere dialogue. Here the competence that comes from knowing well the partner's position will become necessary on hermeneutical grounds.

1. The decline in the churches and the crass materialism which has affected church life call for a *totally* new paradigm. The meditative paths of Asia lead to healing and it is worth our while to examine them, theoretically as well as practically, to see if they can bring about an improvement.

2. "Sects" and "youth religions"—although we consider this over-generalized description inadequate—are arriving from Asia and India, gaining influence in "Christian" countries. The reasons for this are many. One possible explanation is that they are a response to the materialism (and fragmentation) mentioned above and provide new (for Europe) ideas on spirit and community. If we are to understand this phenomenon we must study its background, not polemically, but by entering into its self-understanding. Our

task, then, is to study and understand Indian religions and especially *Indian meditation* and *Yoga.* By analyzing the theological roots of these practical methods we can come to understand their almost magical drawing power and see consequences for our own theology and spiritual praxis.

3. Whatever the expression "responsibility for our world" may mean, it implies that we cannot return to traditional worldviews and interpretations which are culturally exclusive. It calls for holistic thinking and *global* structures of truth, and this will have consequences for particular localities. It encourages us to look for traces of the unity of truth even if this means reformulating traditional concepts.

Thus, dialectical theology's notion of a total difference between God and humanity must be supplemented by the new notion of a dialogical theology, which doesn't contradict the first idea, but rather sublates it into a more complete notion of truth, where the *universal* aspect of a *pax Christi* is realized and the disciples of this Lord become in fact salt, light, and leaven within the worldwide struggle against the power of evil and the evil of power. In no way should this dialogue become the fig leaf of the powerful, who cooperate with one another in order to further their own form of interreligious peace at the expense of the powerless. The experience of the unity of truth should not mask its present disunity! What we will be demonstrating here is not undertaken as a mere gesture to liberation theology, but involves a direct link to a trinitarian notion of God, or an Indian non-duality.

II

The difficulty of a method for dialogue is a hermeneutical problem. It can only be worked out and studied through dialogue. We distinguish different levels and dimensions of dialogue in chapter 13. The unity we envisage here is not just at the level of theories, but a "meeting of worlds."[6] Naturally this meeting also has theoretical consequences, as will be demonstrated in part III.

Our concern is not so much with individual concepts, but with the models or functions which bring these particular concepts together in a system. Thus we aim at a holistic rather than a piecemeal method. Mutual understanding of *symbols* plays a key role here since in the symbol we experience truth creatively. A symbol is the intersection of different subjective experiences. It is the place where truth comes to consciousness, mirrors itself, and unites itself with truth. By our knowledge of symbols we partake in the creative growth of truth. If we wish to understand the totality and unity of truth we must ask about the symbols which represent this totality and make it appear to our consciousness. The trinity is such a symbol. Its function corresponds to what in India is advaitic thinking.

A characteristic of our method of dialogical theology is that it does not try to take a neutral, objectivist position. Dialogue in religion can only be carried on in existential togetherness. A person who is not anchored in any religious tradition has not yet taken the step which all religions try to talk about in their own ways. Only when we are basing our inquiry on faith can we correctly see other faiths. This book represents a Christian viewpoint. It will ask whether the Indian non-dualistic experience can be meaningful for an understanding of the experience of Jesus Christ, and it will discuss the consequences of such an understanding.

The differences between the two experiences and theologies should not be underestimated. They are found, however, in different places than expected. What is especially important at the outset is to realize that India and Europe have quite different ways of beginning their quests for truth and of understanding what truth is. The "spiritual climate" and mentality of each is diverse. Nevertheless, there are amazing points of contact, and it will be our task to show why. Whether Christ or the Upanishads are "true" depends on a personal faith experience. Whether the meaning of the Upanishads can be further clarified in the light of Christ, or the Christian trinitarian experience of God in the light of Indian religion: this is the object of dialogical theology.

The first step in this dialogical hermeneutics is to understand encounter. Just as the human "I" only discovers itself in encountering another "I," and thus comes to maturity as a person in community, so, too, the encounter in a dialogue of religions leads to discovering oneself, and this makes possible *community*. This community is not merely a "common denominator" of different viewpoints, but is present within our personal identity, in a mutual in-and-for-another, and this does not involve giving up one's own identity. These types of relationships will be further examined in chapter 13.

The second step of dialogical hermeneutics is a demonstration of theological method. The individual symbols and thought forms are brought together in such a way that they mirror one another.

This mirroring allows all the particular details to remain clear, whether they are similarities or differences. To avoid the subtle dualism suggested by the image of mirroring (since one could inquire about the mirror as a separate substance) we suggest an acoustical image: If we think of one symbol or concept as in resonance with another symbol or concept, then the relationships between the two are heard as overtones or undertones—produced only by this *mutual* resonance.

In this way different religious experiences and their ideas can be mutually clarifying, without losing their individual identity. This image, originally proposed by Heidegger to explain the relationship between philosophy and theology, was applied to interreligious dialogue by H. Ott in order to talk about the contact between various religions.[7] We attempt to go a step further, since here the symbols and concepts not only touch one another, but penetrate one another, as is clear in the image of resonance. The resonant interpenetration causes the original identity to reappear at a wider, more explicit level. By taking on the particular qualities of the other, the enlightening power of our own thinking is strengthened.

Through interreligious dialogue we are seeking greater community among religions. The result is a differentiated maturing of all partners in their experiences of self as they take on responsibility for the world. This dialogical community can be a sign, as well as a response, to those who hold onto power or take pleasure in devaluing others and using humankind's torn condition for their own interests. Dialogue is a path which starts with and leads to mutual trust. It is not content with coexistence, but seeks *pro-existence.* No further demonstration should be needed to convince us that this being-for-another in dialogical partnership is basically a Christian concern.

Self-discovery means either discovering oneself or discovering one's *self.* Thus, self-discovery means experiencing the self in the broadest sense. We experience the unknown, or it overtakes us, as a lost past. Otherwise there would be nothing to discover. We do not experience what we already know, but only what awaits us. Thus it should not be surprising if what we are to experience here embarks us on a strange journey. Only through deeper experience and critical testing of this experience does the light of *anamnesis* gradually dawn, so that what we learn is finally recognized as our own self which was hidden. Our own tradition becomes clearer. Since distinct lived-experiences are interpreting one another mutually, only through this process do they become fully conscious. But the experience can also be one of completing the other. The dialogue partners can lead one another to their depths. Dialogue is mutual giving and receiving.

What we are, we are according to what our past has been. Thus to experience ourselves we must experience what has been thought before us. Experiencing oneself is only possible by connecting oneself with tradition and by the mediation of tradition. Furthermore, what we are, we are in relation to our future. The future is the realization of possibilities which are now implicit. They belong to us even though we may not be explicitly aware of them. Dialogue is explication. It is an undiminished act of being present. Confronted with the future we make pronouncements that are probable, and this holds true for theological theories which are to be realized in the dialogue of religions.

When we are in a process, we are on a way going towards something. This implies risks and dangers. One such danger would be theological syncretism. Another way which appears to me even more dangerous, however, is complicity in shallow compromises. This way does not perceive or perhaps even suppresses ongoing *spiritual challenges*. The person who avoids being on a way learns nothing. But the one who sets out on a way advances towards his set goal even though he may fail to reach it. "The one who would avoid the risk of praxis also misses out on its opportunities."[8]

III

We must first limit the scope of our study. We will only be able to examine one Indian religious philosophy, Advaita Vedanta. There are many reasons for this choice. The Vedanta, i.e., essentially, Upanishads which are considered part of Vedic literature, the *Brahma-Sutra*, and the Bhagavad Gita, have been interpreted non-dualistically (Advaita), in a modified non-dualistic (*visishtadvaita*) manner, and dualistically (*dvaita*). The great systematicians of these schools were Sankara, Ramanuja, and Madhva. We will be following the advaitic interpretation and mainly (though not only) Sankara (A.D. 800). This philosophical school became known in Germany through the romantics, and especially through the work of Paul Deussen. Advaita Vedanta can easily be discussed because it was systematized in such an exemplary intellectual way by the brilliant thinker, Sankara. In India Advaita Vedanta is widely

known. It is still influential today in discussions about the concept
of God. Its philosophy interests us especially because its thought
process operates in terms of wholeness, and it provides a coherent
model for the unity of truth. Advaita Vedanta also seems to me to
offer the best interpretation of Indian meditation techniques.

Advaita means non-dual. It denies not only duality but every
abstract "ism." Advaita intends to be a way to experience, that is,
to experiencing reality as oneness. We cannot emphasize enough
that it is not an example of monism, but rather of non-duality. The
central question in Advaita Vedanta is: once we accept non-duality,
how can the world of the many appear and be understood?[9]

Advaita Vedanta does not set itself in opposition to other philosophical views, but rather seeks to integrate personalist and dualist
positions. This throws light on its pedagogy which will be treated
below. A pronouncement or statement—and therefore also truth
—depends on the standpoint of the viewer. Seen from a certain
standpoint the world may appear dualistic, and God may seem to
be opposed to the world. At a higher level, that of integrated consciousness, this duality is overcome—dialectically (sublated). This
is the non-duality of reality.[10] The question may arise whether this
is a true experience of being.[11] The dualism behind this question is,
however, either denied by advaitic philosophy, or considered as
overcome.

This is precisely where our interest begins. Our central question could be formulated as follows: what does Indian advaitic experience mean for the Christian concept of God? Can it motivate us
to reinterpret the intentions of the doctrine of the trinity, elevating
it to a more universal level rather than leaving it within its Judaic
and Hellenistic context?

Our study is divided into three parts. Any true understanding
of a dialogue partner involves knowing his or her way of thinking.
Thus in the *first part* we begin by presenting the philosophy of
Advaita Vedanta so that the reader may enter into a dialogue, and
become capable of making a judgment. However, we will not be
able to discuss differences of schools, which would be needlessly
confusing and unnecessary for the task at hand. We focus especially on problems that are relevant to religious dialogue on the
God question. We also study the original texts which are at the
basis of later generalizations, following mainly the commentaries
of Sankara.

In the *second part* we attempt to rethink the Christian trinitarian concept of God. As a necessary preliminary for this we present

the basics of this doctrine, not attempting completeness, but only what is theologically relevant to the dialogue with Advaita Vedanta and what contributes to holistic thinking. We begin historically by presenting the outstanding thinkers who first worked out a trinitarian concept of God or those who creatively reworked it. It might at first seem strange that we pay little attention to the great theological summaries of the scholastics, especially Thomas Aquinas. But there are two reasons for this: first, there are already many outstanding studies by Catholic theologians on the dialogue between Thomas and Sankara, and I do not believe I could add anything (Cf. works by Richard V. de Smet). Secondly, scholasticism's concept of the trinity goes back to the intuitions of Augustine. Only in the mystics and later in Luther do we see explosive new experiences which shake up earlier systems of thought and lead to a new consciousness that will have far-reaching historical consequences. This will involve an unconventional view of Luther, and this view is connected with my conviction that the background of Indian spirituality provides a new appreciation of Luther's experience of temptation. There will be more to say about Luther, but *one* aspect of Luther and *one* possibility of explaining his theology will be considered below in the section devoted to his theology. We will see that his theology offers a way of entering into dialogue with India, a dialogue which, in fact, has already produced fruits in Catholic theology. Hegel's system remains one of the high points in Western holistic philosophical systems. Thus, the fact that the doctrine of the trinity was of great significance to Hegel is not surprising. Chapter 9 is devoted to the problem of totality and unity in present-day trinitarian theology.

In the *third part* we will attempt to work out a dialogical notion of God which enables the advaitic experience and the trinitarian experience to interpret each other mutually. This is the project of a dialogical theology. Its innermost nucleus is the non-dualistic interpretation of the doctrine of the trinity, which thus appears as the universal symbol for the unity of truth. We will conclude with a discussion of the consequences of this for interreligious dialogue and for Christian participation in meditation and Yoga as well as for a dialogical grounding of a universal ethics.

The final impression that emerges from this should not be one of a synthesis which would sublate (*aufheben*) the thesis of Indian Advaita, as well as the thesis of Christian trinity by means of a third, where the final conclusion would be a standpoint higher than either of the previous two theses. Rather, what we have in mind is to make a contribution to Christian theology by means of an advaitic notion of the trinity. The encounter with India would thus have set in motion a process and would follow a direction which would justify the universality of the meaning of Christ in a new way. Our work is an attempt to begin this process. It does not intend to reach definitive conclusions but rather to be a beginning.

For this beginning I am obliged to many theologians who have already set out in this direction. A complete listing of these, mostly Indian, theologians is not possible. But I wish at least to acknowledge Raimundo Panikkar, Swami Abhishiktananda and Bede Griffiths.[12] I have indicated in the text whenever I have used their ideas. Their influence, however, is much more extensive. They have taught me in many ways to judge what the advaitic experience is, how to be sensitive to it, and to recognize its spiritual and theological meaning today. I wish to mention especially my respected teacher, the late Professor T. M. P. Mahadevan, an admirer of Sankara and himself a recognized authority in advaitic philosophy. During countless hours of dialogue he introduced me to Indian philosophy.

A few more remarks about the structure of the third part will help orientate the reader. Chapter 10 interprets the holistic symbol of trinity non-dualistically and reflects on the concept of the *unity of reality*. This is the key to the following chapters which deal with the different dimensions of unity (chapters 11–13) and—in the light of our fragmented experience of truth in a world corrupted by sin—have this unity as a *task* (chapters 13–14).

Chapter 11 demonstrates that the theses of chapter 10 are not theoretical postulates, but verifiable hypotheses which can be demonstrated on the basis of a certain *experience*. Any phenomenologically exact definition of experience (Sanskrit *anubhava*), a notion which is presupposed by Advaita Vedanta and penetrates this work, is however premature. We still know too little about the advaitic experience and can only attain knowledge through personal praxis over long periods of time. The concept of *anubhava* itself points out a path. It is based on the root *bhu* (to be, to become) and describes a becoming near to, a being along with or next to. The advaitic experience is, therefore, knowledge of the ultimate mystery of being which is attained by being fully "next to," or by participating in a truth along with which a person journeys. The idea of practising dialogical theology as a new type of theology of experience was suggested by H. Ott,[13] who however added that it should in no way be construed as a return to subjectivistic psychological experience, where the religious subject is the only source of knowledge. Instead, what we must examine is the experiential event *between* different subjects who participate in the subjectivity of God. The question about the subject of religious experience can, as we suggest in chapter 11, be addressed in a new way by means of advaitic categories. The analyses and reflections on the possibility of verification of advaitic experience is of great importance, since this experience claims to be transformative. As a transforming power it would be an important key for a changed awareness of wholeness and perhaps an entry point into the ontological basis of the genuine Christian ideal of pro-existence—existing *for* the world.

This matter will be treated in chapter 12, for it involves the process of maturing into a person. We consider there the interrelationship of individual destinies and total meaning. Pro-existence is expressed in personal love. If the experience of the unity of reality and individual, lived pro-existence, are to come together in a meaningful relationship, then reality must be interpreted personally and be fulfilled in the wholeness of love. Thus, although we consider wholeness important, we cannot bracket out the question of transpersonal individual human destiny. We thus attempt a Christian interpretation of the Asiatic teachings on rebirth.

The basic thesis of the unity and the inherent personality of truth will be scrutinized in relationship to the core of the Christian message in chapter 13. Christ's salvation as a universal gracious act of God can be recognized as the very essence of the trinitarian self-revelation of God, and therefore it appears as a symbol for the inclusive unity of reality. We will discuss the consequences of this for the church's self-understanding in its dialogue with other religions according to the different vantage points of present theological discussions (on, for instance, the church, mission, syncretism, conversion).

The concluding chapter 14 will at least partially resolve the claims of the thesis of chapter 10, namely that the experience of unity is also at present a task in a world alienated by sin and egocentricity. The essential question there will be: what is holistic Christian praxis?

IV

One of the essential requirements for undertaking this study is to appreciate the difference between Advaita Vedanta experience and the Christian experience of God. The Vedantic experience is the experience of pure being. It is a return to the undivided essence. It is an experience of non-duality with God who is being (*sat*). In the personal trinitarian experience of God there is a growth towards identity, a dynamic identity, which in comparison with the more static identity in Advaita Vedanta is also *concrete*.

Despite this distinction between the two, there are also essentially inherent relationships, which we will try to clarify. What the two experiences mean, no one can say who has not "seen" God—thus, no one (Jn 1:18). But in both experiences there are latent relationships. In the trinitarian as well as the advaitic experience there is an experience of God's working and presence which, when it grasps a person, offers new ground to stand on and grasp truth. There is then a "becoming flesh" of the trinitarian concept of God, on the one hand, and the non-dualistic and transpersonal experience in India, on the other, which can be seen as two possibilities for the one spiritual event of God to become visible to humankind.

All of this is in reference to an urgent problem of our times. The advaitic experience and its meditative realization can give birth to a new consciousness, which is urgently needed everywhere today by responsible people in all walks of life. "We need fearless research on the question of what is meant by the unity of nature, humanity and God in the light of science and an all-embracing ecumenism which includes African and Asiatic ideas on culture. I mean that the churches would then recognize more clearly than they do at present their duty to fill the earth with salvation for all humankind and all creatures—before it is too late. If we wish to tear down the barriers of poverty of nearly two-thirds of all peoples on earth, a revolutionary change in relationships between peoples on earth and of peoples among themselves is needed. The churches of the world must now decide whether they will take part in this revolutionary change."[14]

Certainly one, and perhaps a decisive presupposition, as well as an opportunity for such a new orientation, could lie in the advaitic experience and its practice of meditation, since it creates an integral consciousness and makes possible a holistic way for humans to achieve identity.

I

Non-duality in Hinduism

1.

Absolute Brahman

The history of Indian religion is a history of countless religious phenomena and structures that intertwine to form a seemingly impenetrable thicket. This makes any description complex. Different traditions, cultural forms, and types of religion are so closely intermeshed that to isolate one tradition is something of an art. Theistic and non-theistic forms, action and contemplation, piety based on one or many gods all come together. Almost every caste or every village has its own form of religious life, so that the overall term, *Hinduism* seems hardly justifiable. Nevertheless, there is a difficult to define bond which holds together this diffuse religious world.

One of the most important polarities that frequently threatened to divide the Indian subcontinent was the tension between worldliness and flight from the world. Vedic religion was marked by an exaltation of nature and cosmic powers. The cosmic realm and astrology stirred the imaginations of the invading Aryans. The world of natural powers, such as the strength of horses or the exuberance of tropical vegetation under the bright sun, drew attention to itself and fascinated this people. In it they experienced a manifestation of the divine. It was the principal theophany.

Some time after 1000 B.C. there must have been a spiritual turning point for all of India which brought a radical change and eventually influenced the whole of Asia. The thirst for this-worldly splendor and belief in its constancy were shaken. People turned away from *maya* and began to look within themselves. The macrocosm no longer attracted them. Instead, the wise (*rsi*) sought as source for the manifold sense data a center deep inside, in the microcosm. They discovered *atman*, the true self, the subject and tranquil ground of all.

Furthermore—through a particular spiritual experience—they discovered that it was not different from *brahman*, the ultimate ground of all being. By controlling the body and the senses, the wise (*rsi*) were able to mature in their experience and begin

15

discovering the human mind. Even today this is still in process and influences Western cultures.

A peculiarity of India is that Vedic this-worldliness was never completely replaced by later Vedantic other-worldliness. Both tendencies continue to confront one another in ever-new historical forms. Admittedly, Buddhism and Jainism around 500 B.C. were reactions to a religion excessively oriented toward sacrificial piety. Nevertheless, the attempt to turn away from the world, whether it is prescribed in Vedantic literature, in the Buddhist Sutras or by Patanjali's Yoga-Sutras, is always surrounded by Tantric tendencies, which experience the One not beyond the many, but rather sacramentally in the power of the sensual.

Over the course of time, Vedantic literature has had a significant influence on nearly all religious movements and paths (marga) in India, and has generated various interpretations. Especially influential was the non-dualistic (Advaita) school of the great Sankara (ca. A.D. 800), since it succeeded in uniting the powerful and coherent Madhyamika-philosophy of Nagarjuna with bramanic religion, and thus became the rejuvenating force which countered Buddhism in India. It did this through a process of integration, although in the process the social demands of Buddhism—especially overcoming the caste system—were side-stepped.

Sankara provided a philosophical basis for the Bhagavad Gita's teaching on the unity of the three ways of action (karma marga), devotion (bhakti marga), and intellectual contemplation (jnana marga). On the other hand, he shows conclusively that intuitive knowledge of the One is the pinnacle of spiritual fulfillment. Action without self-interest (naiskarmya), as well as fervent devotion to God (bhakti) are, however, important and necessary elements along the path of unity.

In Sankara's thought reality is contemplated and clarified from two different standpoints: the absolute standpoint (paramarthika) and the relative standpoint (vyavaharika). The absolute standpoint discloses reality as undifferentiated unity and allows this oneness to be known itself, without qualities and as impersonal One (nirguna brahman). The peace and tranquility of oneness sublates the phenomenal experience of the many and of differentiated things in space.

The relative standpoint (vyavaharika) makes possible conditioned knowledge of the One, i.e., according to its visible qualities (saguna brahman). The experience of the many and of history is of relative worth, but is not to be thought of as experience of the real: this is the error of conventional wisdom.

The Basics of Advaita Philosophy

Advaita philosophy is characterized by the non-duality (Advaita) it posits between the experiencing subject and the object experienced, and of God and the world. Transcendence and immanence merge into one at a point beyond the horizon of ordinary thinking and experiencing.

The personal center (jiva) of the individual is essentially the Self (atman), which is beyond the particularities of physical-psychic-mental life or of any changeable things or of change as such. Atman is, in the final analysis, identical with the one and universal reality (brahman). Brahman is immutable, eternal, self-sufficient existence, free from any determination. It is the one-without-a-second (advitiya), true being (sat), pure spirit (cit), and final bliss (ananda). This essence of the macrocosmic as well as microcosmic reality is unity, which only unfolds into many because of human illusion.

The term Advaita is negative. It does not describe a monistic ideal, but implies a negation of dualism. And this negation applies both to two-ness as well as to the attempt to grasp the world as a whole by means of any logical system with rational distinctions.[1]

Because brahman is beyond duality it cannot be known conceptually, nor can it be substantially or qualitatively determined, for this would imply a division of the One. Brahman is immutable and immaterial. "Since it is incorporeal it is aniruktam, ineffable. Anything that has attributes can be expressed in words. If it has attributes it is mutable. But brahman is immutable. Thus it is the source of all modifications. Therefore it is ineffable."[2]

For Sankara, brahman alone is real so that the world does not possess reality in this sense. Humans have their ground in a personal center, (atman), which is a kind of "living monad" (H. Zimmer) underlying their individual self and not different in the final analysis from the Absolute.[3]

The experience of non-duality in Being is the basis of Advaita philosophy.[4] Most people, however, are caught in illusion and live more or less independently, separated from the One. This illusion causes suffering. Advaita-experience is thus closely related to *moksa* (release). Our true Self (*atman*) is identical with *moksa*, yet we are ignorant of this fact. Thus we do not attain something that was not already there. Thus, too, what we really need to do is set aside our ignorance so that freedom may become real.[5]

Brahman is everything and is in everything. The one who knows this *becomes brahman*.[6] We must come to know "that the divine power of life which penetrates the whole world and swells up within each creature is the only indwelling reality."[7] This is the experience of non-duality or *moksa*, which alone guarantees final human interior, spiritual freedom (*santi*).

The basic philosophical question in Advaita Vedanta is the problem of the one and the many, or the relationship of God to the world. *Brahman* is pure, without attributes and indivisible. The world, however, is many and depends on changeable appearances. *Brahman* is bliss (*ananda*), while the world is full of evil and suffering. (*duhkha*). "The problem for the Advaitin is to solve how from the pure *brahman* the impure world of men and things came into existence."[8]

Monistic systems break down before this question, and it would be fully erroneous to interpret Sankara as a monist.[9] Sankara remains unerringly faithful to the narrow path of what, for him, is the one measure: God and the world as not-two (Advaita). Thus he understands *brahman* neither as the immediate creator nor as the material cause of the world. It is not the cause of the world, but is called the cause of causes (*yatah*).[10] It is the fully transcendent ground of the world which, during the process of becoming, is stability and resolution (*janmadi*). The ground itself cannot be encountered. God is not material cause in the sense of a *deus sive natura. Atman*, although fully immanent and infusing all, nevertheless fully transcends empirical reality.[11] Pantheism is out of the question.

Atman is overlaid with various sheaths, manifested from within to without as a series of steps, starting with the most subtle, pure spiritual expression of the one underlying reality and ending in the most gross, the material body. The Taittiriya Upanishad develops this theory as explained in Figure 1.1.

In the Advaita Vedanta there is no soul-body dualism. The structure of reality—and therefore of humanity—is rather a series of levels which are distinguished from one another by their degree of subtlety. That which has a greater range of effectiveness and capability for interpenetration, and therefore influences the other levels is more subtle. The result is a holistic psycho-somatology.

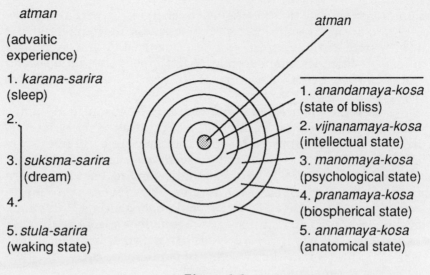

atman

(advaitic
experience)

1. *karana-sarira*
(sleep)

2.

3. *suksma-sarira*
(dream)

4.

5. *stula-sarira*
(waking state)

atman

1. *anandamaya-kosa*
(state of bliss)

2. *vijnanamaya-kosa*
(intellectual state)

3. *manomaya-kosa*
(psychological state)

4. *pranamaya-kosa*
(biospherical state)

5. *annamaya-kosa*
(anatomical state)

Figure 1.1

The five sheaths (*kosa*) are also interconnected psychosomatic
levels which conceal the Self (*atman*), the inner ruler (*antaryamin*)
which governs all without, however, becoming entangled in the
changes which take place in the sheaths. The material body is the
least subtle, and is called *annamaya-kosa*, the sheath of food.
Pranamaya-kosa is the more subtle sheath of vital energy which can
be observed especially in breathing. *Manomaya-kosa* is formed by
the mind and the senses. *Ratio* also belongs here. And beyond it is
situated spiritual understanding (*vijnana*). At this level are situated
rational cognition and intuitive knowledge. But *anandamaya-kosa*
is the sheath consisting of "bliss"—not the bliss which is *brah-
man/atman*, but its appearance in the world of change. The five
sheaths are like garments enveloping the self, the basic ground
which functions as a central power of integration. Its power of
integration seems to be drawn from the outside inwards. But this is
only appearance, since in advaitic experience we know that all the
sheaths are nothing else than *brahman.* The five sheaths form three
bodies (*sarira*); namely, the gross body (*stula-sarira*), the subtle
body (*suksma-sarira*), and the causal body (*karana-sarira*). The
gross body corresponds to the mental area of waking (*visva*), the
subtle to dreaming (*taijasa*), and the causal to deep sleep (*susupti*).
These connections are important for meditation which tries to pass
through the five sheaths to *atman*, and must start with waking

consciousness and then, using all its energies, penetrate succes-
sively to dreaming and sleeping consciousness, until finally, in the
fourth state (turiya), atman can be recognized.[12] This system of
human realities (the microcosmic aspect) applies also, mutatis mu-
tandis, to the overall structure of the world (the macrocosmic
aspect).

God is the Inner Ruler (antaryamin) in all cosmic and human
events of life.[13] He is the hidden subject of all activity (seeing,
hearing, understanding, etc.) and at the same time different from
all activity. Thus he is called the "unseen seer, the unheard hearer,
the unthought thinker."[14] Human understanding operates within
its activities or kosas; however, it cannot grasp its own ground. It
can understand, but it can't understand understanding.[15] Brahman
is all in all. Only where it is seen as saguna (possessing attributes),
as personal God, can it be reverenced. On the other hand, all that is,
is in it.[16] This remains true whether or not humans encounter pleasure or suffering (sukha or duhkha).[17]

The eternal is not outside of time, but in time. The temporal,
therefore, has no existence in itself. Not to recognize this is the
basic error of humans. If the world is seen for what it truly is—
namely, a dependent reality—it is not illusion. The illusion consists in having an unreal concept of reality and in taking what is
only a sheath of the real for the real. Real being (sat) can only be
brahman.

We cannot see the Absolute, basing ourselves on our mental
capacities; rather, the Absolute itself (nirguna brahman) reveals
itself by appearing as determined, qualified and therefore as a conceivable Absolute (saguna brahman). This revelation awakens
what we call reality, which therefore has a symbolic character.[18]
The Absolute is the relative, and the relative is the Absolute. They
are not two sides of one thing, but different standpoints, aspects,
i.e., cognitive positions from which reality can be regarded.[19]

In the experience which is at the core of Advaita, the duality of
God and world, reality and non-reality, freedom and entanglement
are forever sublated to one experience of the presence of the eternal
or the eternal present. Advaita is not subjectivism, but rather attempts to ground that which transcends subject and object.[20] God,
who despite maya is homogeneous, immutable, remains pure consciousness and therefore transcendent to all change.[21]

Despite this apparent unity, Advaita Vedanta does not overcome a certain distance or even hostility to the world.[22] In any case
this remains an ongoing discussion.[23] In the differing paths of Yoga

and the Tantras, which are both based on the advaitic experience, although they reject being interpreted through Advaita Vedanta, the world and the human body are integrated into a total framework of spiritual life.[24] In Yoga, the world as it is is real, but it must be spiritualized and overcome as an object of egotistical greed.[25] Also in the Advaita Vedanta—especially in its neo-Hindu interpretation—the emphasis is not on denying the world, but on recognizing the Absolute.[26]

In order to experience this complex unity and to attain rebirth to full holistic life, each spiritual exercise becomes a rehearsal for death: humans die to the world of the many in order to attain oneness. If they have gone through this "spiritual death," they know that the one is in the many and the many is in the one. Only the ignorant separate these two aspects.[27] The quintessence of Advaita may be seen in the following verse of the Bhagavad Gita:[28]

> He has the right vision who sees
> in all creatures alike the supreme Lord
> Who remains and does not die
> when they die.
>
> For when he sees the Lord dwelling
> in all and everything alike,
> He cannot be at war with himself.
> Thus he is on his way to the highest goal.

Tad Ekam

One of the most ancient attempts of humankind to think about the ground of the world is found in the Rigveda: *tad ekam*, the One.[29] It is undefinable. It cannot be called being, for this would be a determination, which implies a negation and would thus contradict the Oneness of the One. The concept of the Absolute, too, implies two-ness and is therefore unsuitable. *Tad ekam* is one and precedes every beginning and every possible future.[30] *Ekam* unfolds as world and yet remains beyond the world, although it infuses the world.[31] It doesn't remain abstract, but is called a "guest of humankind."[32] The most ancient hymns recognize in it the highest God who unites in himself all powers and forces.[33] Already in very early times *ekam* could be identified with *atman*.[34]

Tad ekam is one only, without a second (*ekam eva advitiyam*).

This is its only determination, for as pure negation it adds nothing.[35] It may become anything that can be thought, but remains "this." Thus the expression, *idam sarvam*, is encountered in many texts: all this, which designates reality as a whole.[36] From the beginning of Indian philosophy this basic experience of *ekam* determines all later developments. Along with *ekam*, there is emphasis on constancy, eternity and repose as the highest values. Everything changing, passing, manifold is relegated to appearance.[37]

The philosophy of the Upanishads develops rigvedic *ekam* by means of *brahman*. The word itself is derived from the root *brh* and means "growth," "expansion."[38] In Vedic times it meant the holy word of the ritual sacrifice or prayer. Thus it is also used to present or invoke numinous power. The root meaning points to a force which unfolds. This meaning underlies later philosophy, which describes *brahman* as without attributes and fully incomprehensible. *Brahman* is greatness—another aspect of the root *brh*—and beyond it nothing greater can be thought.[39] An early text calls *brahman* "that which is the cause of the source of this universe."[40] Or it is reality as such, upon which all other realities are dependent,[41] the great unborn soul,[42] the Lord of all things,[43] the ruler and king of all.[44] *Brahman* is self-illuminating, self-sufficient, and depends on nothing.[45] It is the primal light which reveals all else, while it itself is revealed by nothing except itself.[46] In the Bhagavad Gita all these aspects are joined and sung in a hymnal description of *brahman*.[47]

For *brahman* just as for *ekam*, the problem arises about whether the Absolute is being or non-being. Both possibilities were developed: *brahman* is non-being if it is understood as one object among others.[48] In reality it *is* without a second, *idam ekam eva advitiyam sat eva asti*.[49] *Brahman* is neither being nor non-being; it is beyond this distinction.

Empirical knowledge (*vyavaharika*) deals with the world of the many. It is based on distinctions and conclusions. By means of a higher knowledge (*paramarthika*) the wise recognize that which cannot be perceived (*adresyam*), that which is beyond sense knowledge (*agrahyam*), unbound (*agotram*), colorless (*avarnam*), eternal (*nityam*), infuses all (*sarvagatam*), and extremely subtle (*susuksmam*). It is the womb of all beings (*bhutayoni*).[50]

Although all these terms determine *brahman* analogically, they are not attributes in the strict sense (*mukhyartha*), but only point to it in a figurative sense (*laksyartha*).[51] *Brahman* remains beyond names and form (*nama-rupa*). It would not be the One if it were only knowing, being-powerful, existing, and not knowledge itself, power itself or being itself. For this reason it is said that *brahman* is truth, knowledge and infinity (*satyam jnanam anantam brahma*).[52]

Sankara explains the sense in which *brahman* can be called *cit* and *jnana* (consciousness and knowledge). These terms are not limiting determinations which would cause *brahman* to be in opposition to something else. For "knowledge, which is the true nature of the self (*atman*), is inseparable from the self, and so it is eternal. . . . Consciousness of *brahman* is inherent to *brahman* and cannot be separated from it, just as the light of the sun is inherent to the sun, or heat to fire. Consciousness is not dependent on other causes in order to be manifested, for it is by nature eternal light. And since everything which exists is inalienable from *brahman* in space and time, since (furthermore) *brahman* is the cause of space, time, etc., and since it is subtle beyond measure, there can be nothing—whether subtle or veiled or distant or past, present or future—which would be unknown (to *brahman*). Thus, *brahman* is all-knowing. . . . Nevertheless, the word 'knowledge' points to *brahman*. It is not determined by it. . . . Likewise, *brahman* is not determined by the word *satya* (truth, being), for *brahman*, by its nature, has no distinction at all."[53]

Brahman is power, as we saw above. This special aspect of the Absolute is called *sakti.* The power of the Absolute is distinguished in three forms: life energy (*prana*), the word (*vac*), and thought (*manas*).[54] In the *Agamas* these three powers are identified as the will (*iccha*), knowledge (*jnana*), and the action of God (*kriya*).[55] *Prana, vac,* and *manas* are the bases of all human functions.

Vac has four names which correspond to the four stages of revelation of the Absolute: *para, pasyanti, madhyama,* and *vaikhari.*[56] *Para vac,* the highest word, is the unmanifest *brahman,* the implicit and therefore transcendent force of the Absolute. The *pasyanti* form (manifested *vac*) is the dimension of revelation. It is a self-giving of the Absolute and is associated with the cosmic form of *isvara* (God as personal). The *madhyama*-form (the middle one) is the spiritual mediation and presentation of revelation. In its cosmic form it is associated with *hiranyagarbha* (the golden seed) and in its individual form with knowledge (*jnana*). The *vaikhari*-form is the sensible, audible word, and on the cosmic level corresponds to the manifold of appearances (*viraj*). At this point we may also indicate the correspondence with the four states of consciousness (deep sleep, dreaming, waking state, *turiya*).[57]

Thus, while the Absolute in its *saguna*-aspect appears in the various stages of revelation, so too can *vac*—as the very essence of *brahman's* power—be presented in its various cosmic as well as individually experienceable forms. It is significant that the perceived forms of *vac* perceived by the individual (*jiva*) are explained in connection with meditation.

Since all determinations are inappropriate to *brahman*, it seems empty, *sunya*, to the understanding. "*Brahman*, which is free from space, attributes, movement, effect and difference, which in the highest sense is one without a second, appears as nothing to common understanding."[58] But because of this freedom from all finite determinations it is perfect fullness (*purna*). This is what we find in the famous preface to the Isa-Upanishad:

> *purnamadam purnamidam purnat purnamudacyate purnasya purnamadaya purnamevavasisyate.*
> (That is fullness, this is fullness. Fullness comes forth from fullness. If fullness is taken from fullness, fullness remains.)

Brahman is not a product of becoming, but permanent being.[59] Thus it cannot be connected to or related to anything (*sambandha-anupapatti*).[60] Later we will examine how Advaita Vedanta nevertheless tried to solve the problem of the relationship of God and world in the sense of a specific "relationship of identity" (*tadatmya*).

Generally, *brahman* is the ontological principle of the world. It is not being, but the ground of being. The many is latent in the One, without negating this *oneness*. Name and form (*nama-rupa*), according to Sankara, exist latently within the self. They manifest themselves, but in their true nature remain indistinguishable from *brahman*.[61]

When *brahman* manifests itself—*saguna*—as world, it still remains what it is. Thus we could speak of *brahman's* simultaneous transcendence and immanence. Because the *saguna*-aspect makes it possible to think about the Absolute, there are proofs for the existence of God. Sankara's proofs do not have the same systematic force as Thomas Aquinas', but they are closely related to them.[62] Sankara is aware of the physical-teleological argument as well as the cosmological proof. However, the ontological argument is missing.[63] Perhaps it can be found implicitly in the explanation of the word *brahman*, which in its root meaning is explained as "that than which no greater can be thought." But this etymological explanation is not used as a philosophical argument.

Sankara introduces the physical-teleological proof to refute Samkhya philosophy, which believes it has found the basis of the world in unspiritual prime matter (*pradhana*). Sankara argues that unspiritual essences cannot cause spiritual, finality-oriented, meaningful creativity. Since we undoubtedly find finality-oriented and spiritual structures in the world, there must be a sufficient ground for this.[64]

The attitude towards which Sankara directs his polemics is characterized by a greater distinction between spiritual and material than is found in Advaita Vedanta.[65] In Samkhya's thought there is a basic dualism. The material world is a kind of nature (*prakrti*) from which the world emanates more or less blindly. The contrary spiritual principle (*purusa*) is an inactive subject.[66] In Advaita Vedanta, on the other hand, *brahman* appears as personal God (*isvara*) and, as ultimate ground, is the common principle of spirit and nature.

Sankara proposes the cosmological proof[67] in order to demonstrate that while everything in the world comes from something else, *brahman* was not caused, since this would lead to a *regressus ad infinitum*.[68] Another argument he uses has been called the psychological proof.[69] Since God is the one reality without a second, he is the self of all essences. Humans cannot doubt their own essence, since it is the basis for doubting. Deussen is therefore correct in subtitling his chapter on this, *cogito ergo sum.*[70]

Within the *saguna* aspect we can conclude the existence of God from the world. Analogy is possible. *Brahman*, according to its *nirguna* aspect, however, is beyond concepts. It is unconditional *ekam*, transcendent-immanent reality. Only through the *via negativa* can we say that it is not (*neti, neti*) anything we experience as objective in our world. For it is the unity of subject and object, which is beyond the rational possibilities of knowing.

Saccidananda

There is, nevertheless, a word in Advaita Vedanta which describes *brahman* in its totality and transcendence, without adding any limiting attributes. It is not so much a concept as a hymnic formula: *saccidananda* (*sat:* being; *cit:* consciousness; *ananda:* bliss).

From earliest times this expression has meant absolute reality, although it is not found in the Upanishads. The original form is *satyam-jnanam-anantam brahma* (being-wisdom-infinity).[71]

Both formulas mean the same thing. Another ancient expression is, however, connected with *saccidananda: yo vai bhuma tat sukham* (that which is alone infinite fullness is bliss).[72] *Sat-cit-ananda* is neither a part nor a property of *brahman.* The three united are, rather, the essential nature of *brahman.* That same threefold nature distinguishes *brahman* from the world of name and form (*namarupa*), which is unreal and untrue (*anrta*), unspiritual (*jada*) and filled with suffering (*duhkha*). *Saccidananda* is *brahman* itself. If *sat, cit,* and *ananda* were parts of *brahman* they could be distinguished. But this is not the case. For if being were separated from the aspects of consciousness and bliss, it would be nothing but tragic, suffering-filled nature, not being itself, and thus unreal (*asat*). If consciousness were separated from being and bliss, it would be non-existent and therefore spiritless (*acit*). Thus there can be no bliss which lacks being and consciousness. If *saccidananda* designated parts or modifications, it would be subject to change and would have limits. But a limited reality cannot be called the source of being.[73]

We will now examine briefly the individual parts of this formula:

Sat: The absolute cannot be limited or determined or related. We saw that, properly speaking, it cannot even be said that it *is.* Without either side-stepping the difficulty or complicating our presentation with hyper-concepts, we will speak of "being itself," which transcends being and non-being. Being itself is reality, and the nature of the real is existence, although the concept of existence should not be taken as an appearance nor as one species of the real: "Of the real there is no non-existence, and of the unreal, no existence."[74] Using the concept of reality in this sense is important in understanding Advaita Vedanta. It is related to absolute existence, not to relative existence, which only allows an empirical concept of reality. Each empirical object has five features, which have both an absolute and a relative character. The following absolute features are to be distinguished, and only these encounter *brahman:* 1. existence (*asti*), 2. manifestation (*bhati*), 3. lovability (*priyam*). However, 4. name (*nama*), and 5. form (*rupa*) are different from one object to the next and therefore belong to the inconstant appearances that come from the creative power of *brahman, maya.*[75] Existence, manifestation and lovability are identified as *saccidananda.*

Later Vedantic texts use an example to clarify the latter point:

the first product coming from the power of *brahman* is akasa, space (aether), which is material but also provides space where the material objects of the world can develop. Aether shares in the nature of the Absolute in that it exists (*asti*), is manifest (*bhati*), and attracts (*priyam*). Nevertheless, spatiality is a special characteristic that determines and limits, and therefore belongs to the world of *maya*. When it is said that aether is unreal in comparison to the Absolute, this does not mean that its existence, manifestation and lovability are unreal, but only that all elements that differentiate space do not have reality in the same sense as *brahman*. *Brahman* is absolute reality, while all the forms of existence that are determined by *nama-rupa* are relative reality. There *is* no spatiality (*avakasa*) before the aether (akasa) has become manifest, and also will not be once it (aether) ceases to be. That which is unreal at the beginning and at the end cannot be real in the middle. Beings are manifest only in the process of appearing, not at the beginning and end; that is, they are temporal. But *brahman* is supra-temporal. It is lasting existence, manifestation and attraction of love in the temporal appearances. *Brahman* is the substrate of all appearances.[76]

The use of aether to demonstrate the nature of the Absolute in relationship to the world can be verified in all the objects that are experienced. The reality-concept of the Advaita Vedanta teaches that *brahman* as *sat* is not something abstract having nothing to do with the world of appearances. *Brahman* as *sat* is immanent, and the world is real only insofar as it is *sat*. It is unreal when it is understood apart from its ground in being. Its temporal and spatial relativity is its relative reality.

It is noteworthy that in Advaita Vedanta the term *sat* cannot be discussed without referring to the world of appearances. Thus there is a certain relationship between the Absolute and the relative. But this should not be interpreted as a duality. The world is as it appears, the explication of the one *sat*. Therefore it is not-two (Advaita) with *brahman*.

It would be erroneous to see in the *sat* of *saccidananda* the starting point for an abstract metaphysics which would be rooted in ontology. We must remember that these are hymnic formulas which try to describe the experience of meditation. This experience is an intuition of being whose enlightenment is beyond differentiated rationality.

Cit: Brahman as nothing else than pure consciousness. It does not have consciousness as an attribute which would be determined by a subject, but *sat* is *cit*. *Sat* has no inside or outside. As such it is pure consciousness.[77] *Brahman* is neither the subject nor the object of consciousness, and it has no self-consciousness nor object-consciousness. This is the meaning of *pure* consciousness. R. Panikkar describes *cit* as the force of unity of *sat* which is not different from the One, but can be called its expression. Even in conventional human experience, consciousness can receive the forms of the many and remain one, which clarifies the non-duality in the one (*ekam eva advitiyam*): "In the world of human experience, in point of fact, consciousness is the only power that embraces the manifold without losing its identity and unity. A multiplicity of thoughts as well as the many objects and contents of consciousness do not disrupt but rather reinforce the unity of consciousness."[78] Human consciousness is only the appearance of the cit-aspect of *brahman*. All lights in the world are shining only insofar as they are enlightened by this one light.[79]

Cit is not only the ground from which all human knowledge is derived, but the dynamic aspect of the Absolute in general. All the power which is included in *brahman* without changing it, is *cit*. What appears as a polarity of static-dynamic moments is, in the Absolute as *sat-cit*, one. To demonstrate this the image of a force-field may be helpful.

In the famous episode narrated in the Taittriya Upanishad, the son, Bhrgu, asks his father, Varuna, for instructions so that he can recognize *brahman*. The father answers: bodily energy (*anna*), the energy of breathing (*prana*), sight (*caksu*), hearing (*srotra*), understanding (*manas*), speech (*vac*)—these are the means of recognizing *brahman*. What you must want to understand is that from which all these beings are born, by which, once born, they live, into which they enter when they die. That is *brahman*.[80] The dynamic power (*cit*) of the Absolute (*brahman*) appears in many ways and is found first in the gross forms of nourishment, then in the human spirit as the basis of all becoming.[81] The Absolute is the ground of being for the material as well as all living beings. Likewise it is the principle of all sense knowledge as well as understanding: "All this is set in motion by and built on consciousness (*prajnanetram*); consciousness is *brahman*."[82]

We may call *sat* the intuition of the experience of pure being, an "I am." *Cit* is the aspect of a conscious "I am." To experience that I am and to become conscious of this during the stages of meditation which leave behind the objectification of ego are the same thing.

Ananda: The ananda-aspect of *brahman* is the determination of lovability or attractiveness (*priyam*). This last part of the sacred formula *saccidananda* is the hardest to clarify, at least conceptually. It is the description of a meditative experience. Bliss (*ananda*) grows to indescribable intensity when the ground (*sat*) has become known. Thus bliss is not a subjective, overpowering feeling which the self has, but is an aspect of *brahman's* self-explication, from which it cannot be distinguished. The one who experiences the identity of his own being with that of the ground of the world is taken up into the self-becoming of the One. This is *saccidananda*, being in its consciousness of bliss, or bliss in the consciousness of being. These terms are interchangeable because they describe the one process of realization of the eternal presence of the One.

Reality in itself is not a dead tranquillity, nor a mechanical process, but expansiveness and the attraction of love (*priyam*).

Ananda is the essence of being and its perfect revelation.[83] The knowledge that Varuna delivers to his son, Bhrgu, culminates in the greatest bliss. *Ananda* can be experienced as the basic structure of reality when all relationships of name and form are sublated into one reality. *Ananda* is therefore *moksa*, release,[84] which will be explained later.

The unity of the term *sat-cit-ananda* assumes that *brahman* is dynamic. For *brahman* "appears," "manifests itself," "bestows power on everything." The Upanishads abound in such images. It is true—as the Advaita Vedanta notes—that all this appears only in the mirror of our knowledge. However, when the world is recognized as dependent appearance, when the certitude of the experience of *atman* merges with the experience of the unity of the universe, and when *brahman* is seen as the ground and essence of all that is empirical, then humans have attained *moksa*, release. This is real experience of the real essence of reality: perfect bliss—*ananda*.

In the threefold *saccidananda* there are indications of a certain trinitarian relationship. We cannot properly speak of a relationship of subject and object, nor of a self-consciousness (*cit*) of being (*sat*) in the bliss (*ananda*) of unity. For self-consciousness implies difference. The three terms denote aspects of the One, not relationships.

Nevertheless, we saw that from an empirical standpoint (*vyavaharika*), *brahman* is manifest in different forms. From the absolute standpoint (*paramarthika*) there remains perfect non-duality. Since all descriptions are empirical, we can only speak of the non-duality which appears through the manifold of appearances. Our understanding of *brahman* or *saccidananda* depends completely upon what we mean by the expression *non-dual* (Advaita) and relationship. This will be discussed in the second chapter.

Chapter one can therefore be summarized: "For Vedanta the Absolute is the inner essence or reality of everything and as such it is at once immanent and transcendent. The Absolute is neither one more reality beside others nor a mere synthesis of empirical appearances nor is it empty nothing, it is the real self of everything."[85]

2.

Atman

The Self of All Beings

The four "great sayings" of Vedantic literature (*mahavakyani*) are: 1. *prajnanam brahma*—*brahman* is consciousness. 2. *aham brahmasmi*—I am *brahman*. 3. *tat tvam asi*—that you are. 4. *ayam atma brahma*—this Atman is *brahman*.

These words illustrate in various ways that reality is "condensed consciousness" (*vijnanaghana eva*).[1] The subjective and objective aspects of reality are one. *Brahman* is one and is everything, "above everything, outside everything, beyond everything and yet in everything."[2]

From the analysis of the previous chapter we may conclude that *brahman* is neither a distant, unattainable perfect being from the empirical world, nor a logical abstraction. *Brahman* is the real self of all beings. As such it is called *atman. Atman* is the individual absolute principle. *Brahman* is the cosmic absolute principle.[3]

The absolute self is undoubtedly connected with the principle of unity of reality, a principle also sought by the Pre-Socratic philosophers of Greece. The older Upanishads are testimony to the first hesitant attempts. In these *atman* is something spiritual and no basic distinction is made between spirit and matter. The self is the energy which underlies spirit as well as material processes. In later times, however, there is a growing tendency to depreciate the material, making it more distant from *atman*.[4]

In the earlier Upanishads, *atman* describes the body,[5] as well as the divine breath of life,[6] consciousness,[7] the subject of experience,[8] the human person's true self,[9] the self of the world,[10] the subject of the spiritual path or of cosmic consciousness,[11] and finally *brahman*.[12] It is the *Inner Ruler* (*antaryamin*): "That which lives in the reproductive organ, that which rules (*yamayati*) the organ from within, is the inner guide, your own undying self. It will never be seen, but is the seer, never be heard, but is the hearer, never thought, but is the thinker. It will never be known, but is the

31

knower. There is no other seer but this, no other hearer outside it, no other thinker than it, your own undying self. All outside it is dying."[13]

Atman as *antaryamin* is the center of integration of the individual's spiritual and bodily capacities. It does not depend on the individual appearances, but is what remains constant behind all change.[14]

Atman has been compared to a hub, around which the spokes revolve.[15] Or it is the wagon driver who directs the horses; viz., the senses and thought (*indriyani*).[16] Its relationship to the conventional self is described in the following passage: When a precious gem is immersed in a glass of milk, the gem gives its color to the liquid. Milk will thus appear green through an emerald. So, too, the splendor of the body or of the senses and thinking is in reality *atman* which fills the empirical self and gives it its living force.[17] It contains everything. It is the universal potency.[18] As the Absolute it transcends the universe.[19]

Atman is constant, pure simplicity, eternal and immaculate. It is beyond good and evil and all other distinguishing marks.[20] Movement (*cala*), as well as objectivity (*vastutva*) are all part of the realm of appearances and cannot encounter *atman*.[21] Even when *atman* is described as absolute subject, we must realize that it transcends subjectivity as being set opposite an object. Thus *atman* is transpersonal personality.

It is clear that *atman* is fundamentally different from any concept of soul stemming from Plato.[22] Generally speaking, *atman* is not a special essence existing alongside other things, even if it is given special attributes, such as impassibility, perfection, etc. *Atman* is not soul, but divine power (*sakti*),[23] the all-moving energy of the ongoing world. It is incomprehensible (*agrahya*) and not knowable by sense data.[24] Whoever recognizes in *atman* the unity of reality is free from fear. For fear arises when there is an other who poses a threat. But *atman* is knowledge, and for it there is no other that is not already essentially a self. Non-duality, Advaita, is freedom from fear, *abhaya*.[25]

One of the first things to realize is that the identity of *atman* and *brahman* cannot be attained by speculative deduction, for this identity is a recognition. The means of valid knowledge (*pramana*) is not thinking (*manas*), but meditation or a contemplative spiritual attitude (*upasana*). We become aware of what really is. The one who knows (*veda*) this becomes one with the Absolute in all its forms because, in fact, nothing but this one *is*.[26] In the process of striving for this knowledge, which is not rational knowledge but gnosis (*jnana*), we come up against *the* basis of Indian religiosity.

There is a life-changing experience which gives certainty, fearlessness and the "bliss of a life in God" (*ananda*). It is the experience of being surrounded by, or being hidden in, the wholeness of the unity of being. Thus, the one who experiences this is considered as already saved (*juvanmukta*), even though corporality still imposes limitations and finiteness. These limitations end only with death. Thus even the advaitic experience is called *samadhi*, while death is called the great *samadhi, mahasamadhi.*

In order to grasp conceptually the Advaita of *brahman* and "world," the Sanskrit texts sometimes use the terms *ananyatva* and *tadatmya:* literally, "not-other" and "having this as self." In the first case there is no affirmation, but a negation of difference, just as with Advaita. Reality cannot be described affirmatively. Nevertheless, we can conclude that if *brahman* is the one reality, there can be no second reality outside of it, which would be limited by it. Therefore neither the world nor the individual self can be different from *brahman. Brahman*, furthermore, is immutable, as is *atman.* Since this is so, *atman* cannot be a part of or a transformation of *brahman.* Thus *atman*, in relation to *brahman*, is not-other, which is also true for the relationship of "world" and *brahman.*[27]

Another conclusion follows from the term, *tadatmya.* It means the "relationship of identity"[28]—in itself a contradiction if we begin with a Western notion of identity. However in India, instead of exact equality of two quantities, identity refers to the selfness in the unfolding of the One. *Tadatmya* relates appearance to essence or denotes the inherent connectedness of things. Thus *tadatmya* can also mean the relationship of the species to the genus.[29] *Atman* is thus the self, but this sentence cannot be inverted.[30] *Tadatmya* implies an irreversible dependence within the concept of oneness and therefore a "hierarchy" within reality. In this sense, too, the world is dependent on *brahman*, but not *brahman* on the world. This proves that in Advaita Vedanta we may in no way speak of an identity between the Absolute and the world, using a Western concept of identity![31] *Tadatmya* thus describes an irreversible relationship of dependence between *atman/brahman* and the world. For this reason the relative things within the world have no *tadatmya* relationships between them.[32] The self of the world *is* the absolute; *atman* is *brahman.* Reality has *atman/brahman* as its self, *tadatmya.*

Vyavaharika, atman seems different from the world. *Param-*

arthika, we become aware of the unity of reality. The illusion of difference disappears, and the Advaitin knows that the world of the many is not other than the Absolute self.[33] Thus he can recognize the self of each being through its appearance and say: *tat tvam asi*, that you are.[34]

Analogy and the *Via Negativa*

The attitude of most Indians towards God is determined by two ideas: God is worthy of reverence and above all desires, before whom we prostrate ourselves in total devotion (*bhakti*). Humans must therefore praise God in hymns, using their whole aesthetic imagination. On the other hand, humans know that God is immeasurable. He is greater than any representation of him. He is the incomprehensible Absolute behind all the intimate, analogous names humans use to reverence him, which are ultimately blasphemous.[35] Thus ecstatic reverence is juxtaposed with a profound awe. God in his essence is hidden. But from this hiddenness God effects everything. His actual reality is beyond the reach of our understanding.[36]

Humans can know absolute truth through the categories of experience and thinking, which they superimpose on (*adhyaropa*) the Absolute. But this superimposition is unfitting. For then the Absolute appears as a thing or a person with attributes which stem from our experience. This manner of viewing enables the Absolute to appear as *saguna brahman*, "with visible qualities."

However, the Absolute "in itself" is not thus. Our representations and concepts have a certain justification as analogies, because the Absolute is *also* thus. But the Absolute is qualitatively more, and no predicates may be added to it which would distinguish it from other things and thus limiting it. This would make of the Absolute an object among other objects. Thus finally, the Absolute must be known as *nirguna brahman*, the Absolute without any qualities which would determine it (*apavada*).

Sankara accepted the method of analogy, as long as it was understood that all statements about *atman* include an "as if."[37] What is signified is only symbolically represented. Words have meaning only indirectly, for all concepts are limited. Certain meanings (*upadhi*), however, are propaedeutically more meaningful than others and their use is therefore justified.[38]

Saguna and *nirguna* are basically two ways of knowing. They do not alter the Absolute in the least. Both ways of perceiving are meaningful, although in Advaita Vedanta each maintains its place in a hierarchy.[39] *Saguna* knowing is necessary first before progressing on the path towards spiritual maturity and towards the abandonment of limited images. When we start with the world of experience we can only say what the Absolute is *not.* Thus the *via negativa* corresponds to a higher knowledge.

And yet, grasping the Absolute *saguna* is also meaningful for those well advanced along the path of *nirguna* knowledge. This presupposes, however, that in referring to reality, concepts are not being used in their literal sense (*mukhyartha*), but in a figurative sense (*laksyartha*).[40] But demonstrative or affirmative statements are necessary to facilitate meditation. In meditation we direct all our powers of understanding towards the One, and this is only possible when the senses have been properly satisfied.[41] This, however, is only the beginning of knowledge. There remains the whole process of progressing along a path, before finally reaching the *via negativa.*

Apophatic statements concerning the Absolute (*nisedha-mukhena*) are a second possibility and the one which is preferred. An example of this is the instruction of Gargi by the philosopher Yajnavalkya, recorded in the Brhadaranyaka Upanishad. The master explains the essence of *brahman:* "This is the imperishable, O Gargi, which is reverenced by the wise: it is neither great nor subtle, neither red nor sticky, neither shadow nor darkness, neither air nor space, undisturbed, without taste, without smell, without face, without hearing, without speech, without understanding, without light, without breath, without mouth, without form, without inner or outer. It eats nothing and is eaten by nothing."[42] It is neither this nor that—the famous *neti, neti* of the Upanishads.[43]

The negative way prepares the mind for a specific state of consciousness, which can only be reached through transrational meditation.[44] It is a fourth (*turiya*) state, which is beyond the usual three states of consciousness (wakefulness, dreaming, deep sleep), is called a hyper-rational, object-less, and therefore fully unified consciousness. This state escapes words. *Brahman* can only be experienced in silence.

The absolute negation of objectivity is nothing else than the affirmation of the absolute standpoint.[45] Buddhism especially (*sunyavada*) accepts the consequences of grasping the Absolute as nothing. The Buddha denies all metaphysical statements (affirmations, as well as negations). Even speaking of the Self (*atman*) con-

tradicts a consequent apophatism, which led Buddhism to develop
the theory of the non-self (anatta).[46]

In Buddhism, the term "nothing" does not mean a dead nothing opposed to being. Precisely translated, sunyata means "emptiness," an emptiness of all finite meanings. Sunyata is not a position
which denies, but the negation of any position at all. The anti-
Buddhist polemics in Vedanta[47] could not grasp this sufficiently
because it would have been obliged to recognize more clearly the
similarity with Advaita that denies the possibility of any position.
Sunyata means the interrelatedness of all things.[48]

Mahayana-Buddhism, especially, speaks of the fullness of
nothing, which becomes clear in the Japanese concept mu. Even
nirvana is not nothing, but a dissolving of distinctions and therefore creative fullness.[49] For this reason Vedanta and Mahayana
seem to me to be closer to one another than is commonly recognized. Yet there are differences, which bring out all the more
clearly the standpoint of Advaita Vedanta.

The Advaitin attaches great importance to maintaining the
complementarity of the negative and positive statements on brahman, even when talking about the above-mentioned hierarchy of
the two ways. Brahman is saccidananda. Its ineffable fullness re-
sounds in the all-embracing word of meditation, OM. Vedanta denies that this positivity is necessarily substantialist and rejects
therefore the Buddhist anatta-theory. In both cases substantialist
thinking is avoided because it would imply duality. For the Advaitin negation and affirmation are pictured as being in a reciprocal
relationship. The one position needs the other. Thus they say, saccidananda, but add immediately neti, neti (not this, not this): "the
negation behind which lies a profound affirmation," for the One
"is higher and deeper than every predicate which one could add
to it."[50]

The unity of the via affirmativa and the via negativa was already described by Gaudapada, the great teacher of Sankara, as
follows: Brahman is indeed neither inner nor outer,[51] neither name
nor form.[52] Nevertheless, we should not stop with this emptiness
(sunya), but know that brahman is eternal (nitya),[53] pure consciousness, self-illuminating, and always the same,[54] thus unending bliss
(ananda) and peace (santi).[55]

The one who experiences the fullness (purna) of atman/brah-
man reaches moksa, release or freedom. Moksa is pure non-duality.
For if freedom were opposed to non-freedom, it would not be abso-

lute. Freedom would be under the constraint of non-freedom and would not be absolute freedom, and this would lead to a new duality. This paradox is the most profound intuition of Indian philosophy. It is the mystery of the unity of being and nothingness, good and bad, freedom and constraint, *brahman* and *sunya*.[56]

3.

Modes of Appearance of the One

Maya

Maya enables *brahman*, which is undivided and without qualities (*nirguna*), to appear as having visible attributes (*saguna*) and a differentiated reality. The word comes from the root *ma*, to measure. Whatever is *maya* is measurable, for it brings the imponderable and indefinable into a form. *Maya* stands for power and energy, and in this sense it has the same meaning as *sakti* (power).[1] *Maya* as the measurable is the area of rationality and also of science.[2] This makes possible concepts, distinctions and causality. We make distinctions, think, define and experience things by means of oppositions. Thus we are continually operating in the area of *maya*, where there is no other knowledge than by means of the senses and the understanding. Thus, the concept of *maya* can also stand for illusion: the illusion that holds us when we believe that the world is as we know it by means of rationality and distinctions. Immanuel Kant is the European thinker who reflected on this problem with the greatest precision. His solution, namely the way of practical reason, would not satisfy a Vedantin. For the latter accepts a transrational and transcategorical knowledge, which is possible through the cognitive means of meditation.

Maya works in two dimensions: 1. It is cosmic non-knowledge, for it is the basic cause of the world process that appears as separated from *brahman*. 2. It is individual non-knowing, usually called *avidya*,[3] and here is characterized by the fact that the knowledge is satisfied with appearances.

In Vedic times people saw in *maya* the wonderful creative power of God which, however, could also lead one away from the essential. In order to demonstrate that this is an epistemological, not an ontological problem, Sankara frequently uses the terms, *avidya* or *ajnana* (ignorance).[4] In later Vedanta, however, where there is a greater denial of the world, *maya* is always judged negatively.

Maya is not different from *brahman*. This would imply there was a second reality. Yet it cannot be identical with the Absolute. This would imply that there could be different aspects within *brahman*, which could thus not be grasped as pure being and consciousness—*nirguna*. The ontological status of *maya* is therefore fully incomprehensible and ineffable (*anirvacaniya*).

In the Vedanta *maya* is essentially *brahman*'s freedom to manifest itself or not.[5] It is also the principle of creation.[6] *Brahman* determined by *maya* appears first as *isvara* (personal God). However, the primary cause of the world is not the abstract Absolute, but this God-in-relation. Both, however, are identical, for *brahman* is determined by its own *maya* and appears only as a personal and creator God.[7]

We may compare the functioning of *maya* to a crystal, which splits the one reality (of light) into different individual components. The light is what it is, but it appears in the different colors of the spectrum. This comparison, however, is limited, for *brahman*, contrary to light, has neither components nor a spectrum. As a principle of differentiation and integration, *maya* is inherent to the human spirit. The original wholeness is broken up into individual perceptions, so that a true synthesis of the human mind makes possible a total experience of consciousness. The totality which results from the knowing process is filled with *maya*'s differentiations and temporal changes even though it is not affected by them. The limiting attributes (*upadhi*), which are *saguna* to *brahman*, belong, therefore, to *maya*.

Maya functions according to a twofold process. At first the One is hidden by sense knowledge and understanding: *maya* is the hiding power (*avarana sakti*). Secondly, the limiting determinations of space, time, for instance, are being projected towards the one reality: *maya* is the projecting power (*viksepa sakti*). The appearances are subject to space and time; the Absolute, however, knows no change. This statement implies a soteriology. If *brahman* were subject to change, there would be no absolute certainty of a liberation (*moksa*) which would free humans once and for all from the temporal cycle (*samsara*) and enable them to participate in the eternal happiness (*ananda*) of pure being (*sat*) and consciousness (*cit*).

The empirical world obeys its own laws, and they are not "unreal"—in the sense that a fantastic dream is unreal in relationship to the external world of objects. This distinction is explained by means of humorous anecdotes. For example, it is said that once Sankara had just explained the *maya* theory to his royal pupil when the latter decided to put the philosopher to the test by releasing a raging elephant, which attacked him. Sankara fled to a high tree, and climbed down covered with sweat only when the elephant had been captured. Puzzled, the king asked why the master had taken flight, since the elephant was really *maya* or illusion. Sankara's answer was: "According to the highest truth the elephant is unreal. You and I, however, are as unreal as the elephant. Only your ignorance, which veiled the truth by means of this unreal appearance, saw me seemingly climb into an unreal tree."[8] It is clear that there are two different concepts or levels of reality at work here. The Absolute involves a different kind of reality than the relative.

Maya is without beginning (*anadi*), undeterminable (*anirvacaniya*), and has the structure of existing things (*bhavarupa*). *Maya* is not, however, without beginning in the same way as *brahman* is. For time, which sets down beginnings and ends, belongs to *maya*. Thus there can be no beginning of *maya* in time; rather, time is a given of *maya*. *Brahman*, on the other hand, is absolute trans-temporality. In this regard, rational *maya* is unable to be grasped; it is *anirvacaniya*.[9]

Maya is the principle of the world's appearance. It is both the material and efficient cause (*causa materialis et cause efficiens*), although it cannot really be said *why* it exists. The immutable One cannot be the material cause (*upadana karana*) because this would be the equivalent of admitting that there is change in *brahman*. *Maya* is dependent on a goal; viz., the one set by the *mayin*, and this is *brahman* itself in its *cit* aspect. The classical text concerning this says: "Know *maya* as material cause (of the world), and the highest God as the one who guides *maya*."[10] Although *brahman* is not the direct cause of the world, there is no matter (*prakrti*) existing alongside it from which it creates the world. For then the Absolute would not be without a second. *Brahman* has this power within itself. *Maya* is potentiality pure and simple,[11] neither identical with what contains it nor different from it.

On the other hand, *maya* is related to the world as the root is to the fully grown plant.[12] Thus *maya* can also be described as the primal first cause of the world (*mulaprakrti*), the "original root" from which matter and all forms are developed.[13] *Maya* is the world as not yet manifested,[14] and the manifestation or creation (both expressions are used) is *maya's* process of unfolding. Thus, *maya* can generally be understood as the principle of becoming.[15]

The question about the purpose of *maya* has seldom been asked. Occasionally, however, two arguments emerge. 1. *Maya* is the power (*sakti*) or energy (*vibhuti*) of God which opens up his nature (*svabhava*). God, as it were, eludes us through his own power.[16] 2. God uses his *maya* to hide himself,[17] for only then is human freedom possible, through which we decide for or against God.[18]

Until now we have spoken mainly of the cosmic aspect of *maya*. We will now treat *maya* as *avidya* (ignorance), as an impediment in human life. On the one hand, because of *maya*, the world is seen as appearance: it seems different from *brahman*. On the other hand, humans take the appearance as real and identify it with the Absolute. Thus they project their own images, gained from sense experience, onto reality. Because of *maya* the determinations of the *maya* world (name, form, time, space, etc.) are applied to *brahman*. This is illusion, mistaking projections for reality. Humans are inevitably caught in this web of ignorance and cannot escape from it by sense knowledge and understanding.

An example frequently used to explain the false transference (*adhyaropa*) of finite concepts onto the Absolute is the story of a man who, in the twilight, thinks he sees a snake on the ground, whereas in reality it is only a rope. All the attributes of a snake seem to be verified in this object, and as long as the rope is not recognized as such, it is for the beholder a real snake. The rope, however, because of this false transference of the properties of a snake onto itself (in relation to the other correctly known objects) is not at all affected by this transference or changed. The error lies only in the beholder. We attach predicates to *brahman* which we have received from the projected *maya* world, and the consequence of this is that reality is indistinguishable from the projections. The one who sees an object such as the moon with diseased eyes may possibly see two objects. But despite the perdurance of the two images, it is still an unreal image.[19] The unity of the real thing is not altered.

Here we will not be able to examine in detail the theory concerning error in Advaita philosophy.[20] A few observations are, however, necessary. Each error is based on the confusion of levels of reality. This was already seen to be the case in the above example of the snake and the rope. The same is true when finite attributes are superimposed or transferred to infinite *brahman* and thus absolutized. The simple error of mistaking a rope for a snake can fairly easily be clarified by means of empirical knowledge—by means of a light. For since the snake and the rope are empirical objects, they exist in space and time. This is not the case, however, for the metaphysical error of transferring the structures of the spatio-temporal world to *brahman*. This error can only be clarified by experiencing the whole which surpasses the entire empirical world. The predicates that were added to a substratum need not be real, as may be seen in the case of many fantastic ideas.[21] But now even in this case rationality does not work, because even the unreal, transposed to *brahman*, can seem real.

Humans caught in illusion and ignorance believe that they are separated from *brahman*. This false attitude is the basic cause of all other evils. It produces egocentricity.[22] The one who lives in this separation and continually absolutizes finite dualities is unfree. He worships the projections of his mind and surrenders himself to finite categories. Thus he loses value and freedom which accrue to him in *atman* because of its non-duality with the Absolute.[23]

To summarize: because of *maya* we miss the unity of reality. This results in both a false idea of the world—which is idolized— and a false idea of *brahman*—onto which finite categories are projected. From a relative standpoint, *maya* appears as the power of God, which hides the absolute reality and rejects the relatively unreal. From an absolute standpoint (*paramarthika*) *maya* is that which (*ya*) is not (*ma*).[24] *Maya* cannot, however, be *unreal*, because the world of the many in fact appears. But *maya* cannot be real, for in the knowledge of the non-duality of God and world, it ceases to exist. It is therefore real and unreal at the same time, which is logically problematic. Thus *maya* is undeterminable (*anirvacaniya*). "Any inquiry into *maya* is not to make the concept intelligible, but to enable one to go beyond it. When one has gone beyond, there remains no problem to be solved."[25]

The *nirguna* mode of viewing *brahman* must be added to the *saguna* mode in order to make possible a full description of reality. Whether both are seen as complementary depends on how one judges the *saguna* method; whether it is seen merely as a propaedeutic for the *nirguna* knowledge, or whether it is allowed to stand on its own. Both viewpoints are found in Vedanta.

Theory of Projection

A commonly used comparison shows how the world can be understood as a projection of God. The moon is in the sky. It shines with wonderful clarity. On the earth, however, there are many water pitchers. All of them reflect the single light of the moon in many different ways. The different earthenware jars are the individual forms of this world, which reflect the light of the One.[26] The enlightened mind knows, of course, that the earthenware jars are not different from the one, imperishable reality of the light.

By means of their knowledge humans project finite categories onto the world and onto the Absolute. Knowledge is a projection of a second order, for it depends on the cosmic projection of the Absolute in *maya* (first order). Through the power of knowledge humans gather up splintered reality into a single point. Humans are not just beholders of *maya*, nor just part of the event, but a mirror of the universe. Their knowledge is a reflection and a gathering of all of reality, which in the advaitic, transrational experience breaks through the illusion of the many and returns to the One.[27] Advaitic knowledge has an ontological meaning.

In this sense humans are a true mirror-image of God. They project the manifold, but remain one and also know it, or at least can come to know it, because their true nature as pure consciousness is the integrating power of the One. Humans know the unity of projection and self-knowledge, insofar as this unity is fulfilled within them. For just as the world is a projection of the One, so too every image of God which integrates the many is a projection of humans since it remains attached to *maya*. Nevertheless, humans as *atman* are not different from *brahman*, even when they remain within empirical knowledge which hides *atman*.

All the gods which humans believe they see outside themselves are appearances of the absolute One. They are the highest God, contemplated in spatio-temporal differentiation.[28] At the same time, however, they are only projections of the human mind, for *maya* functions here as *avidya*. The images projected by consciousness—God, heavenly essences, etc.—are, for the purpose of meditation, considered to be real.[29] Their reality has propaedeutic value for advaitic experience. But this objectification is provisional and is only a step on the spiritual path which leads to the experience of all-embracing non-duality. God is therefore an "experimental da-

tum"[30] used for meditation and concentration on the One, and
there alone fulfilled experience knows that the projected God and
the Absolute One are not two different things. The underlying principle is that a person becomes what he meditates. The way we
direct our desires, the way we act and proceed, this is what we
become—*yathakari yathacari tatha bhavati.*[31]

We should note, however, that the Upanishads do not claim
that those who meditate on a certain divinity become this divinity
—in an objective sense. They become like to, or similar to it; they
interiorize its attributes or live from its essence. They imitate the
divinity perfectly by total identification. This is also true of those
who meditate on *brahman* in its *saguna* aspect. They attain (*apyeti*)
brahman; they become *brahman*-structured, but nevertheless—in
the *saguna* way of speaking—there remains a difference between
the two subjects which are personally related.[32]

Whether individual existence "gives itself over to *brahman*"
or "attains *brahman*" has been debated by the various schools in
later literature, and the matter has not yet been decided. Both sides
refer to the Upanishads and both viewpoints are found in the
Upanishads. We will take up this problem in the next section.

For the Advaitin all projected gods, demons, angels are considered to be merely characteristic of human existence: either they
occur to us or are wishful images.[33] This does not, however, imply
an "atheistic" attitude, but is merely a consequence of the advaitic
experience. Images of God—bound to our finite categories with
psychic content, such as fear or joy—are projected by humans, just
as the whole world of the many is projected by *brahman.* The human projection of God is a means of reaching identification with
the Absolute by means of meditation. These means will become
superfluous and obstructive when they have fulfilled their purpose. If we stop here, we remain bound by the limitations of our
understanding and cannot attain advaitic experience.

Furthermore, the one who remains at this stage and reverences
God as merely another essence that is set opposite him/her will not
know the oneness of *atman* and *brahman.* This person is not
merely ignorant, but is robbed of his/her freedom. He/she atro-
phies in heteronomy. For human freedom consists in knowing the
unity of *atman* and the cosmic order. An externally reverenced God
could become an all-powerful rival to us, while the *atman* in us is,
in reality, Advaita with the Absolute.[34]

The idea of God is an interpretation. As *idea* it is a projection of the human mind.[35] It is based on the experience of the unity of reality. That means that it is an idea of *God*, and that *brahman* itself is the subject who is projecting.

Transpersonal Absolute—Personal God

From the beginning a personal God has been worshipped in India. The hymns of the Rigveda presuppose a personal relationship between God and humans. Hymns which understand the highest essence transpersonally as *tad ekam*[36] are probably from a relatively late period. There is however no certainty in relative chronology. A greater degree of abstraction indicates a later date and vice versa. The result is a circularity which no one can verify.

In the literature of Vedanta and the philosophy which has been developed from it—the object of our study—there is both a transpersonal absolute (*brahman*) and a personal God (*purusa, isvara*). In Advaita philosophy the two merge into one thought structure, and the way they are subordinated one to the other is dependent on the various schools. The famous hymn X,90 of the Rigveda uses the notion *purusa* to include the whole range and contains resonances of the later personal expression for God, *isvara. Purusa* is: 1. humankind, especially man, 2. the original type of humankind, 3. spirit, in opposition to the unspiritual nature of Samkhya philosophy, and 4. the highest essence, the soul of the universe, the personal God. The summit of personalism is reached in the (late) Svetasvatara Upanishad, which speaks of the one God who is the cause of the universe[37] and who, as creator, rules the world, remains unchanged and guards and loves his creation. He knows all, but no one to whom he has not revealed it by grace knows him. Requests can be made of him.[38] He is perfectly transcendent and perfectly immanent.[39] As creator he is hidden in the present creation, just as a silkworm is hidden in its cocoon.[40]

The theory of *maya* is used to explain how we achieve an experience of the Absolute One (*brahman*) and the personal God by distinguishing *brahman* as *nirguna* from *brahman* as *saguna*. God is personal in the appearance of his own *maya* in order to reveal himself to humans and make himself present to their worship.[41] The manifestations are because of revelation and because of meditation. In other words, the One is also personal God for the sake of humans. In this personal form, however, he is different from humans.[42]

All of this is related to the *saguna* aspect. God is, as it were, "also" personal, but he is more. The Absolute One in its *nirguna* aspect is not impersonal, but *transpersonal.*

A section of the Bhagavad Gita which is otherwise very important, along with Sankara's commentary on it, explaining the advaitic structure of thinking, demonstrates the delicate balance that is involved in speaking of a personal God.[43] This section speaks of three *purusah.* The first two are related to the empirical world: they are *in* it (*loke*). The first is called perishable (*ksara*) and the second imperishable (*aksara*). The imperishable is the "One who stands on the peak" (*kutastho ksara ucyate*); i.e., the highest being *in* the world. According to Sankara, both of these belong together categorically (*prthagrasikrtau purusau*), for they are subject to becoming and death (*loke samsare*). The third one is to be distinguished from these two, identified by the Gita as the highest *purusa* (*purusottama*) and as such identical with *paramarthika* or *brahman.* This highest One speaks in the first person. He fully transcends the world. But after he has entered the world (*avisya*) he carries (*bibharti*) the world, as its imperishable Lord (*isvara*), without doing harm to his transcendence. He is not subject to change, but as personal God is identical with the Absolute One.

How can the One Absolute personal God be related to the second *purusa*, which is called imperishable, yet is subject to the wheel of becoming and death (*samsara*)[44] and is the highest being although qualitatively different from the Absolute personal God; i.e., the third *purusa*? In his commentary, Sankara gives a descriptive answer. He calls the third *purusa*—the One which is like *brahman*—the exalted One (*bhagavat*), which clearly points to the personality of the Absolute. The second *purusa* he calls *bhagavatah maya-saktih*, which can have two meanings grammatically as well as theologically.[45] 1. "One who has the *maya* power of the exalted One": in this case there would be another, a person for himself, endowed with the attributes of the one, absolute God, something like a second person in the one divine totality. 2. "The *maya* power of the exalted One": in this case there would be an emanation from the absolute One.

In the Advaita Vedanta both of these possible meanings are combined. We cannot (and should not?) decide on one or the other,

and this is not because some answer could not be found and defended—an irrelevant assumption for a clear thinker like Sankara
—but because both possible meanings must be thought at the same
time, which in Sanskrit is easily possible.

Logical clarity in our sense is avoided. Yet it is clearly stated in
this central text that the Absolute is personal God who, however,
qualitatively transcends *all* the predicates which we apply to him
analogously. Because of God's revelation (the *saguna* aspect) we
know that attributes such as all-mighty, are correct in a certain
sense.[46] However, it is important to realize that this is provisional.[47] Furthermore, the difference between the transpersonal
Absolute and the personal God is epistemological, not ontological.[48]

Nevertheless, devotion (*bhakti*) to a personal God is not point-
less for the enlightened Advaitin. Many of the celebrated Advaitins
were fervent Bhaktas and passionate worshippers. Sankara himself
composed beautiful hymns in which he expresses in poetry his profound relationship to the Lord and his love of God.[49] In recent
times the greatest representative of the advaitic ideals, the saintly
South Indian, Ramana Maharishi who died in 1950, also composed
passionate songs reflecting his profound, personal experience of
the God he seeks.[50]

In the end, God's incomprehensibility results in paradoxes.
The understanding is useless when it tries to understand the oneness of the One. Thus, God is described as formless person (*amurta
purusa*).[51] Sankara approvingly cites a text from the Brahmanas,
which says that *atman* is *purusa* and is likewise *in purusa*,[52] and
this reflects the difficulty in Advaita of speaking simultaneously of
identity and personal relationship. *Brahman* is neutral and yet is
self-consciousness, since it is pure consciousness,[53] and in its
aspect of guiding and maintaining the world *must* be a personal
Intelligence.[54] The great liberation (*moksa*) does not necessarily
imply a perfect identity of the redeemed with *brahman*, but Advaita. The texts concerning this allow for an interpretation which
makes the redeemed person closely related to *brahman* or *in brahman*, thus maintaining a difference between them, which is necessary for personal experience.[55]

Because God reveals himself as person, a personal relationship
to him is possible. Moreover, because God is an "I," humans can
grasp him as a "Thou."[56] Redeemed humans are drawn into the
subjectivity of God to the extent that the Advaita of *atman* and

brahman has become for them a transformative experience, in other words, as the unity of reality is realized. In this sense the knower is *saccidananda.*[57] It would thus be completely false to speak of pantheism in the Western sense.[58]

Creation

For Sankara *saguna brahman* has three functions: 1. creation (*srsti*), 2. maintenance (*sthiti*) and dissolution (*samhara*) of the world.[59]

As we already explained, *maya* is the principle of creation. Creation is the appearance of the one as many. It is not the objective result of the activity of an absolute subject, and thus it acquires no autonomous existence. The concept of creation in Advaita Vedanta must be distinguished from the corresponding Christian idea.

Brahman is both the material and the effective cause of the world.[60] However, these notions are not completely the same as in the Aristotelian tradition, and therefore these translations of it lead to misunderstandings. Instead of "material cause" (*upadana karana*) it would perhaps be better to speak of "inner cause" (R.V. DeSmet), but this solution introduces a new term that is difficult to grasp. *Brahman* as *upadana karana* is nevertheless greater and more subtle than that which comes forth from it.

We cannot enter into a detailed discussion of Sankara's notion of causality.[61] But it is clear that God is more than the first in a succession of beings.[62] Since the effects of the first cause are neither different from, nor identical with it, Sankara thinks the world is implicit in *brahman.*[63] Many texts speak of a universal energy: God is in the world as the fire is in wood.[64]

The world is not a real transformation of the Absolute, but a transfiguration of the One in our knowledge. As such it is completely real in *vyavaharika* perspective.[65] Creation texts suspected of dualism are interpreted figuratively and they have less weight than clearly advaitic texts.[66] The sentence, *idam agre ekam eva advitiyam sat eva asit*—this was being *alone* in the beginning, one *only,* without a second[67]—is true because of the particle *eva* (alone, only), while another text with *iva* (supposedly, as it were) is only true in the metaphorical sense: *yatra dvaitamiva bhavati taditara itaram jighrati, taditaram itaram pasyati* . . . (where duality *supposedly* is, there we smell something, see something . . .).[68]

Therefore, the Absolute could be a substratum for an illusory appearance—that which appears separated from the Absolute only to the ignorant.[69] But it would be one-sided to consider only the *nirguna* standpoint. As we have seen, Sankara not only admits the *saguna* standpoint but uses it himself. Therefore we can and must speak of "creation." This results in an ongoing movement between the two standpoints and an ambiguity which is so characteristic of Advaita Vedanta and makes it so rich, spiritually.

Figure 3.1 presents a schematic illustration of the experience of the Absolute, which will be explained in detail.

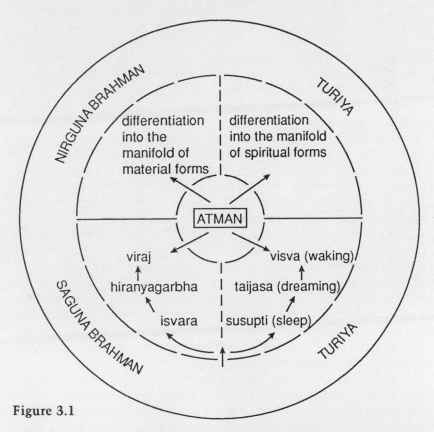

Figure 3.1

Explanation: Brahman appears by means of *maya* as *saguna brahman*. It appears in three cosmic forms, described as *isvara, hiranyagarbha,* and *viraj. Isvara* is the Lord, the Creator. The next and a less subtle form that appears is *hiranyagarbha,* the golden seed, the first-born of creation. In it all things are made. It is the primal potency which was with God before the world was created. *Viraj* then appears as a third and still less subtle form, the manifold of created things in all their material and spiritual forms. As *isvara*, then, *hiranyagarbha*, finally *viraj*, the *saguna brahman* appears—each time more determined and conditioned. There are then individual forms which correspond to these forms of *brahman*.[70] The *turiya* state of consciousness, which is beyond all differentiation and therefore ineffable, corresponds to *nirguna brahman*. The forms of consciousness's appearance which can be qualified—deep sleep, dreaming and the waking state—and correspond in successive degrees of subtlety to *isvara*, *hiranyagarbha*, and *viraj*.

Isvara is the one creator and Lord over all heavenly and worldly beings.[71] It is potency or maternal womb, from which all comes forth.[72] *Hiranyagarbha* is the first subtle realized form of this potency. It is the "golden seed," the bud or kernel, from which all else develops. Everything is already contained in it. It is the same as the one God who can take on several forms.[73] Thus he is identified with primal energy (*prana*).[74] He is the gathered-up energy from which all individual energies unfold.[75] As first-born he permeates all and is not different from *purusa*, but is himself the highest Lord, the source of fullness: "Even a person who is created (viz., *hiranyagarbha*) can permeate all, for as an aspect of the one cosmic life energy he dwells in the bodies of every being."[76] As a manifestation, however, he is also conditioned and cannot be perfectly real in the same sense as the Absolute.[77] Therefore, in another place it is said that the cosmic intelligence of *hiranyagarbha*, which is called *mahat*, is lower than the unmanifest form (*avyakta*).[78] Therefore, a person meditating who remains on the spiritual level of *hiranyagarbha*, which is a very subtle but still a conditioned level of reality, is subject to the same illusion as the one who worships God only in visible or conceptual projections. Indeed, the error could even be very serious, because it is less apparent.[79]

Viraj is described as the cosmic form of the Self, as the full unfolding of all beings. *Viraj* is the gross form of reality: "All things are his visible forms. Each being is a fragment of his cosmic vesture."[80] Thus *viraj* can be described as material.[81] Mythical representations see *viraj* as a splintering of the original personal form (*purusa*), and interestingly *purusa*, too, comes forth from *viraj* retrospectively.[82] The indissoluble relationship, and finally unity, of the two is thus portrayed mythically. The philosophical abstraction resulting from this picture can be seen in the teaching of the Upanishads which sees *hiranyagarbha* and *viraj* as two forms of the same essence, the highest God (*prajapati, isvara, purusa*). Frequently Sankara does not clearly distinguish them since both are more or less subtle manifestations of the One.[83]

Is there any meaning in this process of creation or gradual manifestation of the One? It is sometimes claimed that Sankara saw no meaning, but this is false. The activity of *maya* is the One in its self-manifestation or play (*lila*). If there were not a manifold in the world, *brahman* could not appear as a unity. In the words of Sankara: "If the many forms were not manifested, the transcendent nature of self as pure consciousness would not be known."[84] The world is meaningful because it is the self-manifestation of absolute consciousness.

Prana: Primal Energy

The idea that *prana* is primal energy and all being comes from it is very ancient. Its origin is undoubtedly connected with breathing exercises or controlled breathing (*pranayama*),[85] for *prana* is first of all the life energy that becomes active in the rhythm of breathing. All life depends on inhalation and exhalation, and this can be controlled by systematic exercises which direct the breath into chosen parts of the body. This experience is also experimental, and this has led to the idea that *prana* is the ultimate energy principle of the world.

The word *prana* originally meant life-breath.[86] It comes from the root *pra*, to fill, which is related to the Latin *plenus*.[87] This root meaning undoubtedly links it to the experience of breathing. Wherever there is energy, there are also effects from this energy. Thus *prana* becomes *effective force*. Through breathing exercises in Yoga this force can be increased and this force as such may be transformed either into the vital powers of the body or into psychic-mental energy. This is why in Yoga vital functions are to be curtailed and sexual abstinence is encouraged, for the same energy can be used either for sexual activity or for the psychic-mental processes.[88]

While experiencing *prana* as a life principle, the philosophical search for its basic matter also came to know *prana* as the underlying energy which transcends every individual being. This search for basic matter has its parallels in other cultures, such as that of Chinese,[89] and in Pre-Socratic philosophy.[90] But the Indian solution is characteristic in that it uses introspection and self-experimentation with *pranayama.*

Prana means the "organs" of the self, viz., breathing, speech, seeing, hearing and thinking, as well as the source of these functions.[91] Since all spiritual phenomena are dependent on *prana,* the holy scriptures, too, are essentially *prana.*[92] *Prana* is the essence of everything, but as an underlying force it eludes all direct experience. Only its effects are visible. A very early Upanishad proposes the following arguments for the existence of this subtle energy. Just as there is a subtle, inherent energy in a seed, which makes it produce a great tree, even though this is only seen once, this effect (the tree) has been produced, so too with *prana,* the subtle energy principle of the world.[93] Later systematic philosophy distinguished three dimensions of *prana:* the organ, the life-energy in each individual, and *prana* as cosmic principle.[94]

The cosmic form of *prana* can be identified with *hiranyagarbha,*[95] since this latter embraces all forms[96] which can be thought of as individualized explications of the energy (*sakti*) of *brahman.*[97] In this view *prana* and *brahman* are the same, and this is confirmed by the fact that *prana* is described as the eternal being from which the universe originates.[98]

In summary we can say that *prana* is either *brahman* itself[99] or its manifestation in life-energies.[100] *Prana* is not a principle alongside *brahman,*[101] but the Absolute, understood as the efficacious energy behind everything that happens.[102]

The Unity of Matter and Spirit

Although there are texts which regard consciousness as a special creation of God added to the world, which comes forth from *prana,*[103] Advaita Vedanta regards the world as a unity.

Within the empirical world, both are stages of manifestation of the One, and matter and spirit are clearly differentiated. This differentiation, however, is relative in relation to the Absolute. Thus matter's potential is at first unmanifest. But when this potential is fully explicitated and its relationship to spirit as guiding principle is seen, then *viraj* can be discussed, as we saw above. The whole discussion of *saguna brahman* assumes the connection of matter and spirit. Even God, when he has appeared in our *vyava-*

harika knowledge, is a connection of matter and spirit.[104] Thus all organized matter which we experience is spiritual insofar as an ordering and structural principle (*cit*) has made it real.

The Bhagavad Gita describes the material appearances as a field (*ksetra*) and the spiritual appearances as knower of the field (*ksetrajna*).[105] Both are without beginning,[106] just as our already familiar terms *maya*, as well as *nirguna brahman* are without beginning. Human beings are living beings in which *prana* is at work in material and spiritual ways. Humans are therefore distinct from animals, plants and inert matter in degree, not basically.[107]

Early in the history of India, the earliest ideas of this life force had already led to a philosophy of "living matter," which does not yet know of anything non-substantial and which therefore is as far away from "spiritual beings without a substratum" as it is from "dead matter".[108] This is still implicitly found in some Brahmanas, where nourishment is described as principle of being and the final ground of reality.[109] These ideas, along with advaitic experience, have led to a philosophical system which reflects on the unity principle of spirit and matter.

Karma, Rebirth, and History

The world is a place where all beings may come to moral maturity. It is also the place of *karman* and the effects of our acts.

Karman theory holds that each act is inextricably linked to an effect; thus each act carries with it unavoidable consequences and the whole world is a network of relationships. This karmic network has no beginning, but it does have an end. Temporal existence proceeds towards an end, when all *karman* will be exhausted because the reality of *atman/brahman*, which transcends temporality, will have become known.

The phenomenal world is characterized by the cosmic connection of all things in *karman:* each effect, each event is interwoven in this overall ensemble. Each act has a necessarily determined effect which cannot be lost. The present is thus a consequence of the past, and the future is nothing else than the explication of present *karman. Karman* is inexhaustible, which creates the impression that there is a temporal circularity.

Since reality is subordinated to *karman* there can be no absolute freedom in this area. *Karman* is not so much a universal law with a static structure as it is the accumulated force of habit which develops its own laws as things work themselves out. For example, when an action such as smoking is constantly repeated the consequence is that this act will probably be repeated and so strengthen the habit—smoking will become increasingly more difficult to give up. Habitual dispositions create irreversible structures, not only in the area of conscious human actions, but in the ordering of reality as such, and this is based on the becoming process of *karman*. Thus we may characterize *karman* overall as *the* formative principle of both the material and the spiritual areas of reality.

Karman has no beginning, yet its end can be anticipated through the advaitic experience, which interrupts the circle of habit. By participation in the whole, it breaks the link with *determined* forms (habits, things, ideas). The end of *karman* is the beginning of freedom.

All potential actions which have already been determined by *karman* must all be balanced out. But, since this is not possible in this life, a better rebirth is necessary to reward merits and good deeds or a worse rebirth to punish evil deeds. The *karman* theory is the most important basis for the teaching on *samsara* and rebirth.[110]

The person who has experienced the Advaita between *atman/ brahman* and the whole of reality places him/herself within an all-encompassing ensemble and is therefore no longer subject to *samsara*, which is logically and temporally limited. Everything is non-dual for such a person, and this implies that there is no longer any difference between being in *brahman* and being in *samsara*. This means that in Advaita Vedanta the popular teaching about the wanderings of individual souls, who are caught up in the cycle of rebirth in order to repay their deeds and become subject to ever-new *karman*, must be rejected and reinterpreted: *samsara* belongs to the area of *maya*. Thus in the *paramarthika* perspective it is illusion. Through *karman* psychic-mental dispositions develop, which do not end with the death of the physical body, but leave impressions in the subtle body (*suksma sarira*), although this does not affect *atman* (cf. ch. 1). They form a kind of field, in that life experiences, habits, memories are "imprinted" (*samskaras*). This field modifies the subtle body, which once again has an influence on physical occurrences (e.g., the body of the next incarnation). The new embryo is determined by its genes *and* by this subtle field which is grounded in *karman*.

In fact, there is no independent "soul" different from God and subject to *samsara*. The sole reality, the subject of all physical-psychic-mental occurrences, is *atman*.[111] Sankara draws these conclusions with regard to the teaching of reincarnation: "In truth the only one who wanders in the cycle of rebirths is God—*satyam nesvarad anyah samsari*."[112] This means that God himself is the only one who is constantly "reborn," who becomes in the manifold reality of the world—yet only insofar as he is regarded in his self-determination as *maya*. He himself does not thereby change, his otherness, in his *maya* of which he himself is the Lord (*mayin*).[113]

Because the idea of *karman* implies an ordered relationship between all appearances, it can be described as the very essence of historicity.[114] Historicity does not signify, however, a unified explanation of all appearances in relation to a final coherence with ultimate meaning. The explanation of final coherence is only possible from the end, in the perspective of full realization of *brahman*.

Once humans have attained salvation (*moksa*) by going beyond karmic dependency, the temporal world comes to an end, even though it was without beginning.[115] There is no effort to conceal this contradiction, because the circle of cause and effect *within* the area of *maya* must be an endless process. Any escape from this cycle is only possible from a transcendental standpoint, and this is described by means of *brahman*. Human salvation from mortality and cyclical futility must be transtemporal: by experiencing something qualitatively different we are able to transcend quantitive time.[116] In the Atharvaveda, time (*kala*) is described as the one great energy which gives form to the process of the world. Also, in the Bhagavad Gita God is presented as time,[117] which binds everything together. Time is the principle of mortality, and the world's destructive forces are its tools.[118]

The whole goal of Advaita's meditation spirituality is to overcome the opposition of time and non-time.[119] Temporal differentiation is strongest in the waking state; it weakens in dreaming; it is suspended in deep sleep, only to be transcended in the all-embracing *turiya* state of contemplation. In this life we can reach a quality of consciousness which transcends life and death, for this distinction is one of temporality, which the *jivanmukta* has already overcome.

Thus there is a twofold concept of time in India.[120] The one is quantitative (*karman*) and is related to appearances within *maya*, and the other is qualitative and describes the passage towards *moksa.*[121] Qualitative time is the moment that transcends relativity, when suddenly the universal connectedness of reality as a unity becomes visible, a kind of "heightened moment," such as Goethe's Faust desires fervently.[122] Time is the immediate now, where past and future become present.[123]

India does not think unhistorically, yet it possesses another rhythm of time which is different from that of Western cultures. For the Advaitin God is the subject as well as the object of his own history. But history is never an ultimate value. Thus Advaita Vedanta offers almost no starting point for an incarnational theology.[124] When God appears in the world of human history so that he can be grasped in the fullness of time, this coming into history (*avatara*) is understood docetically.[125] For time and history are relative categories, which are transcended by unity of reality.

Triadic Structures

It is striking that India has frequently thought in triads when describing absolute reality or God's relationship to the world. R. Panikkar has distinguished a cosmic and an eschatological trinity in the Upanishads, which describe the whole of reality triadically, for "everything proceeds in a triple manner."[126]

The *theological* trinity means that God differentiates himself in three ways.[127] This is naturally related to *saguna brahman,* and more particularly to the full cosmic unfolding of *viraj,* which appears as sun, air and fire.

The *cosmic* trinity results from the fact that the universe consists of a threeness of name, form and action.[128] The source of these is *vac* (word)—the self of name, form and action—and in this capacity identical with *brahman.*

The *eschatological* trinity is seen in a protective formula, which humans should recite at the hour of their death to call to mind the non-duality of their own essence with absolute reality and thus have peace (*santi*). They should say: Thou (i.e., the *atman* of the person concerned) art the immortal One, the unchangeable One, the essence of primal energy.[129]

Panikkar indicates that this triadic structure points to a harmony, which summarizes three essential factors of the basic Vedic experience: worldliness, unworldliness and the advaitic integration of both.[130]

It is obvious that the triads we have discussed so far are not properly trinitarian, but mere triadic formulas—at least if we are looking for a specifically trinitarian concept. But this will be different according to the following considerations which we now present.

We saw that *brahman*, under the effects of its own *maya*, appears in a threefold way as *isvara-hiranyagarbha-viraj*. These three moments of manifestation are also reflected when the threefold manifestation of *brahman* is explained as inspiring Lord (*preritr*), object of pleasing sense-perception (*bhogya*)—namely the world— and humankind which rejoices in the world (*bhoktr*).[131]

The Buddhist teaching concerning the three bodies of Buddha (*trikaya*) stems from this same basic experience.[132] Aurobindo describes the manifestations of the One as *atman-purusa-isvara*, and this same triad is also seen in connection with the three moments of manifestation of Advaita Vedanta.[133]

All of these are attempts to understand the One in conjection with the many. They are aspects of reality and therefore the immanence and transcendence of the One, or of a personal God, have to be understood simultaneously.

All the structures mentioned up to this point are related to *saguna brahman*. They describe the relationship of God to the world, the Absolute to the relative, the One to becoming. But we have also become acquainted with another triad, which was essentially different from the others because it was linked with *nirguna brahman*: viz., *saccidananda*.

As we saw, this notion does not mean that being, consciousness and bliss are being attributed to the Absolute, but that absolute reality *in se* is experienced as *sat-cit-ananda*. The three terms do not complete each other, but are all self-declarations of the undifferentiated Absolute, which is also the highest degree of fullness, life, pure consciousness and bliss. We might call these (*sat-cit-ananda*) three dimensions of the One, but only if we keep in mind that the term "dimension" here is used in a figurative sense (*laksyartha*)—from the area of *maya* to the area of the whole. In *saccidananda*, therefore, we would have found an authentic *trinitarian* structure in Indian thought.

4.

Non-dual Knowledge

Advaita Epistemology

A thing may be regarded in two ways: in its essential nature (*svarupa-laksana*) and in its *per accidens* qualities (*tatastha-laksana*). The essential nature is given with the thing itself and cannot be distinct from it. It remains as long as the thing remains. In being of this essential nature a thing is distinguished from all other things. The *per accidens* qualities of things are added under certain circumstances. This makes possible a differentiation which is temporally limited.[1]

If we understand *brahman* as first cause, the energetic principle of development, and the basis for the dissolution or transformation of the world, we would then be making causality a *per accidens* quality attributed to *brahman.*

If, however, we describe *brahman's* essential nature *svarupa-laksana*, a conceptual difficulty arises, for *brahman* in principle is subject and cannot be objectified. It is not knowable by means of the same rationality as empirical reality.[2]

The goal of knowledge is knowledge of the Self (*atmavidya*). The means to reach this goal is study of the revealed scriptures (*sruti*) along with meditation and reflection. We first hear the word of scripture (*sravana*) and reflect on its meaning (*manana*) by means of reason and exegetical principles. In the end the inspiration present in scripture becomes real within ourselves by means of our own contemplation (*nididhyasana*). What the wise (*rsi*) who spoke through scripture have seen is fulfilled in our own experience.

Exegesis involves first and foremost interpreting dualistic texts figuratively in order to be led to a higher, non-dualistic way of seeing.[3] Or else we see in dualistic texts on creation an expedient means (*upaya*) that makes their Advaita teaching understandable.[4] Since all creation texts are meaningful only in reference to the *saguna* aspect of the Absolute, the fact that different, unharmonizable theories of creation are taught by the Upanishads is no obstacle.[5] The later Advaita, undoubtedly because of Buddhist influence, developed a threefold meaning of scripture. In it *paramarthika-satya* (the highest, non-dual truth) and *vyavaharika-satya* (empirical, relative truth) were completed by *pratibhasika-satya* (illusory truth, which is sublated once the illusion disappears).

Returning to our example of the rope in the twilight which is mistaken for a snake, we see that this mistake only holds true as long as the illusion lasts. Once we come to know that what appeared to be a snake is in reality a rope, the original error with regard to true appearance (*pratibhasika*) is overcome. We have now attained a relative truth (*vyavaharika*), which corresponds to rational-scientific knowledge. There is, however, an even higher truth (*paramarthika*), the standpoint of the Absolute. Now we no longer mistakenly consider the rope as existing independently, but know the non-duality of all beings and the totality. This truth is superempirical, transrational.[6]

In empirical questions about things, scientific knowledge—not the holy scriptures—has full authority. Where there is a contradiction between the two, our interpretation must take note of the different levels of reality; namely, the empirical and the holistic-Absolute. It must also keep in mind that all statements about the Absolute are analogous and merely indicate (*laksyartha*). Therefore they are never true in a literal and direct sense (*mukhyartha*). In any case, a given text can only be related to one level and it has *one* meaning and intention (*ekavakyata*).

Empirical science, however, cannot grasp the One or the whole as an object, because the One/whole is not an object. For this reason the holy scriptures are here the final authority in discovering truth.[7] The experience (*anubhava*) of the whole in itself can only ascertain and state the "that" of wholeness, never the "what," which escapes conceptualization insofar as it is void (*sunya*) of all determinations. We learn how to describe positively the Whole/One from the holy scriptures (*sruti*) alone.[8]

Sruti is the experience of others, which serves as introduction, ascertainment, and correction for my own experience, just as the empirical sciences build on the experiences of past generations. Thus the one who has his/her own experience no longer needs the authority of the scriptures. Yet this authority can be a corrective in helping me distinguish between truth and deception in my own experience. The advaitic experience as such, however, is self-evident.[9]

The presupposition for advaitic experience is not ascetics, sacrifice, intellectual study, but one thing only: the self-revelation of the Absolute.[10] Of course, asceticism and study are very meaningful and important in order to achieve spiritual discipline and certain limited goals. But the emphasis is on self-revelation, and this cannot be otherwise in Advaita Vedanta, for the Absolute or God is the one reality which does not stand opposite humans as a second. The subject in advaitic experience is also *atman.* God is thus subject, both of the revelation and of the non-dual knowledge of revelation.

Jnana

Brahman cannot be an object of knowledge. Thus it is not knowable to discursive reason, but is accessible through an intuitive non-dualistic experience.[11]

The goal which Advaita Vedanta strives to reach is *jnana*, intuitive knowledge.[12] It is a knowledge of what already is, an "opening of the curtain" which hides reality. We do not know anything new, but the unity of reality becomes apparent.

Sankara describes knowledge of *brahman* by means of a *via negativa*, thus giving us a methodological indication on how to attain *jnana*: "*Brahma*-knowledge means only giving up identification with external things, such as the body. The relationship of non-duality with *brahman* cannot be brought about, for it already exists. Persons already have this non-duality with it; they only appear to be identified with something else. Thus, the scriptures do not recommend us to bring about a non-duality with *brahman*, but to give up false identification with things. When identification with things . . . is given up, our natural identity with our own Self takes place. This is expressed by the sentence that says, "the Self is known. In itself it is unknowable and cannot be grasped in any way."[13]

The methods to attain *jnana, brahmavidya* or *atmavidya* make use of all our human capacities: food, the eyes, the ear, the understanding and speech are all preparatory means,[14] which are used especially in sacrificial rituals. From external religious rituals of sacrifice (*yajnavidya*), the path towards identification leads us through meditation on various objects, which remains dependent on objects and on the *saguna* aspect of *brahman*, to pure objectless consciousness (*jnana*), which corresponds to the *nirguna* aspect of *brahman.*[15] Thematic meditation on objects has a lower rank than the advaitic experience. Consequently the Advaitin sometimes underrates particular Yoga practices.[16] When, however, *nirguna brahman* is meditated on in an objectless manner, there is no contradiction between meditation and *jnana.*[17] Thus for the Bhagavad Gita the highest ideal is the unity of the knowledge of Advaita and Yoga.[18]

Since in *jnana* the whole thrust is towards simplicity and unity, the first requirement is a childlike spiritual state (*balya*).[19] The one who wishes to make progress along the path of *jnana* must learn especially to be silent.[20] This takes place by means of relaxation, quiet, self-control, withdrawal from the senses and concentration: in other words, the eightfold path of Yoga.[21] None of these "ascetical" means is an end in itself, but an attempt to center the body as well as the spirit in order to achieve both simplicity and unity.

Jnana, in a certain sense, is both the means to liberation (*moksa*) and liberation itself. A distinction is made between the individual stages, which we will not reproduce here.[22] At the basis of all these indications are the three steps: 1. hearing scripture (*sravana*), 2. reflection (*manana*), 3. meditative integration (*nididhyasana*).[23]

Those who achieve perfect non-dualistic knowledge—and they are not many according to Sankara[24]—enter into *brahman*, for *jnana* is knowledge as participation, even to the point of identification.[25] Almost all Advaitins believe[26] that the person who has attained the perfection of *jnana* in this life has already achieved total liberation. This person has attained a goal than which there is no higher.[27] *Jnana* does not come from acts of the will of the empirical self (*jiva*), for we are dealing with the knowledge that *atman* (the self) and *brahman* (the Absolute) are Advaita: thus the Absolute alone is subject as well as object of this process of knowing.[28] We cannot, therefore, speak of *jnana* as a self-redemption, but only of Self-redemption, culminating in the overcoming of egotistic willing.[29]

Thus we cannot "produce" *jnana*, and therefore exercises of penitence or good works cannot bring about non-dual knowledge. There is, rather, a discovery of truth, and the discoverer is *atman/ brahman.* Nevertheless, we can dispose ourselves for this by learning to be silent, to hear and to meditate. When, however, we are led to reality by *jnana*, secondary forces are freed which enable us to perform truly good works.[30]

Grace and Prayer

Jnana is the very essence of spiritual experience. It is *true* experience which alters our life. Since the self is Advaita with the Absolute and the Absolute is Advaita with the empirical, the question of
whether spiritual experience comes from divine grace or from human activity cannot be posed in this way. This alternative implies a
dualism, which Advaita Vedanta removes by sublation. So, too, the
duality between worldly goals (virtues, success) and liberation
(*moksa*) disappears for the Advaitin.

Yogis who are experienced in meditation, as well as the philosophers of Advaita Vedanta are relentless in pointing out the discontinuity of our own capacities, which are linked to the senses and the
power of understanding (*indriyani*), and the non-dualistic experience. This discontinuity is expressed as follows: "This *atman* is not
attained by study, nor by the intellect, nor by hearing. It is attainable by the simple fact that the seeker endures in his/her search. To
him/her this *atman* reveals its own nature."[31] Knowledge comes
from a unified mind and from contemplation.[32] But the experience
itself is described as a *raptus*, as something coming to us from
without.[33]

Are we therefore justified in describing the experience of *jnana*
as the experience of grace?[34] Undoubtedly, in India too, grace is the
presupposition for non-dual knowledge.[35] Thus the Bhagavad Gita
says that God has revealed himself by grace (*prasada*)[36] and by love
and mercy (*anukampana*).[37] Nevertheless, we have to keep in mind
that the notion of grace in Advaita Vedanta and in Christianity,
which bases it on a personal relationship between God and humankind, is to be differentiated. In Advaita our true Self is revealed.
Divine grace is subject and the object in this event, though advaitic
vision transcends these categories in any case. In part III we will
examine whether this insight can be interpreted in a Christian way.

Sankara considers the essential to be a longing for God's revelation, and this comes from trust in his grace. This longing expresses
itself in and is strengthened by prayer.[38]

Also, the Katha Upanishad says that the self, which is manifested by grace, is not known by one's own knowledge, but by
prayer.[39] Therefore our prayer should be concerned, not with
worldly things, but with God's revelation.[40]

In Vedic literature there are all kinds of prayers of petition.
They range from invocations of a personal God to silent immersion
in the One, with which we are united.[41] The directions for prayer in

connection with meditation and Yoga exercises are particularly important.

Also, prayer for the forgiveness of sins is not lacking in the Upanishads.[42] It is an outcry of the person who is overpowered by revelation of truth. The height of this prayer is in the introductory formula to the Taittiriya Upanishad, which is typical of Advaita Vedanta spirituality. After the one praying has requested a blessing from God, addressing him with his various names, he/she continues: "You alone will I call inaccessible *brahman.* You I will name righteousness. You will I call truth. May he protect me, may he protect the spiritual master—OM, peace, peace, peace."[43]

In Advaita Vedanta we find detailed introductions to prayer distinguishing different stages which are closely related to those of Christian prayer. Thus we find prayers of petition, thematic meditation on sacred texts, affective prayer, prayers that express a desire for God's revelation, and the simple prayer of the heart which is carried out either silently or by concentration on certain words of prayer.[44]

Personal faith (*sraddha*) plays an important role. This expression means first of all unconditional trust of one's spiritual guide (*guru*), since the truth of his teaching will only later be confirmed by one's own practice of meditation and any initial doubt would compromise one's readiness to pray.[45] In faith the aspect of unconditional surrender is essential.[46]

The Bhagavad Gita, in particular, develops the essence of faith. God loves all beings with the same love. He doesn't prefer one or neglect another.[47] Nevertheless, God is only present bodily in the one who responds to this love.[48] Thus, in spite of the principles of advaitic teaching there is no indifference in whether one believes or not. The insight behind this is that a person is what he/she believes.[49] Thus faith, just as knowledge, is not an abstract intellectual attitude, but existential realization, and this includes participation in what is believed.

The one who believes enters into God, whether he does what is "good" or not.[50] In the Bhagavad Gita even the bad are accepted into faith: "Even a sinner, if he reverences me and me alone, is to be considered a good person because he has correctly made up his mind," says God.[51] Authentic faith, however, truly transforms a person and makes him/her good.

This corresponds to Sankara's concept of faith. In his eyes faith is a mental attitude which trusts the authority of the holy scriptures to introduce us to the practice of meditation.[52]

The one who has faith will be given a share in knowledge, i.e., spiritual non-dual knowledge (*jnana*), which confirms and justifies the original trust.[53] Faithless doubting, on the other hand, leads to our downfall.[54]

According to the Bhagavad Gita faithful devotion is to be considered as the highest form of Yoga,[55] for faith is sufficient for salvation.[56] The person who is filled with faith should meditate on the visible forms of the divinity,[57] for the invisible is beyond the powers of human perception.[58]

From the teachings of the Bhagavad Gita has come the most popular form of Indian piety, *bhakti* mysticism. It sees devotion and faithful reverence of God as the ultimate good.[59] *Bhakti*, however, also has its place in strict Advaita Vedanta as we saw above in discussing Sankara and Ramana Maharishi. Personal dualism melts away before the advaitic vision, thanks to the teaching of the Advaita of *atman* and *brahman*. Thus we can present the experience of non-duality as a melting away of the human self in the ecstasy of the unity of love based on divine grace.[60]

Nevertheless, the Advaita Vedanta emphasizes that non-dual knowledge, from which faith is finally deduced, must be truly *experienced* and realized. It is neither intellectual nor emotional, but life-changing according to Advaita's transrational mode of seeing.

5.

The Theory and Practice of Meditation

"Persevering practice alone is the secret of success. On this point there is no doubt," according to Hatha Yoga Pradipika,[1] for those interested in attaining spiritual maturity. This is also *the* basic principle for all Hindu as well as Buddhist spirituality. Practice means above all meditative exercises. Practice is not merely applied theory, but rather theory becomes clear when verified in practice, which aims at direct experience (*anubhava*) that either justifies the theory or revises it.

In Indian popular religion, the rituals—especially sacrifices—serve as practice in this sense. Thus for most Indians, the mental attitude regarding surrender and the readiness to identify with the sacrificial object play a major role. Indian religious practice seeks an existential unity of attitude and action.

Cultic activity is a first step on the way to perfection.[2] Sacrifice in the temple, a self-offering which is still external, is later internalized step-by-step in meditation.[3] Cultic activity is the outward expression of an inner event, and as such—at least for the beginner—is the presupposition for *jnana.*[4] The cultic rituals are meant to attune and prepare the believer, and this is the reason Yoga exercises should not be undertaken before performing a ritual or at least saying a prayer. Likewise, the study of philosophy is a praxis of purification and a concentration of the understanding. Ritual prayer, the study of the scriptures, as well as mental exercises all function as physical-psychic purification and are the foundation which makes possible genuine selfless devotion and spiritual concentration. Yoga is nothing else than a preparation of the body and mind for non-dual, intuitive knowledge.[5] Yoga brings harmony and quiet to the psychosomatic system, and this is necessary in activating specific energies (*prana*), which are vehicles for intuitive knowledge. In most schools of Yoga, as well as in Tantric systems, the practice of bodily exercises and experiences play a decisive role.[6] However, this is not generally the case in Advaita Vedanta.

We already indicated that *jnana* is not only theoretical knowl-

edge of non-duality, but existential realization of the Advaita of
atman and *brahman*. In this way human existence is changed. This
type of experience does not happen as the result of intellectual
questions. Instead, the question: "Who am I?" is posed—but by
means of external devotion and concentration, which touch the
whole life of the searcher. This implies the next question, which
concerns the person who is asking the question. This quest for the
subject who exists is called *vicara*, and is part of a method also used
in Yoga and Zen Buddhism. According to Ramana Maharsi, it is *the*
means par excellence in preparing the mind for *jnana*.[7] In Ramana
Maharsi's thought it is particularly clear that theory and practice
cannot be separated. He divides the spiritual way into four stages,
which do not follow one another, but intertwine and penetrate one
another:[8]

1. Instruction (*upadesa*)
2. Practice (*abhyasa*)
3. Experience (*anubhava*)
4. Attainment of the goal (*arudha*)

In Advaita Vedanta *jnana* is a gift and a task which is realized in the
praxis of living.

Moksa

The word *moksa* comes from the root *muc*, to free. *Moksa* is a
release from the ignorance that consists in humankind's experience
of their being as separated from God. Only through the knowledge
of the Advaita of *atman* and *brahman* can humans achieve *brahmavidya*; the freeing knowledge of the non-duality of being.[9]

At this point we must remember the often mentioned basic
law, that the one who has experienced *brahman* becomes *brahman*-
structured. The noetic and ontic levels of reality are inseparable,
for we are dealing with a meditative realization, which alters human existence as a whole.[10]

Moksa—just as *jnana*—is grounded, not in the capacity of the
individual self, but in *atman*, which transcends the individual and
nevertheless is understood as not-different from the empirical personality. It is likewise this transcendental dimension, which we
experience in, with, and under the aspect of the empirical as its
ground. *Atman* is the subject of *moksa*.[11] " 'Salvation' or 'release'

or 'liberation' means that the Absolute, *brahman*, of which we are ignorant (*avidya*) because of our hidden, objective and many conflicting individual selves (*jiva*), is brought to the light. Once awakened, these selves can attain wisdom and return to the true Self. Salvation can thus be defined as a return of Absolute mind to itself."[12]

Moksa, therefore, does not mean that we attain to a beyond which is separate from the world.[13] But rather, by *moksa* a false attitude is abandoned and the unity of reality becomes known. The veil of dualistic ignorance is pulled aside so that what *is* becomes visible.[14] Seeing things as they really are, knowing the formlessness behind the forms, experiencing this as *saccidananda*: all of this is *moksa*.[15] In other words, *moksa* is the experience of the presence of the One or of the one presence. Everything which could be an obstacle to this experience is overcome in *moksa:* reality appears in its total interrelationality as the expression of the One.

The Root of Evil

At this point we must clarify Advaita Vedanta's understanding of evil and sin in order to better understand what *moksa* means. Evil is based on ignorance of *brahman*, which implies that *brahman*—in its *maya* form—is, in the end, the basic cause of this *avidya*, or evil.[16] The one who believes he/she is separated from *brahman* is in error and does evil deeds. Because of their isolation, humans fall into fear,[17] and fear is the root of aggression. *Avidya*, therefore, causes false identification with finite things,[18] which leads to thirsting for (*trsna*) individual being in continuous competition and self-centered struggle.[19] When our common essence in *atman* is not recognized, individuals become hostile to one another. In Advaita Vedanta evil is based on an existential illusion, one which is, however, very real as it emprisons the world in a chain of suffering.

Self-justification and willful self-seeking are the two major false attitudes which are overcome by *moksa*. The Bhagavad Gita explains this in a central passage:[20] Absence of pride and deceit, non-violence are the characteristics of the one who has attained *moksa*. Whoever possesses these virtues, possesses peace (*santi*). Sankara explains the notion, lack of deceit (*adambhitvam*), saying that a person does not show off his/her own virtues or consider him/herself justified (*svadharma prakatikaranam*). In other places the notion *dambha* appears, describing hypocrisy.[21] Sankara says that the hypocrite pretends to be just on his own merits (*dharma-dhvajitva*). This lie is the characteristic of those whose demonic nature is the opposite of those who have found their identity in *atman* and therefore have no need of a lie concerning their worth. Self-justification is another root of evil and is closely connected to *avidya*.

Jivanmukta

It is significant that *moksa* is described not only negatively, as a giving up of duality, but also as *ananda* (bliss) and *santi* (peace), joy and freedom from fear.[22] Peace is composure [*Gelassenheit:* could also be translated abandonment or equanimity—translator] before one's lot in life.[23]

Moksa corresponds to the nature of the self. Thus basically *moksa* can be attained in this life. In India there are persons who are already redeemed while still living in the body (*jivanmukta*). These people are above good and evil, for they are not-two with the Absolute.[24] They are perfectly free and are no longer subject to the cycle of rebirth (*samsara*). To the one who has experienced *atman/brahman* there is no longer any difference between the phenomenal world and *brahman*, body and mind, death and life.[25] "He seems to live in a body only for the unreleased. After a time when the body dies, we say, 'he gains freedom from the body' (*videha-mukti*). But the truth is there is no difference in *mukti* (release)."[26] For the *jivanmukta* there is no difference between present and future eschatology, for what is awaited in the future has become a present experience which transcends the temporal. Normal life with its manifold aspects is a meaningless goal for the *jivanmukta*. This can be clarified in two ways within Advaita Vedanta.

On the one hand *moksa* is not meant as the destruction of, but as the fruition of empirical reality. This is clarified by the famous example of the tiger cub which is raised among goats and therefore remains tame, bleats, and possesses a gentleness completely out of character, for he has fully forgotten his true nature. Only when a wild jungle tiger forces the cub to eat raw flesh does he awaken to his true, tiger nature.[27] *Moksa*, in this sense, is a coming-to-self . . . although in this case there is no difference between "two natures," for everything is rooted in *atman*. The way humans experience themselves is a matter of viewpoint. The *jivanmukta* lives within the *paramarthika* perspective.

On the other hand, there is an important tradition which takes a pessimistic stance towards life and devaluates the empirical world,[28] since it is only *maya.* In this tradition *moksa* implies that everything individual has disappeared. Just as different rivers mingle with one another in the one sea where they are indistinguishable, so too the individual disappears in the Absolute and thus finds peace and perfection.[29]

Both interpretations are based on the Upanishads and influence Indian spiritual life to this day. They indicate the tension between sensuous worldliness and radical flight from the world which is so typical of Indian religions. The *jivanmukta* can reach the goal of spiritual perfection in various ways: by going deeper within the self, by knowledge, by action, and by believing in God.[30] What is common to all the paths is that they all lead to the experience of the Advaita of *atman* and *brahman,* or the self and God. The *jivanmukta* can say without exaggeration the *mahavakya: aham brahmasmi,* "I am *brahman."*[31] It is based on an experience of leaving behind consciousness of an "I" (*aham*). For the "I" implies an object which stands before me, and this disappears in Advaita. Without this the sentence would be meaningless and even a blasphemy. It must be interpreted in the sense of *"atman brahmasti"* (*atman* is *brahman*).

The *jivanmukta* is a fully awakened one (*buddha*). His/her presence radiates indescribable light.[32] Yet there is still a controversy over whether a person can become perfect to the point that no further spiritual growth is possible or necessary. Even the *jivanmukta* has to meditate and so deepen his/her *moksa.* Nevertheless, according to Advaita Vedanta, he/she cannot fall back into ignorance and sin.[33]

Yoga and Meditation

Our purpose here is not to present a detailed discussion of the practice of Yoga, nor its philosophical system—which is quite different from its practice—but only to reflect on the relationship between the theory of Advaita Vedanta and the practice of Yoga.

Yoga is the means of opening up to advaitic experience.[34] Vivekananda described this realization or experience (*anubhava*) as the central idea of the Upanishads. The expression *anubhava* brings up ontic associations: *anu-bhu*—being along with or fitting. Yoga in general is a method of controlling the will and the senses. Through

Yoga, humans place themselves within the rhythm of life and the harmony of being, which makes them aware of a great unity. Yoga and Advaita are therefore closely related.

In very ancient definitions of Yoga found in the Upanishads, the senses as well as the understanding are supposed to come together in a point of stillness, so that all outwardly directed acts of understanding stop; and peaceful consciousness, no longer occupied with concrete images, discovers itself.[35] We saw above that the meaning of Yoga was to give up, as it were, one's false identification with finite things in order to become perfectly in tune with the One. Therefore, remaining unmoved by objects is both the most important condition and the first fruit of meditation.[36] This attitude can be described as equanimity or composure. Yoga signifies that the spirit, as a physical-psychical-mental unity, has been placed in a non-dualistic state.

Yoga practice as such can also be explained dualistically by means of Samkhya philosophy. Here the purpose of exercise is to release the spiritual principle (purusa) fully from its material bondage (praktri).[37]

For the Advaitin the goal of Yoga is the experience of moksa, as an experience of the Advaita of jivatman and paramatman, or atman and brahman.[38] We already examined all these determinations above as characteristic of advaitic experience, and at this point Yoga and Advaita are the same. Yoga is a catharsis in which the husks and masks which surround us are discarded and atman, the true Self, comes to light.[39] Yoga, as a path to radical self-knowledge, consists in total concentration and return to the essentials. Thus Yoga and Advaita have the same goal, and Yoga is considered an appropriate means to realize the advaitic experience.

This connection becomes even clearer when we examine the meditation exercises which constitute the practice of Yoga. Meditation produces integration, and since we identify with the things we meditate, it also produces identification. The meditation of atman overcomes our bonds to the relative.[40] The pranayama exercises of Yoga especially, awaken life energy (prana).[41] In order to integrate death meditatively, Yoga anticipates it[42] and sees it as a particular moment in an overall process. Thus all fear of death disappears in meditation.[43]

Meditation interiorizes the cosmic process of brahman's unfolding in a reverse way: humans advance gradually from gross, external appearances to subtle truth, and finally to the unity of the ground, so that the explication of the world gradually becomes implicated in the unified consciousness.[44]

Advaita Vedanta warns that the one who is meditating on a certain form remains standing in one place, and thus is not proceeding towards non-dual knowledge. Meditation presupposes a visible image of God. For the sake of the meditation the *brahman* has taken on forms and figures as *saguna brahman*.[45] This is, however, only a means to an end; viz. advaitic experience, which transcends all objects.[46] Meditation is a preparation for the self-revelation of *brahman*, which as such cannot come from the step-by-step path of meditation.[47] In the end we have to meditate without forms, symbols and ideas—without objects.[48]

Non-objective meditation—known in the West especially through Zen—is by no means limited to Buddhism. Vedanta recommends it, but only after mastery of preparatory exercises. The beginner needs an image, figure or thought to maintain his/her attention. Without it concentration is impossible. This is called *alambana*, a mental exercise which dwells on the manifold and gross form of *brahman*, the *viraj*. Sankara requires that this meditation as an object (*upasana*)[49] be complemented by knowledge.[50] *Viveka* (discernment or discrimination) contains the rational element. In this way rationality is being placed directly at the service of the overall meditative consciousness which achieves its goal in this way. *Upasana*, meditation as an object, can only attain *saguna brahman*.[51] Only *brahmavidya*, which is based on *upasana* and *viveka* while transcending them, reaches *nirguna brahman*.

Finally, advaitic knowledge (*jnana*) and meditation are identical in the simple meditation of OM, which is the same as *atman/ brahman*[52] since it integrates all states of consciousness. For now there is nothing objective. In its two vowels (a–u), the first and the last of the alphabet, and in the nasal (m), OM (a–u–m) includes the phenomenal world and the states of waking consciousness, dreaming, and deep sleep. The silence which follows OM points to the *turiya* state. "A the waking state, U the dream, M deep sleep, and the SILENCE, *Turiya*; all four together comprise the totality of this manifestation of *atman-brahman* as a syllable. Just as the sound OM manifests itself, grows, becomes transformed in its vocal quality, and finally subsides into the silence that follows . . . , so likewise the four "states" or components of being. They are transformations of the one existence which, taken together, constitutes the totality of its modes, whether regarded from the microcosmic or from the macrocosmic point of view. A and U are as essential to the sound as M, or as the SILENCE against which the sound appears. Moreover, it would be a mistake to say that A|U|M did not exist while the SILENCE reigned; for it would be still potential. The actual manifestation of the syllable, on the other hand, is fleeting and evanescent, whereas the SILENCE abides. The SILENCE, indeed, is present elsewhere during a local pronunciation of AUM— that is to say (by analogy), transcendentally during the creation, manifestation and dissolution of a universe."[53]

OM is the whole teaching of Advaita Vedanta reduced to its simplest form. The meditation of OM is anchored in the world of the many and looks to the physical and psychic energies for its dynamism; namely, in the awakening of *prana*. It brings release (*moksa*) because of the advaitic experience which maintains opposites as sublated. In this way it is possible to attain liberation from finite things—that is, a non-attachment which has no need of external things.[54] It is a freedom from desire and non-desire[55] as well as from sin, since nothing is sought as one's own. In this it realizes our true will, which is unity with the will of God.[56]

This freedom is true freedom, because it doesn't consist in a negation of another's freedom, but is grounded positively in knowledge of one's unity with the other.[57] The ignorant depend on their desires and in this they are unfree. The proficient Advaitin is free, because he knows his self as *atman*, as in harmony with the whole. The Advaita of *atman/brahman* overcomes the opposition of autonomy and heteronomy and makes possible our participation in holistic *ontonomy*. This is the goal of Yoga which is to be achieved through meditation. It is also the very essence of the basic experience found in Advaita Vedanta.

II

The Non-duality
of Trinitarian Doctrine

6.

Development of Trinitarian Thinking

The Theological Basis

The doctrine of the trinity is rooted in a double experience which is inseparable from the work and history of Jesus of Nazareth. One aspect of this experience is the knowledge of Jesus as Christ. In the person of Jesus the immediate presence of God was experienced, and this led to thinking about Jesus' similarity or identity to God. The doctrine of the trinity was thus developed in direct dependence on christology. The other aspect of this experience is the work of the Spirit in the community of Jesus' disciples, as we see it reflected in John's farewell discourse, the Pentecost event, and the overall self-understanding of the apostles. In the Spirit there was certitude about God's presence, and this experience was then communicated by means of the Judaic and/or Hellenistic theological traditions. Thus the doctrine of the trinity was developed in direct dependence on pneumatology. At the same time there were questions concerning the relationship between God as experienced in Jesus and the Spirit. From these questions the whole of later trinitarian theology developed.

The notion of Logos had an important function in the formulation of these questions and their solutions, and it too developed from Jewish wisdom literature on the one hand, and Hellenistic philosophy, inspired by Plato on the other. Especially in the apologists until Origen it would be difficult to overemphasize the importance of the Logos discussion for the development of the doctrine of the trinity. But at the same time, because of certain of these explanations of the Spirit, especially those based on the creative power of *ruah* (spirit) or a heavenly hierarchy, there was a gradual development in the understanding of the Spirit as the Spirit's role in the community. At first the pneumatological themes were not clearly distinguished from the Logos. Only later did a more clearly trinitarian manner of thinking replace binitarian thinking.[1]

In the struggles to portray a trinitarian God, one theme is dominant: the faith that there is one true God, the same God who is encountered in Christ and in the Spirit.[2] For if the experience of Christ or the Spirit were not an encounter with God as he is, but only with an aspect of God or a manifestation of his otherwise inexhaustible essence, we could not be certain of salvation, since the revelation of Jesus Christ would not be absolutely authoritative.

The efforts of the church fathers to account for this revelatory experience rationally, by returning to the metaphysical heritage of Greek, and especially Neoplatonic philosophy, was necessary not only because of apologetical needs, but *also* because of the need for greater certitude about salvation, which was strengthened by rational arguments showing how the relationship of the human to the divine Logos could be credible: *fides quaerens intellectum.*

P. Tillich, bringing together salvation history and the metaphysical heritage, gives three reasons for the trinitarian dogma (III, p. 283).[3] First, the trinitarian dogma is a reflection of the unity of the absolute and the concrete in God. Secondly, it enables us to grasp and proclaim God as living; third, it proclaims the threefold experience of God as creative power, saving love and ecstatic transformation.

At least since Augustine, trinitarian structure of this revelation was seen as corresponding to certain psychological structures, which later dogmatic history described as *vestigia trinitatis,* ontological parallels, images, or correlations.

It is not enough to deduce the doctrine of the trinity from specific biblical passages. Yet the trinitarian formulas of the New Testament (e.g., Mt 28:19; 2 Cor 13:13) are particularly meaningful because they reflect on how God achieves salvation *in* the Spirit *through* the revelation of his love in Jesus Christ. God defined himself in Jesus Christ; thus the effects of the Spirit of Christ cannot be distinguished from the effects of God's Spirit (Rm 8:9; 2 Cor 3:18; Gal 4:6). God, Jesus Christ, and the Spirit who determines the manner and mode of Christ's resurrected presence, are all working the same salvation, as we see in Paul's formulas of greeting (1 Cor 12:4ff.; 2 Cor 13:13; Rm 5:1ff.). Expressions such as "in Christ," "in the Spirit," "Christ in you," are practically interchangeable.[4] When Paul is emphasizing the unity of the Spirit (1 Cor 12:4) and yet speaks of "spirits," he is merely explaining the different effects of the Spirit (1 Cor 14:12, 32; 12:10).[5]

By means of trinitarian thinking Christianity has been able to approach God's work in new ways—from the *logos spermatikos* to the "unrecognized Christ" of the Hindus. Trinitarian explanations provided Christian experience with constantly new ways of understanding its universality in its ever-widening historical development.

Thus the trinitarian problematic cannot be limited to an intellectual task; viz., how "one equals three" or "three equals one." Nevertheless, it is no accident that Parmenides' problem concerning the one and the many has been historically and factually linked with the trinitarian problematic. We live in one reality, which is experienced and explained as multidimensional. The doctrine of the trinity offers a possibility of making the notion of God intelligible within this tension.[6]

Another tension which trinitarian thinking interprets meaningfully without resolving it is the tension between God's absoluteness and his relationality. There is a very real tension between Thomas of Aquinas' sentence, *deus definiri nequit* (God is not capable of definition),[7] referring to God's complete superiority to human thinking, which is the basis of Anselm's ontological argument[8] as well as the reason for continuous warnings about blasphemous *hybris* of the attempt to "grasp" God from John Chrysostom[9] to Karl Barth, and God's revelation of himself through his incarnation as our brother.[10]

Knowledge of God comes from being existentially grasped by God. It allows us no neutral place to stand, from which we would speculate on the trinity. This was especially clear in the life of Athanasius, who more than anyone else struggled with and defended the trinity, for in his eyes the very possibility of salvation was at stake.[11] Hilary gives this same reason for defending the essential unity of Father and Son as essential to Christianity.[12]

The trinity offers a possibility of rising above the dualism of our everyday experience of the world and attaining overall theological knowledge which integrates the seemingly diverse parts of our experience of the world into a total synthesis of meaning and significance. The doctrine of the trinity can be the means of coming to understand our practical experience of a manifold in relation to our meditative experience of unity *non-dualistically,* as we will explain in the following sections. If New Testament theology considers it essential to know Jesus as the crucified and to maintain the identity of God with the crucified Jesus,[13] then this mediation between God as perfect wholeness and God as the crucified one—the very essence of the world's disintegration by sin—offers us a notion of God which interprets and integrates the two experiences non-dualistically.

This is exactly what trinitarian thinking implies. The doctrine of the trinity thinks the unity of reality from within the Christ event, which overcomes the power of sin. Functionally, therefore, it is in continuity with the philosophy of Advaita Vedanta. Trinitarian thinking, just as Advaita Vedanta, is not directed towards knowing an object, but to knowing ourselves as we are known (1 Cor 8:2ff.; Gal 4:9). It is not transitive thinking, but an intransitive becoming conscious.[14] In the final analysis it involves a renewal in the Spirit.

Non-Christian Influences

In the early development of Christian trinitarian thought, there were triadic or neoplatonic ways of viewing reality (perhaps indirectly influenced by India) as well as Jewish tradition, both of which played an important role. The *trishagion* adopted by the church's liturgy was linked with angelic powers, conceived of as word and truth in the original Jewish setting. Both Origen and Irenaeus recall this tradition and identify word and wisdom as the Son and the Holy Spirit.[15] Philo subordinates both angelic powers to God, explaining that they are the highest powers of God. This follows from what he considers as a necessary premise; namely, that the Absolute is revealed in three aspects.[16] He thus understands God as Father of the universe, Wisdom as the Mother of the universe, and the Logos as the soul of the world-body.[17] This three-ness guarantees the unity of the world. We should also mention here the triadic formulas of Jewish liturgies; for example, the prayer of eighteen petitions, which calls on God as one but qualifies him as threefold in his deeds: creator, redeemer and present through the spirit.[18] Finally there is the threefold blessing of Aaron.

Triadic thinking has been found both in the history of religions—including the Indian *trimurti*—as well as in the triadic structure of human thought, for example the syllogism, the dialectical method, and categories of experience such as past-present-future, spatio-temporal-consciousness, waking state-dreaming-deep sleep.[19] Interesting observations could be made concerning these parallels within the spiritual history of humankind. But all these become secondary for the history of Christian trinitarian thinking.

For in Christianity the decisive event was Jesus Christ. This was to be understood by means of any available tradition, whether this tradition was aware of Christ or not, for the use of another tradition could not put into question the Christ event as "once for all."

Early trinitarian thinking was quite naturally affected by gnosticism[20] even as it defended itself against Gnostic enthusiasm and dualism. Gnostics believed that the Spirit was fully realized in them. The Spirit thus became their "possession." They refused any eschatological tension—thereby denying the ongoing presence of the cross. In order to hold this position they had to preach a radical dualism of spirit and body, since this enabled them to overlook the body's insufficiencies and human finitude. In responding to this, orthodox Christianity taught that the Spirit is not the sole "property" of charismatics, but is a gift of God. The Spirit is the "property" of God not of humans, and this leads to trinitarian thinking.

In Gnostic christology's triadic schema of God-Will-Logos (where significantly the middle term is feminine, as is the Aramaic *ruha*) or in Neoplatonism's three hypostases: the One, spirit, soul (*hen-nous-psyche*),[21] Christian trinitarian thinking discovered a dynamism it already recognized from its own religious praxis (Rm 8–9–11; 1 Cor 12:4–6). In the Pastor Hermas, Christ was identified with the Logos as mediator of creation,[22] and this was linked with a subordinationist theology which is very similar to the subordination of *hiranyagarbha* to *isvara*, as we saw above in chapter 3—although this latter does not succeed in understanding the unity of the trinity.

From the very earliest developments in the doctrine of the trinity there was an important difference in the manner of thinking of the Eastern and Western churches. This difference is a reflection of an underlying intellectual tension seen also in their trinitarian thinking, and it polarized the two churches for centuries. While the West reflects on the unity, only then to include three-ness, the East reverses this: it begins with the three hypostases and attempts to understand their unity. Naturally this typology should not be exaggerated, but it helps explain the different emphases in the doctrine of the trinity.

Irenaeus and Tertullian

Irenaeus attacked the Gnostics because they attributed human feelings and spiritual states to God.[23] Irenaeus' task, therefore, was to emphasize God's absoluteness and unity in every possible way. Word and wisdom, according to him, are the two hands of God[24] and are identical with Christ and the Holy Spirit: through them God is visible to the world.[25] Every event is dependent on God's free will, from which (ex) everything exists, created through (per) the Son, in (in) the Holy Spirit.[26]

We see here a tendency towards monarchical thinking: God reveals himself by means of his salvific will in the oeconomy of the trinity. Those who possess the Spirit are led to the Son so that the Son might lead them to the Father, who then shares his immortality with them. Without the Spirit humans cannot see the word of God, and without the Son no one comes to the Father, for the knowledge of the Father is the Son; knowledge of the Son, however, is given through the Spirit. The Son gives the Spirit according to the free will of the Father.[27] The final terminus is always God the Father.

God is the one reality. He is the only reason for all that happens, and is—to combat Gnostic dualism—the creator of matter.[28] The unity of God and the world's complete dependence on him are accomplished through the return of sinful humans to their original *imago et similitudo Dei.* For all is mediated by Christ who, in God's oeconomy, is nothing else than the Father's efficacious work.

Irenaeus defends God's all-powerfulness against every sort of dualism. God is the living unity of power, love and moral justice. These three effects which he wills can be experienced concretely.[29] Naturally when he reflects on Christ's pre-existence with God, and presents God's ways of acting as hypostatized in the notion of the trinity,[30] he returns to the already mentioned concrete soteriological work of the trinity.

Tertullian goes beyond Irenaeus in thinking a trinitarian concept of God. In his eyes it is important to exclude all anthropomorphisms from our concept of God.[31] He is the first to use the Latin term, *trinitas.*[32] His formula is: *una substantia, tres personae.* Here the notions of substance as well as person are understood in a special way. *Substantia* is a translation of (the Greek) *hypostasis.* Both terms describe a substratum, a basis for the realization of being. Substance, according to Tertullian, is the "realized stage of the idea," an "independent existence."[33] In further realizing itself, the substance, as *res* becomes accesible to sense perception. At this stage this realization is called *persona,* for it is an objectively existing thing. Here person means something which can be experienced in itself and is a determinable object or area, which can be differentiated from, yet is not essentially different from other areas.

Tertullian developed his position in opposition to the Sabellian teaching on Logos. In this teaching there were three active modes (*energeiai*) of one person (*prosopon*). The Father was the creative mode, the Son the illuminating mode, and the Spirit the inspiring effectiveness of the one divine person. Consequently, the Son and Spirit were considered to be rays, existing in time, of the paternal sun.[34] Although Tertullian, too, subordinates the *tres personae* to the *una substantia*, the Logos is a real and distinct essence at the moment when God lets the Logos go forth from himself. Nevertheless, there was a time when God was alone.[35] But even then the Logos was with God, potentially, as a thought (*ratio*).[36]

What is important is that, for Tertullian, in opposition to gnosticism, "salvation history" is understood as the natural continuation of creation history,[37] and not as its corrective or a fully new work. The trinity is thought out oeconomically, for God unfolds as three persons in order to achieve salvation. Salvation is thus achieved through creation and redemption. Humans can only look at the sun's rays, not at the sun itself.[38] Only the Son is able to suffer, not the Father.[39] The Father is the totality, and whatever the Son has is given to him by the Father. Thus the Son must be lesser than the father: *filius portio plenitudinis*.[40] All the various images which Tertullian uses to portray his *oeconomical* doctrine of the trinity correspond to this sentence. He compares the trinity to the sun, its illumination, and its rays; or with the root, the branch and the fruit; or again with the spring, the river, and the sea.[41] Thus Tertullian can say that the Son is the projection (*prolatio*) of the Father,[42] but only as having his own dependent existence (*persona*). These expressions are hardly distinguishable from Gnostic presentations,[43] and thus Irenaeus later expressly rejects the expression, *prolatio*.[44]

At this point in our trinitarian discussion it will be helpful to recall the Indian notion of non-duality in order to see how it is both parallel to and different from the starting point in the Christian notion of God. The structural parallels between the oeconomical subordinationist doctrine of Tertullian and the insights of *brahman*, interpreted by Sankara as *isvara-hiranyagarbha-viraj* could hardly be more striking.

We could say that both systems contain similarities in the way they understand the unity of reality, a unity, however, which in

India is seen through intuitive experience, and in Christianity by means of the event of the incarnation. Neither position need exclude the other, since the one is rooted in experience, whereas the other is rooted in the basis of an experience, as we will demonstrate in part III.

Our concern about the certainty of salvation leads us to reflect on the unity of God's activity as the basis for the unity of God in himself. Even though Tertullian has not yet developed the doctrine of an immanent trinity, he is able to distinguish two ways of viewing things—and on this point he is in full agreement with Sankara: that of God as he is in himself, and God as he appears to humans in their rational capacities to know. To simplify, we could say that for Tertullian "the Son is, for the sake of self-revelation, a dis-empowered Godhead—the Godhead (divinity) for the world, whose sphere is identical with the world-thought and with the power which is necessary so that the world order can mediate a powerless God—who is God for the world. From the viewpoint of humanity, this divinity is God; i.e., God as they grasp him and he grasps them, but from the viewpoint of God—speculation can fix itself on him, but not see through him—this divinity is something subordinate and transient."[45]

In Tertullian's work we see clearly the function of the doctrine of the Trinity: maintaining the unity of God in his creative and salvific action. In this way the unity of reality itself can be established. Thus his influence on later historical developments of this dogma cannot be overestimated.

Origen

The first systematic grounding of the doctrine of the Trinity was realized by Origen. He examines Christian faith in relationship to the whole of his world's learning. Cosmology and soteriology form a unity; creation and redemption are two acts of a single drama.[46] God is Spirit and light,[47] the one Being[48] whose substance and spiritual principle is beyond divisions.[49] He is the ground which cannot be explained. Because he is also superabundant perfection, he shares and reveals himself in the Logos.[50] The Logos, however, is spiritual power, above all other forces, and is identified with Christ. The Logos is eternally in God. Through (dia) him all things are created and revealed by (hypo) God.[51] Through the Logos-Christ we know the unknowable One, which in itself is unknowable.

The world, too, in both its harmoniousness and its defects points to its source in many ways. Order in the world, its dependence on being or a ground of being, and the creature's desire for God all point to the One. Knowledge of God and knowledge of the world exist in a correlation to one another.[52]

God reveals himself in three modes, which Origen calls *verbum–via–lux*, and he sees them (in reverse order) as the essence of salvation.[53] The Logos is not only the highest divine power, but is also personal existence, *deuteros theos*,[54] which goes forth from God in a spiritual manner as the will comes from the reason.[55]

In order to grasp the personality of the *deuteros theos* in its special existence, Origen speaks of an *aeterna ac sempiterna generatio*,[56] which is thought of as a continuously verified spiritual participation in the fullness of God.[57] This *generatio* is of a special kind; i.e., not an emanation, for Origen explicitly rejects Tertullian's term *prolatio*.[58]

Father and Son are the same in their essence (*homoousios*), but two in their hypostases, for the Son is related to the Father as light is to the sun. From the Father's viewpoint, the Logos-Son is subordinated. Thus Origen hesitates to address prayers to Christ.[59] The Spirit is called into being by the Son; is under the Logos,[60] and presents a third hypostasis whose property is sanctification,[61] whereas the Son is portrayed as reason. The Father, however, is the principle of being.[62] The trinity thus appears as three concentric circles, with the Father as the most all-inclusive and greatest, while the Spirit is the smallest and most dependent, and the Son occupies the middle.[63] Only God the Father is truly absolute.

Along with this subordination are numerous texts in which the equality of Christ with the Father is emphasized; thus there is no question of subordinationism.[64] This is important for the doctrine of *apokatastasis*. Christ is the prototype of the *theanthropos*.[65] The goal of faith is conformity with Christ. It reaches perfection in divinization (*theopoiesis*). The universal work of the Spirit is to lead humans into this conformity with Christ, who must be fully divine so that conformity with him may accomplish the salvation of the whole world (*apokatastasis*) in the fullest sense.[66]

The only way to understand these two mutually contradictory positions is to say that Origen developed two different ways of viewing things from two different standpoints. The doctrine of the trinity is thought out oeconomically, yet Origen tends toward seeing God's self-manifestation as part of his inalterable essence, and insofar as he accepts this contradiction, he takes a step in the direc-

tion of an immanent trinity. From the standpoint of the world
there is full equality between the Father and the Son, as we could
see from the identity of their will. From the standpoint *of God* the
Son is a subordinated hypostasis. He stands between the uncreated
One and the created manifold of the world, and can therefore be the
mediator.[67]

For the purposes of our study it is important to recognize that
for Origen the doctrine of the trinity is the appropriate means for
reflecting on the non-dualistic structure of the relationship of Father and Son, as well as the relationship of God to the world. He
cannot avoid judging things from two distinct standpoints: God's
and humans'—the same as Sankara. The incarnation of the Logos
brings about no change in the divine being, for God is and remains
immutable and all-present. It is merely an accommodation to our
human capacity of understanding, and therefore can only be explained from the viewpoint of humans. This accommodation on
God's part is not, however, accidental, but corresponds to God's
essence where love, goodness and justice are unified; and this unity
should not be thought of or experienced *only* as an abstraction.

Tertullian and the Alexandrian school[68] provide concepts
which prepare the way for the development of the doctrine of the
Trinity, as it is provisionally stated at Nicaea and Constantinople.
Along with these developments before and after Nicaea, others
who play an important role in understanding especially the Spirit
as person, are Athanasius, and the three Cappadocians, Basil, Gregory of Nazianzus and Gregory of Nyssa.

Athanasius and the Cappadocians

For Athanasius what is especially important is the soteriological motif. He is less interested in conceptual clarity than in the
concept that Jesus Christ is really our salvation. This salvation
must come from God, and therefore the Son and the Father must be
equal in essence.[69] The Son as Logos is eternally present in the
Father and is eternally begotten of him.[70]

Athanasius generally follows Origen in emphasizing the relationship of Father and Son, but does not inquire further into the
details of how the generation of the Son can be understood. For him
it is a divine mystery. It is enough to know that the Son is the very
image of the Father, equal to its origin, even though both must be

regarded as different persons.[71] The Son is the same in essence as the Father and different in essence from creatures. This tension is necessary in order to explain the specifically soteriological function of the Son.[72]

According to Athanasius, *ousia* refers to the concrete being of God and is not the *genus* under which Father and Son are subsumed, as for Tertullian. Thus Athanasius did not at first use *hypostasis* for the persons in the trinity, since in everyday language it was indistinguishable from *ousia*.[73] God is *ousia* just as he is *kyrios;* this applies equally to the Father and to the Son. The Son is the distinct work of the Father—the dynamic principle. He is begotten by him but nevertheless essential being. The ingenious term "generation" explains both the unity and the difference. It is therefore an image of non-duality. Despite Athanasius' many conceptual distinctions, however, the absolute divinity of Christ seems less a theological conclusion than a religious experience.[74] This impression is strengthened by examining his teaching on the Holy Spirit.

Tertullian was the first to call the Spirit "God," and Origen considered the Spirit another hypostasis which stood beneath the Logos. Both treated the Spirit in a way that was completely analogous to the Logos and had no specific theological interest in explaining or grounding the Spirit's *homoousion* (equality of essence). In this regard Athanasius is different. For him the basis of everything was the accomplishment of real salvation, made possible by entering perfectly into the sphere of Christ: viz., by divinization (*theopoiesis*). Communion with Christ leads to communion with God; redeemed humans become participants in the divine nature.[75] This happens in and through the Spirit. For just as God is revealed in Christ, total divinity is possible for humans through the Spirit.[76] What Christ possesses by nature, humans attain through the work of the Spirit by grace.[77] Christ *as* Spirit effects a real renewal in humankind; he grants us communion with God and thus a share in immortality. Athanasius does not ask whether the Spirit proceeds from the Father or the Son, for he accepts the whole Eastern tradition, according to which the Spirit proceeds *from* the Father *through* the Son in a three-part hierarchy.[78] The Spirit's equality of essence is important so that *theopoiesis* may achieve true participation in God, as well as immortality. Gregory of Nyssa describes the work of the Spirit most strikingly: through the Spirit people who are in ecstasy (*ekstasis*) become like to the divine (*homoiosis pros to theion*).[79]

Basil, Gregory of Nazianzus and Gregory of Nyssa worked out a systematic way of presenting the *homoousion* of the Spirit. They stand in the tradition of Origen, yet with the help of Neoplatonic terms they were able to bring about certain conclusions for the doctrine of the trinity. In doing so they created the first great synthesis of faith and understanding.[80] They speak of God's *ousia* which unfolds in three *hypostaseis*. *Ousia* includes a dynamic principle, the *energeia*, which is at work in the *hypostaseis* in certain defined ways. Thus they clearly distinguish between being (*ousia*) and the forms in which being works (*hypostaseis*). The real distinctions of the hypostases are manifested in their names: *patrotes* (fatherhood), *huiotes* (sonhood), and *hagiasmos* (sanctification). Or more precisely: the Father possesses *agennesia*, the son *gennesia*, and the Spirit, *ekporeusis* (procession).[81] The hypostases are ways of being which are defined by their mutual relations. If the Son is *gennesia*, it is only through the Father; whereas the Spirit is *ekporeusis* in proceeding from the Father through the Son.

The Cappadocians begin with the three ways we experience being and then attempt to understand its unity. This is the reversal of Athanasius' method. There the differences of the hypostases were determined from within their divine source, because the unity of God necessarily implies the unity of his work. Gregory of Nyssa sees the unity of *ousia* and *theotes* as the consequence of the one divine *energeia*; the three hypostases have the same *ousia* because the same *energeia* is the property of them all.[82] The unity is *ousia*, their very essence which was understood as a kind of substance. It is common to all the hypostases. It is not a fourth, added to the three, but their unity.[83] The Cappadocians could not overcome this problematic substantialist thinking, and perhaps this is the reason they revert to a Neoplatonic emanation theory to explain how the Father is the completely transcendent source of the godhead from which the Son and the Spirit proceed.[84]

There is *one* transcendent God, with *one* will and center, who reveals himself in the concrete work of his hypostases. Significantly, the overall way of describing this is tri-unity. The Absolute remains Absolute in his hypostases, and therefore within this hypostatic unity, no subordinationist hierarchy may be understood. But in claiming this the Cappadocians are not convincing. Help came once the unity of God was explained by analogy to the human mind's unity of *nous*, *Logos*, and *pneuma*.[85]

The formula *mia ousia en trisin hypostasesin* means that God is understood as a dynamic unity without a multitude. "It is always the same thought, that Father, Son and Spirit are related to one another as principle, effective power, and fulfillment, or that the triad God, the effective principle, also involves a twofold presentation of this principle. But beyond this, they do not attempt to draw any conclusions concerning the essence of the hypostases. In other words, the connection between the experienced oeconomic trinity and the constructed immanent trinity remains unclear."[86] It is our thesis that this lack of clarity stems from insufficient clarity about non-duality and about how to understand it in ontological categories.

A very important step in this direction was to be taken by John Damascene. He added the idea of the hypostases' mutual permeation, using the expression *perichoresis*.[87] This descriptive word means *dance*. Accordingly, the trinity is a process of perfect interrelationality which achieves unity in the circulation of divine life. For John, the divinity is *one* reality which, because of our manner of seeing it, appears in different hypostases which are perfect in themselves.[88] The perichoretic dynamism of God creates reality and realizes its unity in rhythmic, everlasting movement. This view of the unity of reality using the image of dance, in which the dynamic and the static are in polar unity, was the high point of non-dualistic thinking in the early church.

We may now summarize: the decisive content of understanding is the unity of reality, for both Advaita Vedanta and the Christian doctrine of the trinity. Both start with different assumptions. But in the end, they can be allowed to interpret one another, so that we attain deeper insight.

In India the "hypostases" *isvara–hiranyagarbha–viraj*, are held together in subordination. But this subordination can only be grasped "oeconomically," because it is only present in the field of the *saguna* manner of seeing: from *our* vantage point we perceive different effects. When, however, we accept the *nirguna* standpoint of the Absolute, there is only one reality and one effect, with which we are Advaita. In the distinction of an absolute (*paramarthika*) and a relative (*vyavaharika*) standpoint, the indissolubility of the hypostatic union emerges as an apparent problem. However, the difficulty returns when we ask how the one, unmoved Absolute can become dynamic in its *saguna* manifestation, or how the relationship of *nirguna brahman* and *maya* is to be determined. The same problem occupied the Cappadocians: how can the one Godhead be understood in union with the principle of his effectiveness (*energeia*). India solves the problem by pointing to non-duality:

this non-duality as Advaita acquires a specifically ontological status.

In Advaita Vedanta, however, the many cannot truly be integrated into a unity: the many has a lesser ontological status than the previous unity. In the symbol of *perichoresis*, however, the many and the one are seen as polar moments in the one process of divine life, so that the unity of reality has a status equal to its dynamic unfolding in the many.

Augustine

In Augustine's thought everything revolves around the immutable unity of the absolute God. This is the basis for his doctrine of the trinity, and in this he relies on the theology of the Cappadocians and Nicaea. For him, God is absolute, simple being—being itself in which there can be no differentiation, participation or dependence. Thus his preferred way of describing God is as *essentia*, indeed as *summa essentia*, and as purely spiritual—thus reflecting his Neoplatonic background.[89] God is being without accidents, for he is fully immutable and as such not affected by his effects *ad extra*.[90]

Augustine distinguishes between the *ad intra* and *ad extra* effects of accidentless *essentia*.[91] The concept of the trinity comes from this area of effects. The unity of God means that he is *one* being and *one* will and must be *one* subject in relationship to the world—*inseparabilia sunt opera trinitatis*.[92] The individual effects of the *essentia*; i.e., of the one Godhead, cannot be divided among Father, Son and Spirit. From this it follows that the trinity cannot be deduced from differentiation in the *oeconomia* of revelation. While we may consider the Father as the one who sends, the Son as the one sent, Augustine's position is that the whole trinity was incarnate; thus the Son actively takes part in his own *missio*, which is nothing else than the *verbum patris*.[93] In God the word was timeless and was God. In him the word was spoken timelessly and announcing when it should enter into visible and temporal existence.[94] The eternal Son does not thereby cease to be Son. He appears in a body (*in creatura corporali*), but remains essentially a spiritual nature (*intus in natura spirituali*); i.e., as the transtemporal, second person of the trinity. The same is true of the Holy Spirit,[95] since Augustine maintains the highest equality (*summa aequalitas*): they are one in being.[96] This has two consequences.

1. Neither the Father nor an *essentia* abstracted from the three-ness, but rather the trinity is God. 2. This is a unity which is differentiated within itself. The differentiation is based, not on different outward effects, but on interior relationships. In order to explain this, Augustine uses the notion of *relatio*, which operates in two ways. First, God in himself is in relationship within himself. These relationships are immutable: they *are* God. They don't happen to God, and thus they do not change his essence, which is unity. There are no substantial or qualitative or quantitative differences among the "persons." Rather, their differences consist in their relationships to one another and only then and as a consequence in their relationship to the world.[97] Since being and being a person are the same in God[98]—for he is a unity to which no accidents can be added[99]—God is never Father *or* Son *or* Spirit. Rather Father, Son and Spirit are three mutually dependent *relationes* in the being of the one God. For this reason God cannot be triple (*triplex*),[100] but is always, in every case, to be thought of as one. Each of the persons is as great as the whole trinity.

There is mutual dependence of the relations on each other. The Father begets the Son, and the Spirit is the communion of the two. Since Augustine says that this relation is not accidental,[101] he must speak of an eternal generation (*sempiterna generatio*).[102] The Spirit is both communion of Father and Son (*spiritus sanctus ineffabilis est quaedam patris filiique communio*)[103] and the *donum commune of both* of them to creatures.[104]

In the oeconomy of salvation, we speak of the sending not of the Father, but of the Son. The only reason for this is that the essence of the Son is to be sent by the Father. The Son is not, however, less than the Father, nor is he of another substance. He represents that aspect of the relation which is related to us: being-sent.[105] The *proprium* of the *relatio*, being-sent, belongs only to the Son, not to the Father. The determinations of the relations within themselves are relative. But this does not influence their essence which is the identical essence of the whole trinity, for this, as a unity of relations, is the one God.

Augustine uses the notion *persona*, not however because he thinks this would be an appropriate term, but in order not to remain silent. *Dictum est tamen tres personae, non ut illud diceretur, sed ne taceretur.*[106] The one thing that is important is this: to grasp the unity of God to which no change or particular determination can be added. This unity is not an abstract idea, but contains in itself the fullness of life, knowledge and communion.

In order to explain the inner trinitarian relations Augustine uses various anthropological-psychological analogies. They can be justified theologically by the teaching on *imago Dei* and on the basis of this assumption can be seen as *vestigia trinitatis.* Figure 6.1 presents the analogies, which stem from careful psychological observation, schematically.

Father	Son	Spirit
esse Being	*nosse* Knowledge	*velle*[107] Will (Love)
1. *aeternitas* 2. *memoria* 3. *mens*	*veritas* *intelligentia* *notitia*	*voluntas-caritas* [108](*beatitudo*) *voluntas*[109] *amor*[110]
4. *amans*	*quod amatur*	*amor*[111]

Figure 6.1

The eternity of the Father, who is Being itself, is proclaimed in the *memoria,* a storehouse of past experience. The mind (*mens*) is reason and as such the "from where" of psychic life. Nevertheless, the Father as *amans* is the loving subject, and thus the *causa* of the inner-divine love event.

The Son is the self-knowledge of Being, and as such is truth (*veritas*). Corresponding to this, the *intelligentia* is the human person's spiritual process. Because it is the reflexive presentness of all events and because of its capacity to form concepts (*notitiae*) self-consciousness is possible. The Son is also "object" (*quod amatur*) of the Father's love.

The *Spirit* is the intentional movement between Father and Son, the force-field that describes the activity of the other two in the area of the human spirit or mind. Thus he is the principle of community, love (*amor*), and the goal of the divine will: the happiness (*beatitudo*) of God's own self-sustaining life.

Augustine uses analogies to describe the inseparable unity of divine life. The three persons interpenetrate one another as aspects of one and the same thing.

Just as unity consists of these aspects, so the aspects in their relatedness constitute a unity;[112] or in other words, "The divine life is like a self-generating subject as a self-generated object, and in the constant exchange of these two, one God."[113]

God as unity of subject and object transcends rational knowledge. For this reason the trinity cannot ultimately be understood, even by analogies.[114] Thus Augustine's attempt ends with an impasse which he cannot explain satisfactorily concerning how the three persons can have their own identity while still being the whole. There are also other contradictions which remain unsolvable within his system. The personality of the Spirit cannot be grounded convincingly, for the *spiratio* is on the one hand the expression of love between the Father and the Son and thus the *proprium* of the Spirit. But on the other hand the Spirit as *donum Dei* is the gift of the triune God to creatures.[115] Augustine finds some help in describing the whole triunity as Spirit, but this term must be distinguished from the third relation.[116]

For Augustine the trinity is the expression of the dynamic unity of reality in which God draws us to himself.[117] The meaning of this movement is the eschatological fulfillment by which humankind participates in the inner trinitarian life and the event of love in the *visio beatifica.*

We hardly need to emphasize how much Augustine's discourse on the unity of God recalls the ideas of Advaita Vedanta in part I. His contemplation of the One under three aspects, which are not properties but relational moments by which the whole becomes present in each of the particular notions, has parallels in *saccidananda* as the expression of the essence of the Absolute. Being (*sat*)–consciousness (*cit*)–bliss (*ananda*) are not far from Augustine's *esse-nosse-velle* (*amor*). The *cit* aspect of *brahman* reveals the same thing as Augustine's attempt at trinitarian analogies in consciousness. Consciousness is one and identical with itself insofar as it comprehends a multitude of contents.

On particular points, however, Augustine's psychological analogies are quite different from the Indian picture, because India has no notion of soul comparable to Augustine's. For our study, the most important viewpoint that leads to differences is this: Sankara understands *brahman* as that which is in itself at rest, in which no movement would be thinkable. The dynamic principle, *maya*, could never be integrated into this unity. Augustine's notion of the trinity stems from a dynamic One, which is life itself and yet has calm within itself because it undergoes no change. The dynamic element *is* the being of God, which is then expressed in mutually dependent relations. That which Sankara separates—not fully, but imperceptibly—in order to understand the notion of pure *brahman*, Augustine joins together, in order to present the Godhead in its fullness by means of the notion of the trinity.

7.

Non-duality in the Mystics and Luther

While Aristotle was accepted by Christian theologians—especially Thomas Aquinas, the Neoplatonic tradition, represented by Dennis the Areopagite, Scotus Eriugena, and Bernard, greatly influenced the fourteenth-century mystics. Meister Eckhart is the outstanding representative, and his theology is extremely fruitful in comparisons with Asia. Nevertheless, since the basic theological work of comparing to Sankara's Advaita Vedanta[1] as well as to Zen Buddhism[2] has already been done, it would be superfluous to study him here.

As a bridge to Luther and modern Protestant thinking, we will examine three important mystics, who either indirectly (*Cloud of Unknowing*) or directly (Suso, Tauler) depend on Eckhart. Their importance for understanding the theology of Luther can hardly be overemphasized.

Regarding trinitarian theology, the mystics, by grasping God's self-differentiation as an outpouring of his living love, accomplish the important task of opening up the scholastic notion of relation, which had become fixed in abstractions. To Ruysbroeck the Spirit, the unifying power of the trinity, is the fire of love, and Richard of St. Victor deduces personhood from the superabundant fullness (*plenitudo*) of love. The *Cloud of Unknowing*, as well as Suso, Tauler, Luther and the Spanish mystics of the sixteenth century continue this development.

The Cloud of Unknowing

The *Cloud of Unknowing* was written by an unknown English author around 1320.[3] Among other works by the same author is the *Book of Privy Counselling*, which is more speculative than the *Cloud*. The author stands in the tradition of Dennis the Areopagite, Richard of St. Victor, Bernard, and Thomas Gallus, whose works he partly translated. His influence on John of the Cross was considerable; indeed he has been lauded as John's predecessor.[4] In its emphasis on apophatic thinking, the *Cloud* is likewise in close relationship to Rhineland-Flemish mysticism, especially Ruysbroeck, Suso, and Tauler.[5]

The main theme is darkness, the darkness which fills the mind, enabling it to shake itself loose from rational-discursive thinking. In this darkness we experience God. The same example of Moses climbing the mountain to encounter God in a cloud, which was already used by the Cappadocians, Dennis and later Eastern Christian theology, returns here with a spiritualized meaning. Climbing the mountain is the mystical way and involves forgetting all sensations and ideas, being isolated from everything, in order, finally, to attain unified vision (ch. 5). Even pious thoughts must be hidden by the Cloud of Unknowing, so that consciousness may reach stillness and unity, for all such thoughts are the product of discursive reasoning. In the beginning they are useful, but later along the path to perfect unity with God they are a hindrance.[6]

The author identifies two ways of knowing: discursive logical thinking (scholasticism) and non-conceptual, contemplative knowing (mysticism), which fills the person's mind when all images and concepts have been silenced (clouded). Contemplative knowledge lifts up rationality dialectically: not because *ratio* as such is incapable, but because it is insufficient in relation to God. Transrational consciousness presses forward in the deepest recesses of the soul, where the capacity for love is rooted. Love for God is the decisive moving force in understanding and is given along the way of self-forgetfulness, under the Cloud of Unknowing. Love is nourished by faith, which receives its certainty from the truth revealed in Jesus Christ. In this way, the *Cloud of Unknowing* joins mystical apophatism to orthodox piety in answering scholastic supernaturalism.

Love for the human Jesus is the starting point for this mystic. He can therefore be compared not only to Luther, but also to Teresa of Avila.[7] In the later stages of spiritual development, however, this attitude must be given up, for the humanity of Jesus is creaturely. Infinite love for God does not allow itself to be limited by this figure, but thrusts beyond to Christ as the second person of the trinity. The significance of the ascension of Christ is that he has become inaccessible bodily to the disciples and has withdrawn himself from encounters through the senses, so that they might not remain attached to his human form. This refers also to Christ's human soul which—according to Ruysbroeck—never forfeits its conditioned form, and therefore cannot serve as a means to meditate on the essence of the trinity.[8] The *Cloud* argues similarly, citing Augustine and Thomas Aquinas.[9]

The kataphatic way leads to the apophatic, and this leads to loving knowledge which gives participation in the mystery of the trinity. Practically, this means first of all meditating on Christ's sufferings in all their gruesomeness. Those who are advanced forget all this, so that they may experience in their souls the "blind stirring of love" in its pure form as a gift of God's *grace.* This love leads to contemplative prayer, which is without images and given only by God (Chs. 37, 39, 71).

The technique recommended by the author of the *Cloud of Unknowing*, whereby humans enter into a state of perfect self-forgetfulness and become aware of the "stirrings of love," is described in terms similar to those of the mystic, Ruysbroeck, whose works had been entrusted to this English mystic.[10] The person enters a state of perfect spiritual calm quite naturally, once sense images have been abandoned and the content of his/her thoughts has ceased to exist, thanks to concentration. The one who learns to harness the mind attains this emptiness, which is neither good nor bad in itself (Ch. 68ff.). Where there is not a will confirmed in virtuous living and a mind filled with love, however, people fall into pride. Genuine mystical prayer is based on love-filled spiritual peace which God gives. He alone leads us along the spiritual way. Mystical experience is grace.[11]

With regard to particular points, what the *Cloud* recommends is not suppressing distractions, but letting them lie along the way towards concentration. Short words such as 'God,' 'love,' etc., are to be repeated continuously with full concentration so that the mind becomes unified. Above all our *motivation* for being on the mystical path is important. "For it is not what you are or what you have been that God sees with his merciful eye, but what you would like to be" (ch. 75).

Forgetfulness of all the content of thoughts is the way of self-surrender, composure, and inner freedom, so as to become independent of every material or spiritual tie outside God himself.[12] Since the attraction to knowledge is the root of all other desires, it must disappear in the *Cloud of Unknowing* so that—free from concupiscence—the power of a knowledge motivated by love may make its appearance.

The goal of human life, of which the mystical path is merely a particular form, although according to the *Cloud* it is also the highest if not the only realistic form, is *unification with God.*

This unification is achieved in the soul or "in the souvereign point of the spirit," as the *Cloud* says. The presupposition to attaining this is total self-forgetfulness. The often repeated prayer of the mystic expresses it as follows: "All I am as I am unto Thee as Thou art."[13] God is the human person's true being. The *Cloud* uses the analogy of clothing: the soul clothed with the self throws off this garment and is clothed with God. This image involves a contradiction, however, for in it God would remain external, while what really happens is a transformation of the *core* of consciousness.

It is important that unity with God be experienced as a perfect harmony, which the author of the *Cloud* does not interpret monistically: the difference between God—who is loving union by nature—and human beings, to whom the same is given by grace, holds true. God is the being of humanity, but humans are not the being of God: "He is thy being and thou not his."[14] This is not pantheism, but perhaps a kind of panentheism, which is compatible with Thomistic metaphysics. The unity with God allows for interior differentiation without explaining more precisely how the relationship of unity and difference is to be understood.

In all of Rhineland-Flemish mysticism, the *Cloud of Unknowing,* and the later Spanish mystics, becoming one with God is understood as a gradual divinization, which reaches its peak in the *visio beatifica.* This *visio*—contrary to early church or Eastern Christian ideas of *theopoiesis*—emphasizes the cognitive element, and this fact is in a special sort of tension with the constantly repeated theme of love as *participation,* which is found especially in the *Cloud.* But since it is talking about a gift of grace, it would be wrong to conclude to an ontological sameness with God.

This is also clear when the author of the *Cloud* compares the unity with intratrinitarian love. The persons of the trinity empty their being mutually on one another and are thus one. We humans participate in this love through Christ's sacrifice. Insofar as we fulfill this sacrifice in ourselves (by emptying, self-forgetting, self-giving) we enter with Christ into the trinity, into the abyss of divine love.[15]

The author of the *Cloud* always treats intratrinitarian unity as the prototype for the unity of reality. Just as God is one with himself: by *nature* he cannot be separated from his being, so too the soul by grace is not divided from what it sees and feels in deep mystical experiences; viz., the movement of God's all-encompassing triune love.[16] In love there is such an interior unity that the soul can be called "a God."[17] This bold idea will resurface in John of the Cross and Teresa of Avila, who express it in striking images that come close to a non-dualistic interpretation. The soul descending into its own depths sees a ray of light (God) through a pane of glass (the soul). The clearer the glass, the more it disappears so that the light may shine through with perfect clarity. Teresa adds to this explanation concerning the relations between God and the attentive soul: It is like rain, which falls into a well where both waters are united so that the rain water cannot be distinguished from the well water; or like a river which flows into the sea and is no longer separable from it.[18]

These comparisons correspond to Indian ones even in their wording. But the theological interpretation is different. For the Christian mystic God is what he is *by nature*, whereas the soul is divinized *by grace*. The original relationships, therefore, are unequal.

Suso and Tauler

Meister Eckhart had described God as superessential being and superessential nothingness and thus overcame the simple negation of the concept of being in relation to God.[19] The fact that abundance of negations in our concept of God still determines and limits God was already seen in Eastern Christianity by Gregory of Palamas,[20] and the consequences of a double negation were examined—which describes nothing else than the *fullness* of God—by people ranging from Nagarjuna in India to Hegel in Europe. Eckhart is thinking similarly when he contemplates God through the image of a quiet desert, on the one hand, and as the incarnate fullness of the Lord of grace, on the other.[21] Eckhart's language points to the transcendence of God beyond categories which at the same time, as the most interior essence of each being, is fully immanent. It is clear that Eckhart is not leveling out the difference between transcendence and immanence.[22] In any case, the relationship between the two has been understood in a similar way by the Rhineland mystics, as well as by Luther, Ignatius, and Eastern Orthodox thinkers.

Henry Suso (1295–1366) was Eckhart's most important disciple. He was a friend of Tauler, and both had a great influence on Luther. For Suso, God is a "dark stillness" and a superessential spirit, in whose ground humans find fulfillment. In order to share in divine being, humans must practise abandonment, and moreover "an abandoned person must be de-imaged of creature, imaged with Christ and super-imaged in divinity."[23]

Suso develops his teaching about God, which is derived from the mystical experience of becoming one, in the *Book of Truth*, which is extraordinarily similar to Indian Advaita. The following is an overview of this important writing.[24]

Immersion in God reveals to humans their very self (p. 331), for it is a "taste" of God in which every obstacle and all otherness disappears (p. 338). In this immersion we learn God's simplicity, which is without any determination and which is thought of as an eternal nothing (p. 333). The essence of this calm simplicity is life, and this means in particular that it is "reason existing in itself" (p. 333), without any attributes. Rather, it is its own self-presentation of the One, and is very similar to the *cit* of the Indian formula *saccidananda.* Both terms, nothing and life, are seen as polar opposites and are mediated trinitarily. While Eckhart tended towards a transtrinitarian Godhead, presented as a *higher* notion of the Absolute in its perfect calmness beyond the manifestations of the trinity,[25] Suso understands the "power of discernment" and the "ground of unity" non-dualistically (ch. 2: *Book of Truth*).

The correspondence with Advaita Vedanta is sometimes word-for-word: the drive towards effectiveness of the Godhead gives it its natural "creative power" (*sakti*). This is responsible for the multitude in God, which expresses itself in the multitude of the world. "In its ground and basis this multitude is a simple unity (p. 336),"[26] which corresponds to the *nirguna brahman* in its identity with *saguna brahman.* In the abyss of nothingness the divine nature is "pregnant with fruitfulness and works" (p. 335). The essence of the Godhead is a ground in which "the three-ness of persons is immersed in unity and therefore where, in a certain way, any multitude loses itself" (p. 334).

This corresponds to the non-dualism of *saccidananda,* where being—consciousness—bliss, were understood in their inner dynamism, without their relations which destroy the unity, as it were. Suso says this explicitly, stating that this *nothingness* (i.e., the trinitarian mystery—or *saccidananda*) is in itself reason (*cit*) or being (*sat*) or tasting (*ananda*). He adds that this expression cannot grasp the essence. In it we have hardly gained any more knowledge than "if someone were to call a beautiful pearl a butcher's block" (p. 347).

This carefulness seems strange. If it were only a matter of the inadequacy of analogous concepts, it could be construed as a return to a common theme of mystical literature. But here it is a return to Eckhart's notion of "God above (the trinitarian) God." Suso seems to intuit, rather than understand fully in all its notional consequences, the non-dualistic polarity in trinitarian language. This would be left to Nicolas of Cusa, who makes *coincidentia oppositorum* a key concept in knowledge of God, thus stating conceptually what Suso intuited.

Intratrinitarian unity is the direct grounds for the unity of reality, for reality is not outside God. Suso distinguishes *twilight knowledge*, which is filled up with the multitude of created things, from a *morning knowledge*, in which "humans see creatures without all their differences, without individual images, denuded even of all sameness in the One, which is God himself" (p. 351). This imaged description refers to two polar ways of knowing and corresponds exactly to Indian relative (*vyavaharika*) knowledge and absolute (*paramarthika*) knowledge. The two condition one another, just as morning and evening presuppose each other. For Suso—and naturally also for Indian non-dualism—there is no doubt that the unity integrates the many, and therefore only from its vantage point can a holistic notion be formulated. Thus unity is held in higher esteem.

Both ways of knowing return directly to a trinitarian notion of God, for God as creative power is form that creates structures and shares this essence with them. As potency in God this form-essence is more all-inclusive than any explicit order. After "going forth from God," creatures have their own special life, although all have "the same life, being, power in so far as they are in God" (p. 336). From the viewpoint of eternity, each creature is *ideally* in God; God's actualization gives them creatureliness, which is "more genuine and useful than the being which they have in God" (p. 337). For in creatureliness God's formative order is expressed; that is, his creative life gives itself away and thus discovers an apt expression of its essence in *perichoresis*. Before creation, creator and creature were the same, thus were not unified; when creatures return to God after having been individuated, they are now *unified* as a *result* of trinitarian love (p. 349). This is a higher form of being.

The soul that has entered into God is fully one with him, yet there remains a difference between the creature and the creator.

Unity is not sameness. Humans can not simultaneously be creatures and God. "God is threefold and simple. Thus in a certain way, humans too, when they have entered into God, are one in the process of losing (themselves), even while, seen from without, they are still contemplating and appreciating, etc." (p. 349). The one who is united with God has a consciousness (*cit*) of unity and enjoys bliss (*ananda*). This is different from the drop of water which has mingled with the great body of water which is the ocean—to cite the example frequently used in India.

The "eternal nothing," super-conscious being, produces a differentiated order—in other words, reality—by means of its generative power (p. 356). Differentiation is not, however, division (p. 357). Thus the intratrinitarian unity is the unity of reality. Using a comparison, Suso refers to an organism's interconnectedness of limbs and organs, or he talks of the mutual intermingling of body and soul: neither can be separated from the other, and yet they can be distinguished. They are a psychosomatic unity (p. 357).

The mystic goes through stages, which lead to unity with God. Only in death can he enjoy "lasting" unity; in this life only a "foretaste" is possible (p. 348). Suso is therefore distinguished from the Indian ideal of *jivanmukta*. The "shared community" with God, which is attainable in this life, is distinct from "complete and perfect unity, beyond anyone's power" (p. 342), which is also *hyperspiritual*. Nevertheless, *present* mystical experience transforms life fully in that it leads to composure and this in turn to love and freedom. For everything is seen in the light of unity.

Composure is the ego's letting go of ego. Suso speaks of the ego in five ways, and these distinctions are important in order to understand the continuous insistence by mystics of all religions on ego-lessness. 1. The "I" as an expression of being. Here humans share what is common to all beings. 2. It can mean a "growth," which we share with the world of plants. 3. It refers to "feeling," which humans share with animals. 4. It refers to our common human nature. 5. It stands for the specific body-soul unity which individuates each person (p. 339). According to Suso only in the fifth sense is the "I" a hindrance to spiritual development. For the individual self asserts itself as ego in claiming for itself, on the basis of its own self, what is only apt for God. Instead of "returning to God," it believes in its own independence. This blindness upsets the correct order and is the essence of sin, as well as the root of all evil. In general, this is what happens: "Since the creature, gifted with reason, which should have been turning its gaze towards the

One, instead turns it outwards, impertinently gawking at its own being," it therefore brings forth "sin, evil, . . . the devil." In Asia this is called *avidya* (ignorance or blindness) and there, too, it is considered as the primary cause of evil.

The blindness decreases when the self learns to leave behind and overlook itself (p. 339). Only when we experience our nothingness can God be experienced as the ground of the self. In this regard suffering can be helpful, and it is praised by Suso as the initiation into the mystical way of contemplative unity.[27] This is likewise the central insight of "Theologia Germanica," and we will show that Luther's experience of temptation has a very similar meaning for him.

The path of self-abandonment is characterized by a threefold view of the deeper self. 1. The "I" abandons itself and plunges into its nothingness, which is God. 2. The true self comes back from its immersion impregnated with God and returns to the world and now no longer loses itself in the world, for it has found its medium. 3. The self goes out of itself and re-forms itself anew in the form of Christ (p. 339f.).

Suso lists six steps along this way: the mystic 1. "loses himself in God with all his force," 2. gives up his self in an irreversible manner, 3. "in this way becomes one with Christ," 4. "works always in complete accord with Christ," 5. "stands (detached) in the face of all," and 6. "contemplates all things in such simplicity" (p. 340).

Humans are being unclothed of their human nature and are transformed by the *light of God.* Just as a drop of water poured into wine loses its own characteristics and takes on the color and taste of the wine, so too for the one "fully possessed by happiness": his "I" (in the fifth sense), i.e., especially his covetousness, is lost, and he is immersed in the divine will. "He maintains his essence, but in another form, in another (viz., a heavenly) light, and in another, power. And all this comes from an ungroundable giving up of self" (p. 341).

Suso does not clearly define what he means by essence and nature, nor show how they can be distinguished. Nevertheless, it is clear what he means. The one who is immersed in God is perfectly one with God, (yet this is an awareness of this bliss which is a super-formation in God-nature). In a certain way he/she does not lose his/her identity. He/she attains oneness of form with Christ, drawn into intratrinitarian love. But no human is completely the same as Christ. Suso mentions two reasons for this: 1. Christ is the only begotten Son, who is like God in his nature. He is the very image of the Father. We, however, are formed in the image of the trinity and become like to the divine nature by rebirth. 2. Christ is the first-born, while our unity with the Father is *through* him.

Whether humans can attain unified contemplation of God on their own, or whether it is the effect of divine grace is a question that cannot be raised, even for Suso. The alternatives are false. Our essence or our works are good insofar as we open ourselves to God. Our essence is super-formed by God, and thus the one who remains in unity with God can only be of God; this person's will is free from covetousness and distraction. He concentrates on divine love, which expresses itself in action (p. 353). The mystic is not subject to any laws, "for he does with calm freedom what common people do only when forced" (360). "He lives in community with others without allowing their images to determine him, shows them love without clinging to them, and has compassion without worrying in complete freedom" (361). Thus he does not continually project his own wishes and ideas onto reality, but allows reality to freely work on him, because in reality he encounters God. Only when this is the case is he truly capable of love.

The non-duality of this attitude stands out most when Suso says that a person in the state of rapture no longer acts merely as a human, for he/she has "entered into the One and become one with it" (348). "And so we must understand that this person *possesses within him/herself all creatures in their unity*, and beyond that, all joy, also in the body's works, without implying a bodily or spiritual action, for he/she realizes that he/she exists within the unity which we already discussed" (348). On the basis of the self all creatures dwell in God. Thus they experience themselves as not-two, Advaita, in relationship to one other, as well as in relationship to their ground. What Indian advaitic experience tries to express through the teaching of *atman*, is seen here in Suso in a form that is mediated by the trinity: the Advaita of reality.

John Tauler (ca. 1300–1361) was especially effective in his preaching and, by means of clear language, brought the non-dualist experience of Eckhart and Suso to the people, for his field was spiritual pedagogy about the mystical experience. This Strasburg Dominican was a favorite, not only of Luther, but of later Protestant theologians, especially the poet, G. Tersteegen (1697–1769). Tersteengen hoped to use Tauler as the basis for an ecumenism of mystical experience, an idea which Tauler himself had attempted to develop many times. He hoped for an ecumenism which would even transcend the boundaries of the church to include especially Neoplatonism.[28] Since Neoplatonism is likewise an important bridge to Indian culture, Tauler has special importance for our study.

Tauler's preaching was very pastoral, although it included attacks on the visible church. He criticized out of love for the church, a church he wanted to renew by means of mystical experience. For him the church never loses its sacramental character. Although many of his ideas and motives were similar to Luther's, in practice his methods and goals were quite different.

Tauler places great emphasis on the discovery of the *interior* world. He distinguishes "those who are attached to the senses, those attached to reason, and those who are formed by God interiorly in a hidden way, i.e., the truly spiritual."[29] The ground of the soul contains the kingdom of God in us, and this is likewise the essential ground of the trinity, out of which our human being "flows." In this ground the Holy Spirit works, "drawing" us and "turning us" to God. "The Spirit transforms people and divinizes them, returning them to the wellspring where they were from eternity, "God in God."[30] Here Tauler is saying no more than Suso. He emphasizes even more, or least more straightforwardly, that it is only because of a gift of the Holy Spirit that the mystic is lifted into unity with God, the original ground. For Tauler, too, the experience of our own nothingness, which consists in knowing oneself sheltered in the nothingness of God, is the decisive point along the way to discovering the interior world.

This way begins and ends in silence, out of which all exercises touch the essential ground. The first step is meditation on one's own nothingness and sinfulness. The second step is meditation on Jesus, the prototype who then, thirdly, brings us into transtemporal contemplation.[31] Everything is an allowing-oneself-to-be-transformed by the reality of the triune God. God is *in* all and when we seek him with a pure heart, he *must* be there.[32] Nevertheless, God also remains fully transcendent. Yet to ordinary eyes he is only experienced as hidden.[33] God is pure simplicity, and humans have to bring to him their world of the many, so that God may unify and make possible true distinctions, which only exist *in* the unity, just as the trinitarian persons exist in the unity of the Godhead.[34]

God's birth in humans corresponds to the prototype of the first paternal birth in which God bears the Son: "The Father in his personal way returns within himself with his divine power of knowing and with clear insight plumbs for himself the abyss of his eternal being; and consequently, after this single act of comprehending himself, expresses himself completely, and this word is his Son, and this act of knowing himself is the generation of his Son in eternity; he remains in essential unity within himself and pours himself out in the distinctions of persons."[35]

Thus God is understood as the dynamism of his own being, in the process of his consciousness. When this triadic coming to consciousness grasps the ground of the soul, God is born in us. Consequently God's birth is a beyond-conscious immersion in the unity of being. "Then the Father's power comes to call humans to themselves through the only begotten Son, and just as the Son is born of the Father and flows back to the Father, so too humans are born in the Son by the Father and flow back to the Father, and become one with him. . . . And thus the Holy Spirit is poured out like a stream of inexpressible love and joy, and overflows our human ground with his delightful gifts."[36]

Humans are drawn into likeness of form with Christ, into the unity of the trinity, and thus they realize their own being which finally is not different from the being of God. For Tauler the difference consists in the fact that what Christ is by nature, humans are only by grace.[37]

Oneness with God is achieved in "the most interior love of God," which is distinguished from sensual love of God in that it is "contemplative love present in one's soul" and a "striving love" coming from the unity which encompasses all of creation. Interior love of God and exterior love of neighbor are therefore two aspects of *one* love. The one cannot exist without the other.[38]

The original non-duality of God and soul consists in a "relatedness which surpasses all measure"; herein is the ontological ground for the unity of reality. "For God is spirit and the soul is spirit, and consequently the soul has an everlasting tendency towards and insight into its own original ground. From its likeness in spiritual things our spirit tends towards and inclines towards its origin, which is God. This inclination never ceases, even in the damned."[39] This last sentence indicates a universality, i.e., the perfect unity of reality in the spirit.

We might consider these ideas of Tauler to be nearly identical with Indian *atman/brahman* if it were not for the fact that Tauler, as a Christian mystic, necessarily adds that God is uncreated, while the soul is created by God—even though this difference is part of a unity: "Just as humans, before their creation, were eternally God in

God so now, once they are created, they must be totally immersed in God. . . . When the human spirit is immersed totally in its own interior being and melts into God's innermost being, it is imaged anew and renewed; and the more ordered and pure its passage along this way and the more clearly it has God in mind, the more this spirit overflows with and is formed by God's Spirit. God pours himself out in such a spirit in the same way the sun pours out light into the air. All of the air is penetrated by light, and the eye cannot distinguish light from air nor see where the two are divided. Thus who could divide the divine, supernatural oneness by which the spirit is implicated in and drawn into the abyss of its origin? You would know, even if someone could see the created spirit in the uncreated, he would doubtlessly believe he were seeing God himself."[40]

As Luther already realized, *Theologia Germanica* is completely within the tradition of Tauler.[41] Along with the Bible and Augustine, this unknown mystic was the next most important source of inspiration for Luther, the reformer, who could fully identify with him.[42] The main theme here is grace-filled divinization by means of "the life of Christ," with whom the Christian is so fully identified that his/her self disappears completely. (ch. 44, 49 etc.).[43] When the Self's pretensions are given up, God grants pure knowledge (ch. 51), a knowledge of the wholeness of reality. Its individual parts have been annihilated (ch. 18). Interestingly, *Theologia Germanica* is much closer to Sankara than non-duality which is mediated by trinitarian language. In the eyes of this author the individual (ego) Self is "illusion" and "delusion" (ch. 5). It is created by God to make possible reason and will, but only when God remains the subject. The world of the many, of forms, is sacrificed for the sake of unity, exactly as in Advaita Vedanta; and in both cases the root cause for this deficit is the fact that a certain polarity in God is not properly understood.

Luther

There is no one summary text to show Luther's ideas and thought forms on the doctrine of the trinity. An early Christmas sermon from 1514[44] and one on the trinity,[45] as well as a later work, *The Last Words of David* (1543),[46] and a few Disputations from 1539 until 1545[47] may be used to study the continuity in his

thought.[48] However, we have to go beyond these writings in order
to bring out the relationship between Luther's trinitarian understanding of God and other elements of his theology.

Already in the Christmas sermon of 1514, Luther uses new
analogies to understand the trinity which go beyond Augustine,
since they no longer refer to the human soul but to the whole of
created reality. On the one hand, he presupposes the special place
of the soul as *imago Dei*, just as Augustine does. On the other hand,
however, he discusses God and the world in relationship to the
whole of creation. It is not true that Luther is only using this analogy casually,[49] for he repeats it in other sermons.[50]

For Luther, God is the same in all his actions. This unity is
grounded in the intratrinitarian relationships. To humans, however, God can be distinguished as creator, redeemer, and faith-in-
stilling Spirit.[51] God is triune. There is a relationship between the
personalis pluritas and the *unitas naturae et essentiae*.[52] God can
only be known through revelation. We do not know him as he is in
himself. In revelation, however, we encounter his essence. The
starting point, therefore, is the oeconomical trinity. Luther reflects
less than Augustine on the consequences of this starting point for
the immanent trinity, because he considers it less important for
certitude about salvation. Thus in his thought there is an unmistakable tendency to grasp the Father as absolute God, even though the
essential equality of the persons is not denied.[53]

The desire to know God *extra revelationem* is human pre-
sumption, for humans do not stand on the same level as God. Besides, humans would merely find there the projection of their own
wishes and desires. (*applicuerunt pro votis et desyderiis suis*).[54] By
themselves humans can only know their projection of God, which
is the product of their ego.

In revelation, however, God presents himself as capable of being grasped by human knowledge. There we know him in his being
pro nobis. This is enough for certitude of salvation. God reveals
himself in Christ as love and gives himself freely by grace. And yet
he is an almighty and predestining God.[55] Humans should therefore relate to the revealed God, who as incarnate is the promise of
salvation.[56]

In order that all God's work be understood as the action of the
whole trinity creation, too, must be interpreted in a trinitarian
way. God as Father is the source of creation. As Son he is the word
which calls creation out of nothingness, and as Spirit he is the safe-
guarding love with which creation returns into the heart of God,

thus renewing its Being and receiving continuity in the word.[57] The appropriations do not disturb the unity of action in three persons.[58]

Reconciliation also is the work of the triune God. The Father is the source from which a person lost in sin is called back by the word and renewed in the Spirit and so returns into the Son.[59] Thus, creation and reconciliation are merely two moments in the one process of salvation history. In the Son, God gives himself; in the Spirit he maintains everything.[60] God as Spirit is the bond which unites creation.[61] Because God is united in himself he acts as unity and establishes unity. Thus distinctions such as creation, reconciliation, and redemption, etc., are *sub specie Dei*, meaningless.

Luther emphasizes the humanity of God in revelation. Here we know and understand him.[62] The person who humbly knows the man, Jesus, and follows him, will be given the gift of divine knowledge through him.[63] Thus we are led away from ourselves to God.[64] The *sacramentum incarnationis is essentially the crux Christi*, where the Father's will is perfectly united with the Son's. When we recognize the cross, we are freed from our own ego and become united in our will with God, and therefore we are in community with him.[65] Because the cross leads humans to self-knowledge—in that they discover themselves as egocentric sinners[66]—it is the way to *fides sola gratia.* Thus, in Luther's eyes, *crux sola est nostra theologia.*[67]

Luther applies what to him is the central insight deduced from both a theology of the cross and the doctrine of justification: namely, that God's grace works through contradiction (*sub contrario*), to the whole of the divine-human relationship. Thus a *theologia crucis*, the doctrine on knowledge of the trinity by means of the humanity of Jesus, the distinction between law and gospel, his ideas concerning *opus proprium et opus alienum Dei*, are all variations on one and the same experience.

The distinction between law and gospel brings us to the center of Luther's experience of God. It describes the double encounter with God, which can lead to either life or death. On the one hand is God's wrath; on the other, grace. By means of law, God leads humans to the nothingness of their self, since law destroys egocentric pride (*usus theologicus legis*). By means of the gospel, humans who have died to themselves experience the grace that God is all in all and affects all, giving, especially, new life beyond the egotistical ensnarement of sin.[68] In order to describe the unity of these two aspects, Luther uses the formula *opus alienum et opus proprium Dei.*[69] Law is the *opus alienum*, through which grace (*opus pro-*

prium) works in a hidden way. Thus, the two works are not of equal weight theologically, since in both works God loves us. The tension between the two is only overcome eschatologically *sub specie Dei.*

God is free and absolute will, which determines everything necessarily.[70] This does not mean that Luther teaches absolute determinism.[71] On the contrary, in *De servo arbitrio* (1525), he is only calling attention to God's all-powerfulness[72] as excluding the free and cooperative will of sinners in relation to the realization of salvation. Without God's grace humans can do nothing which is good or just *coram Deo.*[73] This position does not imply metaphysical determinism, a position which Luther neither affirms nor denies.[74] Likewise, the doctrine concerning *Deus absconditus* is not related to theoretical knowledge of God, but rather demonstrates that God works salvation *sub contrario,* despite human pride and illusions concerning the ego. Direct knowledge would nurture pride; the ego would be fortified, and therefore fall more deeply into the ensnarement of sin.[75] For this reason a *theologia crucis* is the only viable way. Thus Luther's term, *deus absconditus,* means that God is not object, but the subject of our knowledge of God.

The teaching on the *word of God* returns to the same idea, but in another form. To Luther, the word is *the* image for spiritual self-communication, as seen in the fact that a diminutive breath can have the most powerful effect, just as the helpless child in the crib is *sub contrario* the Lord of the world.[76]

Christ is the word of God which becomes present through the mediation of the Holy Spirit. This is the trinitarian key to a proper understanding of the *word* in Luther's theology. The word is creative power, for reality *is* through words. And through the word God transforms us into his own being.[77] In the word we acquire a share in God and the sacrament is merely a type and mode of the word's expression.[78] This rules out any intellectualistic understanding of the word in Luther.

We must distinguish various dimensions in Luther's understanding of word.[79] Everything that God does and creates takes place in his word. Thus all creatures *are* words of God.[80] Luther speaks of an internal and an external word of God. God first speaks an external word (*verbum externum*) to humans, especially through the incarnation of Jesus Christ. But also human speech— especially human speech recorded in scripture—is God's way of speaking as external word.[81] The internal word (*verbum internum*) is in God and remains in God. It is God's power and wisdom, through which he draws all to himself. The internal word is Christ in his divine nature and is one with the Father in the intratrinitarian relations.[82] The internal word of God is the true word of God, which can be given directly without external mediation, through the power of the Spirit in human hearts. Thus it is a divine, illuminating presence. The Holy Spirit thus belongs essentially to the internal word.[83] Normally, however, the external word mediates the internal word, for the external word is produced because of the internal.[84] In any case, hearing the word produces faith, which transforms our being. God becomes man, so that man can become God.[85] The external word (e.g., the sermon) penetrates only to the ear. The transformation of the heart is thus the work of the internal word.

We may easily distinguish four stages in Luther's understanding of the word:

1. The internal word that *is* God and is present in the intratrinitarian relations.
2. The internal word expresses itself in the external word in revelation; i.e., in the incarnation of Jesus Christ.
3. The holy Bible is the mediation of the external word of Jesus Christ.
4. The external word of the third stage expresses itself in spoken language, the *viva vox evangelii.*

The decisive step is from stage 1 to stage 2, for stage 1 describes the immanent trinity, while stages 2 to 4 concern the forms of manifestation of the word in the area of the oeconomical trinity.[86] Luther's deepest experiences and thoughts concern what he calls temptation (*Anfechtung*) or *temptatio.* God works *sub contrario* by his wrath through the law, the cross and even our despair. The *usus theologicus legis* forces humans to give up their selfish demands which oppose God. The ego must die again and again so that the renewed person may be raised up in Christ.[87] *Mortificatio* leads to *vivicatio.*[88] In connection with what was said concerning the term *opus alienum,* it becomes clear that temptation is finally an effect of grace.[89] Thus Luther can speak of God's wrath as *benignitatis ira.*[90] The moments of temptation are truly *God's embraces,*[91] for the *opus proprium* can be experienced behind the *opus alienum.* God himself makes and sends temptation to break down the pride and illusions of the sinner. Temptation makes humans fit for God's grace.[92] Temptation means experiencing existentially the loss of a certitude which was based only on an ego-centered, ego-projected idea of salvation. This is painful, for humans first experience it as God's absence.[93] But it is precisely in this absence that God is near. This fact will only be revealed, however, when the ego has vanished. The tension remains until death; it is unsolvable in this life.[94] As humans we remain sinners, i.e., ego-centered, even when we are justified by God's grace: *simul justus et peccator,* justified and sinners at the same time. Luther is also aware of a gradual *sanctificatio.* But it reaches its fulfillment only at the end of time. To live in faith is to live in the beyond, i.e., in the tension between both poles of the *"simul."*

In the light of God's all-presence humans are aware of their nothingness (*nihileitas*).[95] But besides this, the accusatory power of the law and the cross are places where humans may experience the absence of God in terrifying fear (*deus absconditus*). This is the terror of *nothingness.* The experience of temptation is a total end, a complete break, a radical death of the "old Adam." This is what Luther is describing through such expressions as *descensus ad inferos,*[96] *resignatio ad infernum,*[97] and—the strongest—*excessus in nihilum.*[98]

These terms, as well as the context in which they are found, point towards a very profound experience of temptation. Were we not to take Luther seriously at this point, we would be losing the most important key to understanding his personality and his theology. When the ego experiences its nothingness, God is revealed. Humankind's nothingness, *coram Deo,* implies that only God *is* and is acting. The person who sinks into nothingness turns back to God, for he gives up his false identity.[99]

The death of the ego is a total rupture. Thus the experience of grace is a totally new beginning—it is the creation of a new person, who is as unique as the original creation of the world out of nothing.[100] The nothingness of our human ego is an experience of temptation, until faith reveals a new dimension of being, received Being. Here our identity comes from grace alone. Faith is by no means mere *fides historica.* On the contrary, by means of faith in Christ, our hope develops in the very midst of temptation. This hope is the work of the Holy Spirit. It makes us capable of waiting for and becoming receptive to the transforming grace of God.[101] This does not contradict Luther's emphasis on justification but interprets it as more than just a forensic act: it now becomes a transformation through the power of the Spirit.[102] While justifying grace is still *iustitia imputata*, it is also a process which changes our life.

Luther's thoughts on temptation are closely related to Rhineland-Flemish mysticism's understanding of *mortificatio* and *vivificatio*. The most important thing that Luther adds is that *mortificatio* as *opus alienum Dei* comes from God alone. Otherwise it is not authentic. God appears in mortification and is perfectly present— but *sub contrario*. We know that God is acting by means of the revelation on the cross, which has opened a path leading us out of our nothingness. We can now trust God to sustain the spiritual process of dying to ego; i.e., to overcome the temptation. Only then will we be able to attain new life in communion with God.[103]

The more the ego is annihilated through temptation, the more God's grace can renew us.[104] In this renewal, humans experience their true personhood. Only those who are not trapped in egotism, but determined by God are truly persons, for they are free to be in relationship to another being. True personhood comes totally from God. The process of transformation begins now and is complete eschatologically.[105] Only as a person in this sense are humans truly free because their ego-centeredness no longer holds them bound. The ensnared person who is held by the power of sin and greed has no free will (*liberum arbitrium*), unless slavery is to be called freedom.[106]

There is a certain dualism which runs throughout Luther's thought, as we have seen in considering the contradiction between law and gospel, such as *opus alienum* and *opus proprium Dei*. In it is reflected the relentless struggle of Christ with the powers of darkness or with Satan. But God uses these forces so that grace may conquer.[107] To Luther, the battle between Christ and Satan is a very real battle between two powers,[108] which belong together insofar as both are subject to God's will.[109] The battle between them is the means God is using to work our salvation. But just as in the case of wrath and death, they are not two equal principles.[110]

In temptation God leads our human will towards integration with his. Just as Christ suffered the wrath of God on the cross and in doing so could unite his will completely with God's, so too the believer should now be united to Christ in perfect discipleship. Luther calls this *conformitas*.

In the incarnation God became man and entered into a conformity with the human. Because of this we can now enter into conformity with God. When humans recognize themselves as sinners, they reach conformity with the will and judgment of God.[111] Only when this is presupposed is it possible to talk of a *conformitas* between God and humans. Luther speaks of *Christum mortuum in se transformare eique conformare.*[112]

The *conformitas Christi* also includes the event called *vivificatio*, for we also have a share in Christ's resurrection. The death and resurrection of Christ "are a present reality in conformity with Christ, which is given to us in the working of the Spirit."[113]

At the basis of Luther's idea of conformity lies a stark realism. The Spirit really creates a new person through communion with Christ's being. "To Luther, *Fides Christi* means life in and from the redeemed reality of Christ as actually present. In faith the Christian is so unified to Christ that he/she possesses salvation through Christ as an *immediate* reality (italics added). Through faith in Christ we possess the reality of his work of salvation as our own reality. His victory is our victory. And this is not to be understood figuratively, but really. . . . The *fides Christi* is a real unification with the living Christ as saving reality."[114]

Yet the question remains: How is this "real unification" to be understood? We said that being a person means conformity with Christ. In the *unum cum eo fieri* we achieve the very essence of what we are. From the *conformitas* comes true knowledge of God. If at first, by means of *sapientia carnis*, humans were only projecting a false god which came out of their ego and its concerns,[115] now once the ego has died the light of the Spirit may be seen. For now we are *totally* of God. Our knowledge is *sapientia spiritus*, for our natural senses have been transformed.[116]

Conformity with Christ, however, never means complete identity.[117] The *fides Christi* is not *our* holiness, but God's action alone.[118] It is by no means an active *imitatio Christi* through ethical actions, but a reality that *becomes* real through God who works our redemption, who creates anew, who saves in Christ and transforms us in the Spirit into new beings, so that we now have a *new*—this is an essential point—identity, which is *God.* This is Luther's understanding of *conformitas.*

Luther understands God as the living, acting, and above all redeeming—i.e., trinitarian—God. In Luther's overall treatment of God the soteriological moment is the starting point, and thus his understanding of the trinity is characterized by the experience of salvation offered in Christ *sub contrario.*

The Father is linked to creation in a special way, the Son to redemption, and the Spirit to sanctification.[119] In each work, however, the whole trinity is present, as we have already seen.[120] The distinctions of persons come from the various works and are therefore oeconomical.[121] Abstractly, the Father is the original ground, the Son is the formal ruling principle, and the Spirit is the individual lifegiving and driving activity.[122] In another place Luther expresses the same content through images, saying that Christ is the door to the Father and the Holy Spirit the watchman of the door, who opens it and assures humans that they can enter it.[123] Because we experience God as differentiated by his works, even though "all are works of the one God",[124] we conclude to the intratrinitarian relationships of the persons, which Luther proceeds to do.[125] In doing so he is at pains to emphasize the personality of the Spirit, who is really God himself.[126] For the realization of our salvation depends on the work of the Holy Spirit, who makes Christ really present to us. The Spirit makes us into new beings.[127] Through the work of the Spirit God's presence in us is a real power of *conformitas Christi*. Thus humans are also called to a *cooperatio*[128] with God in his salvation history and the true agent in this is not the human self, but the Spirit of God.

God's trinitarian activity in salvation history appears as a process only to *us*, who see the separate moments of creation, redemption and sanctification. But for *God*, these moments of salvation history are an eternal present. They are all simultaneous. They are related to one another as the persons of the trinity are related. To God, says Luther, the Last Day is already present, while to us it is still to come.[129] Thus the different ways of seeing things—God's and ours—result in different expressions. From the human viewpoint God is most changeable (*deus est mutabilis quam maxime*). But in reality God remains one and the same; the changes are only from without, i.e., according to our human perspective (*verum hec mutatio extrinseca est*).[130]

Luther discusses the relationship between God and the world especially in connection with the doctrine of the real presence of Christ in the eucharist. As creator and sustaining power God is present in all of reality. He is the all-powerful force *welche zu gleich nirgent sein kan und doch an allen orten sein mus* (which at once can be nowhere and yet must be in every place).[131]

Luther accepts Nicolas of Cusa's notion of *coincidentia oppositorum* in order to show that God's all-presence is not bound to our spatial ways of picturing reality.[132] God is present most interiorly as well as most exteriorly in every creature.[133] Thus he can be "deeper, more interior, more present than a creature is to itself, and yet in no way can he be held or fixed, for he oversees all and is within. But no one oversees him or is in him."[134] God is therefore perfectly immanent within reality, but he is also perfectly transcendent, "exterior to and above all creatures."[135] Luther speaks of God in this way in order to overcome the "ordinary alternative of transcendence or immanence as a totally false way of regarding the matter," and this already reveals the *extra nos* of God's work in its main contours.[136]

But the manner and mode of God's presence in creatures is hiddenness. God is an overall presence, yet a presence that cannot be contained or pinned down because God is free and unbound.[137] Thus God is known wherever he lets himself be known; viz., in his word or the revelation in Jesus Christ.[138] Revelation alone casts light on God's omnipresence in reality.

Luther's theology is closely related to his personality. Therefore we must conduct our dialogue with him very carefully, especially since the historical situation in which he found himself plays such an important role in the development of his thought. On the other hand, since Luther's thought is permeated by a profound spiritual experience, there are, deeper links between his thought and meditative contemplation, whether these are developed against a background of Neoplatonism or the Indian path to salvation. Equally profound, however, are the differences which each side brings to the deeper penetration of the problem.

Now that we have become familiar with the most essential traits of Luther's theology we will relate them to Advaita Vedanta in order to see both their common ground and their characteristic differences.

1. To Luther, faith is a complete transformation through the indwelling Christ. Faith is *conformitas Christi.* The "first Adam" disappears and Christ becomes the center of our life; he is now the real subject (Gal 2:20). There is a process of identification, participation, and fusion.

Justification is an event from without. It breaks into our life and must continually be realized anew in faith. Justification in faith thus means a giving of oneself to the transforming power of the Spirit, who, in Eckhart's words, is our "is-ness."

The Holy Spirit is God indwelling, who creates and renews life everywhere and in every time. The Spirit, in fact, is the subject who acts. Thus Luther speaks of *spiritus creator.* Humans are determined either by the Spirit or by their human ego. Authentic life, prayer, meditation are always works of the Spirit. God is the subject who leads our life.

Without detailing each point made in part I, we see here the same basic similarities to Advaita Vedanta's spirituality. *Atman* is the center and ground of the personality. Here it is the Holy Spirit. Finding one's true identity means bringing about the reality of *atman/brahman*. Here the human ego is not the subject. In both instances there is an illusion to be overcome concerning the independence of the human subject. This position is especially well articulated by Rhineland-Flemish mysticism.

The task of humans is to be silent and listen, and thus interiorize the "standpoint of God" (*paramarthika*), as well as letting themselves be changed. What Luther calls faith corresponds largely to Vedanta's goals of *participation* in and fusion with the One— which leads to the discussion of the differences between the two ideas. Basically there is a becoming one with the universal presence of the One.

God is subject of the process of salvation, or freedom. In India, *atman* is the subject in salvific knowing. We only know this, however, when we contemplate reality from the standpoint of God, i.e., *paramarthika*—or, in faith. In *vyavaharika* the distinctions remain: such as, space-time distinctions. With the same intention in mind, Luther says: *sub specie Dei* there are no differences, no time. For the day of the last judgment is already here.

In other words, the experiences at the basis of these thought patterns may be similar. Still, unlike Luther's *donum Dei*, *atman* is not freely given by a personal God. No contingency may be attributed to *atman*; rather in *atman* reality appears as what it really is. *Atman* is the being of reality. Nothing outside it is.

Nevertheless, this argument may not be that foreign to Luther, for he too understands the unity of creation, redemption, and sanctification as the unity of the trinitarian God, who is universally and eternally present.

2. The opposite of spirit is flesh or human ego-centeredness, reflected in the physical as well as the psychic-mental areas of human reality. Paul's insight, that human pride and self-glorification must be overcome by being in Christ (Rm 3:27; 15:17; 1 Cor 15:31), is the basis of Luther's doctrine of justification, which he has made the center of the Christian's self-understanding.

In Advaita Vedanta a similar experience, along with the Bhagavad Gita's interpretation of it, has great significance. The one who forgives in order to be righteous (*dambha*) and wants to be something on the basis of his/her ego, instead of being totally immersed in God or in *atman*, becomes demonic in nature and a hypocrite (*dharma-dhvajitva*). Such a person must first experience the nothingness of her ego before being able to attain the advaitic experience, as we saw in chapter 5.

In Luther's terms, this would mean that a person must first have an experience of temptation by which he becomes aware of his *nihileitas.* Then he can attain communion with God or *conformitas Christi*, by the experience of justification. He will realize that God alone is and is active.

3. According to Luther everything can be viewed either as gift (*donum*) or as our own (*proprium*). It depends on a person's viewpoint whether her holiness and ongoing salvation are judged according to the hope of resurrection or under the curse of the law.

The relative standpoint of humankind must be raised to the absolute standpoint of God. This is especially evident in the light of the debate of *liberum arbitrium:* humans have relative freedom in relation to the things of this world, but *coram Deo* they are completely unfree.

The capacity for freedom is the decisive characteristic in the human person both for Luther and Advaita Vedanta. Its basis is not any quality that could be developed through what is empirically available, but God or *atman/brahman.*

Once again there is an undeniable similarity between Luther and the distinctions of *paramarthika/vyavaharika.* To temporally conditioned humans, things seem to be based on their own decisions and actions. In reality—*sub specie Dei*—there is a transtemporal unity, the divine will, the gift of the Spirit—or *atman.*

4. God's presence in the world is described by Luther advaitically. In the world God is being and a driving force. Yet God is not identical with the world. He is beyond the differences of transcendence and immanence, and thus beyond objectivity and subjectivity. Luther and the mystics, as well as the non-dualist argumentation of Vedanta are all characterized by a unity of the concepts of immanent transcendence and transcendent immanence.

To Luther God can only be known in his revelation. Revelation corresponds to his essence, which must be explained by trinitarian language. In India the same problematic is explained by means of the notions of *nirguna brahman* and *saguna brahman*, which are "not-two." Revelation is experienced in the word. Luther describes four dimensions of the word, which correspond to the advaitic understanding of *brahman*, which manifests itself in three stages wherein it becomes ever more concrete. These may be interpreted as stages of revelation: *isvara-hiranyagarbha-viraj* (cf. ch. 3).

We could continue to find parallels. In light of the fact that Luther is within an entirely different tradition from Sankara and that both representatives have their own particular historical development, we cannot speak of any identity in their theologies, but only of underlying structures which express common human, spiritual relationships. In retrospect, these different traditions can be related to one another without denying the individuality of each.

We would like to point out two important differences, however, which have been chosen because they are typical distinctions which can be used generally in judging Indian spirituality.

1. For Luther, God's revelation can be experienced in Jesus Christ. He is not just an example and a teacher, but the *bearer* of God's love revealed. This is the paradigm for all God knowledge in Christian faith. The Spirit makes present the historical person of Jesus, so that faith is something totally different from a pure *fides historica.* The historical figure of Jesus Christ took upon himself the human condition and now, by means of this, makes light shine forth. By means of human relativity and weakness he reveals divine, absolute, forceful and true being. For Luther, overcoming also implies *integrating.* This is a general characteristic of Christian mysticism.

In Advaita Vedanta the emphasis is different, at least in evaluating historical reality. The world of *maya* is not. It simply disappears once reality is known. In the end it is not integrated. Nonetheless we should not overlook an integrating tendency in the advaitic vision. It may, however, be judged as inferior at the level of the historical, since it lacks the integrating power of the incarnation. And this may lead to a negative or even a disintegrated view of history. Yet it must be asked whether this is a *necessary* consequence of Vedanta's starting point. Nevertheless, historically, this has been its position.

2. The second difference is equally serious. Luther allows the tensions between law and gospel, wrath and grace, *mortificatio* and *vivificatio*, temptation and the overcoming of temptation, egocentricity and new being to remain until death. Spiritual growth and conformity with Christ in faith take place on the basis of the power of the Spirit. Humans may realize their true identity more and more and thus overcome their egocentricity and isolation. Their being is from God. On earth, however, fulfillment is impossible.

In Advaita Vedanta and in almost all the paths of Indian spirituality, humans strive for the ideal of *jivanmukta*, which can be achieved completely in this life, within our conditioned, temporal existence. To the *jivanmukta* who has achieved the bliss of being-one, no return to selfishness and ignorance is possible. Against the background of Luther's experience of the power of sin, this ideal of *jivanmukta* would seem unrealistic.

To Luther, existence in the Spirit of God—as non-duality between God and humans—is and remains "simultaneous existence," a tension-filled unity. In Advaita Vedanta, on the other hand, the existence of the person who has realized in him/herself the non-duality of *atman* and *brahman* is free from all tensions. Human "conditionedness" is overcome; it is recognized as illusion. Thus the *jnanin* lives in a perfect non-duality of God and humanness: the empirical person has disappeared.

8.

Completion of the Synthesis: Hegel

Although Hegel's treatment of the doctrine of the trinity remains traditional, on some important points he clarifies it brilliantly. The doctrine of the trinity is an integral part of his system and can only be understood in connection with this system. We wish to point out only a few of its facets.

Being and Nothing

Hegel's starting point is his criticism of Kant's dualism. The "thing in itself" remains something abstractly opposed to the world of appearances. It remains for itself and the result is, reality is split into two areas that cannot be united.[1] This is the point where Hegel's dialectical logic begins. It is the exposition of the Absolute in its unity, before the opposition of matter and spirit. Its content is this One, the "true matter."[2] The Absolute is the unity of being and nothing or, on the level of reflection, the unity of identity and non-identity.[3] The fact that both, being and nothing, are to be understood as a unity means that they cannot be abstracted from one another, so that one could be defined by the other, and an essential relationship of the two could be explained: "What is the truth is neither being nor nothing. But that being does not pass over, but has passed over into nothing, and nothing into being."[4] Both are simultaneously distinguished and inseparable. Each moment is sublated in its opposite, and what we think is the result of this process: a becoming. The Absolute is this becoming, whose abstracted moments, being and nothing, can only be thought in complete relation to one another, identical and yet distinct. Thinking the difference between being and nothing implies introducing certain determinations, which would be relative and not absolute. In this case neither being nor nothing would have been thought.[5] Thinking the unity involves a dialectic, which is "the higher movement of reason in which such seemingly utterly sepa-

119

rate terms pass over into each other spontaneously, through that which they are, a movement in which the presupposition sublates itself. It is the dialectical immanent nature of being and nothing themselves to manifest their unity, that is, becoming, as their truth."[6] What Hegel means here becomes clearer when we understand the antithesis to this, which Hegel himself names: Parmenides. Parmenides only wants to think being. Non-being is not. This results in a dualism of being and nothing which will be rich in consequences for the whole history of Western thought. Being is the absolutely indistinguishable One. Concerning this being nothing can be said. It is indeterminable and therefore cannot be active. This being must therefore remain empty. It cannot be made clear how anything can be thought out from this starting point; that is, how reality is to be interpreted on the basis of it. And in fact—at least in Plato's Parmenides—this being has to be abandoned in favor of a new, more differentiated starting point. This implies a certain dualism. When being is understood as an abstract oneness, any continuation or movement must come from outside, from a second, possibly relative principle. There is an unsolvable contradiction.[7]

Becoming and passing penetrate each other just as being and nothing penetrate into each other and then disappear into the other. Becoming and passing are the same because they describe the process caused by the relationship of two opposites, now seen from another standpoint. Becoming is "an unstable unrest which settles into a stable result," which however is not nothing, for that would be an opposition to being. Rather it is this simplicity that is a unity of being and nothing.[8]

From these considerations Hegel deduces his own counter-thesis to Kant's. The In-itself is *in* the appearance. This is an ontological statement. The In-itself is the true essence within the appearance, it is the infinite within the finite,[9] as such not divided from the appearance or the finite. The infinite is the essence for the finite itself. It is not outside it, not a second. Were it a second, we could not have thought the infinite, but only the relativity of two quantities and this would destroy the concept of infinity. The Absolute is the negation in the appearance and vice versa. As negation it is essential to, not foreign to the finite.[10] Indeed the finite only acquires intelligibility from the infinite, through which it is determined.[11] If we wished to think of the infinite *alongside* the finite, a dualism would result; there would be a "bad infinity," which would only be a quantitative prolongation of the finite and would remain dependent on relativity. It would be a "finite infinite."[12] These manners of viewing things must basically be surpassed.[13]

For if the dualism between the infinite and the finite, between God and humankind is not sublated there can be no human freedom. If God is the all-determining reality, this reality meets its limits in human self-determination, and this contradicts the absoluteness of God. If, however, the infinite appears as the true essence of the finite, and if the unity of the two is known, then human freedom is conceivable as the form of realization of God's freedom.[14]

Trinity

It was Hegel's intention to overcome this dualistic division. He works out his solution using the trinitarian concept of God. This enables him to think reality dialectically. The infinite present in the finite does not mean it is an alien force, but rather the finite sublates itself and transcends itself: this is its infinity.[15] Hegel sees the true infinite within the becoming of a trinitarian God, whereby three-ness brings forth and makes present particular moments of the process. The whole of the Logic explains this becoming, which becomes intelligible as God's self-exposition and is identical with revelation. The Logic is the science of revelation.[16] The whole becoming process of the world is the revelation of God and can be seen by means of its three determinations.[17]

The *first* determination is God in his eternity before the creation of the world. Here God thinks himself, he is "unmoved silence." This is the realm of the *Father*.

The *second* determination is God who creates the world and with it division and distinction. God appears as the particular. He denies his being in and for itself and enters into the world of appearances, which is appearance when it is thought of as an other alongside God. The dialectic of infinite and finite developed above is at work here, all the way to the death of God. For the difference that was set up in the particular must be sublated in a negation of the negation.[18] This is the reconciliation of the infinite and the finite leading to unity. This second determination is the realm of the *Son*.

The *third* determination is the result of the negation of particularity. What appeared as historically particular in the second determination is now sublated within the Spirit of community. The particular reconciliation is sublated as a general *consciousness* of the reconciliation of God and humankind. It is the negation of the negation. This is the realm of the *Spirit.*

God is Spirit in the constant movement of coming-to-be-self. And "God as Spirit is essentially God revealing himself for an another. He does not create the world only once, but is eternal creator, eternally creating. He is this, this *act;* this is his concept, his determination."[19] Creation and redemption are moments in this one process of self-revealing, just as the three persons of the trinity are determinations in the process of God's bringing-himself-forth. God as Spirit is a presupposition for this process, but as Spirit he is likewise the result insofar as he has integrated the infinite and the finite in the third determination. Or, as Hegel says elsewhere: "(He)It is the subject of the movement and is equally the *moving* itself."[20]

God is the event in which he is bringing himself forth. He is the subject of this event. This accounts for the doctrine of the *unity* of the trinity, which is then differentiated into three moments. This is likewise the manner and mode by which the infinite is mediated with the finite without causing a dualistic distinction. With Augustine, Hegel sees the first instance of trinitarian reality in self-consciousness, the result of a being-reflected-in-itself, as a process which is immanent to the trinitarian determinations presented above.[21]

God is Spirit and as such the subject of becoming, in that he brings forth himself. This means: God is personality.[22] Personality here does not mean an individual center—thus, a separate being—but absolute subjectivity, a center of freedom which has power over itself. Person is relationship. The personality of God is perfect interrelationality, whose structure is understandable by means of dialectical logic. There is no division between God and the world, only interrelationship and interpenetration of the two. But since God is in no way dependent, he has to appear as the center of all possible relationships. He determines the interrelationality. This means he *is* freedom.

As subject reflected in himself, whose individual moments are the three trinitarian persons, he is, however, only *one* personality. Within the distinction of Father and Son as well as the mutual going over into the other, there is love.[23] Thus personality is only the trinity as a whole, because personality implies the notion of freedom, which is the result of God as self-mediating, not of the individual moments.[24]

By means of the relational unity of the trinity, God can be understood in such a way that he both differentiates himself and is identical with himself. The unfolding of this identity takes place in history. Hegel sees God as trinitarian history in three forms:[25]

First, God is "eternally in and with himself": he is in and for himself since he has not yet entered the world of appearance. In relation to spatial ideas, this means that he is thought of as outside time, "as eternal idea in the element of the pure thought of eternity." He is God the *Father*.

Secondly, God is the form of appearance, particularization, and Being for the other. Thus he is relationship to the other, intelligible and concrete. He is historical being, spatially conditioned by history, temporally subject to past, present, and future. He is God the Son.

Thirdly, God is the form of returning from appearance into himself. He is God as subject of becoming, which in finite appearances—that is, in the community—is present as ongoing reality, which strives for completion in the future. He is God the Spirit.

God is activity insofar as he determines himself, becomes concrete, and then dies to this concreteness, to shed his finite appearance and bring about a universality of spiritual reality. Hegel comments on this in the *Phenomenology:* "The death of the Mediator as grasped by the Self is the *supersession* of his objective existence or his particular being-for-self: this *particular* being-for-self has become a universal self-consciousness."[26] This is the same, earlier idea of theopoiesis in the form of dialectical logic!

It is true that Hegel understands his trinitarian thought on the basis of a revelation which is concrete in Jesus Christ. But only in the context discussed here does this revelation become meaningful for Hegel. "The reconciliation in Christ, which is believed, has no meaning unless God is known as triune: he is, but also he is other, as differentiating himself, so that this other is God himself and has within it the divine nature, and the sublation of this differentiating being-other, this return of love, is the Spirit. In this consciousness it is implied that faith is not a relationship to something subordinate, but to God himself."[27]

The trinitarian God is Spirit: both the initial determination and the result of the determination of the third person are called Spirit. The third is the first, and the first is the third, for the process which divine life goes through is not extrinsic, but intrinsic. It is therefore, "nothing other than a drama of being-self, a becoming conscious of self."[28] The result of the intratrinitarian process is that God comes to his own self-consciousness by means of history. World history, as seen by us, is nothing other than the extrinsic form of the intratrinitarian process. The controlling principle here is a perfect non-duality with regard to the whole and the individual moments of historical reality.

Non-duality and Freedom

Hegel sees in the doctrine of the trinity the possibility of overcoming ontological dualism. The Absolute, God as Spirit, is the one reality which unfolds in three-part self-movement, and thus comes to be Self. God is at first pure substance or the content of his own pure consciousness. He then enters into otherness: i.e., in the synthetic conjunction with finite determinations, which he himself produces—he is incarnate as human. Finally, he returns from being-other into the spiritual unity of self-consciousness. Thus, in each of these moments, which Hegel thinks of as a perfect circularity, God is fully God. For: "his complete movement is therefore this, to diffuse his nature throughout each of its moments as in his native element."[29]

In the terminology of Advaita Vedanta this would mean: the eternal self-movement of the Absolute (brahman) proceeds through the moments of saguna brahman in such a way that in a third, mediated stage it comes to know itself and thus sublates the objective character of saguna brahman in the pure subjectivity of what is reflected within itself, but now within a wholeness which is at rest. This third step, significantly, is not, however, recognized in Advaita Vedanta, and in addition, only with great caution could we speak of a self-movement of the Absolute, for the modes of appearance are relegated to maya and by no means imply a history of the Absolute.

To Hegel the Absolute is subject of its own self-movement, its history, through which it comes to be itself. To Hegel Indian nirguna brahman would be substance, which only rests because it remains alone;[30] thus it never becomes completely the concept of subject.

Nevertheless in Advaita Vedanta there are strong indications that brahman can be subject in Hegel's sense, namely, when the Absolute appears as being (sat), which is likewise consciousness (*cit*), and in this self-knowledge enjoys complete bliss (*ananda*). However, these determinations apply only to *nirguna brahman*, not to the relationship of *nirguna brahman* and *saguna brahman*.

In order to understand God's self-movement as a unified process, Hegel must accept a binarian tendency in his doctrine of the trinity, and this is related to the problem of freedom. He understands the relationship between Father and Son as a being in one another, thus in the sense of the *perichoresis*. The Spirit, as love, is the unity of the two, but is not thereby constituted as the third person of the trinity, since he only clarifies the relationship of the first two. This was also a problem that, as we saw, Augustine could not solve in a satisfactory way.[31] Since Hegel grasps the whole of trinitarian becoming as Spirit, he cannot think of the third determination as "person" in the same sense as the first two. This has wide-reaching consequences for understanding God's freedom.

In order to understand God's freedom of choice, there must be a distinction between knowing and willing in God, and this distinction was made by scholastic theology.[32] Only if there is a priority of the known over the willed in God can we understand how creation is freely chosen as one possibility from many known possibilities. When there is no distinction made between knowing and willing in the trinity, creation cannot be seen as a free act of God, for freedom implies choice. God's freedom would then be less than human freedom; that is, the notion of freedom would have no meaning in relationship to God. Hegel's philosophy can be interpreted in such a way then that, at least in relation to this unsolved problem—which is eventually set aside—it does not sufficiently take into consideration the unity of the threefold distinction in God.[33] This is directly connected to the problem of the Spirit. The revelation of the trinitarian God is "the decisive condition of possibility of present, full freedom,"[34] because human freedom means that humans give themselves into the objective becoming of spirit and are thereby determined. Therefore, particular existence is sublated into the universality of the Spirit. Human freedom is experienced as participation in God's trinitarian freedom, as he participates in it himself. This sharing happens in the Spirit. The Spirit is the continually new result of a spiritual process, not an already determined outcome, as Hegel implies.

The individual has infinite worth because he/she is sublated into God, but as individual moment in the process of God's own self-realization. Yes, the activity of human freedom is the appearance of the dimension of the infinite in the finite. In this way—ac-

cording to the dialectical logic presented above—any dualism or
any mutual reduction of divine and human freedom is overcome.
Divine freedom realizes itself by trinitarian becoming, and human
freedom is the realization of divine freedom under the determination of finite being-other, so that acting in freedom already implies
a sublation of the finite. The return from the particular to God's
infinite thus demonstrates this: that human freedom is the expression of and the form of realization of God who is Spirit.

Man is not God. But humans are one moment in the self-realization of God. Humans are relative to God, but in their individuality they are of infinite worth, because in them the freedom of God
is determining itself. Thus for Hegel, God and humans are neither
identical nor different. They are not-two. The Advaita-category
takes this fact into account.

Individuality and History

For Hegel, history as trinitarian is real. It is the self-realization
of absolute Spirit becoming itself. Thus there are progressively
three phases of the Spirit, who is both the process, and the finality:
The *first phase* is the stage of a consciousness which is still pre-
conscious perception. It is the area of nature, which is God in his
being-other, or potential Spirit. The world appears as object without any mental mediation.

In the *second phase*, the Spirit is awakening to self-consciousness in humans. As such, Spirit is the area of *mental understanding*
(*Verstand*). As understanding it becomes "unfortunate consciousness" or divided consciousness alienated from itself. This is the
egocentricity of Adam who, to use the mythical image, ate from the
tree of knowledge.

In the *third phase* the Spirit returns to itself as absolute knowledge, which is also humankind's highest knowledge. This is a stage
of reason beyond discursive mental reasoning, a higher consciousness (*Vernunft*), according to Hegel. It is the synthesis of objectivity and subjectivity. The Spirit which knows itself as Spirit is consciousness aware of its non-duality.

Since this history unfolds by means of dialectical negations,
the former stages are "sublated" in the latter. The development
starting with *consciousness*, then *self-consciousness*, finally *reason* corresponds to the Indian categories of a pre-conscious area
(*annamayakosa/pranamayakosa*), a conscious area (*manomaya-*

kosa), and an area of higher-consciousness and super-consciousness (*vijnanamayakosa/anandamayakosa/atman*), as we explained in chapter 1. It must be added, however, that the Advaita Vedanta, as well as Buddhism and other psychologies that describe the meditative experience which corresponds with the Hegelian area of *reason*, are much more subtle in their exposition, especially in detailing the various parts.[35]

The history of nature is a phase in the history of consciousness, which in turn is a phase in the history of the Absolute subject which is Spirit, as seen in the symbol of the trinity. Thus in Hegel's eyes, the unity of reality is the dialectical "sublation" of dualisms conditioned by process.

To Hegel the sublation of those dualisms in world history is a real process. The differences are already sublated. The question is whether this thesis is verifiable and actually corresponds to our historical experience. The Hegelian "left" contests this and attempts to set aside the differences in reality. For within our actual experience "we cannot eradicate . . . the moment of difference without turning reconciliation into a cynical, reactionary statement."[36] Hegel understands reality as history, but he is not thinking of real history. Thus the dualism which Hegel wanted to overcome emerges elsewhere.

Vedanta does not identify God with his own unfolding in revelation. The two are neither identical nor different, but rather nottwo (Advaita), as aspects of our way of viewing things. This is dependent on the degree of realization of Spirit in us. This degree of realization is still not perfect, so that Advaita Vedanta can look forward to what is still to be realized without thereby being obliged to split reality dualistically. The price of this, however, is that God's self-movement, from God's standpoint, is not real in any finalized sense, but only appearance. The Hegelian understanding of God's self-movement as a play of love within God's self could also be understood by the Advaita Vedanta, namely, as the work of *maya*. But in this case the movement of *maya* would be considered as different from the unmoved absolute *brahman*, thus not the *self*-movement of the Absolute. To Hegel it is important that the movement proceed as a constant negation of one element passing into another.[37] In this way God's becoming is a becoming-other, until the "death of God" which is in fact the end of an "empty beyond," and thus the end of dualistic metaphysics.[38]

This latter idea cannot be realized in Advaita Vedanta, especially in Sankara. To Hegel non-duality is the result of a real process. To Sankara non-duality is the experience of what is eternal, once the veil of our dualistic ways of viewing has been torn away by the advaitic experience.

This is the most important difference between Hegel's attempt to grasp the unity of reality as the history of the absolute subject and Sankara's doctrine of non-dualistic *atman/brahman.* This difference is further seen in the fact that Advaita Vedanta does not understand individuality as an essential moment of the Absolute. Humans who have recognized their essential determination as *atman,* as identical with *brahman,* and have thereby returned advaitically to the Absolute, are not part of an overall process of becoming-self. They have merely overcome the appearance of being individual. In Advaita Vedanta, human freedom could not be a dialectical counterpart of God's freedom. Instead, the only place human freedom is found is when humans are one with God and when all individual particularity which differentiates them has disappeared.

9.

Unity and Self-differentiation: The Ongoing Discussion

The project of thinking the unity of God in his self-revelation also implies answering the fundamental human question concerning the unity of existence.[1] This unity has implications for God's relationship to himself in his subjectivity, as well as God's relationship to the world. If reality is not to remain shattered and broken up into discrete parts, contingently determined and thus threatened by meaninglessness—which would also imply fragmentation in our lives—we need to speak of a subjectivity which includes everything. The *meaning* of life depends on the *unity* of reality.

The difficulty begins when we try to understand the unity of God in conjunction with his self-differentiation—a necessary task since revelation implies a differentiation. Understanding the unity of the trinity involves walking the tightrope between modalism and subordinationism. The modalist tendency eliminates the real differences. It dissolves them and thus only reaches an apparent solution. It does not, however, deal with the very real oppositions. Subordinationism, strictly defined, reaches a fourth level: a "God above God" which is supposed to unify the differences. However, this only postpones the problem. In principle it leads to a *regressus ad infinitum* in reaching a final level of unity. It is an unsatisfactory solution to the problems of unity, meaning and subjectivity. Neither of these one-sided positions were helpful. Yet both continue to plague theologians today.[2]

Unity as Subjectivity

Since Plato it has been acknowledged that it is not possible to think the unity of God, since thinking is limited and remains linked to subject/predicate differentiation; thus it always implies duality. God as subject can only be explained by means of a predi-

129

cated determination. Since the area of the predicate must be larger than the subject, there is no way out of this dilemma.

According to Plato, God is simply one (*hén estin*). "Is" in this case is only a copula, not an explanation, for then the One would participate in being, and there would be a duality.[3] The One has no name and cannot be known, since it is the subject of knowing.[4]

This is the starting point for a *theologia negativa*, as it was handed on by Neoplatonism to many Christian fathers of the church such as Clement, Origen, the Cappadocians, and especially Dennis the Areopagite. It comes from Plato and need not be attributed to Indian influences, although it is striking that the Upanishads also ground the unknowability of *atman* in its being-subject.

Understanding the unity of God in the strict sense means understanding God as the One (*to hen*; Sanskrit *tad ekam*), which is logically impossible since the One is above being, just as it is above every determination. In order to speak about God we must think of him as an existing One (*hen éstin*),[5] which implies that God participates in being (*metechei*). But this results in a duality, and thus the One has not been thought out. The Absolute is relativized when we think it. Thus God's absoluteness means that he cannot be thought.

There is a relationship between Plato's first expression, *hén estin*, and the second: *hen éstin*, which is very similar to the relationship between *nirguna brahman* and *saguna brahman* in the Advaita Vedanta. Neither Plato nor Advaita Vedanta could describe or make comprehensible the passage from the first to the second. In Advaita Vedanta the middle term is *maya*; in Plato—at least in the Parmenides—the one stands opposite the other without any mediation.[6]

The trinitarian notion of God, interpreted non-dualistically, could bring us closer to a solution. This is what Hegel saw; this is why the trinity has a central place in his onto-logic.

In confronting the same dilemma of Plato's Parmenides, Karl Barth accepts Hegel's solution. According to Barth, unity can only be understood in and from the self-manifestation of God in revelation: "By being the Father in Himself from eternity, God brings Himself forth from eternity as the Son. By being the Son from eternity, He comes forth from eternity from Himself as Father. In this eternal bringing forth of Himself and coming forth from Himself, He posits Himself a third time as the Holy Spirit, i.e., as the love which unifies Him in Himself."[7]

The problem with this statement is in the way it determines

the Holy Spirit, who (in connection with the Western church's *filioque*), is seen as the unifying bond between the Father and the Son, and thus in effect is not really a hypostasis—as the Eastern church relentlessly observes.[8] The consequence of this is a binitarian tendency—from Augustine to Hegel to Barth.[9]

God is subject, a subject who is active. In this subjective activity, God is eternally coming to be and remaining himself. This is what Barth means when he speaks of the trinitarian God as revealer/revelation/revealedness.[10] Revelation is the whole event which we experience as creation, redemption, re-creation. This total event is God's self-interpretation. Since this determination constitutes the subject-object unity of his essence, God's being is *in* becoming (E. Jüngel), without becoming other. The fact that God interprets himself in the historical figure of the Son does not, however, mean that the being of the Father is lost in the being of the Son. That one is prior to this. Insofar as God's being-subject, identical with himself, and his being Father as first of the modes of being are identical, Barth still has not answered whether the unity and personality of God lie in the three modes of being or in a monarchical fatherhood.[11]

Still, Barth states much more clearly than Hegel: God's essence *is* trinitarian self-movement, which is deducible only from his eternal differentiation. Thus it follows that the Father always remains Father. As such he is not at our disposition and is not merged into his revelation.[12]

Barth's presentation of the unity of God becomes especially clear in his arguments against the teaching of *vestigia trinitatis*,[13] which he rejects because this would assume the *analogia entis.* To Barth an ontological correspondence implies ontological dualism, which he therefore avoids, although he falls into it in some cases. The duality of transcendence and immanence *is*, however, overcome in Barth's eyes: immanence is sublated in transcendence. This is how he explains the Christ event. Barth speaks of its irreversibility in the following way: revelation can determine language, but language cannot determine revelation.[14]

In another argumentation Barth demonstrates that our knowledge of God represents a moment in the being of the triunity, where the Holy Spirit pours forth as the light in which reality appears in its true nature. He distinguishes the *analogia entis* from the *analogia fidei*, not in order to add another analogy, but rather to show that the possibility of analogy is only given *ex fide*. God alone is subject; i.e., he is also subject of knowledge of God and thus of authentic knowledge of reality. Being-known (*gnosthenai*) precedes knowing (*gignoskein*).[15] This means that the unity of God in the trinity and knowledge of God are related. Barth offers the following descriptive example: "We can see a stick dipped in the water only as a broken stick. But unapparently for us, invisibly and yet really, it is the completely unbroken stick."[16] The empirical impossibility of seeing it does not change the fact. But in faith, God himself gives a glimpse of the non-duality of reality, and this is a *sort of certitude*, because God the triune eternally creates it anew.

God did not differentiate himself once for all in the past, but is infinitely a becoming-one and is differentiating himself in this process as threefold.[17] Since we exist in relation to this event, we recognize the unity in the circulation of divine forces: a perfect mutuality of God's intrinsic relatedness. This is what *perichoresis* means to Barth.[18]

On this basis it is correct to distinguish God's triunity from the identifications of identity-philosophy. They see an identity between empirically known reality and God.[19] According to Barth *we* can only know God's differentiation within a broken unity: i.e., our knowledge stands within dividedness, sin and the cross (1 Cor 13:12). In reality, however—*sub specie Dei*—opposites are already unified into a wholeness: they are overcome by the reality of the cross, and as Luther says, the "last judgment" is already here. But Barth—unlike the mystics and naturally the Vedantic thinkers—is unable to see the possibility of an experience which would be transrational, yet still knowledge.

Self-differentiation as Personality

Since Tertullian, the Western tradition has used the term *person* to designate God's self-differentiation.[20] The Eastern tradition did not reject this term, but interpreted it on the basis of its understanding of *hypostasis*.[21] The Greek term *prosopon* and the Latin *persona* are by no means identical with the modern concept of personality although certain characteristics such as individuality have always been connected with this term.[22]

Nevertheless, starting with Augustine, who clearly explains these connections, the difficulties of using the notion of person became apparent, especially with regard to the personhood of the Spirit. Augustine tried to understand the Holy Spirit as the holiness of the Father and the Son,[23] and this tended to take away his personal individuality.[24] This binitarian tendency characterizes the whole Western tradition to this day, as we have already seen.

The scholastic theory of relations made the notion of person even more abstract. Nevertheless, another theme appeared in the mystics and later in Luther: God, experienced as living love and therefore related within himself. The fulfillment of love becomes the basis for speaking of three persons.[25]

An interesting development occurs with Luther, one which brings out the interrelationality of personal Being. God is seen concretely in the humanity of Jesus, and this is the basis of Luther's portrait of the human person. Humans are persons insofar as God is present in them. In other words, being a person consists in being-grounded-in-God.[26] In the absence of this determination, *liberum arbitrium* becomes impossible. Only when God remains as absolute subject is freedom possible, and thus also personality. Personality implies being determined by another. This is also the formal structure of love. If God is love, he is also person and the differentiation of persons within God is determined by the other divine persons.

The notion of person used here refers to relationships. When these relations are understood substantially, using anthropomorphic images, it becomes impossible to understand the unity of God. The misunderstanding comes from the notion of person, since person implies individuality and historicity, today just as in the times of the church fathers.[27]

For this reason Karl Barth insisted on talking about God's three *modes of being*.[28] In all three it is the same God, but each way describes a particular state of being which is essential to God. To describe these states, Barth returns to substantial images, which show what the notion of person refers to.[29]

The properties of the three ways of being are deduced from the relations, which are mutually interconnected: "Father, Son, and Spirit are distinguished from one another without inequality in their essence or work, without increase or decrease in divinity the *original relations* in which they stand to one another are unequal."[30] Barth speaks of *genetic relationships* in God, which are the grounds for the distinctions of three modes of being. They are the only ground for speaking of three modes of being. The anthropomorphic character of these images is evident: in Augustine we have already seen the difficulty of using *generatio* or *generatio sempiterna* in a way that does not endanger the unity and perfec-

tion of God. The presentation of modes of being, grounded in genetic relations, is no less problematic than the concept of person,
since it reifies functional relations.

Since Augustine the notion of person has been linked to relationship. Thomas Aquinas could not define the trinitarian persons
without referring back to the less problematic notion of *relatio:
relatio ut res subsistens in natura divina.*[31] Every "thing" is concrete. As its etymology indicates, it is a "collection." A thing is the
intersection of relationships to other things; i.e., it is what it is *in
relationibus.*[32] Nothing exists for itself. For reality consists of interrelationships or mutual "in-ek-sistence" of elementary parti-
cles, from subatomic things all the way to the integrated
personality.

God in himself is relational; that is, as living he is continuously
constituting himself through relationship. He is *not* the movement
this implies, but his being is *in* this movement.[33] The relations
describe mutual dependence and do not thereby signify any hierarchical subordination.

There is also a proportion between the relations in God and
God's relationship to the world.[34] Just as God *is* as self-differen-
tiating, so too God is in differentiating himself from the world:
viz., in a dialectical integration. As long as there is such a proportion, God cannot be understood without the world, nor the world
without God. As Pannenberg has pointed out,[35] this is implied in
Hegel's as well as Barth's teaching on the trinity.

To Pannenberg the doctrine of the trinity enables us to think of
God—including God in his subjectivity—by means of a specified
difference from the world. Furthermore, this concept of God is not
dependent on a negation (namely, of the world), since in the trinity
the relationship between God and world—a non-dualistic relationship, as we explained—is "prefigured."[36] Yet it remains unclear
what Pannenberg means by "prefiguration," since it obviously
cannot imply any temporal or ontological priority, lest a certain
kind of subordinationism creep in again!

What we are proposing, then, is a non-dualist solution. The
trinitarian self-differentiation of God not only *enables* God to be
related to the world, but contains this relationship *implicitly.* Prefiguration would therefore be one pole of the tension between possibility and a reality which constitutes itself within this polarity;
i.e., in the process of a trinitarian self-differentiation.

Since a trinitarian understanding of God includes an opposition between God and the world (as well as between the One and

the many of Platonic and Vedantic philosophy) and also goes beyond this opposition, because it is formed in and beyond the trinitarian perichoretic event, Christianity's concept of God successfully thinks both the unity of reality and God's infinity, without falling into abstract theism.[37]

Pannenberg's critique of Hegel and Barth culminates in the observation that grounding God's unity in his subjectivity (which is identical with the notion of *concept* for Hegel) demands a priority of subject over its unfolding, and thus leads to a theory of God's *one* self-consciousness over three persons. This in turn leads to a Godhead beyond the trinity (Eckhart) or God above God (Tillich) or the modes of being *of* the one subject (Barth). The flaw in this thesis is that it *deduces* the trinity from subjectivity. Yet in reality the three persons (or modes of being) *constitute* a trinitarian unity.

The notion of personality, which has been psychologized since Augustine and then interpreted in the sense of an autonomous self-consciousness is, in fact, a highly problematic transposition of the human experience of self to the infinite reality of God. Only with great difficulty can it be successfully applied to the trinity.[38] For the trinitarian persons are what they are both in and from the other persons. They maintain non-dualist relationships of mutual indwelling to one another, and thereby constitute a process of *perichoresis*, which is a unity. This process is an *explication* simultaneous with *implication*, since the real and the possible both indwell in analogy to the trinitarian persons.

We can also accept (and go beyond) Pannenberg's critique of Hegel's thesis concerning the necessity of an unfolding in God, on condition that we understand the *perichoretic indwelling* of the moments of reality as *the* basic datum of reality. This point will be developed in chapter 10.

Since self-differentiation is in a general way something we experience in love—and this is the essential to the person, who is constituted through and in other persons—God's self-differentiation describes and prefigures (Pannenberg) an ultimately personal structure of reality. Therefore, the *perichoresis* of the trinity is the appropriate symbol for the non-duality of reality.

Although the clear Indian notion of Advaita has no exact equivalent in Christian theology, nevertheless Tillich's notion of *participation*, as well as his ontology of *love* are similar and can be helpful for understanding Advaita Vedanta.

Tillich begins by opposing individualization to participation, and understands the two as polar elements of being.[39] The courage to be oneself is the polar opposite of the courage to be part of a whole. Apart from the actual term, individualization, there is advaitic structure in what Tillich understands by individualization: "In all these cases participation is a partial identity and a partial nonidentity. A part of a whole is not identical with the whole to which it belongs. But the whole is what it is only with the part."[40] In order to understand the "dialectical nature" of participation, Tillich wants to think, not in terms of substances, but in dynamic terms: the power of being, a power which can be shared by many different individuals. "The identity of participation is an identity in the power of being. In this sense the power of being of the individual self is partly identical with the power of being of his world, and conversely."[41] It is clear that the participation of the relations in the trinity expresses this symbolically, as described by the dynamic term, *perichoresis*.

A further question is whether Indian *atman/brahman* can become more understandable through Tillich's categories. Tillich believes that all of mysticism is caught in contradiction since it does not take seriously the concrete.[42] To him this applies also to Indian mysticism.[43] Since Tillich sees the mystical and the personal as opposites he can reach no other conclusion. However, if we understand *atman/brahman* mysticism in its non-duality and personality as essentially interrelational, another picture emerges. Realizing *atman* means experiencing personality *in* participation. Personality would be the term that encompasses the two poles of individualization and participation.

The trinity is the very reality of what can be termed personality in participation. By calling the Father *sistence*, the Son *existence*, and the Spirit *insistence*, the unity of the trinity is an "in-eksis-tence," which is also characteristic of participation and Advaita. In the personal unity of *in* and *ex* God's "life" is fulfilled as *perichoresis*. Divine self-affirmation and human being are not opposites, but human being is a being-joined in the *perichoresis* of trinitarian non-duality.[44] This term of the mystics includes personality and corrects Tillich's overall conclusion.

Further clarification comes from Tillich's ontology of love. Love is the overcoming of the division of one self and an other; i.e., reunification of what is usually divided, one individual and another. Love thus assumes a basic unity of being. "Love is being in actuality and love is the moving power of life."[45] This is also what the doctrine of the trinity emphasizes, that God is not dead identity, but unifying love.[46] What is clear in the case of the trinity can also throw light on the essence of *atman/brahman:* each person is an *atman* who is neither identical with nor different from the Absolute, but in a peculiar relationship of non-duality to it. We would therefore understand Advaita as expressing the ontological structure of love.

Tillich sees the superiority of Christianity "to any other religious tradition"[47] manifesting itself in the fact that Christian love "preserves the separation of the self-centered self," while Asia strives for a complete identification of the person with the Absolute. This judgment is overly general. It applies only to a few forms of Asian religions. Even in these instances it is only correct when there is no distinction made between individuality and personality.[48] However, in Advaita Vedanta the personal consists in a nondual polarity, or in the karmic overcoming of individual isolated being. It is a process which sublates the karmic mechanism, and is therefore creative, in the sense of Tillich's "creative justice."[49] That this is in reference to a spiritual experience and to a kingdom of God which integrates concrete history can be seen from the fact that in India there is also a *perichoresis* between the "first and the third persons," *brahman* and *atman,* while the *maya* state must remain undetermined, as we saw above, since India is not aware of the incarnation. The Christian trinitarian God integrates both alienation and suffering within the trinity's self-movement. This is the meaning of the second person. In Advaita Vedanta, alienation is the consequence of human illusion and is sublated in the realization of what we *are already in God.* The trinitarian God overcomes alienation by submitting himself to a transtemporal process of integration, or he *is* this temporal-eternal process, and therefore he remains identical with himself. This trinitarian notion is an Advaita of the concrete: a perfect integration.

Another work in trinitarian theology which can provide important clues for understanding the trinity non-dualistically is Jürgen Moltmann's *The Trinity and the Kingdom of God.*[50] Moltmann asks how God's unity can be understood within a trinitarian history of God. It will be a unity of *community in God.*[51] This assumes, however, that the triunity is open enough so that the whole of creation may be united by it and find unity in it.[52] "Community with God" and "community in God" are ways of expressing the relationship that is portrayed in the community of Jesus with his disciples. However, the notion of community, i.e., the supposed ontological basis, remains unclear—at least if we understand him correctly.

Moltmann considers the Spirit as "new presence of God," as "God's indwelling," so that "the whole of creation will become illuminated by the indwelling Lordship of God.[53] He sees here a "pantheistic vision:" *God in the world* and the *world in God*, which is the meaning of a world illuminated by the Spirit. It is the *home of the trinity.* If the world has been transformed and illuminated by the Holy Spirit, creation in the Christian sense can only be understood in a trinitarian way."[54]

We agree thus far. However, Moltmann does not explain in detail what his notion of the trinity is. Yet this is precisely what our comparison of trinitarian concepts with Advaita Vedanta involves.

In understanding the process as a unity, Moltmann refers to the teaching of *perichoresis*,[55] which is a symbol for a "social trinity." Interestingly, he describes the history of the trinitarian God as an "eternal process of generative, responding, blissful love."[56] This corresponds approximately to Indian *sat* (generation)-*cit*-(responding)-*ananda* (blissful), as we saw in chapter 1. In connection with his teaching on creation,[57] Moltmann discusses the possibility of understanding *perichoresis* as the dance of the triune God. However, these images are different from Indian images because in Christianity there is an eschatological, irreversible goal, whereas in India there is an eternal cycle. But what the symbol of an irreversible goal could mean regarding Indian ideas of the Absolute is not discussed. The specifics of the notion of *moksa*, which describes the eternal and ongoing presence of the Absolute beyond or behind the veil of *avidya* could, at least implicitly, shed new light on these apparent contradictions (so that the myth of Siva's dance could also be interpreted differently). But it is precisely with regard to the all-important term of *perichoresis* that Moltmann's understanding of the trinity is problematic. He has difficulty avoiding the basic problem of substantialism.

Moltmann detects Sabellian modalism in Barth's three modes of being or Rahner's modes of subsistence, which he rejects. But at the same time his thinking reveals a certain tendency towards tritheism when he speaks of God's history as in three persons. For he would assume three "distinct persons and subjects in the 'history of the Son,' "[58] and this neither takes into account the appropriations nor is logically meaningful. Indeed, it tends towards tritheism. Moltmann speaks of three subjects, and refers to Rahner's

position that the three persons of the trinity should not be understood as "personalities with different centers of activity."[59]

Naturally the problem goes back to the notion of person. Moltmann makes his definition more specific in saying that there can be
no univocal concept of person that applies to Father, Son, and
Spirit.[60] But in this case what does person mean, specifically in
connection with the trinity? We agree with Moltmann that person
cannot be an individualized, subjective center, but must be relational. Rahner, who puts too little emphasis on this point, mistakenly places personal being in the *unity* of the three modes of subsistence, and this leads to a static concept of God or even to the
dissolution of the trinity. Moltmann sees that Rahner's problem is
in his notion of person, which has been reduced to individual self-
existence, but then thinks that the *unity* of the trinity is already
realized in the *community* of the three persons.[61] This is possible
only with great difficulty, since there should be an ontologically
coherent basis for the community of three "subjects."

Moltmann himself, however, refers to the notion of *perichoresis* as a possible way of overcoming the alternatives of tritheism
and modalism. He understands it as a "process of perfect and intensive *empathy*."[62] We agree with his intentions. But what does
perichoresis mean? To Moltmann it means no more than the community formed by the three independent subjects. The trinitarian
persons depict "by themselves their own unity within the circle of
divine life."[63] A clearer notion of *perichoresis* could, however,
complete this generally correct statement. For *perichoresis* does
not constitute only the *unity* of the trinity, but also the differences
within it; i.e., the three-ness of persons. The three persons cannot
be understood without or outside of the *perichoresis*, for their *be-
ing-persons is this perichoresis.* Only in this way is it possible to
overcome the tendency to tritheism in Moltmann's notion of three
independent subjects and the strange idea of the "history of the
Father" which endangers the unity of the trinity.[64] Unless this is
the case, he falls into substantialist categories, which become necessary to support the unity of the trinity in Barth and Rahner.

The argument that we suggest here makes understandable the
mutual implication of unity and differences: the two remain in a
non-dualistic relationship. The notion of *perichoresis* is the advaitic category par excellence. It does not confer personal being
either on the whole trinity *or* on the three persons or modes of
being, but rather being-subject is constituted by the movement of

three moments, which posit unity as well as self-differentiation. In other words: subjectivity is neither in the unity nor in the distinctions, but in the non-dual process constituted by the two poles. This would be Advaita's important contribution to the whole Sabellian-tritheistic aporia. We will demonstrate this understanding of *perichoresis* concretely in chapter 10.

III

The Unity of Reality

10.

The Trinitarian Unity of Reality

In the chapters that follow, we will develop our understanding of a trinitarian notion of God in dialogue with and by means of insights from Advaita Vedanta. This will not be a synthesis, but rather Christian theology, placed in the context of the worldwide dialogue of religions and using Advaitic categories, in order to rethink the specific Christian experience of God, measured by God's self-revelation in Jesus Christ, in a more universal context.

In doing this we presuppose the Christian faith. The faith of a believer is already part of the phenomenon of religion. Advaita Vedanta is seen here in the light of Christian faith, acknowledging that the faith of the knower influences the knowledge of the phenomenon.

Therefore, what our method dictates is that we enter the other area and allow ourselves to be drawn into the religious experience of the other, in order to understand the basic advaitic experience from within, insofar as this is possible. This takes place mainly by means of meditation and the practice of Yoga, since these practices, we repeat, are presupposed by almost all Hindu and Buddhist systems. It is important also, however, to bring Christian history to bear upon these practices, since it may furnish tools for reflection and point to possibilities of bridge-building, either for those who have already embarked on this practical path, or for others who could profit from it by deepening their Christian life.

Advaita and Trinity

Advaita is neither monism nor dualism, but the negation of two-ness in a specific third: non-duality. We saw how on the one hand God was regarded as Absolute without qualities or relationships (*nirguna brahman*). In relationship to this Absolute, the world necessarily appears as a second, and thus contradicts the absoluteness of the Absolute. On the other hand, the Absolute appears in relationship to the world (*saguna brahman*), or as first

143

cause. God unfolds in the world (or as world), in the stages of the creator's manifestations (*isvara*). He is first manifested in potential realization or the prototypical model of the world (*hiranyagarbha*), and then in material-spiritual reality (*viraj*).

1. *Brahman* is the "whence" (*yatah*), the primal ground of the world.[1] This is, of course, a statement about the *saguna brahman*, since here the Absolute appears in relationship.[2] God as the "whence" from which comes the world is mediator between the Absolute and the relative. He is neither identical with the one nor the other, nor different from the two, but Advaita. This means, first: God is not an "other" over against the world, for then there would be two. Secondly, it means: God is not identical with the being of the world. God's being must be different from the relative determination of beings. Both aspects taken together provide the first meaning of the relative distinction between Absolute and relative. God exists *as world*, and he is *simultaneously transcendent* and different from the world. Advaitic thought thinks the unity in this contradiction.

The trinity performs a similar task: it mediates the absoluteness and the relativity of God's eternity and his history, his *in se* and his *pro nobis* in revelation. The advaitic character of reality was most clearly stated by Hegel when, in the dialectic of finite and infinite, he understood infinity, not as a numerical quantity of the finite, but as a quality which is realized *in* the finite, but then sublates it and is thereby an eternal bringing forth of itself. This is also the meaning of three persons or modes of being, in which God eternally brings himself forth. They are understood as the inexorable event of a *perichoresis*, which presupposes the unity of God, on the one hand, and on the other hand—because this unity is in the movement of three-ness—engenders it.

2. Another peculiarity of Advaita Vedanta makes it especially interesting for Christian theology. It is based on spiritual experience and intends to be a means of spiritual experience. It recognizes that in the end God can only be reverenced in silence, since all human categories fail in the light of his fullness. But this is by no means a mere feeling or vague dream. It constitutes a specific experience of unity with God, and can therefore be described as mysticism. But it is reflective contemplation, which not only takes responsibility for the critical distinctions and concepts it experiences, but also considers that the power of knowledge itself serves the advaitic experience. Advaita is "a mysticism that teaches,"[3] knowledge and the critical use of reason *on the basis of* transsensorial and transrational

advaitic experience. Thus, what we have is not only a theological method, but also a union of faith and understanding, of contemplation and the critical use of *ratio*, which is considered necessary for either spiritual life or contemplative experience.

Since Christian theology has the task of understanding the Logos and applying it to the whole of reality, it is also implicated in this insight. Christian spirituality, in the sense of a contemplative life, has not always been aware of this insight and has too often believed it could attain its identity while upsetting this unity.

3. Advaita is characterized by its understanding of reality under two aspects: reality viewed as a whole (*paramarthika*) and viewed relationally (*vyavaharika*).[4] In the latter, reality is viewed relationally from the standpoint of the infinitely many and relationship. The former, however, sees it as one, without denying the differences within the relative standpoint. Its unity does not sublate the individual and the particular. We can compare this thought structure to a circle, which can be infinitely differentiated in itself, yet remain whole and perfect. The wholeness of the circle remains. The differentiations—the many—are relative to the wholeness. Without the wholeness there would only be divisive lack of order, and finally no circle. Yet the circle would still be a circle without the differentiations.

These two aspects stand in an advaitic relationship to one another. The standpoint of the whole is the higher in Advaita Vedanta, because it is more comprehensive and can imply the relational, as our example of the circle makes evident. Because of this implication, relational language cannot simply be given up in favor of holistic language.

These two aspects correspond to the two moments of God's unity and self-differentiation in the trinity. The advaitic character of the trinity becomes clear when we see that the unity of God is understood *in* the self-differentiation of the relations and that the mutual permeation of the relations *is* the unity. Neither the one nor the other aspect has meaning in itself; rather the one defines itself by the other.

The fact that there is a tension between the aspects or ways of viewing the trinity was clearly explained by John Damascene: God should be one, but in our ways of viewing him he appears as differentiated in himself, as the particular hypostases of Father or of Son or of Spirit.[5] Yet since reality must be understood as a unity, the aspects acquire ontological meaning. Trinitarian faith implies that we can trust revelation and the possibility of knowing it. It is real.

This does not mean that we can have a notion of God which creates God's being. But, on the other hand, our concepts are not false, assuming that we conclude to him from his revelation of himself. Despite his immeasurability, he is measured, for God himself appears in his revelation. The church was able to avoid a basic agnosticism by maintaining the unity of the oeconomical and immanent trinity.

To Advaita Vedanta reality is the *one* being, *brahman*. Yet *avidya*, or ignorance, consists in regarding the differentiation and the relationships as real. Naturally it looked for the ground of *avidya*, and it was found in *maya*, the creative power of God, which likewise creates an illusion of many. *Maya* is therefore an ontological principle, but its origin and relationship to *brahman* cannot be demonstrated (*anirvacaniya*). On the basis of a basic non-duality, reality as such would be knowable, since it is based on *maya*, but *maya* is not in duality with *brahman*. This consequence is not, however, referred to in Advaita Vedanta, or it is only mentioned with hesitation. The reason for this lies in the lack of clarity concerning the ontological status of *maya*.

In the doctrine of the trinity, distinctions and relations are considered to be real because God is really differentiated within himself and is relational. God himself is the principle of differentiation (*maya*); he is perichoretic *in* this differentiation and so remains identical with himself. The ontological status of *maya* could therefore be clarified by means of the trinity: God is the One, *brahman*, by being one in *maya*. *Maya*, the principle of differentiation, is what it is in expressing a "place" for the being of the one God. *Maya* is the "how" of God, who is infinite fullness as well as love, and must therefore be thought of as trinity. His "what" is a being-one; viz., the self-integration of a self-movement that remains eternally identical with itself. An advaitic interpretation of the trinity offers a solution to the unsolved problem of the ontological status of *maya* in Advaita Vedanta. It thinks Advaita consequentially.

4. Furthermore, the trinity enables us to understand the concept of *saccidananda* in a non-contradictory way. We have seen that *saccidananda* cannot be an attribute or determination, since this would introduce differences into the One. Thus the One expresses itself in these three dimensions. The *cit* aspect is not a determination added to *sat*, but both are the same One in its different aspects. *Saccidananda* does not say something *about* God, but is God's statement of himself. It can only be received in contemplation by humans and repeated. Thus, when Advaita connects God's

self-expression and human expressions about God, or the divine ways of being and human ways of viewing, these relationships are very precisely defined.

A non-dualistic interpretation of the trinity and of *saccidananda* can grasp the modes of being of the one God as relationality and as a dynamism, and thus it thinks the ontological unity between modes of being and modes of manifestation without doing violence to the concept of God. The inner dynamism of God as a "place" for his being is of great importance for soteriology, as can be observed in the history of the term *homoousios.* The reason that the concept of a trinitarian God broke down frequently in the history of Christian theology, being interpreted either modalistically or more often tritheistically, is that the advaitic character of the trinity was not sufficiently understood.

5. Conversely, an important problematic in the doctrine of the trinity can be understood more clearly by means of an advaitic explanation: namely, the necessary distinction between God as "abyss" and as principle of self-manifestation.[6] In this regard we must return to Luther's distinction of the hidden God (*Deus absconditus*) and the revealed God (*Deus revelatus*), since it is frequently discussed apart from trinitarian discussions, to the detriment of a possible clarification in the trinity, which would also result in a better understanding of the differentiation in Luther's notion of revelation.[7]

The distinction of *Deus absconditus* and *Deus revelatus* makes a statement about the relationship of God to humans. It says that even in our experience of being abandoned by God we are still dealing with God. The trinitarian differentiation, on the other hand, holds that the finally validating, ontological truth of revelation is guaranteed. Only in the context of this revelation is the opposition of *Deus absconditus* and *Deus revelatus* tenable. Only when we assume that God is One in his self-movement can we reconcile the annihilating judge with the merciful Father who loves freely (Barth). Here, for the first time, the tensions of law and gospel, despair and faith,—in other words, our human experience— are described realistically as moments in the gracious activity of the One God.

6. The interpretation of God as advaitic trinity is coupled with another pair of terms which have accompanied the history of Western philosophy from the colonnades of Athens to the Tübingen school and beyond: the question of the ontological primacy of reality or possibility. Here we will introduce only a few of many fac-

tors, through which the transparency of the problem for an advaitic teaching on the trinity will become apparent.[8]

The Aristotelian tradition decides in favor of reality (God as *actus purus*), and this position has dominated the Western world. Nevertheless, the mystical tradition as well as Schelling's philosophy of potentiality develop the idea that God must be interpreted as creative energy, realizing forever new possibilities. A return-to-the-ground implies grounding the real in the possible: perishability is a return to possibility. The concept of possibility permits self-movement and a return to origins in God; i.e., God can be understood as trinity.

Our hypothesis is that the doctrine of the trinity teaches the advaitic character of possibility and reality. God is the very essence of or structure of reality, and simultaneously the source of creativity. Creative newness is not the realization of a preexisting idea, but the transformative structure of reality itself, starting with its ground, made possible in the trinitarian process of *perichoresis.* Creativity and law are thus related in the coming to be of the unity of reality, which God continually integrates. An imaged way of expressing this is: God is in himself the event of love. The unity of trinitarian reality comes about as possibility set in motion by intra-trinitarian love.

This implies, first that the temporal is dialectically sublated in the trinitarian God. Time is not a quantitatively limiting category, but a medium for this expression of the One in its trinitarian history. Secondly, it means that God's historical acts are the realization of his love *ad extra*, which is already *ad intra*—in the Advaita of possible and real—a continuous engendering.

7. The advaitic teaching on the trinity seeks to ground theologically the dialectic of the trinitarian and an apophatic concept of God.

A basic datum of Christian theology is awe before the depths and immeasurability of God's being (Rm 11:33ff.; 1 Cor 13:9ff., etc.). God is beyond our perception (Jn 1:18). The Alexandrian school anticipates later *theologia negativa* when, for example, Clement claims that God must be understood by means of ever more-widely extending abstraction.[9] For all our concepts are material and finite. Dennis the Areopagite converts this into a theological method. We can only say what God is not, because all our descriptions are necessarily finite and remain dependent on creatures; i.e., they are the opposite of God. Dennis, of course, adds the *via eminentiae* to this apophatism, yet what is common to both methods is that our concepts of God are only achieved by overcoming the em-pirical-visible as well as the logical.

All of this is closely connected with yet another tendency in Western Christian thinking: language is brought into relationship with the Logos. The Logos, however, is God's manner of being and his form of appearing. Language as well as thinking are therefore essential. Naturally this insight goes back to a pre-Christian tradi-tion, the famous identification of being and thinking, and the *Par-menides* remains the classical statement of this, despite all the various ways it is later expressed. When Christian tradition began using the term Logos in its christology, it joined this tradition, even though its incarnational theology prescribed a very specific under-standing of the essential role of language. In any case, Logos philo-sophy, all the way down to Hegel and Heidegger, and Logos poetics in Dante, Goethe, and Hölderlin both imply a confidence that we can attain truth if our thinking is precise enough or if we penetrate into the primal ground of language.

In India as well as in Buddhist Asia everything mental, includ-ing language, is consigned to the world of the senses. Language is relative and lacks the capacity to mediate absolute truth. Truth can only come to light by means of a meditative experience of unity which transcends rationality.

Thus, just as the three persons in God are defined by their mutual indwelling, so too our ways of viewing God exist in mutual dependence and can be sublated dialectically. Statements about God as being are the reverse side of statements about non-being. The two not only imply each other as opposites, but describe phases in the trinitarian process of God. The negative in a state-ment about God is nevertheless a statement about *God*, because the God-statement corresponds to a negative form, which it fulfills perichoretically within itself: the negative is thus positive.

In this way the greatest universality and freedom can be at-tained in relationship to speech about God: because God is beyond all form and seeing, God can be known and named[10] in *every* form and visible appearance. Because God is not the object, but the sub-ject of knowledge, his subjectivity can be known in, with, and through every objective appearance.[11]

The non-duality of the apophatic and trinitarian views of God has become known especially through Christian mysticism. The mysticism of Ruysbroeck, for example, can be cited as the "perfect synthesis of extreme apophatism and deepest trinitarian contem-plation."[12] The non-duality of affirmation and negation within the

reality of God does not point to an incapacity of understanding, but
rather reveals a participation of human mental activity in God's
own trinitarian revelation of himself![13]

8. A remaining question: How do we describe the trinity more
precisely as a unity of three aspects in our experience of God?
Richard of St. Victor, as well as Melanchthon who follows him,
describe the trinity as a "creative conversation of self-forgetting
love."[14] It is interesting that this description corresponds almost
perfectly to *sat* (creative being)-*cit* (language)-*ananda* (self-forgetting love), although the concrete meaning of this imaged way of
speaking is left unsaid.

The metaphor of language points to the creative power of the
Spirit in the word. The word is God's power to reveal himself. An
interesting parallel may be found by comparing the oldest Indian
texts (p. 23) with certain images of Luther (p. 108f.).[15] In both, the
word has four stages in its appearance, which can also be seen as
steps by which it manifests itself, thus localizing the three aspects
of our experience of God in the trinitarian notion of God himself.
The four stages are illustrated in Figure 10.1

The "word" as the essence of God's self-revelation thus encompasses the whole of reality in all its possible dimensions and
aspects. The different aspects of the experience of God are therefore modes of experience, and are grounded in the multidimen-
sionality of the revelation of a trinitarian God. We will now discuss
the mutually indwelling moments of reality as they are found in
the trinitarian symbol. The trinitarian dimension of the *Father* is
the experience of the origin of being; the dimension of the *Son* is
the experience of being, realized; the dimension of the *Spirit* is the
experience of the renewal of being by means of creative acts. The
three dimensions enable God to appear *above* all (*epi panton*),
throughout *all* (*dia panton*), and *in* all (*en pasin*) (Eph 4:6).

As origin, God is not yet being as it truly is, but the eternal
source of all becoming. He is neither past nor present nor future,
but the ground of temporal-eternal wholeness. He is infinite possibility: i.e., fully "not yet," as well as the infinite abyss of "no
longer."

As realized being, God is eternally present; i.e., infinite reality.
Through him all things participate in being (1 Cor 8:6). He is the
mediator of creation and at the same time the way to the Father.
Just as all things are created through him, so too all created things
are directed towards him.

As the creativity of new becoming, God is perfect divine imma-

1. The interior word ≙ *para vac*
   Word or power not yet manifested, the inner self-move-ment of God

————————————————————————————

2. The external word ≙ *pasyanti*
   Revelation in the incarnation of Jesus Christ, transcen-dence in the dimension of revelation and enlightenment. The universal form of the self-manifestation which contains the process of the world, the world is created through (*dia*) Christ (Eph 3:9) = *hiranyagarbha* or *bija* (seed) as poten-tiality, not yet realized in the many

3. Sacred Scripture ≙ *madhyama*
   The word mediated by historical tradition; mental articula-tion of revelation: i.e., the human mind set in motion by these steps of God's revelation

4. *Viva vox evangelii* ≙ *vaikhari vac*
   The mediation of the external word in (2) and (3) by the spoken word; the word as language, which in itself ex-plains the realized manifold of the objective world.

Figure 10.1

nence. He is the realization of the original source in the world of the many; i.e., the eternal unity of the many, and therefore the way back to the Father through participation in the being of the Son. He is the unity of possibility and realization insofar as he creates con-stantly what is possible in reality and returns the real to the state of fullness of possibility. Thus he is eternal renewal of being from its source.

Origination in the Father

God is the "whence" (*yatah*)[16] of being. The Father's relation-ship to creation must be defined in a certain way: not as the struc-ture or form of matter, but as *creatio ex nihilo*, a principle which insists on God's indivisibility in making being real. In Advaita Ve-danta we find the same idea of indivisibility, understood as *maya* —*anirvacaniya*. Although this is implied in Vedanta, the doctrine of the trinity describes it concretely by means of God as Father and answers the question "whence," or from where, being comes without denying the reality of the world. God as Father is the power of revelation to reveal; i.e., "ek-sist." He is also the source and origin of the nothingness from which he engenders himself and creates the world. Thus he is infinite potentiality and perfect freedom.

Because of this original indisposability we can make no statements about this dimension of God. The spirituality of the Father is the experience of silence. The objection could be made that God the Father is nevertheless creator and that this determines him. But this overlooks the fact that creation is the work of the whole trinity. In the overall event of creation (*creatio et creatio continua*) we experience God as Father, Son and Spirit. Because God is trinitarian "in-ek-sistence" he can bring forth creation out of this *coesse* without endangering his immutability (Jas 1:17). He is unchangeable in change, unmoved in the movement which he himself is. As the source and origin of the other trinitarian moments[17] he is also the source and origin of creation, though not yet the "is" of being. Thus he encompasses even nothingness and is truly "all in all" (1 Cor 15:28). Thus any metaphysical dualism is excluded.

The trinitarian Father-symbol describes God's perfect simplicity. As such God transcends all other types of knowledge, which— as in a mathematical formula—seek a simplicity, yet always remain linked with the duality of determinations such as subject and predicate, constant and variable, etc.[18] To this extent the Father is comparable to Indian *ekam* or pure *sat*, the origin and not the realization of being.[19] As subject of his own existence without properties he corresponds to Sankara's *nirguna*-aspect.

Realization in the Son

The Son is being, realized. Through him everything exists (Rm 11:36; 1 Cor 8:6; Col 1:16). This statement implies a temporal eternity or eternal temporality, i.e., *tempiternity*, in the Son.[20] He is the realization of the Father and therefore the visibility (Jn 14:9) or the being of the Father. He manifests God's perfect transcendence as immanent and through his being points to transcendence. As immanent transcendence he is being's eternal transcending being in the trinitarian self-realization of God.

Creation as the aspect of the Father was *creatio ex nihilo*. Creation as an aspect of the Son is *creatio in participatione*. Creation, as participation in the divine nature (2 Peter 1:4), is in the Son. It is a sharing in being, which "ek-sists" from its origin. Thus the Son is mediator of creation or the "where" of being. *Creatio in participatione* truly makes possible the power of the Father's being. This realization cannot take place apart from its origin; yet the origin does not exist without realization. The two permeate one another, since otherwise the Son would not be God.[21]

The Son is reality which "ek-sists" out of possibility. He is the function of being. Insofar as he is in being and being is in him, he is differentiated from creatures; viz. as the mediator. He is the primordial image of creation.[22]

In its aspect as Son the ground of being is revealed as creative power. The Son, as the concrete form of God's life, is the density of essence mediated by historical human form. The trinitarian unity demands that the incarnate, original image be no less than the Father. Thus he is called the exact image (2 Cor 4:4; Col 1:15; Heb 1:3), the incarnation of the Logos, the only begotten Son (Jn 3:16, 18) or God himself (Jn 20:28; Rm 9:5). In the Son each individual figure of reality experiences its *ontological dignity*.

We must also distinguish between what is historical and realized from the source. Thus Jesus himself points to the Father as "alone good" (Mk 10:18), the one who, as source, predestines what happens to beings (Mk 10:40), and thus he alone is the subject in future realizations of the possible because he is the aspect of freedom and thereby the ground of creation (Mk 13:32). Insofar as the freedom of the origin is greater than the concrete realizations of this freedom, the Father is greater than the Son (Jn 14:28). The Son's reality is from the Father, whereas the world is made through the Son. The Son is not "first creature" but God, the creator of the reality which thus shares in his being. But as the human being, Jesus, he is creature and participates in its limitations. Thus there are steps (1 Cor 3:21–23; 1 Cor 8:6),[23] and they are nothing else than the self-presentation of the trinity:

God Father

↓

Son/Jesus Christ

↓

Manifold of the world

These steps can be described very precisely by means of expressions from Advaita Vedanta, which describes the stages of manifestation of *saguna brahman.* In it God is seen in three stages:

	isvara	(Lord)
Son	↓	
	hiranyagarbha	(Golden Seed)
	↓	
	viraj	(differentiated material world)

The unity of these three stages corresponds to the trinity in its aspect of Son. The Son is the *isvara,*[24] God as creator. However, he is also first-born of creation (Col 1:15), which corresponds to *hiranyagarbha.* Thirdly, he is the power of Christ dwelling in creation, working in the present as resurrected. The individual particularities are the aspects of the Son as *viraj.*

By means of this constellation of terms borrowed from Sanskrit terminology, we are able to understand the trinitarian work of God in his aspect as Son by means of stages of manifestation, or as an unfolding of an ontological order of mutually implied stages that constitute the unity of reality. Perhaps these suggestions will enable us to formulate more precisely what was intended when Christian tradition proposed the somewhat confusing teaching of two natures, or when it developed a representational christology (Christ as representating God and humans).

The notion of Logos also is subject to the ambiguity sketched above in relation to the identity and distinction of the Son and the Father. The Logos *is* God, but also stands *before* God (*pros ton theon,* Jn 1:12). The Logos has been assigned a creative function and is thus also wisdom (*sophia*), since the Father as source is in this aspect without movement or determinations (*nirguna*). The preexistence of the Logos therefore gained acceptance, starting with Tatian.[25] On the ground of Jewish wisdom speculation and Greek views of the Logos, it was believed that God had always possessed a creative potentiality, as we see in Tertullian.[26] But only when the preexistent Logos entered into reality as creation was he considered as real. Before actualizing his potentiality to be real he led a "shadowy existence."[27]

On the basis of Logos philosophy, the Son was understood as the projection (*prolatio*)[28] of God. This projection should not, however, be interpreted dualistically, as happened in gnosticism. Nonduality offers a satisfactory solution. Thus we can argue as follows:

The Logos is the reflection of being-in-itself and thus corresponds to the *cit*-aspect of the formula *saccidananda*. In reflection, being experiences the highest form of organization of its potentiality: consciousness, whose intrinsic power of relationship surpasses being by far. Similarly, Advaita Vedanta says that in *cit* nothing is added to *sat*, but one determination is comprehended and constituted by and in the other. In translating this sentence into trinitarian terminology, we would add that there must also be a reflection on the unity of *saccidananda*, just as there has to be a trinitarian unity which makes possible God's oneness *in* differentiated moments.

The significant difference remains the same: the role they assign to history or to *maya*. In Advaita Vedanta, history is never real in any complete sense. Yet the illusion—*maya*—creates a division from the truth of the one being. This need for mediation should not be minimized by claiming that all this is only seemingly a problem since the world *is* not. The *vyavaharika* viewpoint describes *maya* as literally real, and this is true even when it considers that *sub specie Dei* nothing is real in itself.

The mediation we are suggesting here is the specific aspect of the Son, visible in the incarnation. The incarnation is more than a gnoseological necessity following from the fact that God can only be known by means of God, as Hilary teaches—nearly docetically —using Empedocles' knowledge-theory.[29] But, rather, the incarnation is a moment in the real process of God's self-mediation, a point which was first explained systematically by Gregory of Nyssa.[30] God's self-mediation was most conclusively formulated through the doctrine of *kenosis*. (Phil 2:7)

The deepest expression of kenosis is the cross: in Jesus Christ God empties himself of his Lordship and takes upon himself the sufferings of human existence in order to overcome the seemingly unbridgeable gap between God's fullness and human nothingness. God himself becomes human, so that humans might become divine (*theopoiesis*). In other contexts this same idea is expressed in such a way that true life is promised to those who overcome their present existence which is apart from God (Mt 10:38ff.; 6:24ff.; Lk 9:23ff.). Taking upon oneself the cross means overcoming the attitude of duality in order to conform wholly to the one divine reality, or to let oneself be determined by God, the one all-determining reality.

Just as God empties himself and takes the form of the other—sufferings, the finite, the cross—in order to integrate it in himself, so, too, must humans who enter into the spirituality of the

Son empty themselves of their egocentric will. In their egocentrism they continually project their own wishes, expectations and ideas on the world and thereby deny things their own space. Humans take over as sole occupants, seeking only their own realization. They form an idea of God according to their wishes which mirror their egoism. They also form an image of other humans that does not allow them to be themselves, but sees them according to their own needs. In other words, egocentrism is an aggressive stance towards reality that believes reality must be mastered lest it master humankind.

The cross overcomes this separation from the whole. It is essentially a giving up of oneself in order to experience a new identity in God, a rebirth (Jn 3:3ff.). Being crucified with Christ in order to share in the resurrection produces a new advaitic identity beyond our denial of self. I am no longer cut off from others as an individual self, but am now joined to the process of God's self-realization: this is the ground and goal of my life (Jn 12:25; Rm 6:3ff.; Gal 2:19f.; Col 2:12f.).

In this sense we experience the spirituality of the Son as conformity with Christ. Through God's action we become like Christ (Rm 8:29; Phil 3:10) or acquire Christ's form within human reality. The transformation (Phil 3:21) involves the *whole* of human life.[31] In their conformity with Christ believers experience their true identity (Eph 2:5ff.; Phil 3:10). This has two consequences for dialogue with Indian spirituality.

1. The interpretation of the cross and resurrection as a *kenosis* which we accept, thus acquiring a new identity given by God, is nearly the same as the Indian experience of *moksa*, where we recognize the ego as illusion and this leads to a deeper identity grounded in non-duality with the Absolute. In both cases the experience is a gift that comes from beyond the ego. This was explained in chapter 4 and is self-evident in any interpretation of the cross (Eph 2:8f.).

2. God's revelation in the incarnation, cross and resurrection describes a concrete historical event. This means that Christian revelational theology must reflect on the historicity of revelation. The world cannot be regarded as an illusion which demands little attention, but is God's creation and, as such, a determined moment in God's self-realization. The world's fragmentation and sufferings will be overcome when it is sublated into God's trinitarian unity.[32] Christian revelation demands that the advaitic relationality of one reality be regarded as a mediated process which *integrates* history. History then becomes salvation history.

This second viewpoint comprises *the* decisive difference between the Son in the trinity and the *cit* aspect of *brahman*. Advaita Vedanta can understand history and historicity but it cannot understand them as the history of God; nor can it grasp the historical work of God as a moment in the supra-historical reality of the Absolute.

The advaitic interpretation of the trinity, however, leads to a specific interpretation of history. History cannot be meaningful by itself. It is not "open-ended time,"[33] which would be understood outside a system of relationship and meaning, but it has meaning within the "unity of time" rooted in God's trinitarian process. Time is one by virtue of a oneness *in* the relations of differentiation of the trinitarian event. The relational structure of individual temporal moments however—in other words, the eternally becoming trinitarian unity which also remains identical with itself—is the full circle of God's dynamic being. The advaitic doctrine of the trinity makes possible a concept of history in which linearity (time as open-ended) and the circularity of being's unity are joined together, so that linear time appears as a moment in the dynamism of the One. Temporality is interpreted on the basis of the One.[34]

The dimension of Son realizes the Father's origination as a "where" which is the "whence" of the unity of reality. The Son makes the Father real. By the *nihil* of his death—which corresponds to the *nihil* in *creatio ex nihilo*—he brings creation into being (as *creatio in participatione*) in the historically real. Thus, the particularity of history is released from its particularity and is sublated in the creativity of the original act, which is fulfilled *universally* by the work of the Spirit. The particular (historical reality) is and remains real, but it appears as a moment in connection with the unity of reality. This unity gives it meaning, and this is the ontic meaning of resurrection.

Creativity in the Spirit

The dimension of the Spirit is God as the "whither" of being. In the Spirit God is experienced as renewal of the real from the source. The Spirit is "God *in* all," i.e., the Spirit is the complete immanence of divine power which demonstrates itself in its self-movement as life-producing, renewing, and fulfilling Spirit. Just as creation in the aspect of Father was called *creatio ex nihilo* and in the aspect of Son *creatio in participatione*, so in the aspect of Spirit it is the *actus participationis* within the creativity. Through the Spirit each being participates in the dynamism of God's trinitarian being.[35] The Spirit is the principle of individuation and manifests the universal trinitarian movement in individual form. Thus the Spirit realizes unity in the individuation of individuals. The Spirit makes possible the unity of the many in return to the paternal source, through the reality of the Son. In the Son divine, trinitarian being is realized, whereas the aspect of God as Spirit signifies the continual possibility of new reality, the realization of the possible. The Spirit is God as source present in each existing thing.

In the Spirit the Christ event is released from its historical limits in order to attain its essential universality. The experience of this release and its universality is *the* experience of the Spirit (Jn 16:7).[36] The Spirit is Christ's everlasting presence remaining in humankind. In the Spirit we know the meaning of God's revelation as incarnation-cross-resurrection.[37] This knowledge caused by the Spirit is itself a moment in God's trinitarian self-manifestation. It can therefore really include new becoming, which is as unpredictable as the *creatio ex nihilo* of the world's beginning.[38] Spiritual knowledge not only reflects reality but transforms it. For it is *actus participationis* in the creativity of the trinitarian God. This participation became visible at Pentecost. The "becoming-divine" (*theopoiesis:* 2 Peter 1:4) or "corresponding in being" are exact translations of the Sanskrit term *anubhava,* which is usually translated "experience" and describes the advaitic experience. Hence, Christian experience of God is an advaitic experience of participation in the trinitarian event of the Spirit.

The creativity of the Spirit is a relational event of the trinitarian God and originates there, not in our experience! Creativity is the emergence of the ground in new forms. The new forms end by sinking back into the ground and thus fill the original form with newness. The consequence of this is a new, altered explication. We therefore propose regarding creativity as a moment of *irreducibility* or as the newness in connection with a moment of *continuity*, insofar as the process of reality constantly engenders itself anew according to its own immanent structure. The term, *transformation*, brings this into view, for in transformation there is a tension between continuity and the leap to a new level of reality. Stating this in trinitarian terms we could say: God in his aspect of Spirit brings about a new creation in continuity with the revealed, realized being of God in Jesus Christ: *spiritus ex filio procedit.* Reality created anew by the Spirit is also a leap, since it is joined with *creatio ex nihilo* and has its source in the Father: *spiritus ex patre procedit.* In our opinion, this is the sense in which *filioque* must be interpreted. Today's discussions of *filioque* should take into account this twofold fact which is dialectical.[39] When *filioque* is rejected in favor of the Father's monarchy,[40] the all-important aspect of the irreducibility of a creative framework is stressed. It is undoubtedly true that the Western church's *filioque* led to neglecting a non-dualistic realism and that this gave rise to alienation and an exclusivity in the way we understand the Christ event.[41] When, however, the dimension of the Son is understood universally as the ordering level of realization in the trinitarian process, and when creativity appears as the new becoming in the process of three dimensions, then it is possible to understand both the unity which assures continuity and the creative break within the trinitarian reality.

An example of *transformation* is the freedom from the law which is brought about by Christ, yet becomes *my* freedom by the work of the Spirit (Gal 5:1; Rm 8:1ff.). The law, as a universal power which involves being bound by structures that are related to our ego (e.g., when we achieve), is overcome when we find our true identity in God. All "fruits of the flesh" which humans produce under the power of the law are connected with works achieved for oneself (Gal 5:19ff.), while the "fruits of the Spirit" are, significantly, love, peace, joy—in other words, attitudes which involve community and the abandonment of egotism. Here the foundation is the certitude that God and humans are not-two. Anxiety over our own identity and the meaning of our lives has now been abandoned.

In another image the Spirit is the indwelling of the Father and the Son in us (Jn 14:23). Even more to the point is the image of the vine (Jn 15:1ff.). Christ is the one life-energy which determines our whole being and produces fruit. The fact that Jesus Christ is speaking of himself and not of the Spirit is not a difficulty if we assume the unity of the trinity.

In spiritual experience the transparency of an historical presence bursts forth. The Spirit is not something supernatural, but an irreducible dimension *in* the real, *in* every created form; i.e., creativity coming from the source. The Spirit is, as the image of the vine suggests, the life-energy within everything, which comes forth as infinitely many. As energy the Spirit grounds every appearance, yet remains transcendent and irreducible to any of them. God as Spirit is the ground and mystery of creation who binds himself to forms yet is not held bound by them.[42]

The Spirit as this one energy, manifested in material as well as spiritual events, is parallel to the Indian *prana. Prana* is basic energy and is not different from God. This holds true for the Spirit, who is not only connected with the Christ event, but as *spiritus creator* is the universal creative power of the trinitarian God (Gen 1; Ps 33:6; Ps 104:29ff.; Is 59:21). The Spirit is the breath of life (Gen 2:7; 6:3; 6:17; 7:15; Ps 104:29ff.) or soul, even of animals. The Spirit is life-giving creative power in general (Rm 8:11; 1 Cor 15:45; Gal 6:8).[43] The work of the Spirit is holistic since it is seen in material as well as psychic and spiritual ways. Thus a certain realism is involved when setting one's heart on the kingdom of God— i.e., being in the reality of the Spirit—includes material things as well (Mt 6:33). This realism, which understands God's universality advaitically, overcomes any dualism of spirit and matter.

To think of *prana* as Spirit in connection with one overall trinitarian reality could be an important starting point for bringing the Christian experience of the Spirit into dialogue with Asiatic meditation techniques and Asian cultures in general.

It is important to point out that in India the Spirit has sometimes been dualistically elevated above matter. This was not, and at present is not, any different from what can be found in Christianity. Certain schools of Yoga, as well as some tendencies in Vedanta go in this direction. However, it would be false to claim that India's understanding of the Spirit is generally dualistic and implies "hostility to matter."[44] Wherever *prana* is a fundamental element, as in Tantric interpretations of Yoga and coherent Advaita Vedanta, the thinking is holistic.

Creativity in the Spirit is generally characterized by a sense of being grasped. The Spirit seizes us within our everyday surroundings (Nb 11:25; 1 Sam 10:10; 19:19ff.). We do not possess the Spirit but are possessed by the Spirit. The Spirit is neither a semantic nor a psychic reality, but the transcendent power behind the psychosomatic (1 Thess 5:23). In the Old Testament as well as in several parts of the New Testament the experience of the Spirit is a strange experience. It is the experience of freedom within our normal, ongoing, psychosomatic as well as social determinisms.

In Indian philosophy *atman* performs the same functions as Spirit. *Atman*, just as Spirit, is the center of authentic existence. Of course, it cannot of itself be grounded, yet it is not deducible from the empirical; i.e., it is realized by grace. The experience of *atman* is the experience of the true self. We find our identity not in ourself, but in participating in the Absolute or God. This corresponds to Paul's "Christ in us" (Gal 2:20).

The experience of the Spirit as *atman* implies the same dimension discussed above as a liberation and was seen to be part of the Christ event of reconciliation and salvation. In the Spirit, creation appears in a new relationship. Creation no longer constitutes an area over and *against* God, but is an act of participation (*actus participationis*) in God. It is the experience that reality is one in God. In other words, in the advaitic experience of *atman*, as well as in the Spirit, the kingdom of God is experienced *in us* (Lk 17:21).

Creation, reconciliation, and salvation now appear as unified in the experience of *atman* or Spirit, for the Hindu on the grounds of a "realization of experience," as well as for the Christian, on the grounds of Jesus Christ's mediation. For *atman* is the reality of creation, reconciliation, and salvation. In it the trinitarian ideal is fulfilled. The difference between Hinduism and Christianity lies in the mode of mediation, as we have just seen.

The dimension of Spirit or the experience of *atman* results in three ways of being or moments of one trinitarian reality.

Father	Son	Spirit
(*nirguna brahman*)	(*saguna brahman*)	(*atman*)

When we say that *atman* corresponds to the Spirit, this does not mean that the two notions are identical in every detail. The correspondence is based mainly on a specific, common experience which is apparently known in India as well as in Christianity. *Atman* is the absolute dimension within every experience. This means that the experience of *atman* or Spirit does not necessarily have to be an extraordinary event. On the contrary, there is a perception of the whole or of what is more profound in everyday life, as we will see in chapter 11. This seems to me to be the basis of the principle of incarnation, which we know as historically mediated. But insofar as we overcome the limitation of the historical we are under the power of the Spirit, which is very important for John, Paul and the mystics, as well as Luther.

Even when humans experience spiritual realities, they still tend towards egocentrism. We are "justified and sinners" at the same time (*simul iustus et peccator*). There is an important and unforsakable realism in this statement. It frees us from the drive towards perfectionism which only leads to ever-increasing, egotistical ensnarement.

The Indian *jivanmukta*, on the other hand, believes he is lifted entirely outside human ambiguity. He has been freed from egotistical clinging. This, undoubtedly, is the reason for the grotesque self-divinization of many gurus, who are totally egotistic—victims of an inflated ego. There is also another aspect of the typically Indian disinterestedness in social evils on the part of those on the spiritual quest: viz, the effect this has on social mores. Philosophically, this attitude could be explained as a lack of consistency in carrying out the advaitic principles. But on the other hand, this Hinduistic tendency results from the fact that the experience of the Spirit (*atman*) does not stand beneath the reality of the cross, which is the specificity of every advaitic-trinitarian experience in Christianity.

This judgment must be made more specific, because in Advaita Vedanta and especially in Sankara's thought humans are *not* identified with the Absolute. Sankara speaks of a relationship of *tadatmya* (p. 33); i.e., humans have God as their self; or the world has the Absolute as its self . . . but this cannot be reversed! Yet in simplified interpretations the tendency we have just summarized is frequently encountered.

The experience of the Spirit *first* encounters intratrinitarian love, and this is an experience of God as life and as being in movement and therefore the love of God is the unity of reality. *Secondly*, it encounters human love, which can be interpreted advaitically as the work of God's trinitarian love. The result of this double experience is a twofold praxis, based on the twofold commandment to love (Mk 12:29–31). God is love in that he is Spirit, and therefore the one who dwells in love knows that God is in him and he in God (1 Jn 4:9ff.).

The trinitarian love of God that is experienced in the Spirit is an expression of the work of the whole trinity. An advaitic teaching concerning the trinity cannot understand the trinitarian event of love without connecting love to the reality of the cross. Within the historical condition of sinfulness—i.e., where egocentric self-will prevails—love can only make its appearance in the powerlessness of the cross,[45] which annihilates egocentrism and the despair that accompanies and thus leads to a new creation by means of the Spirit or in the realization of *atman*.

Because God manifests himself as love in the unity of the Spirit, the trinitarian movement of God can be described as the "intrinsic interaction of love" (Hegel), if this presentation includes the reality of the cross.[46] This means God needs no other to be perfect love. Thus God as Spirit in the event of love is "the ever new relationship of God to God," the "relation of relations."[47] It is also the *ananda* aspect of the Indian *saccidananda* formula: bliss which grows in perfect love community of the one, conscious being. Since God is this event of love, he gives us a share in his reality and draws the world fully into his light.

God's love is realized universally. Thus, wherever there is an event of the Spirit the newly won unity of reality is being celebrated. This happens in a striking manner in the way Pentecost is pictured (Acts 2:1 ff.). Here human divisions, expressed as confusion of languages, are overcome by the unifying force of the Spirit. The division was the result of humankind's egocentric attitude, which according to the Yahwist account began with the first sin, then led to fratricide, then to the abominations that resulted in the flood, finally to the tower of Babel and the consequent confusion of languages. In the experience of the Spirit which comes from the unifying love of God, this division is overcome.[48] Thus the gift of the Spirit is linked to forgiveness of sins (Acts 2:38). For sin *is* this division, and is the result of egocentric separation and fragmentation.

Unifying love fully reaches its goal in a suprahistorical being-with and being-in that involves both God and humans. For God is so fully present to and in all that no other source of light is needed to enable us to live and be enlightened (Rev 22:5). A temple is no longer needed (Rev 21:22) where external acts of worship are performed—a sign of our dividedness from God. This vision is completely Advaita!

Through the unifying power of love of the Spirit, creation reaches completion; i.e., it attains its essence. The eternal trinitarian event of love is not a lack (as is Plato's *eros*), but a fullness, which appears in its perfection as the peace of God (Heb 4:1 ff.) because it is *in* the dynamism of trinitarian love. This peace of God is a unity which is realized in the process of love. It builds a new person in a new world, a person who allows him/herself to be perfectly determined by this unity (Ez 39:28f.). God is the source, the realization, and the fulfillment of the unity of reality.

The Unity of Reality

The three moments and aspects of the trinitarian reality should not be considered as isolated from one another. All three together in mutual indwelling must be the basis for saying how God's being can be understood on the ground of its self-revelation. God exists *in* this event. Seen from the human standpoint this event has an internal and an external aspect. The internal aspect has been described as the immanent trinity, the external as the oeconomical trinity. From the viewpoint of God's wholeness the internal is the external, for God exists as life and love—in other words insofar as he manifests himself and remains identical with himself. Thus the concept of God is not static, but energetic.

God's being is movement and cannot be described by a concept (which would tie down being to a static result). What we know are the individual moments of the movement, which are likewise, and in advaitic relationship, aspects of our experience of the world and God. Even the concept of relation and relationality is not without problems because it could make us think of a connection between different things. This would substantialize God's movement in its stopping points, and, by analogy with spatial images, set up a duality. God is relationship within the moments of one movement which constitutes his being. A substantialized notion is unsuitable to describe a God who is always energetic happening.

The three moments continually bring forth this one reality by their perichoretic relationship. Figure 10.2 can be read horizontally or vertically. Vertically we see different entry points to the question of ultimate reality or God, while horizontally we see the movement of God's being in its different moments. The unity in this movement, which is achieved either from left to right or right to left, describes the trinitarian unity of reality in the process of its *perichoresis*. The unity of the horizontal and vertical dimensions is what we have called the advaitic doctrine of the trinity.

The fact that we are dealing here with an *experience* which is trinitarian, and one in which humans are involved in the becoming of God's own self-movement, is clear from the advaitic starting point. At a few important points the advaitic experience corresponds to the mystical experience of becoming one (*henothenai*). Starting with Paul, the Johannine writings, and the influence of Neoplatonism this influence has determined, not only trinitarian theology, but all of the church's spirituality. It leaves its mark especially in the notion of divinization (*theopoiesis*) in Eastern Chris-

Father	Son	Spirit
Ground, source of being	Being, realization of being	Return of being, meaning, renewal of reality from the source
Above all transcendence	Through all immanent transcendence, being transcending	In all Immanence
One simplicity	Many The manifold	Unity of the many as the way back to the Father through the Son, realiz. of the one in the many
Possibility	Reality	Making possible new realization or realization of the possible
Creatio ex nihilo Principle of universe	*Creatio in participatione* Principle of history	*actus participationis* the principle of individualiz.
Source from beyond time	Eternal present	Presence of the source in reality
Whence Wellspring Power of revelation Freedom Inexorability	In what Wisdom Act of revelation Commitment Making available	Whither Life = Love The effect of revelation Being free Availability
Source of inspiration Need for decision	Content of inspiration Gift of decision	Act of inspiration Act of deciding
nirguna brahman	*saguna brahman (isvara, hiranya-garbha, viraj)*	*atman*
sat	*cit*	*ananda*

The various possibilities of experience of the trinitarian God ↑

← ────── Moments in God's trinitarian self-movement ──────→

Figure 10.2

tianity, and the beatific vision in the West. The Eastern Christian teaching of *theopoiesis* establishes the non-dualistic character of reality more precisely than the Western Christian *visio*. The Eastern church thought that the *visio beatifica* limited our unification with God to the gnoseological and that it was rooted in Platonism. They describe our becoming-one in the incarnation of Jesus Christ as an "unending, continual transfiguration of the whole of creation" until "final unity."[49]

Theopoiesis takes place as a human synergy in the process of transfiguration.[50] This does not depend on what humans merit, but solely on the indwelling of the Holy Spirit. "Synergeia means that God has chosen to work through us."[51] God remains the immeasurable ground since he is the one who chooses. Insofar as his work is through us, however, he is held bound. He is not identical with humans, but is the transformative subject-power which he will never withdraw, for his choice expresses his perichoretic essence which is love.

The Eastern Christian teaching of uncreated energies, which are God himself in his work, enables us to grasp God as the subject of what is done by humans without thereby making him identical with them. These energies are his grace, God's "presence in us,"[52] and this clarifies the mystery of how grace simultaneously coexists with human freedom. While Western spirituality has found no exact way to express this simultaneity, it is very important in the Eastern tradition as well as in Advaita.[53] The perichoretic notion is advaitic. The perichoretic unity of the trinity corresponds to human love, the "work" of the Spirit. In the terminology of Advaita Vedanta this is the experience of *atman*.

In summary: trinity and Advaita are not only related notions, but each helps interpret the other. The one helps understand more deeply the essence of the other without thereby being identified with it. This is the great advantage of dialogue which we will demonstrate concretely in the following chapter.

11.

Non-dualistic Experience

Experience is the act of participating in an event. The difficulty of defining religious experience is connected with the more general problem of analyzing religious phenomena systematically. There is no commonly accepted category which takes in *all* religious phenomena. Categories which are geographical, historical, sociological, as well as value standards based on theological premises, all turn out to be inadequate since they use one particular tradition as the basis to judge all the others.[1] There is no religious meta-language and thus no general, undisputed methodology for the study of religions.

Since the very definition of religion is a subject for debate, it is not surprising that religious experience cannot be defined clearly. In Europe the definition of religion is usually theistic (although this term is understood quite differently in the different disciplines), following the emergence of the Christian tradition which used the categories of Platonic philosophy. But this is not the case in Indian, Chinese-Japanese, or African, American and Oceanic cultures.

For this reason sociology and psychology have been brought in to help develop coherent religious notions grounded in the *humanum* of humankind, which apply to all cultural forms. Religion is therefore a "system of thought and action shared by a group which gives the individual a frame of orientation and an object of devotion."[2] It is easy to agree with this definition. However it remains so general that it allows for no *definitum*.

We could remove some of this generality by saying that all humans long for a wholeness which is never completely grasped, since reason continually imagines new possibilities. This results in a necessary and ongoing tension between possibility and reality.[3] This desire for wholeness would be the basis for religion. But this does not state to what extent the many religious phenomena correspond to this need. Besides, religion does not simply spring from a desire to fulfill a need, but is rather a creative force based on the

fullness of experience, which in turn increases through further
contact with wholeness. This type of thesis is phenomenologically
verifiable.

Let us presuppose an encounter with complete wholeness. The
different moments of religious experience begin, for example, with
Plato's *wonder*. Then there is a being-led towards the "ultimate" or
a being-grasped by, and a becoming one with the whole in certain
states of consciousness.[4] All of these elements imply a departure
from the divided self and the attainment of a greater unity or a kind
of wholeness.

If the experience of wholeness as explained in the previous
chapter is the heart of religiosity, we must explain how this experience is possible and whether it is common. We will assume that it *is*
common, without claiming that this experience of wholeness is the
heart of religiosity, and we will further postulate that it is something very decisive.

What do we mean by an experience of wholeness? The normal
definition is: an act of participation in the whole. This leads us to
think of the mystical tradition, which is built on such an experience. Our descriptions of Advaita Vedanta, Tauler, Hegel, and
others provided us with examples of this tradition. Insofar as the
trinity is a symbol of wholeness, the whole of trinitarian theology
—if it is truly trinitarian—is important here.

But has not modern rationalism destroyed the myth of wholeness? And is it possible to speak of experience without considering
the sciences and their method of quantification, which explicitly
excludes a holistic view?

Yet we *must* speak of experience in one sense which transcends
the empirical, and this is true for the following reasons. Not only
mysticism, but the whole of Western metaphysics shows that a
kind of "intuition of God" is decisive for knowledge. The thinkers
who state this *explicitly*, such as Plato, Aristotle or Hegel, are in
agreement with those, such as Descartes and Spinoza, who implicitly hold that the idea of God or of the whole is inborn or necessary
for understanding in general. It makes possible the relationship
between the subjective idea and the content of this idea. The mystics, however, are to be distinguished from the metaphysicians in
that they link their experience of God to a "seeing" or "tasting";
that is, with *sense* perception. In other words, at the beginning of
modernity, the question was not whether there was religious experience, but rather what psychic-mental powers it should be linked
to. This question was to be answered phenomenologically. Both in

the area of cognitive perception, imagination, and reason, as well as in the area of desires there is an experience of wholeness. Thus there are qualitative steps towards the experience of wholeness starting with the senses, later involving the understanding, finally in pure spiritual vision (*Cloud of Unknowing*, John of the Cross)[5] or: in the eyes of the flesh, the eyes of reason, and the eyes of contemplation (Hugo of St. Victor, Bonaventure). The distinction of three levels is essential for correct experiential verification, as we will see later. Because of its immediacy, vision (Sanskrit: *vidya*) characterizes this experience, and this is true in all cultures.[6]

Experience has been defined as "a form of knowledge which arises from the direct reception of an impression from a reality (internal or external) which lies outside our free control."[7] It is the beginning of knowledge, but also, in its integrating structures, the goal of the meditative and mystical way.

Experience is interior empiricism. Religious experience deals with something "comprehensive," whether this is an all-encompassing value, an all-encompassing power or all-encompassing reality in the widest sense.[8] It is distinct from *observation* which perceives things from a distance and then determines what they are by objectivizing them. By contrast experience is, as we said, *participation* in reality. The subject who is experiencing is changed to the extent that he/she attains unity with the object. The experience which radically changes us is merely the highest step of religious experience, which began with the experience of wonder (Plato), and interiorization.

As participation, experience is also *communio*. It overcomes rationalism's dichotomy of *res cogitans* and *res extensa*.[9] It makes our basic participation in being concrete, starting with particular events that relate to us and extending to participation in reality in general.

Since reality is an interrelational whole, we can only speak of objectivity (in the classical sense) by using abstractions; i.e., in relationship to particular subsystems. Every experience is subjective, yet relates to a transsubjective reality. Subjectivity increases as it increasingly abstracts from the sense level, while shedding the precisions just mentioned. This becomes clear in experiences of love and freedom. In relation to the limit notion of wholeness, the imprecisions just defined have reached their maximum: this corresponds to perfect subjectivity. Experience, therefore, cannot simply interpret (and verify) itself, but needs language and a community, which make possible a community of experiencers

and sets up criteria, as we will see below. But first we will recapitu-
late the phenomenon of non-dualistic (advaitic) experience.

Meditative Consciousness of Wholeness

All experiences of wholeness are not by any means identical, as
the phenomenology of mysticism demonstrates. Thus, too, the
ways meditative and rational consciousness are related can also be
quite different. Just as European mystics often had difficulty re-
conciling their experience with rational systems of thought, so too
Indian mysticism has a very restricted relationship to *ratio*. Thus
Advaita Vedanta, in describing non-dualistic experience assumes,
as it were, that it was through the holy scriptures that the revealed
truth of non-duality was transmitted, believed, reflected on, and
therefore experienced in meditation. The experience itself corresponds to a certain state of consciousness which is considered to be
a power higher than rationality in terms of its integrative capability, without making it superfluous.[10]

The Indian term *anubhava* (experience) means literally "being
along with, or proportionate." Thus there is a likening and a meld-
ing of subject and object which makes possible a direct consciousness beyond the subject-object dichotomy.[11] Reality is universal
consciousness. *Anubhava*, therefore, is the expression of cosmic
reality's knowledge of self in a consciousness that is unified within
itself.[12] *Anubhava* is a means of knowledge (*pramana*). It allows
direct entry to the essence of *brahman*.[13] Just as the senses are
oriented towards the external world, *anubhava* is oriented towards
the internal.[14] Knowledge is possible on the grounds of a correspondence between the subject of knowing and that which is to be
known: everything shares the same nature as *brahman*.[15] In meditative consciousness we become what we meditate (*brahmaiva san
brahmapyeti*: being very *brahman* to *brahman* does he go; BU IV,
IV, 6). This is not therefore a simple cognitive act, but a realization
of being. The subject of meditative consciousness is therefore, as
Christian mystics also realized, God himself. Thus Eckhart says:
"God tastes himself in all things," or in another place: "Ego, the
word 'I,' is never myself, but God in his selfness!" According to
Nicolas of Cusa an *ablatio omnis alteritatis et diversitatis* (the re-
moval of all otherness and diversity) precedes the *deificatio*.[16]

The same connections are valid in the trinitarian experience of
God which is participation in the divine nature (2 Peter 1:4) or the

unity of knowing and being known (1 Cor 13:12), and thus a total transformation of human existence into perfect wholeness. Christian meditative consciousness culminates in being-in-Christ (Gal 2:20) or in perfect determination by God.[17]

The experience of God can be defined as follows: it is perfect advaitic conformity with God. Indeed, it means a becoming similar (homoios); i.e., there is a unified consciousness and knowledge of being not-two with God (1 Cor 13:12).

Meditative consciousness is knowledge of the ground of unity, the cosmic self, atman or humankind's true ground of being. This is not knowledge of an object, but the subject of every possible act of knowing knows itself.[18] What is appears in the light of wholeness.

The Christian idea of trinitarian experience of God corresponds in large part to the idea of jnana (gnosis) in Advaita Vedanta. Jnana is the unity of being and knowing. Once again this does not mean knowledge of an object, for the subject-object duality fully disappears in jnana because the one subject is—without a second. It is worthwhile citing in full the classical text concerning this:

> For where there is any semblance of duality, then does one smell another, then does one hear another, then does one speak to another, then does one think of another, then does one understand another. But when all has become one's very self, then with what should one smell whom? With what should one see whom? With what should one hear whom? With what should one think of whom? With what should one understand whom? With what should one understand him by whom one understands this whole universe? With what indeed should one understand the understander?[19]

Here, too, the deepest knowledge is a being known. This experience is related non-dualistically to the conventional forms of consciousness of the waking state, of the dreaming state, and of the sleeping state. It is a fourth (turiya) form, which can be described as being-grasped in the non-duality of spirit (atman). Meditative advaitic consciousness is the Advaita of thinking and being.

A few basic elements of non-dualistic experience are: 1. intuitive vision of the One as the internal reality of all, 2. consciousness of a transformation into the divine sphere, 3. the feeling of perfect peace (*santi*) and bliss (*ananda*), 4. transrationality, and therefore awareness of paradox, 5. self-evidence.[20]

All five characteristics are true in an unqualified way for the trinitarian experience of God, although here one important characteristic must be added: the One (God) differentiates himself as trinity and, in the creation of the world the One is *in* the complementarity of static and dynamic, so that God can appear as creator (in Vedanta: *mayin*) without being changed. In other words, his activity is temporally-eternally dynamic and unites all opposition in itself (*coincidentia oppositorum*). The trinity is the creative source of reality, as well as the world's immanent power of being: thus wellspring (Father), reality (Son), and finality (Spirit) in one.

This trinitarian character is the ground for a meditative consciousness that includes concreteness. Thus the corresponding Christian experience of meditative consciousness is essentially *incarnational.* Incarnation does not remove the Advaita, but deepens it. The Christ event as God's self-determination can only be meaningful and fully clarified within this context, as we saw in chapter 13. This releases it from its historical determination and individuality, but only by integrating them at a higher, more comprehensive level.

If non-dualistic meditative consciousness can reach a certain level of being aware (we could also speak of energy levels of consciousness)—a state that can be induced by means of meditative exercises—we must ask how to clarify the many within the one experience of wholeness and the many interpretations of these many. This is essentially a question about the relationship between experience and tradition/interpretations.

Experience and its interpretations are mutually interdependent. The first argument concerning the holistic experience is obvious: if the unity of reality could be known by means of a certain intensity of consciousness, which in turn would be connected with other states of consciousness (e.g., rationality), in this case the experienced or rationally postulated non-duality would mean only one thing: that both analytical understanding and intuitively unified consciousness are moments of one and the same process of awareness. As such they are interrelational. Indeed the experience of wholeness as such forbids the thesis of a unified mystical consciousness which would only become many in its interpretations—in other words, secondarily. Thus identity and pluriformity must come forth as non-dual poles of one and the same experience.

Another viewpoint would speak of a breadth in the spectrum of experiences of wholeness, and this cannot be denied, even when there is a single tradition in the background. The possible argument that mystical statements are ineffable and therefore exempt from rational criteria is itself a rational argument. In Advaita Vedanta this *implicit rationality* is important for the practical path of meditation, just as it is important in many schools of Buddhism, which are very sophisticated in their theoretical depiction of non-dualistic experience. They have developed an appropriate paradoxical language and symbolism, which is not irrational even when it subordinates the principle of non-contradiction to the principle of identity.[21]

All of this has far-reaching consequences for present-day encounters between the Christian West and the Hindu-Buddhist East. The attraction of Eastern methods of meditation is understandable as a remedy to rationalistic reductionism in European and American civilization, and expresses a justifiable criticism. Yet in the light of Advaita Vedanta and Buddhism's *rationally based and responsible mysticism*, the anti-rational attribution to the East is mistaken. This is often overlooked. The goal of Eastern meditation is not irrationality but superrationality, and this makes an enormous difference.[22]

Furthermore, it is to be noted that liberation (*moksa*) brought about by the non-dualist experience is an overcoming of *concrete* determinations, whether psychological or sociocultural and theological. There is a background which has left its mark on the reality with which we are consciously uniting ourselves before any secondary interpretations. This is very clear in C.G. Jung's theory of collective archetypes, which are truly collective, yet they are also culturally and socially determined. Dreams, visions, and intuitions give witness to the limitations which integrating consciousness must accept and unify at the various levels of becoming aware.

This also means that cult on the one hand and rational theology on the other hand co-shape the non-dualistic experience. Preconscious contents are at work, not only at the conscious level, but also influence the transrational. Conversely, however, transrational, non-dualistic experience not only has an effect at the mental (rational) level, but also manifests itself preconsciously (including bodily changes)—which is easy to verify in oriental cultures which have paid close attention to these points.[23] There is a perichoretic relationship between the different levels of consciousness. Therefore we can speak of a mutual projection and injection.

Verification of Non-dualistic Experience

Verifying the truth of religious experience is *the* problem of religious epistemology. India determines truth differently from Europe: *Satya* (truth) is a direct unfolding of *sat* (being), while European *aletheia* is an active discovery by the understanding, which encounters an existing object or being as an object.[24] For India there is no difference between ontology and epistemology, while in Europe the correspondence between the two determines truth. Since it is difficult to find an objective criterion of truth for the religious experience which is subjective, the search has largely been abandoned, and the utility of the experience—to integrate the personality or establish social harmony—has become the measure.[25] This is obviously insufficient since illusions are equally useful for bringing psychological stability, at least temporarily.

By using different arguments and models it is quite possible to distinguish meditative consciousness produced by the power of intuitive truth from mere subjective illusion. Gurus in the East as well as the masters of Western cloisters are adept at this. This is also an important task for present theological reflection.

Since non-dualistic experience unifies oppositions in itself so that subject and object come together as *one* transsubjective ensemble, the commonness and potential universality of this experience has become an important argument for proving its truth. There is no denying an intercultural consensus here, for whether the experience is described by Sankara, Eckhart, Suso, Luther, or a Japanese Zen master, there is always the same characteristic of a non-duality, which is experienced within the complete awareness of meditation as happiness.

All experiences (including love, artistic appreciation) are at first singular and then generalized. The reason they are not the same for *all* people is due to cultural and psychological conditions. Only those who submit themselves to the tried and proven methodology for achieving a given experience will be able to have and repeat the experience described by others. This holds true for each kind of knowledge, from scientific to meditative.

The argument of a *consensus populorum* should not be underestimated, although at the same time it does not offer any precise keys to a solution, due to the definitional imprecision and the difficulty of verbalizing experience. Thus, in itself, it is insufficient in evaluating a *particular* experience.

W.T. Stace, therefore, uses a second argument; viz., *order.* "An experience is objective when it manifests order both in its internal as well as its external relationships."[26] Order means subject to laws, regularity in repeating itself, structural similarity among different related samples, etc. Whereas hallucinations are unordered in this sense, religious experiences reveal a distinctive degree of order and are therefore *transsubjective.* In non-dualistic meditative consciousness the element of a wholeness which transcends all content is the form of the experience, not a secondary interpretation of it. This grounds the certainty which the one experiencing has in the face of all doubts. In addition this transsubjective, self-evident nature of religious experience has a parallel in aesthetic experience, which was seen especially by Max Weber and Rudolf Otto,[27] but was already implicitly stated in Kant's "Critique of Judgment."

The danger of error and self-delusion is nevertheless great. Christian mystics as well as Eastern teachers of wisdom are in agreement that the authority of scripture, the experience of spiritual masters (gurus), as well as rational arguments (though not always), all have great importance in excluding error. It is interesting that the famous list of ten sources of error found in the "Ten Precepts of a Guru" in Tibetan Yoga is very close to what Patanjali says concerning Yoga, as well as what Advaita Vedanta says with regard to its praxis.[28]

1. Desire may be mistaken for faith.
2. Attachment may be mistaken for benevolence and compassion.
3. Suspending the stream of thought may be mistaken for the quiescence of infinite mind, which is the true good.
4. Sense perceptions (or appearances) can be mistaken for revelations of the One Reality (or as a transitional enlightenment towards it).
5. A transitional enlightenment of the One Reality may be mistaken for the perfect realization of being.
6. Those who know religion externally but do not live it may be mistaken for true believers.
7. Slaves of the passions may present themselves as masters of Yoga who have freed themselves from all conventional laws.
8. Actions based on self-interest may mistakenly be seen as selfless.

  9. Deceptive methods may falsely appear as truthful.
  10. Charlatans may be mistaken for wise.

These are truly rules! These ten warnings can be verified by critical analysis, proof from scripture or by a guru. Verification of meditative experience thus follows specific hermeneutical criteria. In this we can see the community of those who experience as a more or less coherent basis for verifying meditative consciousness hermeneutically.

But the viewpoint of theoretical and analytical reflection demands that the truth claims of meditative experiences of wholeness also stand as *hypothesis.* For though tensions and polarities may be dissipated for the experiencing *subject,* they must at least potentially be resolvable for all human beings (and the whole cosmos).

W. Pannenberg calls this "subjective anticipation" of fullness and wholeness. It is the self-evidence of religious truth which is present in faith and mediated by conscience.[29] In this case the temporal aspect of *anticipation* involves setting aside the spatial aspect of *participation.* Both, however, point to the *mode* of human experience; that is, its inherent dualism. While Pannenberg is true to Lutheran tradition in seeing conscience as the mediating "organ," this does not address the problem of how conscience, relativized by social or psychological factors, can make its leap out of duality and ambiguity (of good and evil) into the dimension of wholeness. Anticipated wholeness as self-evident certitude would only be possible if human consciousness already possessed the possibility of the holistic perspective and experience. This latter perspective we call meditative consciousness. It is the very ground of certitude with regard to the all-comprehending reality (H. Ott) or the certitude of wholeness and fulfillment (Pannenberg). Thus we must describe the problem of verifying mystical consciousness in relation to knowledge theory.

Sense Knowledge—Mental Knowledge—Spiritual Knowledge

  The various levels of human existence correspond to different modes of knowing. We already encountered an example of subtle epistemology in the Indian tradition in chapter 1 and it relates to our discussion here. The Taittiriya Upanishad develops a model of different bodies (*sarira*) and levels (*kosa*) of reality, as well as corresponding steps of consciousness making the identification. The one who identifies himself with the material body (*annamaya-*

kosa) experiences the world materially and as corresponding to his own material being. The one who identifies himself with life-energy (*prana*)—that is, in using this measure over all others, at the level of consciousness—will be a vitalist who sees the origin of all things as creative *élan vital*. The one who identifies himself with psychic powers (*manas*) will come close to subjective idealism, which considers the human mental system as the ground of reality. The one who comprehends himself as pure understanding (*vijnana*) considers this understanding as a creative principle, to be the summit. The one who identifies himself with the transcendental experience of blessed mystical vision (*anandamaya-kosa*) will view the spiritual level of experience as ultimate reality. Finally the one who experiences the advaitic ground, *atman*, which sublates all the differences in itself, clarifies the undefinable wholeness, experienced as transcendent immanence and immanent transcendence, in a finally-integrated experience.[30]

This schema is subtle and far-reaching. It is striking that rationality and spirituality are not seen as opposed, but as steps in an integral process. It is important to emphasize this, because over and over, in comparisons between European and Asiatic cultures, one or the other of these ways of knowing is erroneously left out, which leads to understanding this knowing as being in opposition to European rationality. This error becomes apparent if we understand the context of Hindu or Buddhist theories of consciousness.

We should notice, further, that mystical vision (*anandamaya-kosa*) is distinguished from the advaitic experience of *atman*. This is very important! In the former, we attain a conscious state which is relative. But the latter, advaitic experience, cannot be differentiated from other steps. It is therefore undefinable. How then can it be meaningful and considered as knowledge? We will return to this point later.

In order to simplify the many levels, we will abridge the schema of the Taittiriya Upanishad by setting aside the distinction between the physical and biological structures, as well as the different areas of the mental, and we will analyze only three levels:

1. Sense knowledge (*sensibilia*)
2. Mental (symbolic) knowledge (*intelligibilia*)
3. Spiritual (meditative) knowledge (*spiritualia*)

How can these distinctions be justified? Since the eighteenth century the predominant concepts of experience and knowledge have developed in conjunction with the scientific (quantifying) method. This is a reduction of everything to level 1, which in effect leaves out the other levels.

In everyday rational consciousness we experience reality as a tension between polarities and this is enounced logically in the principle of non-contradiction. Rationality corresponds to a two-dimensional perception based on the object as an either/or. It thus leads to a choice between alternatives. It needs limits to determine the object. The consequence of this is that rationality is inadequate as a way to present wholeness, a wholeness which is reached by meditative consciousness.

All of this can be clarified by means of an example. Reducing the surface of dice to two dimensions would not adequately represent to an observer who had not yet seen dice *the experience* of dice. He could determine some of the parameters of dice, but he could not comprehend in what way real dice are different from their two-dimensional projection.

So, too, our ordinary images of space, time or causality are predetermined by certain mental constructions: e.g., those of Euclidean geometry. They are only approximations. This is the price of making them plausible at the level of rationality. The geometry of Riemann, which depends on Einstein's theory of relativity, is more comprehensive. Here the polarity of space and time is bypassed and united as a continuum. Space and time appear in a circular structure, and the circle is the symbol of the whole. This geometry is unimaginable to everyday consciousness, operating in polarities. The question is whether holistic meditative consciousness produces an experience which can be presented as a "trans-Euclidean unity."

It is too early to tell whether this is possible. But theology has to pose the question and cannot continue to speak of time, history, causality as though we still live in a world controlled by Cartesian thought or Newton's scientific paradigm. Theology must become dialogical, as we are attempting to show here, not only by considering various "trajectories," but by examining the underlying experiences.[31] Thus our acceptance of Eastern and Western experiences of meditative consciousness is of great significance in our theoretical considerations.

Is the meditative experience of wholeness a form of knowledge? And if it is, is it true? In order to render our argument more understandable we must give greater precision to the concept of experience, since we are using it differently on all three levels of knowledge. I depend here on the excellent work of Ken Wilber.[32]

All knowledge is based on experience. Experience, however, is not merely sense experience, as empiricism claims, but can exist in relationship to the *intelligibilia* and *spiritualia*. Thus I experience not only my sense data (*sensibilia*), but also my stream of thoughts, ideas, etc. (*intelligibilia*). These are more subtle than sense experiences, but they are still experience; i.e., immediate perception of direct data (yet not sense data), which belong to the content of thinking.

There is likewise direct experience of the spirit through the spirit in contemplation and in states of enlightenment. No one disputes the fact that a mathematical *a priori* is not deduced from sense data, and yet it is experienced. The idea of experience is therefore meaningful outside the sensual. It follows that the mental level cannot be reduced to the sensual. It is properly an area of experience. So too meditative consciousness is not reducible to the mental level, but is its own proper area of experience at a spiritual level (*spiritualia*). This however must be explained.

Every experience is a procedure in which an object and its perception come together by means of an act which conjoins subject and object. The *house* which I see and the seeing of the house are one in the act of perceiving. This means that data are directly grasped in the sense experience, and this holds true also in relationship to experiences mediated by symbols and language, as well as in spiritual experiences (*spiritualia*). In symbolic-mental knowing the *meaning* of the word "house" is not drawn from the sense impression of the letters h-o-u-s-e, but is immediately perceived as a symbolic or collective whole which is communicated by means of sense data yet qualitatively different in a fundamental way. Similarly with meditative experiences of the whole, whose complexity allows for the greatest differences, yet in each case the immediacy and irreducibility of the experience is a decisive factor.

The distinction of three levels (*sensibilia-intelligibilia-spiritualia*) is important in order to understand both the unity and the differences in the process of verifying any given experience. To avoid methodological objections during the verification process, there are three characteristics which are common to all three levels:

1. Using a fixed method.
2. Understanding the data joined on the basis of this method.

3. Verifying the results by comparing them with those of other researchers; i.e., through a consensus of the community.

In principle this is W.T. Stace's argument from consensus and order, but here it has a precise theoretical framework.

The *concrete* methodology, in other words the application of these three characteristics to three different levels of knowledge is, however, somewhat different. Concerning *sense experience* we are dealing with objects. The normal method of verification is to use repeatable experiments as the fact that certain results can be foreseen. In *mental* experiences there are symbols, language, concepts, values whose *meaning* is knowable. The truth of a meaning depends on an intersubjective hermeneutical structure. Its verification is through the consensus of a group which participates in a given symbolic system or at least shares its premises. The one who *shares* in a commonly accepted symbolism knows, or at least recognizes, the truth of certain *intelligibilia.* Intentionality, values, and meanings are specific mental phenomena which are *directly* experienced and verifiable by a human community using hermeneutical methods. They are subjective insofar as they come from mental or subjective areas of reality. However, they have a transsubjective structure and can be compared with other data.

Intersubjective understanding is universal and is normally presupposed, even by empiricists. It is based on an ordered, reproducible intersubjective structure of the *intelligibilia.* This is at the basis of the experimental testing (accumulating and verifying data) and is as necessary as the empirical data. The two modes of knowing are both based on a three-part process of indicating what is to be tested, collecting data, and then comparing the results of the data.

However, the empirical testing process is much simpler in the case of *sensibilia,* since it depends on a relationship of subject and object, whereas the testing of *intelligibilia* involves two equal subjects as symbolic centers. Subjects or symbolic centers (i.e., in language) react to one another and interact *with* one another, and this leads to the well-known hermeneutical circle. Reciprocal relationships result, which complicates the structure enormously. Objects, by contrast, can be abstracted and are passive things which we can picture and manipulate. But this difference does not by any means imply that all knowledge can or must be reduced to *sensibilia* in order to be regarded as true. For example: a mathematical statement is true when it obeys the laws within mathematics' own symbolic logic, not when it corresponds to sense data. In mental knowledge, consciousness is not related to the material data (*sensibilia*); rather, consciousness relates to consciousness (*intelligibilia*). In sense knowledge there is a structural monologue. In mental knowledge there is an intersubjective dialogue.

The three-part process of verification (indicating what will be tested—collecting data—verifying by comparisons with other experiences) also holds true for meditative experiences of the whole (*spiritualia*). Meditative knowing is experimental knowing. The person who meditates follows certain tested directives in placing him/herself in a state, which is a presupposition necessary for the experience (or the spiritual peace, the concentration). In contemplation itself, data are being collected while the meditative experience of the whole is *consciously* going on. The verification procedure follows in the presence of a master or a given traditions's scriptures—thus, by means of a hermeneutical process.

There would possibly be a confusion of categories with regard to the *spiritualia* if we were to insist on a *rational* verification of the experience. The *ratio* can *point towards* the whole which unites polarities, i.e., the transrational area, by means of analogies, negations and paradox. But it cannot grasp the whole and therefore it cannot verify, for these are two different kinds of knowledge, each with a different form of subtleness. Thus the instrument of verification here is not reason, but contemplation. The proof is direct and cannot be mediated by concepts.

To continue our presentation meditative experiences are sufficient as a non-reductionist notion of experience. Whether a scientific concept can be used here depends on definitions, and this is the problem at this second (mental) level. It is the problem of hermeneutics, history, and the science of the mind which was discussed by Dilthey and others.

We can now summarize: the sensual, mental, and spiritual levels of knowledge correspond to levels of reality as matter, understanding, and spirit. Each level can be related to itself, as well as to the others (see Figure 11.1).

Each level describes a real field of experience. Each kind of knowledge has its own methodology within the framework of the basic structure: indications on what is to be tested—grasping the data—comparing the data with other results (communication). Each level of knowledge has to follow its own process of verification: Level 4 works through classical experimentation of the natural sciences. Level 3 makes allowance for a hermeneutical verifica-

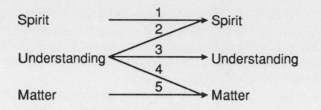

Level 5   (matter → matter) signifies sensual-material action and reaction (*pre-rational*).
Level 4   (understanding → matter) produces empirical-analytical knowledge (*rational*).
Level 3   (understanding → understanding) is hermeneutical and phenomenological knowing (*rational*).
Level 2   (understanding → spirit) is the understanding thinking *about* spirit, which leads to paradox (*rational*).
Level 1   (spirit → spirit) is direct spiritual (meditative) experience (*transrational*) or *resonance* in the spirit in which the subject/object dichotomy is overcome.

(According to Ken Wilber, *The Holographic Paradigm and other Paradoxes*, p. 267. Cf. note 33.)

Figure 11.1

tion which assumes a community of interpreters. Level 1 is tested by transsubjective agreement and interpretative (holistic) ordering.

According to this model knowledge is not just mental knowledge, but includes a prerational reaction as well as transrational resonance. Knowing is therefore an attunement with the "rhythms" of the whole, which is variously reflected in the levels of reality, each of which acts in accordance with its *own relative* structure. Knowing is resonance.

It is therefore impossible to speak of a spiritual science (level 2), which would demand theoretical consistency and univocity, because although understanding can grasp the material level which lies beneath, as well as its own mental area, it cannot grasp the spirit, which transcends understanding. Thus paradoxes, analogies, and negations are the various means used to point to the meditative experience (level 1), or to anticipate by concepts (level 2) a wholeness which is *coincidentia oppositorum*, and finally to transcend all concepts in silence.

Trinitarian Consciousness of Wholeness

Meditative consciousness of wholeness, in the highest/deepest sense, is beyond all polarities and therefore comprehends all the other levels and permeates them in a subtle way, producing a transformation of the whole of lived and experienced reality. This consciousness of wholeness does not stand in a relationship of complementarity to the other levels of experience, as is sometimes claimed, but encompasses them integrally. It is another quality which is not deducible from the steps of psychic development. Meditative consciousness of the whole is not a broader, but rather a transformed consciousness. We return, therefore, to *ekam eva advitiyam* (one without a second), which is by definition limitless. Consciousness of wholeness cannot be limited.

Since this experience has no limits, it cannot be a *specific* experience of awareness which we could attain at a certain time or in certain conditions. This experience cannot be had or reached, and the essence of this experience would be precisely that it cannot be had!

This absurdity is well-known and has been dealt with in Hindu as well as Buddhist philosophy. Here, it should be noted, we are not dealing with an expression or interpretation of the experience, but with the very essence of the experience itself. Since we are *atman*, we cannot reach it. *Atman* as *the* subject would already be there before any "reaching."

There is clearly, however, a difference between the enlightened person and those who identify themselves with the sensual and/or mental spheres, and this difference cannot be clarified by epistemological categories, since the difference between ontology and epistemology is overcome in *ekam*.

Thus, the only solution to the problem is when *ekam eva advitiyam* is understood not as a statement, but as a self-realizing process; in other words, when a dynamism is recognized in the Absolute. In Advaita Vedanta this is precisely what must be avoided. Yet in the Christian trinity it is the key described as *perichoresis*. Meditative consciousness of wholeness is therefore direct participation in the becoming-one of the various aspects of reality, as well as the different levels of consciousness. One never enters into wholeness, not even in deep contemplation, but one is taken up into it. Polarity and duality manifested at the mental and sense levels are not dissolved, but transformed in the continuous process of becoming whole. Advaita is process, not a result. God and humans are one, but not identical. They are in a temporal-eternal becoming one. It is this fact which the symbol of trinitarian *perichoresis* considers. The doctrine of the trinity is an attempt to explain the experience of this dynamic consciousness of the whole and thus portrays the unity of reality symbolically.

A distinction must be made between: 1. wholeness with regard to the interrelationality of the empirical world, and 2. wholeness which describes the transcendent mystery of unity *beyond* and likewise *in* experienced reality.

This distinction is based on the qualitative difference between levels 2–5 and level 1 in the epistemology that was developed above. The distinction is based on the paradox that God is at one and the same time and in the same circumstances the *ground* and the *goal* of reality.[33] This can be illustrated in the following way: we frequently imagine reality as a ladder of cosmic evolution. God is not only the highest rung of the ladder, but also the material out of which it is constructed as well as its structure and its transcendent ground that makes everything possible.

This unity cannot be grasped by the understanding in any non-contradictory way. But it is directly given in the experience of wholeness which we are discussing. For once the self has been overcome and fulfilled by the one subject (God, Christ, *atman*), our human spirit is taken up by the Holy Spirit, and the Holy Spirit is reflected in and permeates the human spirit non-dually. This is the "transformation" spoken of by the mystics. The two are fully united, but they do not become a lifeless identity. On the contrary, identity and non-identity become one. This asymptotic drawing near to the Father *in* the Spirit *through* the Son is the Christian symbol of wholeness. We could also speak of enlightenment as the process of participating in God.

The trinitarian distinctions are developed from operations which constitute the reality of the personal self; namely, knowing and loving. Trinitarian *perichoresis* is the full entry of one consciousness into another without any loss of itself, and this act is constitutive of every personal relationship.[34] When the ultimate ground of reality has the character of a conscious self—which is also implied in Indian *saccidananda*—this self must be understood as a type of unity in self-differentiation. It is a transpersonal happening, which implies the moments of *perichoresis*. Thus we have a symbol of unity which includes all possible explications of reality and has overcome every reduction. In this most comprehensive sense it must be called holistic.

In summary we can now say that the symbol of trinity implies three things:

1. The unity of reality is simultaneously *beyond* and *in* each experience. The experience of this paradox depends on an intensity of awareness or the degree of participation in God. The Absolute is *in* all experiences for there is nothing which is not an explication or manifestation of what we call the Absolute. It is *beyond* every possible experience, for as the finality or goal of reality it is perfectly transcendent in relation to all dualities which constitute the reality of experience. The Absolute is not the sum of all the parts, but the unity of part and whole.

2. The unity of reality is expressed in and through all material as well as spiritual processes. The unity of the trinity approaches thinking of a non-dualistic relationship of *sistence* (Father), *ek-sistence* (Son), and *in-sistence* (Spirit) which integrates all the partial processes of the various levels of reality. Since the ground of reality is consciousness or a personal self, it can be concluded that manifest reality takes part in the nature of this ground in various degrees. Therefore all dualism of spirit and matter disappears. We can now view reality as a gradual manifestation of consciousness. The degree of integration between parts or individuals and the whole or the "being-in-and-from-another" refers to the degree of realized participation in the one consciousness.

3. The unity of reality is known in its innermost nature by the act of participating. This nature is perichoretic; i.e., unity in distinction or the process whereby complex structures become one. God's unity is *in* this process, so that language about a "God above God" (Eckhart, Tillich)—a static unity above the trinitarian dynamic—becomes meaningless. God is beyond time and yet in time; i.e., he cannot be fixed in motionless identity. The various essences have different degrees of participation in the trinitarian *perichoresis*. Thus they are situated at different levels according to their realization of their true nature. Their nature is essentially *kenosis*, a constant emptying of ego-filled selfishness realized in and from another. Personality is relationality. Perfection is therefore attained when this whole reality is fully attuned to the trinitarian "dance"; when, in harmony with the rhythm of the trinity—which is also its own rhythm—reality realizes its essence. Perfection is uninterrupted resonance in God.

Paths of Experience: Prayer-Yoga-Meditation

As we saw in chapter 5 the non-dualistic worldview of Advaita Vedanta is connected with a certain practice of meditation, and this is regarded with increasing interest in the Western world. Christian churches are often skeptical about attempts to relate Eastern meditation and Yoga to Christian practices, because they feel this fails to take seriously the personal encounter with God in prayer. Besides, they consider this as another attempt to achieve salvation through self-realization. We will respond to this second concern in the next chapter. We begin here with the question of prayer in relationship to meditation.

Anyone who prays and/or meditates will eventually come up against the problem of human receptivity within the spiritual area. Vedanta's meditation is not so much concerned with trying to experience something strange, something that enters into our realm of experience at a certain time, but rather with *becoming aware* of what is already there surrounding us. This is not really different in Christianity, even though the Latin tradition frequently puts inordinate emphasis on the distance between us and God, including dialectical theology's exaggerated term, God as "wholly other." If Christian faith is trinitarian, however, it is clear that God as *creator* cannot be experienced in any other way than as an "ever present milieu"; and this tradition, starting with Augustine and continued in the mystics and Luther, has never been lost. *Redemption* is an event which happens. It implies, always and everywhere, a present offer of *salvation* through the universal power of the Spirit. The Spirit *is* here, presently. God's grace is here. The path of spiritual experience consists in becoming *receptive* to the saving, i.e., all-effective, power of God through faith, love, and hope. Faith is the discovery of the ground of existence, a becoming aware of what truly is. There is at least a spiritual correspondence between the experiences of transformation or *metanoia* in Vedanta and in Christianity.

Our problem is not that we actually *are* alone, abandoned and godless, but that we are not *aware* of salvation. Awareness is not just a cognitive act, but rather a change in our basic experience which transforms all aspects of being human. Becoming aware of God—in Sanskrit, *vidya*—cannot be reduced to an intellectual insight: it is *metanoia*. This reduction occurs not only in modern Christian circles, but also in India where we find similar problems throughout the history of Vedanta.

In becoming aware or awakening there is no new content of

which we are conscious, but consciousness as such appears in a new, more all-encompassing relationship. There is no doubt that Christianity, too, has used the metaphor of awakening (*grego-reite!*) to describe the moment of *metanoia* (Eph 5–14; Mt 24:42).

The cause of our normal experience of brokenness or of sinful reality is not God, but humans, who are incapable of breaking through to truth/reality (in Sanskrit, *one* term: *sat*) by means of their shattered consciousness and this is caused by their egotistical preference for self over God (biblically: disobedience). Thus humans are not receptive and are not grasped by the Spirit. They continually project their own wishes onto reality. This false attitude can be characterized as a *mental grasping* or as cognitive aggressivity. The methods of the natural sciences have been very successful in eliminating the causes of this faulty awareness, but only in their limited area. In personal relationships, in questions of value and meaning, the problem is more serious. The consequence is that humans no longer live in harmony with the One, but produce disharmony. What is lacking is a holistic perspective. Instead there is "perceptive provincialism," which tears asunder the sensual, intellectual affective and emotional areas. In other words: humans are sinners.

In order to reestablish contact with the "rhythm of God" and become receptive to the reality of the whole, humans pray. Prayer is essentially a form of human receptivity to the wider dimension that encompasses us. Prayer is a series of steps which are learned through the experience of praying.

The Christian tradition has distinguished many possibilities and forms of prayer and ordered them in a hierarchy of exterior to interior. Here we will not present the different models, but will give a very general schema that will help us understand more or less all the forms of prayer.

Prayer of petition
↓
Praise
↓
Personal prayer
↓
Contemplative prayer

1. Prayer of petition, which grows out of weakness and need, is generally placed at the beginning. Just as the newborn infant cries out for its mother's milk, so too the Christian calls out with

Jesus, "Abba," which simultaneously expresses a need and expec-
tantly hopes it will be fulfilled. This prayer brings everyday experience before God and relates God to the whole of life. God is addressed as *being outside* us, and the way this act of praying is
portrayed is undoubtedly marked by early childhood experiences
of one's parents. Prayer of petition presupposes a relationship with
God. It is more interested in "things" than in God himself and
reveals a more or less naive egocentrism on the part of the one
praying. Jesus' warnings in this regard (Mt 6:7–8:25ff.) have seldom been heeded in the actual *praxis pietatis.* However, in a specific form of this prayer of petition, the prayer of intercession,
altruistic motives become important. But here, too, God is understood as one who fulfills our wishes from the outside.

2. On the basis of experiences in the prayer of petition, we
now advance to prayer of thanksgiving or praise of God. This
prayer is less an expression of need than an experience of receiving
fullness and joy. Here, too, God is experienced as outside us, although the person praying enters into an area of interior experience
and feels that joy and praise are not just a mood, but the working of
grace and the Spirit. God, however, still appears in the third person,
the one to whom we owe our respect.

3. In *personal* prayer the feeling of power through the Spirit
grows stronger. God becomes a "Thou." This stage of prayer corresponds to the I-Thou experience of God's relationship to humankind, and has been forcefully presented by Martin Buber. God is no
longer imagined as outside, but is a partner living within who
enters into internal dialogue with the person who is praying. He/
she spontaneously experiences a fullness welling up within, and in
this internal dialogue there is a regeneration. Although God is now
fully present as an inner force, this intimate encounter is still based
on a duality. The one praying during this stage seeks nothing less
than community with God: all "things" have become secondary.
When the immersion becomes deep enough the presence of the
"Thou" becomes so strong that it completely determines the "I"
who prays. The duality of subject-object begins to disappear. From
the experience of an inner bond with a personal partner there gradually develops a *trans-personal*, living unity. We could fill many
volumes with examples of this from Christian literature as well as
the prayer books of all religions. However, this experience leads to
and in fact is already part of another stage: contemplative unity of
consciousness.

4. Contemplative prayer begins and ends in silence. The initial

silence is a quieting of the spirit which increasingly overtakes the whole person. This leads to a heightening of spiritual receptivity. When the content of our images has completely disappeared and the Spirit, concentrated within our self, has brought inner peace, a sudden or gradual transformation of the ground of consciousness takes place.

In the early stages of contemplative prayer the spirit normally concentrates on God or Jesus; thus an objective content fills our consciousness. In our concentration we penetrate so deeply and perfectly into Jesus that he is no longer an object. Our own willing and knowing also disappear and all normal everyday duality is dissolved. The subject of this "happening" of knowledge through love is now Jesus in his own consciousness. Everything is perceived in "his light," as though one had passed through the narrow door of forced concentration into a new room, where the world of the many is given up because of the new perspective of unity.

Strangely enough, however, our own personal consciousness does not disappear. We are still aware of our self, but it is fully permeated by Jesus. It is as though two conscious beings, i.e., two personalities, grew together into one life process. The driving forces of all psychic-mental activities are united, synchronized, and brought into a unified rhythm with divine power.

In the second phase of contemplative prayer there can be a further deepening of unity with God as an immersion process. Not only does the person see reality in another light, but she sees this light "from inside." In other words, Jesus' consciousness not only transforms the consciousness of the person praying, but the gathered powers of awareness are so perfect in their penetration into the divine consciousness that we experience Jesus as he experiences himself; namely, as a center within the trinitarian love, during our giving-self-fully-to-God. God is in no way an object. There is only pure subjectivity, which reflects itself and thus experiences. Once again the person's own self does not disappear, but achieves its fullness in this perfect unity of love which is participation in the divine nature (2 Peter 1:4). In this unity there is neither two nor one, but the very actuality of non-dualistic *perichoresis.*

The initial personal experience that began in duality pushes forward by the force of its own dynamism and goes beyond itself towards a transpersonal non-duality. A complex non-duality is the characteristic of full personal community.[35] Here the one being is perfectly conscious of itself in its community within itself, which appears as glory, beauty, and bliss—*saccidananda.* In contemplative prayer human weakness is transformed into strength, for the power of the Holy Spirit is the fulfillment of authentic human existence. The perfectly united consciousness has not therefore returned within itself to an inert nothingness, but rather integrates all of reality in contemplative receptivity. In other words, it experiences the *unity of reality.*

This is how several great teachers of prayer have described their own experience. Jesus himself prayed all night (Lk 6:12), with such intensity that physical changes were perceived in him (Lk 22:44). Everything that exists, exists in God whose life it shares. This is the intratrinitarian creativity of which Jesus was so perfectly aware that he experienced himself as "Son of God" (Jn 14:10–11, 16; 15:10, 26; 16:25; 17:5). Prayer means unlocking oneself to this presence of God so perfectly as to make possible participation in God's intratrinitarian life (Jn 17:21ff.; 2 Peter 1:4). This participation is the fulfillment of creation so that the N.T. often develops the idea of Jesus who is *in* God, or believers are in God *through* Jesus, or other people are *in* God through Christians, who show them Jesus; and finally the whole of creation is *in* God *through* humanity redeemed by Jesus (1 Cor 15:23–28; Jn 17:20ff.; Rm 8:20–23).

For Augustine and Luther God was more "interior" to the soul than the soul is to itself. Teresa of Avila and John of the Cross are special witnesses to the non-dualistic experience of contemplative prayer. To Teresa, prayer of petition already begins the path of greater union with God, for the mere recitation of words without meditation and concentration on Jesus or God would be fruitless.[36] Her ideal is to join meditative concentration with vocal prayer, at least for beginners.[37] Prayer in her eyes is the language of love. Recollection and self-knowledge are therefore important steps on the way towards recollection and the outpouring of grace; then prayer of unity, finally to the life-transforming experience of a mystical marriage which is nothing less than an expression of *indwelling trinitarian love.*[38]

Thus, concentration is not just a help in dualistic prayer, but a *step* along the way of prayer which leads to unity with God. This becomes clearer when we consider Paul's exhortation to *constant prayer* (1 Thess 5:17; Eph 6:18). Prayer is not a part-time occupation for Christians, but a basic attitude that infuses the whole of their lives. But how can this be achieved? Precisely at this point Yoga and meditation[39] as forms of spiritual praxis provide invaluable help for everyone including, of course, Christians.

Meditation is the spiritual aspect of Yoga's holistic spiritual-psychosomatic approach. *Yoga* (Sanskrit: *yuj*, to join) means recollection, integration, unification of various aspects and polarities. Normal everyday rational consciousness frequently experiences reality as disconnected, disintegrated, and therefore not in harmony. The result is loss of identity and anxiety, the root of aggression, and this only increases the disintegration. This becomes a vicious circle. Today, especially, people will agree on this and readily see it in their own lives. Psychosomatic illness is a way of expressing deeper sickness. Yoga sees a corporal-spiritual unity not just in humankind, but in the whole of reality. There is a universal ecological organism that must be integrated and kept in harmony. This is *the* task for humans, who are more or less directly responsible for the whole cosmos. In Yoga this task is realistic since there is no chaos, forsaken by God, but only the one reality as an ordered whole, filled with divine power, even when human guilt and ignorance (*avidya*) produce disharmony.

Belief (*sraddha*) in the goodness of God and the yet to be revealed harmony of reality is the starting point of Yoga. The witnesses to this are the revealed scriptures (*vedas*) and the experienced masters (*gurus, rsi*) of the past and present, who confirm it in their own authentic experiences. The yogi must first learn to hear (*sravana*) what revelations say, and then reflect on (*manana*) whether these teachings are meaningful in the light of his own experience. *Manana* is a kind of discursive spiritual activity which can lead to knowledge of truth. As long as knowledge remains external it is useless. It must be applied to our lives so that in concentrating on the essentials we may change our lives. This happens especially in contemplation (*nididhyasana*), which penetrates into everyday reality and transforms it. Since the world is understood holistically, every change in one level or in one area has an effect on the whole. This is the theoretical criterion for Yoga's effectiveness. Naturally the various metaphysical interpretations of this path to wholeness differ greatly in their details, even in India. This will not occupy our attention here, but should rather serve as an encouragement in our attempt at an interpretation that is appropriate to the Christian trinitarian experience.

Patanjali, whose *Yoga-sutra* was and is the classical text for all systems of Yoga, gives an overall definition. "Yoga is the restriction of the fluctuations of consciousness" (*citta*). *Citta* is not just intellect or the stream of thoughts, but describes the ground of all psychic-mental-spiritual activities. Thus it includes the heart and the understanding. This quiet is seen especially in a capacity for perfect concentration of the mind "on one point" (*ekagrata*). Consciousness is compared with the sea, whose surface is agitated by the stream of thinking. When perfect calm has been attained, consciousness appears in pristine clarity: the bottom can be seen and the essence of consciousness is revealed as not-two in relationship to God (*atman-brahman*). This stillness is also a capacity for perfect acceptance. Apart from the fact that deep water is a basic symbol of consciousness (including the subconscious) in many cultures, this disorder of surface interferences also demonstrates what an unconcentrated state of consciousness looks like.

The immersion into deeper consciousness is achieved by various concentration exercises. In a few especially gifted persons this plunge takes place spontaneously, and it is more often seen in children. Basically every non-reflective spiritual opening can help in this submersion process (as in momentary peak-experiences or when one is grasped by great music). In concentration there is an "emptying and unification" of consciousness which hinders an "intrusion of distracting experiences" during this process of deeper immersion.[40]

There is frequently a confusion concerning the relationship between concentration and meditation, or in terms of Yoga psychology between *dharana* (concentration) and *dhyana* (immersion). Here, too, Patanjali offers clear advice: "Concentration is the focusing of the mind on one point" (III, 1), while meditation is "the continuance of knowing therein" (III, 2); i.e., the *enduring* character of concentration on the part of unhindered consciousness.

In language more familiar to Christian ears we could say that the intention of Yoga is purely and simply the achievement of perfect *silence* so that we can *hear*. This is not the place to begin a detailed discussion of the practice of Yoga. We would merely note that: consciousness is not quieted by *striving* or by *controlling* our thoughts, for this only leads to more agitation of consciousness. Regulating one's breathing (*pranayama*) is an important help, but in order to achieve unhindered, rhythmic breathing we must perform exercises in certain bodily positions (*asana*), and these can be learned. Silence, concentration and receptivity are dispositions in which the *whole* psycho-somatic system may open itself to the spiritual level and be formed by it. Yoga ends in a perfect equilibrium of all the parts of human life from which contemplative stillness grows. *Yoga is a preparation for perfect spiritual receptivity.*

In their deepest essence meditation and prayer are identical.

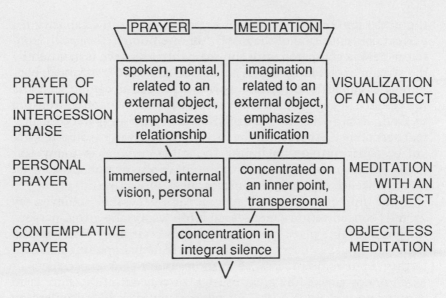

Figure 11.2

They are, however, distinct at the surface; i.e., at the beginning of the spiritual way (see Figure 11.2). The details of the steps are open to various interpretations, and there are also intermediate stages. We are not by any means claiming that this schema synthesizes the whole reality of prayer and meditation and its different elements. The diagram intends to provide a typology for the relationship of prayer and meditation that brings out one fundamental fact: *prayer, Yoga,* and *meditation* are not *opposed to,* but *rather need one another to reach their full depth.* The opposition only appears at the first stage of prayer. We already saw why meditation is of great significance for a deeper life of prayer. The reasons why prayer is important for meditation will be seen in the following chapter, when we discuss the question of self-redemption and redemption by another.

Here, however, we must clarify in what sense the personal experience of God presupposed by prayer can also be understood as part of the non-dualistic experience of meditation. The question, we repeat, is: Where is the *personal self* in the advaitic experience? Our clarification may begin by distinguishing between the individual and the person, or between the "I" and the self. All conceivable variations on this have been imagined both in Christian eschatology and in Indian philosophy. Above we linked individuality with the "I" as center, in order to distinguish it from personality which can be portrayed as the result of, or the substantial unity of a relationship. But the question remains, in our immersion in God (the Absolute, *brahman*): Is there a conscious center which is on the one hand in *continuity* with everyday human consciousness, and on the other hand is part of the whole individual course of a life? In other words, can everyday, awakened experience be integrated into Advaita or is it to be excluded? And how can/cannot individual life and the totality of life experiences have meaning for the supra-temporal, death-transcending level of reality?

In Advaita Vedanta (but not in all Indian systems) this question is denied on principle. For *atman* can in no way be influenced by the *jiva* (individual center of each life). Although *nirguna brahman* appears as *saguna* (personal) it does not possess this personality in and for itself. The personality, indeed, is the result of *maya*. Other Indian thinkers (e.g., Ramanuja) try to transpose the personal dimension into the Absolute, and Advaita Vedanta contains sentences which support this. But this usually involves sacrificing a coherent non-dualism. To me a successful, but too little known, synthesis has been reached by Abhinavagupta and other thinkers of Kashmir Saivism.[41] But it has not generally been continued. Yet the whole of Buddhist thought of the Mahayana tradition explains with Nagarjuna: when the Absolute is considered as impersonal, there remains an opposition to the personal and thus we have not understood the unity. Thus the Absolute (*buddhatva*) is *neither* personal *nor* impersonal, but integrates both aspects in a synthesis, which logically leads to the famous four-part logic statement of Nagarjuna.

Elsewhere the objection has been raised that while a yogi in the state of unified consciousness (*samadhi*) recognizes *atman* as the deeper self, this is not identical with *paramatman* (i.e., God). Therefore this is merely a deeper experience of self and cannot be called an experience of God. This would be the basic objection to a monistic interpretation of the *atman/brahman*-reality. While this monistic interpretation is to be found in India, it is not the only one possible. A truly non-dualistic (*a-dvaita*) view, on the other hand, recognizes the unity *in* the distinctions and thus warrants speaking of their subtle relationship—also manifest in the state of *samadhi* upon careful examination: Total meditative absorption is not unconscious or subconscious, but *beyond-conscious*. Discursive thinking ceases, but there is a higher *consciousness* which has shaken itself loose from all the ego-projected distractions (striving,

wishing, emotions, cares, doubts, etc.).[42] The true nature of consciousness: pure consciousness, as it is called in India, has become
manifest. It is consciousness (*cit*) which has experienced being (*sat*)
in its state of bliss (*ananda*) as a unity. These subtle distinctions
should not be overlooked, although, significantly, they do not
correspond to the perichoretic relations in the trinity. Our whole
study is a plea *for* this position and against (Indian) monism or
(Gnostic and sometimes also Christian) dualism.

Advaitic integration as it is truly experienced in Yoga and meditation, I would suggest, is an apt expression of the Christian experience as seen symbolically in the trinity. Personality as relationship
is attained *through* the individuation of Father, Son, and Spirit.
Thus it occurs continually as a kenotic process of a self-giving over
into the event of the trinity. In relationship to our question, this
means that the individual, or the historically concrete, or the individual experience—in other words, each person's destiny—is truly
integrated into a final beyond-individual and transpersonal connectedness of the one reality.

This is an essential point in interpreting mysticism in a way
that is appropriate to the Christian experience. There is always a
suspicion of "enthusiasm" when this interpretation is not maintained. To Luther the general criteria for discernment of spirits
involved the spiritual dimension of the "word" via the incarnation,
scripture and everyday living. Thus there can be no abstract spiri-
tualism, but only a mysticism of the concrete. In Advaita Vedanta,
as well as in much of Christian "pop" spirituality, this point is not
made clearly enough. At the conceptual level this becomes apparent in an ignorance of the meaning of Christ as second person of the
trinity. In practical everyday living it is a lack of integration of
holistic consciousness, which demands unity in all areas of reality.
For Hinduism this would be the often-demanded, but seldom realized unity of *jnana* and *karma-Yoga.* In Mahayana Buddhism it is
the basic teaching of the unity of *prajna* (contemplation, wisdom)
and *karuna* (living compassion, solidarity with all beings). And in
Zen Buddhism it is the "personalizing of Satori" or the "return to
the market place," once consciousness has been transformed. In
other words, Christians are not alone in regarding the integration
of the concrete through an advaitic experience as *the* basis for authentic religious progress.[43] Yet in the light of the Christ event, this
task becomes one of central importance.

Only through the contemplative stages of prayer can the whole
of life be infused with this spiritual attitude. Prayer—of petition,

thanksgiving, and personal prayer—is one of consciousness's activities, even though this activity works with increasing intensity on other activities. Contemplative non-dualistic consciousness cannot be limited temporally. Increased exercise in meditation causes it to be effective during the whole day. Indeed it "becomes part of" dreaming and sleeping consciousness. It gives a basis to all other activities and motivates them. It *transforms* all individual contents of consciousness and all human activities. This is the "personalizing" of the enlightenment experience in Buddhism or the spontaneous exercise of the *samadhi* state commonly found in Indian masters. The best example of something similar in Christianity is the Jesus prayer, as explained and practised in Eastern Christianity.[44] It is the true sanctification of being Christian, the gradual growth towards God's unity, which reaches its perfection through the experience of unity.

12.

The Personality of Reality

Person and Transpersonality

The Christian experience of God is personal. In Advaita Vedanta, however, the Absolute is a neutral reality, *brahman*, which is impersonal since personality implies limitation and this contradicts the notion of an Absolute. Furthermore, personality presupposes a massive dualism between two subjects which can be opposed to one another, and this contradicts the basic intuition of Advaita.

In rethinking this important problem for interreligious dialogue with Asia, we must first ask what we mean when we speak of a personal experience of God. Secondly, we have to consider whether and in what sense advaitic experience can be called personal.

1. An important terminological problem involves the distinction between individual and person.[1] The *individuum* is an inseparable ontological unity which is distinct from other individual unities. It can be meaningfully defined in itself. *Person*, on the other hand, is a center of relationships. This personal center unites within itself a theoretically infinite number of relational structures. The person is centered on and structured according to a mode or type, which orders and joins together its relationships. Thus the notion of person integrates. The person is unique as an unrepeatable kind and manner of ordering a network of relationships.

Our proposed interpretation, based on these facts, is this: Person is the center of the integration of reality. As a center, person is the point in which all the energies and experiences of reality become meaningful and interrelated. Person can therefore be regarded as the structural principle of *prana*, the basic energy principle. Let us explain. Reality may be seen as an infinite quantity of lines, points, shared networks of those points and lines. The unifying, ordering power of the personal crystalizes a whole quantity of

unordered lines and points in such a way that they are all structured
and fused together in a qualitatively new way so as to form a continuum which is relatively different from other individuals (or individual crystalizations). We could also state this in a more imagina-
tive, but less precise way: reality is like a huge net interconnected
by a series of knots. The reality of the net depends on how well and
where the net is held together by the knots, (= the persons).

Four insights into an understanding of the person can be drawn
from this image:

a) The structuring power of the personal is a new quality of
that which was unstructured. Person is not something that is
merely formal, but a special kind of reality that emerges through
relationships with others.

b) The person's continuous being is constituted by the developments in the process of self-imaging. Being a person implies becoming; the person is a centered continuum which exists insofar as
it develops.

c) Within the person is hidden an experience of its becoming
as a "memory." What the person is, is determined by its past becoming and its future possibilities of integration as well as its ongoing present process of structuring.

d) Realization of the personal implies freedom and creativity.
For while new relationships are integrated by being brought into
meaningful connections with the present crystalized forms (without which no integration would be possible), integrating the new
also alters the structure of the person: the person *is* the alteration,
and its continuity is dialectical.

Person, therefore, is a unity that is becoming and which integrates within itself the process of becoming; i.e., it stores up "experiences." Any complete concept of person, therefore, includes consciousness and consciousness of self, for it is only here that
relationality can be realized as a reciprocity. Less perfect forms of
the personal occur everywhere in reality where energy is held together in a relatively constant pattern. The power of integration
increases as the degree of perfection of the personal increases, leading to consciousness as a storehouse of experiences, and consciousness fulfilled as self-consciousness. *Reality is thus a hierarchy
of gradually differentiated levels of integration of universal
consciousness.*

In this sense the being of a trinitarian God is perfect personal being. Indeed God, who is the perfect unity of all integration by means of his trinitarian self-movement, from which the movement of the world is deduced, is the *only* person in the full sense of the word. He is the unity of being and consciousness. His trinitarian existence is *persona personans.* We are persons to the extent that we are determined by this personal integration of God's being. Our personal being is the reality of the Spirit (*atman*) which sublates individuals in their individual self, yet at the same time integrates them into God's being advaitically.

The trinitarian self-movement is God's everlasting self-manifestation as person. It corresponds to the four moments of our notion of person, and we recall the mutuality of the three modes of being or moments of the trinitarian God.

a) God is creator. He creates the world and conducts it towards perfect self-integration in the trinitarian movement of creation, redemption, and sanctification. Thus God is the only subject of the integration process, and as such is a specific quality in contradistinction to the duality of the world.

b) God is *in* the trinitarian event. Insofar as he is realizing himself therein, he has experiences which, of course, do not add to his essence because he *is* the event itself which, nevertheless, is in the process of being explicated.

c) God is the unity of all moments of time and is therefore above time. In him the past is future and the future is past, and thus the perfect presence of all integral works of power is what constitutes his being as personal. God is the "absolute now."

d) In the trinitarian event of his self-becoming, God is perfectly integral continuity and freedom, or structure and creativity, for he is and continues to be God in freely manifesting himself as relational. His continuity is in the achievement of freedom of trinitarian being. He is perfectly self-conscious because the trinitarian process takes place as being reflecting itself.

God as *persona personans* is the principle of being a person, as well as its highest realization. The resulting *transitive character* of being person in the trinitarian God makes us all the more clearly aware of the personality vs. impersonality of God since personality is the principle of inclusivity in the trinity. This means that the personality of the trinity can be directly applied to the personality of reality.

The unity of reality is an all-encompassing advaitic notion. It

includes the personal. From the many possible relationships implied in the total interrelationality of *karman* there is a *crystalization of structure* that takes place creatively. This crystalization of
structures in central points[2] implies a storehouse of experiences,
for on the grounds of a basic unity or karmic interconnectedness of
all things, nothing can be lost, nothing can be outside. This "storehouse of experience" is significant in order to understand any new
becoming as realization, coming from a source, which is the characteristic of the power of the Spirit. The crystalization, consequently, is a becoming-person, which we see in the relatively high
forms of integration called human consciousness and consciousness of self. On the other hand, the process of integration of the
trinity in the three moments of Father-Son-Spirit is a perfect advaitic personal integration.

If we consider reality in general in all its created forms, personality is already present in lesser forms of integration. "The personal
is not an exception, but the paradigm of all creation."[3]

Advaita Vedanta links the notion of person to limitation and
individuality and therefore avoids using it of the Absolute. The
vyavaharika standpoint enables the Absolute to be known as personal God (*isvara*), but—*paramarthika:* from the Absolute standpoint—God is described as non-personal or beyond-personal. Naturally God is not less than personal, but qualitatively he is
infinitely more. Thus we can speak of the *transpersonal person.*[4]

Clearly this hesitation of the Advaitin with regard to the use of
the anthropomorphic image of "person" is not limited to Vedanta,
but is also true for Christian theology and is correct. Also, the
universality of personhood is not a new tenet.

2. In the notion of person relationality is used to understand
the essence of divine being, and the discussion with Indian Advaita
Vedanta culminates in the question: Can God be understood as
relational?

This question cannot be answered in a general way, for even
within Advaita Vedanta different schools answer differently. Nevertheless, the notion of *purusa* is, after *brahman* and *atman*, one of
the three basic descriptions of the Absolute. The Katha Upanishad
says there is nothing higher than *purusa*, and Sankara understands
this to mean that *purusa* is the fullness of pure consciousness, the
culmination of subtleness, and the grandeur and interiority of the
self (*atman*).[5] This text should be studied in connection with the
explicit identification of *purusa* and *paramatman* in the Bhagavad
Gita.[6] Strict Advaitins such as Sankara and recently, Ramana Ma-

harsi, have always held to devotional prayer (*bhakti*). This assumes a relationship. Besides this, the fact that the Absolute is described as *saccidananda* presupposes a kind of relationship within the Absolute. This would lead to inquiring into the Absolute "in itself." More importantly for our discussion here, Vedanta speaks of a *tadatmya* relationship between *atman/brahman* and all beings (cf. ch. 2). The beings possess this (the *atman*) as their self. But this reflects a specific relationship, for there is no question of identity, but of Advaita.

The experience of Jesus Christ describes this same non-duality with God (cf. the Farewell Discourse in John's gosepl). It is an advaitic experience, which is continued in the faith experience of Christians. Wherever God is experienced as the relationality of love we can talk of an advaitic personalism or a personal Advaita. Personal experience and advaitic experience are not in opposition, but fulfill one another. However, this implies that our egocentric and individualistic understanding of person has gradually been sublated in the way explained above. Therefore we may speak of the transpersonal.

The doctrine of the trinity explains how we can speak about *one* reality. Within and under the three aspects we acknowledge a unity. The notion of the unity of reality is something which transcends the dualistic-theistic images of God *and* the world. It is undoubtedly a *paramarthika* thought, for only from the standpoint of the whole can we grasp the whole as non-duality. Since the whole is neither an object of sense knowledge, nor of intellectual knowledge, the notion of one reality or the unity of reality is grounded in revelation—to which humans can become holistically receptive, as was explained in the previous chapter. The standpoint grounded in spatio-temporal images and distinctions (*vyavaharika*), which inevitably projects the contents of knowing onto what is to be known, will not be able to overcome the difference of God and the world. The best it can do is explain the interior intimacy of God and the world.

How then can we understand the relationship of these two ways of viewing? Is the personal experience of God a preparation for the advaitic vision? (Sankara) Or is the advaitic-personal love relationship between God and humankind the more comprehensive insight, since it exposes the impersonal standpoint as bland and "empty" when taken for its own sake (cf. most Christian theologians, *bhakti*, etc.)? Or is it possible to integrate the two?

It could be argued that the two ways of viewing are complementary, for both truly reach their "objective"—and from different perspectives. The notion of complementarity could make intelligible such tensions such as *nirguna-saguna*, impersonal-personal, if it were not inadequate, and for a very good reason: it remains within the two-ness and this two-ness does not change. The complementary ways of viewing condition one another, but their complementarity does not change the basic attitude of the viewer.

It is precisely this need for a change in the one who experiences, which is characteristic of the path of experience in Advaita Vedanta. It would therefore be better to talk of the *implementarity* of the two ways of experiencing, for this expresses the dynamic experience of Spirit, whether personal or impersonal. One implies the other and transcends its present standpoint in going towards the other, and the result is a circularity; one which however, makes possible an end-oriented growth in the unity of love.

On theological grounds, which would discover a Christian controversy with Sankara, the notion of implementarity must be completed by means of the notion of *simultaneous modes of speaking* with regard to both ways of experiencing and viewing. We speak *simultaneously* of the impersonal advaitic view of reality and the personal relationship of God to humans because here we experience ourselves *simultaneously.* And we experience ourselves simultaneously in two ways because human existence within the advaitic experience of the trinity is *simultaneous existence.* This will be explained in the next chapter.

Sin, Freedom, Love

Simultaneous existence comes from the fact that the one reality appears as broken, and this is so because the Advaita of God and world is not yet fully realized. The experience of Spirit is not yet the all-determining experience. *Atman* is still hidden beneath the *aham* (ego). Simultaneous existence is also the result of the eschatological tension between what is "already" and "not yet." Within this eschatological differentiation we only see through a mirror (1 Cor 13:12), which reflects the original image in a conditional way. Reality is one, but under the conditions of sinful human existence it appears as broken.

Our brokenness expresses itself in the fact that on the one hand we are gripped by the Advaita of divine reality which the Spirit is realizing in us—in other words, we are justified through our faith, as Luther says. But at the same time our egotistical self-recommendation, which keeps us from unity, is also at work in us. Thus we are both justified and sinners. Luther's *simul iustus et peccator* is an interpretation of this tension.

Evil is not the result of God's absence, but of human turning from God, which leads to a judgment.[7] Moreover, sin can only be viewed in a radical way, as a distance from God, when God is perfectly interior to us, i.e., truly *present*.[8] The root problem of evil and sin is that humans exclude this reality and this presence; they lack receptivity to it and replace it with ego projections.

Simultaneous existence and the implementarity of the two forms of knowledge of God is not a static complementarity or a duality, but rather expresses a tendency in the direction of the *iustus* or the full realization of advaitic reality.[9] This is the process of spiritual maturing, and finally the very meaning of life.

This is the only way, we suggest, that the existence of the *jivanmukta* can be explained in a Christian sense. In Advaita Vedanta he is said to be perfectly *above* reality as determined by dualities. Consequently he is not involved in choices between good and evil. Thus he is seldom or never occupied with "worldly things." Even charitable works are at a distance. He seeks no disciples, but works through his quiet presence on those who seek him. He is—according to the Indian metaphor—"on the other shore."

To Christians this outlook appears unrealistic and, in addition, it may not be completely non-dualistic in every respect. For while it proclaims an end to all ontological dualisms, at another level it does fall into an *existential* dualism: the *jivanmukta* in his life is clearly *separated* from normal history and society. We will pursue this problem in the last chapter.

Indissoluble simultaneity within human life leads to a simultaneous structure for the experience of God, and thus to speaking simultaneously *paramarthika* and *vyavaharika*.[10] Beyond this we can say no more. Even the advaitic experience is bound to the simultaneous structure of human existence. The notion of the unity of reality is therefore never more than a *notion*; i.e., it depends on meditative experience. But exterior reality is still torn. *Unity* is a *goal*.

Nevertheless, the *vyavaharika* standpoint is sublated in the *paramarthika* standpoint. Personal relationship to God as we experience it in a conditioned way, is eschatologically transported beyond itself to a transpersonal mutuality between God and humankind. Humans are perishable, but are sublated in God.[11] Since it is only this latter which truly expresses our infinity, perishability is only a determined moment within the greater whole of unity. And here once again we encounter Sankara.

In Christian tradition redemption from our ensnarement in sin is experienced as the realization of freedom and love. But what do we mean by freedom and love when we interpret the advaitic experience of the trinity as the experience of one reality in which the distinction between God and world has been sublated into a transpersonal unity?

This question becomes even more crucial when the unity of freedom and love is to be understood as part of a specifically Christian notion of God.[12] Our interpretation of the one reality must be tested by whether it can understand the Advaita of freedom and love.

Earlier we said that the trinitarian process of one reality was determined by the moments of origination, realization and eternal renewal from the source of this realization. The consequence of this trinitarian characterization of reality was *interrelationality*. In India this idea is expressed by means of the notion of *karma*, which unites actions and the effects of actions and thus allows reality to appear as a network of relationships where all events are closely interwoven.[13]

From the congruency between the essence of the trinity and the law of interrelationality in reality we can now draw a conclusion about what God's absolute freedom means in relationship to the freedom of reality: *The freedom of reality is the eternal self-determination, to realize interrelationality.*

In this sentence, the moment of the Father is represented by the term, freedom. The moment of the Son by the term, self-determination, and the moment of the Spirit by the term, realization of interrelationality. This could not be otherwise, since our simultaneous language concerning the trinitarian self-movement of a personal God and the trinitarian structure of reality is an expression of an advaitic experience of reality. This one reality is no other than the realization level of the trinitarian God. It describes an integral notion, which also sublates the relative opposition of God and world, advaitically. Thus, the freedom of this one reality is grasped in the same sense as the freedom of trinitarian self-realization: as the "free steadfastness on the part of God's fidelity,"[14] by which he realizes himself. This shows that freedom and imperishability constantly influence one another and consitute one another anew in the dynamism of one reality.

The consequence of this is: our freedom is not just an insight into an abstractly conceived necessity. Nor is it an unrestrained, individualistic way of acting. But freedom is the awareness of the basis of life and life lived in rhythm with this basis. Freedom is the overcoming of dualisms stemming from the ego (greed, compulsions, projections, etc.). It is a being involved in the perichoretic love of God.

Human freedom is therefore participation in God's freedom. Those who act freely through the reality of Spirit are in an advaitic relationship to the universe. They recognize themselves as moments in its history and can therefore be conscious; i.e., integrated as much as possible in the final goal and the structure of realization of the unity of reality.

Their identity is the whole, and therefore they no longer picture a "small counter-world" in their egocentric imagination, which they, misusing their freedom, would have to continually experiment with and build up *against* the universal whole.

God's trinitarian communion and self-movement is God's love. Love is relationship or polarity, and depends on the non-duality of partners. In this notion of love neither a dualistic nor a monistic interpretation is possible, since both are one-sided.

When the doctrine of the trinity reaches a notion of one reality, this means that reality is one in love insofar as it is interrelational. This notion of love is ontological and surpasses misleading, edifying metaphors. Here love is the very structure of the one reality. For love as interrelationality integrates within itself justification and justice, as we see in the notion of *karma* as well as in the dimension of the cross.

We said that the freedom of one reality is eternal self-determination to realize interrelationality. Now that we have interpreted the notion of interrelationality as love, we can add a corollary: the *freedom* of the one reality is the *self-determination* to realize *love.*

This sentence portrays the trinitarian structure of reality. The Father as source (*sat*) is freedom, which is seen in the Son as a will towards self-determination (*cit*), and is realized in the Spirit as love (*ananda*); i.e., as the interrelationality of reality. We summarize this important relationship in Figure 12.1.

Within the framework of simultaneous language, we can now understand the Advaita of absolute freedom and love:

God is the continuity of freedom in the event of his love. The one reality is the continuity of freedom in its eternal self-determination towards interrelationality. Since this simultaneous lan-

```
                    ┌─────────────────┐
                    │   One Reality   │
              ┌─────┴────────┬─────────┴──────┐
```

Freedom	Self-determination	Interrelationality
		(Love)
Father	Son	Spirit
Source	Will	Love
sat	*cit*	*ananda*

Figure 12.1

guage is advaitic, we can also say: The one reality is continuity of freedom in the event of its love. God is the continuity of freedom in his eternal self-determination towards interrelationality.

Human personal becoming is therefore the paradigm for the process of integration of reality. Human personality is in the same relationship to the transpersonal character of reality as is each realized structure to the whole of trinitarian reality; viz, in an irreversible relationship of dependence (*tadatmya*): the human person has as self the transpersonality of the trinitarian God, i.e., it is a moment in the transpersonal character of the one reality.

The Guru and Community

In this section we will explain how the dialectic of personal transformation leads to transpersonal structure, as seen in *community*, or, conversely, how the quality of the community is dependent on a readiness for this transformation.

The non-dualistic view demands that the transformational experience not remain merely individual, but that it be realized in communitarian living. For Jesus, too, the reign of God is a reality both within us and among us (Lk 17:21).

Egocentrism, which the Bible calls sin, is the fundamentally false human attitude which produces disharmony. Humans put themselves in the place of God instead of being centered in the One. This confines us to the area of individual experience and prevents receptivity to deeper stages of consciousness and readiness for social integration and love.

Consciousness which is separate from the whole (in other words, sin) is visible in today's society in three problems: 1. the overemphasis on material goods, i.e., the economic principle of life, 2. the authoritarian struggle for power of individuals and groups, and 3. the lack of consciousness of the wholeness of reality. Although humans have always suffered from these forms of alienation, the problem is especially severe today because of the technical possibilities of modern culture, which deepen our alienation. Alienation is in direct proportion to lack of consciousness of the whole, as we saw above.[15]

This fundamental alienation can be overcome by faith and prayer, but the previous chapter has shown that only the deeper experiences of prayer effectively open us to new being in Christ. Superficial religiosity is an illusion of faith, as when people think they *have* or use faith, rather than exist *in* faith.

In spiritual experiences, as well as in realizing authentic community, there arises the problem of authority. In Asiatic cultures the guru wields unquestioned authority because he embodies and lives according to a higher wisdom. The word "guru" means teacher, but teaching is not his primary function. The guru is not an instrument for dispensing wisdom, but rather his *whole* life embodies truth. In the spiritual power which radiates from him the disciple gains entrance into an area of spiritual realities. Thus the disciple does not receive instruction, but rather *lives* with the guru, shares his everyday existence as part of his family (*gurukula*), and in this way, he/she exercises him/herself in spirit-centered living. Only when the disciple has become selfless enough to receive higher learning will the master initiate him/her into the practice of meditation. In this sense the guru himself is, above all, a self-experienced person while he directs others, one who enables the darkness in the heart of the disciple to come to the light. The guru communicates his wisdom directly to the disciple by means of spiritual powers of a special kind. The authentic guru must be free from every form of egotistical striving and should not promote a cult of his person, nor be authoritarian in his behavior. By this measure alone pseudo-gurus are not correct. These latter sometimes mislead the ignorant, who are not aware of these criteria. But it is only seldom that such pseudo-gurus gain support in India. Indians, it is true, may identify the guru with God, they may reverence him and accept what he says and does, but there is rarely any social or financial dependence on him. It is taken for granted that the experienced disciple separates himself/herself from the guru. In this way there is a recognition that God alone is guru, even though God manifests himself in the wise to make possible direct spiritual instruction.

We could continue by describing the qualities and characteristics of the guru. The most important thing is that he himself lives out of his experience of meditative consciousness of wholeness. There must be a complete unity between his teaching and his praxis. Only then does he have authority, which comes entirely from within. Any spiritual authority based on an exterior power structure is not highly regarded in India.

This picture of the guru is very similar to the spiritual masters and guides in Christianity. Besides the mystics mentioned in chapter 7 we could add Teresa of Avila, Francis of Assisi, and especially the Russian staretzes. Only in rare cases did they influence the overall life of the church, just as in India with the authentic gurus, who are rare exceptions.

In early Christianity the problem of spiritual authority led to a well-considered, yet in many respects harmful solution: viz., the office of bishop, based on an *external* authority which became more and more powerful and often hindered the free development of spiritual gifts and movements; i.e., by changing Christian faith into an ideology of those who were holding power.

Jesus resisted Jewish messianic expectations and *lived* his authority as suffering servant of God. He rejected struggles for power and the hierarchical ambitions of his disciples (Mk 10:35 ff.). Paul's letters are filled with the overwhelming immediacy of spiritual living and experience, which afterwards is quickly harnessed. Clement, bishop of Rome (A.D. 90–100), warns of "rebellions" against established authorities, which certain young men were fomenting against the elders in Corinth. He even considers the death penalty. His argument is significant: just as God rules with authority from above and demands unconditional obedience, so must humans obey the "bishops, priest, and deacons," for God gave his authority to princes and leaders on earth.[16] What began as an immediately present experience of the Spirit among the first Christians had become an authoritarian religion, which was then supported by a monarchical and completely untrinitarian God-image. Spiritual experience became dogma, faith became obedience, the irruption of the Spirit became political calculation. Anything "Gnostic" had to be suppressed, and the N.T. canon of scriptures is itself a witness to this development, as E. Pagels has shown with the aid of the discoveries from the Nag Hammadi library.[17]

Luther tried to reestablish the priesthood of all the faithful on the basis of true spiritual experience. However, despite some breaks with authoritarian political structures and reductionisms, the Reformation returned to rationalism and the external authority it engenders. The modern refusal of authority is a reaction to this, but it is superficial, as is proved by the success of "gurus."

It is no accident that the search for spiritual masters is so strong and that even minor lights gain so much influence. Once we have lost sight of authentic spiritual experiences and turn to substitute idols (film stars, athletes, publicity symbols), false gurus have an easy time. Here, too, the blame falls on Christian praxis, which has neglected to make authentic spiritual experience a thing of value by providing *living* examples of it. The true guru embodies freedom, love, and wisdom. He never wishes to have his opinions prevail, but rather leads others to their own experience. Since he knows that in the end (*paramarthika*) truth is one, he is able to tolerate great pluralism at the level of differentiated consciousness (*vyavaharika*) without feeling that his identity is endangered. On the basis of the *experience* of unity he risks action towards unity without thereby secretly preferring his own views or those of his own group (nation, religion). He is *free* to love.

Only when we learn to distinguish pseudo-gurus from authentic ones will we be able to master the present situation. And pseudo-gurus are by no means limited to the founders of sects, but may also be found in the form of political ideologies, rationalistic pressures, and theological dogmas. Just as true trinitarian experience of reality can expose our self-made limitations, so too can gurus help the *communio sanctorum* crystalize its truth. Thus the ideal guru is relativized by the community, which itself becomes a guru. The trinitarian structure of reality prohibits belief in an authoritative hierarchy, starting with the area of spirituality!

Community is necessary, for we are not recommending anarchy. Institutions and offices are unavoidable, but they should be rooted in *spiritual* experience and spiritual authority. Uncontrolled egocentrism must be overcome, and there are two quite different possibilities for doing this: community or collectivism.

Collectivism is a form of organization by individuals who find their identity in the collective form. The individual has to develop according to the collective identity in such a way that he/she resembles all the other individuals. The ideal is uniformity, and there is no room for pluralism. The mechanisms of advertising, which appeal to certain impulses to buy or to other behavioristic determinisms, use this principle, as do those who claim totalitarian power within nations. The dogmatic claim of being in sole possession of the truth can also further the goals of collectivism in this sense, and this is a problem which ecclesial institutions have to struggle with. Needless to say, such a collectivism is not desirable, for it cannot allow for creativity nor can it rejoice in differences. It hems in the holistic development of personality.

Community is understood as a free relationship of persons who develop unity without losing their special characteristics as individuals. This is possible when the real center is outside the community itself and can thus integrate various polarities. Community is based on freedom, relationship, and pluralism. It involves an ongoing process of integrating, and the results of this process are not determinable beforehand, lest a renewed uniformity, dogmatism or intolerance once again take hold.

It is to be feared that either the torn human condition or the enslavement of the personality are unavoidable, if *integral communities* at all levels of human existence cannot be realized.

Community is grounded in the personal maturity of integrated individuals and likewise becomes an important part of reaching this maturity. Community can help integrate differences. It repeats, is a prototype of and provides examples of the basic pattern of reality, which we saw in the symbol of the trinity. God is integrated community and as such is both the source and the goal of reality. Community expresses the fact that the structure of reality is the interrelationality of love, fulfilled in transpersonal integration.

The symbol of trinitarian *perichoresis* was analyzed in detail above. This symbol can lead us along a communitarian path, which not only leads to Christian community, but also—because of the universality of the trinitarian promise—helps overcome the problems of isolation, exploitation and destruction on our earth.

This is what Moltmann attempts to show by means of a "social doctrine of the trinity."[18] Starting with the early Christian notion of *communio sanctorum* he points to the third thesis of the Theological Declaration of Barmen, which understands the church as "community of brothers." The notion of brother/sisterhood means not only a strong emotional bond, a responsibility, and a community among the members of Christ's body, but, since the French Revolution, it also awakens social hopes which have neither been achieved nor given up. Moltmann explains: "The community of brothers/sisters announces the kingdom of God in a new and alternative lifestyle to our present social environment."[19] What this means remains open and must be learned through concrete instances, which join social and individual transformation, for the two aspects involve one another and end up within the other since both are situated within a whole.

We said that the community's center is beyond itself. This means that the unity and identity of the community do not come from within the community itself nor are they based on its goals nor its own powers. Unity and identity come, rather, from the participation by each individual in a wholeness which is fully immanent and fully transcendent at the same time. Such a community lives a spiritual experience of sharing in the "divine dance" (*perichoresis*), in the self-realization of God *through* each form of interrelation and community.

Thus, community is grounded in the process of divine self-integration on the one hand and in human participation in this event, on the other. The community's life comes from meditative experience of the whole, which in the eyes of rational consciousness is a creative *u-topia*. Community never *has* or *is* this whole, but *participates* in it. Since it never is the whole, but only approaches it, community is free to manifest itself in many, even imperfect, forms. This *freedom for imperfection* is essentially the basic attitude of abandonment, without which the individual cannot overcome his/her disharmonious egotism. A compulsion to perfection cannot be a spiritual letting-go in receptivity (the gospel), but only an ideologically motivated, egotistical striving (law).

Community grows out of participation in the trinity and this becomes a life-transforming power as it penetrates more deeply into the stages of non-dualistic consciousness. The integration of personality by means of meditation is therefore an important preliminary for the coming-to-be of community where the transpersonal dimension of reality appears. At the level of dual-rational consciousness the dream of the French Revolution must remain a dream if *at the same time* freedom, equality and brotherhood are to be realized, for a dream transcends rational waking consciousness, but cannot integrate it. In the experience of meditative wholeness, which integrates the dreamed of unity and the concrete realization in the process of transpersonal *perichoresis*, we find the key for realizing also the communitarian dimension of Spirit. Though here the brokenness and simultaneous existence of *all* human reality, as described above, are taken into account. In other words, we remain grounded in the bedrock of biblical realism. For an illustration of this kind of *perichoresis*, see Figure 12.2.

(aspect of the Father)   COMMUNITY   (aspect of the Son)
FREEDOM   (anticipated)   EQUALITY
individuality   wholeness   collectivity
particularity   unity in
                                           the body of Christ

(aspect of the Spirit)
BROTHERHOOD/SISTERHOOD
Advaita

Figure 12.2

Everything is grounded in consciousness of the whole. The whole is always there and awaits our receptivity. It is present *in* pluriformity. When this pluriformity is upset, the experience of the whole disappears. When we are aware of the whole we see in it the worth of the particular. We allow it to be as an expression of the whole and our identity is not threatened by the otherness of the other. The whole encompasses all things, but all things cannot exist without the whole.

What does this wholeness and personality of reality mean for the individual destiny of each person, whose being—i.e., possibility of realizing wholeness—is threatened by death? Is there a transpersonal integration of individuals in the unity of reality?

Rebirth or Continuous Manifestation?

The theme of rebirth or transmigration of souls is usually not discussed in Christian theology. It is an emotional theme and is undoubtedly of great significance for everyone. This alone would be a reason to take it seriously. Beyond this, there has been an increasing number of psychological, thanatological, and parapsychological publications on this question. Theology cannot continue to maintain that this theme has no meaning since the Bible excludes rebirth. Aside from the fact that rebirth has always been on the periphery of Western thinking (although mostly outside the churches), the number of those who believe in the transmigration of souls is increasing in Europe and America, and this should impel us to analyze it thoroughly, at least out of pastoral concern.

Christian apologetics in this regard would have to be characterized as largely irrelevant, since it has done little to distinguish the different ideas on reincarnation or to differentiate the philosophical and logical problems involved in order to bring about a certain clarity. A few exceptions to this rule include the studies of John Hick[20] for the English-speaking world, and in Germany, Adolf Koeberle, who has recently considered anew some of the arguments for and against transmigration without, however, sufficiently taking into account ideas developed on Indian soil.[21] To an extent this lacuna has been filled by H. Torwesten, who however does not enter into a systematic, theological discussion.[22]

In the dialogue with Asiatic cultures, the theme of rebirth is central. In India all the native religions (Hinduism, Jainism, Buddhism, Sikhism), as well as the related religions of the Parsi treat reincarnation, even though they differ in details with regard to content and mode of argumentation. Our intention is not to discuss Indian or Western rebirth generally. Instead we will present the very sophisticated theory of Advaita Vedanta and bring it into a dialogue with trinitarian theology in order to suggest a possible Christian solution.

Christian theology has four objections[23] to rebirth: 1. It is not biblical, 2. It obscures the meaning in this life of a faith *decision*, 3. It contradicts the biblical teaching of resurrection of the body, 4. It cannot be reconciled with the individuality of Christ's saving work.

1. It is a fact that the teaching of rebirth cannot be drawn from biblical sources, and it has *never* been part of orthodox Christian teaching. Claims to the contrary are due to faulty interpretation of tradition going back to Origen.[24] However, this argument does not preclude the possibility that the theory *could become* Christian teaching, if it could be demonstrated that it does not contradict the basic intention of the Bible and indeed could help explain Jesus' teaching. There are other Christian *theologoumena* which are not explicitly found in the Bible or in early Christian tradition. Theology is always an ongoing process of making explicit what was once implicit. It allows for creativity and new insights in the clarification of revelation for the ongoing context. The rejection of the teaching of rebirth by the early church was directed at a certain idea of reincarnation. It would be inadmissible to forget this fact and

apply unquestioningly this past rejection to arguments developed in Advaita Vedanta.

2. The argument that rebirth minimizes the role of a faith decision in this life has been over-generalized. A. Koeberle's supposition concerning India's basic pessimistic attitude—since it tolerates a cycle of rebirth—is an often-heard judgment, which is false.[25] Also, the claim that Indian *karma* and the theory of reincarnation are responsible for the material misery of India today (in classical times the social structures were most probably similar to those of Europe at that time!), since they encourage economic and social lethargy, is unconvincing and perhaps ideological. It hides from the fact that European colonization is largely responsible for the misery in South Asia.[26] The fact is that the teaching of rebirth talks of the polarity of necessity and freedom in order to *increase* human responsibility; i.e., it places a decision for the good (interpreted differently) within the realm of our human freedom within *this* lifetime.

3. The Christian interpretation of the resurrection of the body undergoes a development because our ideas of what matter is change. As we will demonstrate, the Indian belief in reincarnation depends on the idea that matter and spirit form a continuum. Thus, what is of great importance here is an "intermediate" state, a kind of field of psychic energy. Far from having to contradict this idea, Christian imagery may deepen it and vice versa.

4. The notion of the "uniqueness of Christ's redemption" needs to be interpreted. Within the horizon of today's world, especially the holistic theory of reality which is used here, this notion will have to be reformulated, both qualitatively and quantitatively, in order to address a world which is no longer merely the product of Judaism and Christianity. In the previous chapter it became evident that our model of the trinity is essentially *inclusive*, and we will interpret this in relationship to the uniqueness of Christ's redemption in chapter 13. Here we will assume an inclusivity. It includes all the levels of real and possible temporality. Simply stated, this means that Christ's saving work cannot be confined to *one* temporally limited lifetime, but encompasses the whole "cycle of rebirths" (*samsara*).

There are two reasons to reconsider reincarnation today, even in Western theology, and completely apart from a third reason, which is dialogue with the religion and theologies developed in Asia:

1. The problem of theodicy is being discussed again. Given the

possibility that "Christian civilization" is destroying itself, theodicy is gaining in urgency—and has different presuppositions behind it than in the time of Leibniz. There is much undeserved suffering and inequality which cannot be rationalized, even by social theory. In India also, at least since the time of Buddha, it was known that *karma* cannot interpret away inequality and oppression although it can help us to understand them better.

The popular images in Hinduism and Buddhism (as well as Christianity) are naturally mistaken in depicting a better afterlife or a more favorable rebirth in order to make the oppression by the powerful more bearable. This does not mean that rebirth as such is mistaken, but rather it alerts us to possible ideological misuses of it, which can and do accompany certain eschatologies. Whether the pathos of rebirth theory can bring intelligibility to *de facto* inequality and injustices is another question, which we will ask later. But here also, we must distinguish between the various theories.

2. Doctrines of *karman* and rebirth are first of all an expansion of the indissolvable interconnectedness of reality. Science itself recognizes today the interrelationality of the universe. Relativity theory, quantum physics, post-Darwinian models of evolution, psychosomatic medicine, parapsychological research, biofeedback and, most of all, experiences with Yoga and meditation support this basic vision. Therefore it is no surprise that theories of reincarnation are gaining ground. There are now countless publications along these lines, and while the quantity of studies is certainly no proof for the theory, they demonstrate the need to think through interrelationship even with regard to the fact of the individual. Contrary to John Hick's guesses (1976) that Eastern reincarnation theories must ultimately give way before Darwin, it is to be noted today (1984) that certain forms of Darwinism are losing ground to holistic models of evolution which are now being developed. These models may even be reconcilable with certain ideas of reincarnation.[27]

Karman

The theory of *karman* is at the basis of all Asiatic ideas on reincarnation. *Karman* is basic to faith in Asiatic culture and is more widespread than anything else. The Rigveda's notion of the cosmic order (*rta*) prepares the ground for the later doctrine of *karman*. *Karman* is by no means a late discovery, part of the sudden

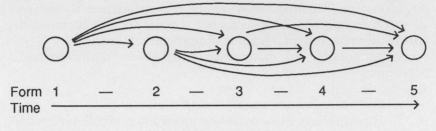

Figure 12.3

change to a pessimistic attitude in Indian culture.[28] It is true that an essential shift took place during the time of the Buddha and the Upanishads. But to call it pessimism is quite inadequate. It would be better to speak of a new phase of *introspection.*

In the earliest texts, *karman* usually means holy action, especially sacrifice, which determines and maintains the status of the world. In the Upanishads *karman* is the cosmic law of conservation of energy and includes, especially, human physical-psychic-mental activity. Through their actions humans are in conformity, not only to their individual structures—in other words their habits which increasingly determine them—but to the forms which change things universally. This is the basic insight of *karman:* human activity has ontological significance. What we *think* is what we become. By our actions we structure ourselves and this has an effect on the whole.[29] And it is in meditation, especially, that this is experienced. The total interrelationality of reality is the basic ontological structure. *Karman* is the law of order, formed by the already elapsed forms (habits) of past actions. Thus present forms also will influence the future. This applies to all parts of reality. Thus, for example, the laws of nature are understood as already having become karmic "habits." The *repetition* of an act or a certain form strengthens the tendency that it will be repeated and will acquire an enduring stability, as we can easily verify in observing human behavior and morality. Thus it is worthwhile considering whether this is also true in the area of physical-biological reality.

We have pictured the effects of *karman* in Figure 12.3 (using R. Sheldrake's model, presented in *A New Science of Life,* p. 97[30]). *Karman* as a formative principle determines the individual, but has transindividual consequences. It is a way of expressing our historicity and therefore points to the transhistorical meaning of history insofar as karmic connectedness goes beyond the individual and the species, and indeed goes beyond every possible form. In the tradition of the Upanishads, *karman* has consequences for personality: the way a person sows is the way he/she reaps.[31] Yet nowhere within all these Indian images is *atman* encountered.

It is possible to distinguish three basic anthropological positions:[32]

1. Our essence is transtemporal (Indian *atman*),
2. Humans have a temporal beginning but not end (Greek culture and orthodox Christian teaching).
3. Humans have a beginning and an end (modern secularism).

In India the second of these is felt to be logically contradictory. The argument resembles Kant's. The doctrine of *karman* brings together the first and third arguments: thus the *implicit* reality of *atman* as subject is accepted, while the appearance of *jiva* (individual "soul") involves limitations, both logically and spatio-temporally. The relationship between *atman* and *jiva* is interpreted variously in different Vedantic systems, but in every case *atman* is not subordinated to the karmic order.

Belief in *karman* is not, therefore, an inevitable law of absolute necessity. On the contrary, while there is *relative* necessity in the order of temporal structures, not only can this necessity be overcome within the area of freedom (*atman, moksa*), but this is the goal of all life. *Karman* is only one pole in the bipolarity of *karman* and *moksa: moksa*, the other pole describes a higher order which alone is absolute reality. Belief in *karman*, therefore, at least in its Vedantic form, is anything but a fatalism,[33] as we will show further in chapter 14.

Karman as the ontological principle in the formation of habits, creates stable structures and thus recognizes the total interdependence of all parts of reality. R. Panikkar distinguishes seven aspects of *karman* theory, which summarize what we have been saying here:[34]

1. *Karman* as the expression of cosmic interdependence avoids an individualistic image of the world, for karmic communion breaks through "ontological monads."
2. *Karman* gives a precise expression in the limitations of human freedom and thus stakes out an area of freedom.
3. *Karman* frees us from the illusion that there is something absolutely my own. In karmic conectedness nothing is exclusively mine, for it is also related to another.

4. *Karman* gives an intelligible basis to the solidarity of all beings, for all processes and actions have universal meaning and effects. Each being has a share in the destiny of the whole universe. Each being thus has universal responsibility.
5. *Karman* does not inquire into the nature of evil, nor does it explain it away, but rather seeks to detect the beyond-individual elements and *manner of functioning of evil.*
6. *Karman* describes the mutability of the world, thus its historicity and contingency.
7. *Karman* acknowledges the difference between the Absolute and the relative, or between God and the world. God is Lord of *karman* and as such is the only transkarmic reality—the Absolute.

It is obvious that karmic interconnectedness cannot stop with death, for death is a moment in the karmic process. This sentence is self-evident, since *karma* describes the physical-psychic-spiritual continuum of reality. Physical death is a change *within* the karmic network and not its end. Since *karman* is essentially temporality, the end of *karman* cannot be temporal; this can only be the trans-temporal spiritual reality, God—the Absolute, the reign of freedom. All of these notions do actually appear in one or another Indian text to describe what is *not karman.*

We will now outline briefly the popular belief of rebirth in order to distinguish it from the Vedantic teaching of reincarnation (which is similar to the Buddhist theory, yet not identical with it).[35]

Popular Theories

In India the claim is never or only seldom made that belief in rebirth is based on direct phenomenal evidence. It is a belief which, however, appears as the only plausible explanation of certain observable phenomena. In general, rebirth is thought to be so self-evident that it cannot even be doubted. An apologetics for it has only developed because of Islam and Christianity.[36]

There are essentially four arguments which support the doctrine of rebirth:

1. Rebirth is taught by the sacred scriptures (*sruti*).

2. The doctrine of rebirth provides a rational explanation for the undeserved inequalities among humans.

3. It corresponds to the testimonies of the enlightened, who in their intensive perceptiveness are able to bring into awareness experiences of earlier existences.

4. Since the whole of reality is to be understood as a unity, there must be interdependence, not only of the micro- and macrocosmic, but also at the level of morality. But since the moral order is disturbed from the perspective of a single lifetime, rebirth is needed to reestablish the equilibrium.

1. With regard to the first argument, the Vedas do teach an order (*rta*) similar to *karman*, but not an explicit rebirth. Only in the later scriptures, which belong to the *sruti* (Vedanta), is it fully formulated. It is not necessary to cite individual texts. The original source is unclear. Since ideas about reincarnation are also found in Eskimo, African, and Polynesian cultures, it is a universal human phenomenon. Israel and a few other cultures are noteworthy exceptions. In India the earliest witness to it is Jainism, which is older than Buddhism or the Vedantic scriptures. Since the sacred scriptures are considered as a revealed and unquestionable authority, this argument alone is sufficient for a pious Indian.

2. It is clear that guilt and atonement for guilt cannot be rationally accounted for, either individually or collectively. There is, for instance, an individual *karman*, a collective *karman* of a people, a karmic destiny which outlasts individual generations. All are interconnected. The connections are so complex that the *ontological ecology* of *karman* goes beyond any possibility of summarizing it. Since unjustified inequalities exist, they must finally be the responsibility of the creator—assuming that God is all-mighty. Rebirth is an attempt to deal with this burden (as a theodicy). Its coherency is still to be tested.

3. It cannot be denied that gifted *mediums*, or people who experience intensive states of awareness through Yoga or meditative exercises, are suddenly able to speak unknown languages without making any errors, or give coherent summaries of past events without having any apparent spatio-temporal relationship to them; thus they are remembering "an earlier life." In India such phenomena are more common than in Europe—presumably because this culture does not marginalize them. But in Europe also, parapsychological research has gathered enough material of its own which requires some explanation.[37]

But there are explanations other than rebirth for such phenomena, although these appear no less suspect to rational thought. Thus, for example, specially gifted or trained people could be immersing themselves in a collective "heritage" or "the deep sea of the unconscious," which—distinct from Jung's collective unconscious—would not be composed primarily of archetypal symbols, but of conscious experiences of the past. Whether this explanation is as plausible as the teaching of rebirth remains to be seen.

4. This argument presupposes cosmic harmony, which is true for the area of morality as well. Since it is a postulate of practical reason, this insight can neither be logically grounded nor denied. For, why must the moral order be consistent within itself? As a theological argument it would require further distinctions. Also the cycle of rebirth is not the whole. This will only become evident later when we see that the cycle is dissolved on the basis of the expansion of *karman* or through the grace of God (as seen in many places in the Bhagavad Gita).

The problematic brought up by the last argument is similar to the second argument discussed by Hick.[38] Inequality in *this* life is clarified by a previous one and each depends on a previous . . . *ad infinitum. Karman* brings out the problem of an intraworldly texture of guilt and sin, but does not give the final reason for inequality and suffering. The Vedanta's reproach against Christianity is that it has succumbed to a logical error, since the soul is seen as created (in the beginning) and likewise infinite (at the end). This reproach must be taken seriously. Conversely it is equally unsatisfying to claim that *karman* has no beginning, but does have an end. Thus this form of rebirth doctrine has difficulty in achieving a satisfactory theodicy.

To clarify some individual points, the various ideas on reincarnation must first be distinguished. It would be more accurate to talk of a *mythos of rebirth*, reflected in different theories.[39] Popular beliefs accept that the "soul" wanders from body to body. But what is the "soul"? And how is it continuous?

Whatever soul means, there must be a conscious self which is the carrier of the person's characteristics and memories, if indeed the idea of reward, which is required by morality, is to have any meaning; i.e., some "cathartic" function. The continuity must be either within a physically similar entity or in a grouping of psychically similar dispositions, or in an enduring memory. No claim is ever made for bodily similarity. The psychic dispositions are for the most part so general that no individual continuity could emerge from them. In general, i.e., in the case of average people, there is no continuity of memory. Thus the arguments for rebirth are deficient in their moral aspect, for if we cannot recognize the guiltiness of a previous life, we cannot atone for it, in order to overcome it by *insight (jnana)*. In this case sin would only be a mechanistic occurrence—which many interpreters readily admit, although not the overall tradition of the Vedanta. Continuity of memory would make *karman* intelligible in relation to the moral components of the person. But this only becomes explicit when the karmic circle is completed: in the enlightened, or in *jivanmukta*.

It could be said that there is a "soul monad," which implicitly contains within itself all previous existences and, by means of *partial* explicitation in the present or in future lives, makes possible a continuity. The whole burden of proof for continuity between incarnation A and reincarnation A_1 depends on this explicitation, i.e., on the realization of higher consciousness by the *jnanin*. The *jnanin*, however, knows that individual souls (*jiva*) are unreal, since reality is only found in *atman*, which is not subject to *samsara*. Since the cycle of rebirths is also unreal for the one who is on the path of *paramarthika* knowledge, it becomes difficult to explain how the knowledge of the *jnanin* can prove the continuity of this cycle. For the soul, which had been wandering up to this point, does not have a transsamsaric reality. How then can it reach the necessary intensive state of consciousness from which it can view all the past hidden lives? Where else but in *atman* would its center of memories be, which would ensure continuity beyond death? But then *atman* would be subject to the modifications of *jiva*, which Advaita Vedanta emphatically forbids. Thus a contradiction results: the popular theory must appeal to the Vedantic *jnanin*, but this latter denies the reality of individuality.[40] It holds a completely different theory, which we still have to present.

Whether a person will return as human, or will either descend, returning in the animal or plant realm, or ascend to higher divine spheres is explained differently by the various Indian traditions. This problem is secondary in relationship to the basic principle of rebirth and need not concern us here.

In conclusion: individual identity beyond death cannot be clarified by popular theories without accepting an infinite number of existent wandering monads, which do not necessarily possess self-consciousness. But this is precisely what is rejected in the Vedantic notion of *atman*.

The argument sometimes employed by Christian theology that

karman excludes the reality of grace is not tenable. The whole of
Indian religion teaches the opposite, even though human striving
may be more emphasized than God's favor towards humans—as
we see also in the history of Christianity. The Bhagavad Gita is an
example of a balanced position, and typical of expanded Indian
sensitivity is a famous sentence from the Sikh scriptures: "*karman*
determines how a person is born, but grace opens the door to salvation."[41] We will return to this discussion in chapter 13.

The Vedantic Theory

For our study, what is more important than the contradictory
popular theory is the Vedantic notion of reincarnation, which is
advaitic and which opens up possibilities of interreligious
dialogue.

Sankara himself formulates this classical theory with unsur-
passable precision: "In truth no one else besides the Lord is reborn"
(*satyam nesvarad anyah samsari*).[42] This statement directly contradicts the idea that an endless number of souls wander through the
cycle of rebirths (*samsara*). Instead it is the Lord alone (*isvara*), i.e.,
the personal God, who continually and in various stages of manifestation subjects himself to *samsara*. Because of the Vedantic insight into the unity of reality this could not be otherwise. In very
truth (*paramarthika*) there *is* nothing else than *brahman*, which is
qualified under the influence of *maya*; that is, *saguna* the *brahman*
appears as *isvara*. This *isvara* is manifested in all forms of reality.
The individual soul is nothing other than this manifestation of
isvara. In and of itself it has no being (*svabhava*) and therefore
cannot undergo *samsara*. The quintessence of ignorance (*avidya*) is
the illusion of independent existence. Thus individual souls are not
reborn, but one and the same God manifests or "births" himself in
a continual succession of individual beings of reality.[43]

However, such an interpretation of Sankara is only defensible
if we understand the difference between the absolute standpoint
(*paramarthika*) and the relative standpoint (*vyavaharika*). To our
ordinary knowledge (*vyavaharika*) things appear as many, and thus
it is meaningful to speak of a cycle of rebirths. From the absolute
standpoint (*paramarthika*) however, which is attained by means of
a unique transrational experience, all of this is seen as an illusion.
Whether our presentation of Sankara's interpretation will seem
convincing is thus connected with the basic question of Advaita

epistemology concerning the relationship between the two stand-points. If we could immediately know and speak in one way or the other, there would be no need to bring the levels or standpoints into relationship with one another. We contest this approach and hold that the insight into the ultimate unity of reality (*paramarth-ika*), once it has been seen, also alters everyday knowledge. Thus it is no longer possible to speak of rebirth of "individual souls." We believe that Sankara must be interpreted in this way because other-wise *jnana marga*, the goal of freedom, and enlightenment (*moksa*), achieved by intellectual meditation would be useless.

The continuity from one manifestation to another is guaran-teed by the doctrine about the subtle body (*suksma-sarira*), which was presented in chapter 1. Since body and spirit are in a contin-uum of degrees of subtlety it is superfluous to ask whether this subtle body is material or spiritual. It is intermediate: characterized by a certain structural density of the spiritual, which becomes less subtle in the area of the material. The subtle body contains above all psychic powers: the cognitive intellect (*buddhi*), understanding joined with the will (*manas*), the five elements of perception, the five powers of action, and the five subtle life-energies. In summary, it embodies the moral, aesthetic, intellectual, and subtle-psychic (*prana*) dispositions of the human person,[44] which are partially in-herited and partially acquired. Each activity produces an impres-sion in the subtle matrix in relation to one of these elements. If the impression is repeated, dispositions or habitual patterns emerge which have effects on a person's thinking, willing, and behaving. These impressions are called *samskaras* and, in analogy to the law of conservation of energy, are not extinguished with the dissolu-tion of the physical level of manifestation (i.e., death). The subtle body continues to put its stamp on material forms on the grounds of its being God's power of manifestation. The karmic structure, therefore, has a relative continuity by means of the *samskaras* in the subtle body. The *samskaras* tend to imprint new forms (re-births) with their pattern. They produce mental dispositions which have an effect on the next manifestation of life (the new individual).

Memory (individual or collective), therefore, is not stored up in the brain, but is a kind of subtle field which, of course, needs the brain for normal operation, but without the brain it might exist in a different way expressing itself at other levels of reality. It is mem-ory which causes tendencies to build up new structures. Through meditation and *jnana* it is possible to experience this subtle level of reality. The one who enters into it and is united with God's consciousness can look upon the whole and therefore "remembers" the whole subtle karmic field. This person recognizes earlier forms; i.e., the whole of spatio-temporal reality becomes present in a single moment. Thus, there is no recall of earlier individual existences, but a *becoming aware of a universal collective connectedness.* Karmic interdependence is only recognized when it is surpassed. Only the redeemed (*jivanmukta*) know and see the whole, because they regard all with the consciousness of the Absolute.

Figure 12.4 is a diagrammatic overview of Vedantic theory. The *key to the diagram* is as follows:

The absolute ground of wholeness (*brahman, atman*) manifests itself. It does not change in doing so. It is completely unmoved by the manifestation. This thesis is worthwhile discussing and has been criticized in the previous chapters because of the doctrine of the trinity. The manifestation brought about by *maya* creates levels of reality which are distinguished from one another by their subtleness or capacity for interdependence. The *jiva* is predisposed by tendencies which put a mark on the self as it traverses the subtle levels (*samskara*). The self has other experiences, and the sum total of these activities (either as active or passive impressions) is an altered individual memory, and this manifests itself in habits, which in turn are stored up in the karmic collective memory. But it is especially the unfulfilled wishes in our life which have potential in the subtle area. These structuring elements, along with other mental dispositions, become important factors for new creative manifestations of the divine. Individuals, therefore, are not only formed by an eternal and divine idea (in the Platonic sense) or at least organized according to its dynamism, but also their structure depends on the structures of previous individuals.

The Gita uses a striking comparison:[45] "When the Lord acquires a body and then departs from it, he goes, taking these (subtle impressions, mental dispositions) with him, as the wind carries off fragrances (of flowers)." The fragrance is the subtle essence of individuals, formed by means of *karman* which God reinserts within the material in his next manifestation. The Gita concludes: "Whatever state of being he remembers upon giving up his body at death, to that he attains."[46] The one who thinks of God approaches God. The one who has worldly desires creates mental dispositions so that these—because of the basic law of interdependence—survive within corresponding material forms. Naturally the last thought

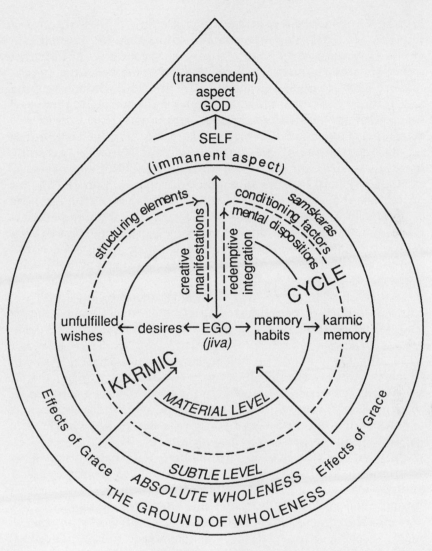

Figure 12.4

before death is not to be taken in isolation, but is in continuity with the whole of a person's life which is present at this moment. The one who trustfully remembers God in the last moment, erases the other dispositions and shares in a redeeming unity with God. Knowledge of the Absolute which Spirit accomplishes, love for God, and belief in the power of the Most High dissolve all the *samskaras,* if indeed this attitude is authentic. This is the end of *samsara,* the redeeming integration into the absolute ground.

It is important to notice that this "return"—in Christian terms, the world of divine grace—is *always* possible since, in fact, it alone is real. Starting from the level of absolute wholeness, grace penetrates the subtle areas and extends all the way to the material forms. However, only in the human form of existence is there free decision, and therefore it is very valuable as a "springboard" out of the karmic into the divine order. In Advaita Vedanta, therefore, there is very little speculation on the intermediate states or on the existence of hell, because it is within human existence that the promise of final salvation is concealed. Even a person who is reborn as an angelic being (*deva*) must first return to a human form because of the freedom within the knowledge that is found there. Where there is no longing for material things, there is no corresponding mental disposition and therefore no renewed bond with material structures.

This is a general outline of Vedantic teaching on "rebirth," which is very different from a doctrine of restless wandering by restless souls. What does it imply for intercultural and interdisciplinary discussions?

1. Advaita Vedanta is an example of a holistic worldview, in which the whole of reality is one and the various levels of reality are distinguished from one another by their degree (greater or lesser) of subtleness; i.e., by an interaction with forms from their own level or with others. The highest subtleness corresonds to the greatest interaction and interdependence.

2. God is *the* reality, purely and simply. He is *implicit* in his manifestations and is also—as a completely transcendent ground—*explicit* in individuals and their karmic change which does not end at death, since the subtle body is not subject to the laws governing materiality. The karmic dispositions are formative energies, which create relatively stable substructures (i.e., individuals). Ultimately "God himself comes and goes when 'we' are born or die."[47] Human individuality is an illusion from the transtemporal standpoint.[48]

3. Relative becoming is in itself a continual process of deaths and rebirths, and these are the basis of the creative impulse that comes forth from the absolute ground into all levels of reality. If the subtle levels may be considered as having their own relatively

independent substructure, in this case bodily death is nothing more than a passage within the overall life cycle; i.e., a moment *in* a process of becoming. Only when the material level is isolated does death appear to be the end of becoming.

4. The end of the cycle, *moksa* or freedom, is the complete breakthrough of consciousness integrating the spiritual as well as the material in a kind of "rebirth in the spirit" which dissolves *samsara.* Whether at this point the material is transformed and as such included (the *bhedabheda* school) or revealed as illusion and simply ceases to exist (strict Advaita Vedanta) is a much debated problem for Vedanta.

This leads us to our critique of a certain Vedantic position. The problem of individuality or the destiny of material reality is by no means secondary, but is essential to guarantee the consistency of Vedantic theory. For if there is no individuality, then the karmic connections are not real. And if these are not real there can be no real manifestation of the Absolute, and thus no real life which breaks through and dissolves the karmic bonds. If there is no incarnation there can be no reincarnation, not even when *isvara* is recognized as true *samsarin.*

The Advaitin can indeed argue that the whole karmic cycle is an illusion, for only *brahman/atman* is real. But then—and this is the Advaitin's conclusion—the whole subtle network of interrelated karmic connections means nothing. But this would imply that it has not correctly clarified the nature of the evil, and thus the whole laborious argument was useless. Furthermore, it is problematic to accept the *atman/brahman* reality as the only reality and at the same time to claim that there is no beginning to the karmic cycle. That which is without beginning stands above the laws of time and cannot be overcome by temporal karmic procedures. But then are we not denying the conditions for *moksa* and allowing for a transtemporal karmic becoming which exists *alongside* the Absolute? We thus end up in either dualism or absurdity.

If there is no relatively consistent personal center as a *relative wholeness* in relationship to the *whole* (God), there can be no knowledge which transcends karmic structures. If we are to avoid splintering the unity of reality, the dispositions formed by means of materiality must have some meaning in the Absolute, even if it is not absolute meaning; i.e., the Spirit must give new form to and not merely eliminate the material.

Even Vedantic teaching on reincarnation cannot resolve this contradiction, which is immanent to it, and this is not surprising considering such a difficult theme.

How then can we clarify the undeniable phenomenon of "memories" of previous, beyond merely individual existences? John Hick makes a suggestion which may help clarify the memory of a "previous life" and other intermediate appearances, without bringing in reincarnation theory. After death there would be a "mental husk," which remains longer than the physical body and could be perceived by gifted mediums. Since this mental constellation is grasped while it is dissolving, memories of a "past life" are mostly partial. "With such a theory the idea of reincarnation becomes, in effect, a matter of degree. There is no rebirth of the full living personality. But there is a kind of reincarnation of parts or aspects of the personality, such attenuated reincarnation being equally compatible with the extinction of the personality as a whole or with its continued life in some other sphere, leaving behind only a mental 'husk' which becomes entangled in the mind of a living child with whom it has perhaps some kind of affinity and through whom its remaining quantum of psychic energy is discharged."[49]

It is to be noted that this theory assumes a relatively stable psychic level of reality which is not joined to bodily manifestations, or only in a conditioned way, but at the same time it is not identical with the spiritual. Hick's thesis can help clarify paranormal phenomena, which Koeberle also enumerates and agrees are genuine.[50] But the difficulty with this theory is that it cannot clarify why the "mental husks" survive longer than the body or what gives them stability and coherence. Also, the idea of fragmentary recall is very imprecise. There could be selective psychic mechanisms, which would operate in a way analogous to normal forgetting. Of course, the cultural environment is very important, since it creates paradigms for what we are able to experience or direct our attention to and say.

We will now attempt to describe a model which takes these problems into account and, at the same time, can be discussed theologically and enter into dialogue with physical theories (David Bohm's interaction of an explicit and implicit order), as well as biological hypotheses (Rupert Sheldrake's morphogenetic fields, viz., immaterial characteristics that control the formative processes and transcend space, time and biological death: thus very similar to karmic ideas.)[51] The following presentation is hypothetical.

Continuous Manifestation

The following is in the form of a proposal to enable this topic to be at least discussed by Christian theology, even if the proposal itself would require greater precision. It begins with Vedantic theory and our critique of it, and maintains the relationship to the above developed non-dualistic interpretation of the trinity.

Even according to Vedantic theory it is not meaningful to speak of "rebirth" and "transmigration of souls." This is also true of our proposal, which speaks rather of *continuous manifestation.* It links (a) the doctrine of *creatio continua* with (b) a basic non-dualistic attitude, and (c) the relative autonomy of the psychic-subtle level of reality. We are thus using the biblical distinction of bodily, psychic, and spiritual levels of human existence, which in modern times has been given up in favor of a matter-mind dualism. The psychic level is relatively independent, because it may not be reduced to material processes nor identified with the spiritual level. If this level is not maintained as separate, phenomena such as clairvoyance and telepathy, as well as certain meditative experiences, can easily be misinterpreted. Likewise, there is the danger of mistaking a pseudo-guru for a spiritual master if we judge only on the basis of his psychic powers (e.g., telepathy), not his spiritual maturity—in fact he could have an inflated ego. A lack of discernment in this case could have disastrous results.

We consider it theologically valid to reopen the whole question since the interrelationship and interdependence of the *whole* of reality is at stake in the Christian message of God's absolute love. If God is love, and injustice is against his will, there *must* be further possibilities of purification and maturing beyond death. Otherwise the majority of humans would be damned, and this would have to be attributed either to God's will or to his powerlessness, which in this case would contradict his love. If grace worked in such a way that all evil were taken away *without* a cleansing process, love and justice would end up in an inadmissible and completely unbiblical opposition. Traditional church teaching has thus included a further saving, cleansing process after death, either in the form of purgatory,[52] or through other mediate states between death and eternity; i.e., positing a space for the subtle force-fields (*suksma sarira*) of the psychic level.[53]

Basically it would be sufficient to hold that the person is purified after death in a subtle field of reality. Thus the evildoer would go through—on the other side—all the sufferings he had imposed on others, thus overcoming karmic tendencies by living through them. Justice would be accomplished and a renewed linkage of *samskaras* with their material forms would not be necessary. True compunction and forgiveness would not be in opposition to justice.

According to the viewpoint of the unity of reality, however, it makes no sense to divide the "intermediate state" (imagined in all possible ways) from other levels of reality or, in other words, to see interrelation working only in one direction. The connection between the material and the psychic allows for reciprocal action in the literal sense: action effected in both directions. If this is the case, it would follow that each level would provide stability for its *own* interrelational structures, even if they were simultaneously in relationship with other levels. In order to maintain coherence it seems plausible that mental dispositions which correspond to material structural laws also "work" at the level of the material. Each level is real when it is actualized by the subtle forms of the next highest level. In other words, for the case at hand, the mental psychic tendency is the form of the material. An example of this would be that the mental disposition of "desire for sensual fulfillment" would have to be overcome karmically in the specific area where it is situated: viz., in the sensual-material area. If, however, the unfulfilled psychic desire were sublimated or spiritually transformed, this disposition could then be integrated at a higher level. In the case of a psychic sublimation, for example, the egocentric quest for worth would be experienced and overcome within the collective-psychic framework. In the case of spiritual transformation or "love of God," there would be participation in the divine which transcends *karman*.

This argument is not a *proof* of the linkage of mental dispositions to material (bodily) processes, but rather suggests a certain, difficult to quantify, probability.

Thus we understand the *samskaras* to be self-accumulated dynamic formal elements or general tendencies in the way reality is organized; i.e., changeable formative structures. They are formative and make real—in the Aristotelian context of form (act) and potency. But this says nothing about the ontological basis of the *samskaras* or its first form. Although at the non-material level of reality the *samskaras* stabilize and have effects, they also have repercussions on the *whole* of reality. Figuratively we could say that the one energetic potentiality of reality is "condensed" in various degrees and thus creates sublevels and substructures (namely as levels of manifestation), which in a secondary way interact.

A Christian teaching—as opposed to a Vedantic theory—on continuous manifestation would also have to include the following points:

1. In the light of Christian belief in the incarnation, which leads to the teaching on the resurrection of the body, the material level cannot be extinguished in the reciprocal action of the various levels of reality. The transformation of *all* levels by the Spirit implies the end of *karman*, because all of the conflicting mental dispositions are now sublated in an integration within the whole or in God. This genuinely Christian argument of a material transfiguration could be especially fruitful in showing that the "purification" process after death cannot merely be relegated to a dematerialized sphere, but is to be seen as real in, with, and beneath the surface of the material manifestation of a divinely willed creation. In other words, we must now take a serious look at a renewed embodiment of psychical powers, unfulfilled potential desires, etc.

2. In every kind of Hindu reincarnation theory the non-human forms of reincarnation mean that *karman* requires a place of satisfaction. This would point out a more mechanistic process and humans would have little influence on it, since *brahmavidya*—the spiritual experience of release—can only be attained within human existence. For a Hindu, actual experience is necessary for salvation, which is not the case for Christian eschatology, since God's grace-filled saving action takes place at every level and is present and actual under all circumstances. Thus purification, too, can take place at all levels of reality, not just at the human level.

3. The person is not dissolved into mental dispositions, nor unaffected by his/her own historical circumstances. Instead each person is formed—materially, psychically, spiritually—and this formation has transtemporal significance. Thus finally, the karmic area is not meaningless for a Christian, but it is an unfolding of the Absolute or the creative power of God. The continuity and coherence of a self-conscious personal center is a necessary presupposition for finding meaning in the karmic continuity in the *samskaras.* Mere mental-psychic tendencies would be too general as a way of guaranteeing an ontological and moral order. The personal center

must be able to integrate memories and impressions if the whole
cycle is to have any meaning. The person can be understood as the
center of this integration. The person *is* this process of becoming
conscious. It is not a mere accumulation of *samskaras* within a
"mental husk."[54]

Experiences and impressions which are not integrated form a
"wall" around the person, and this leads to lack of freedom and
subsequently a "rejection by God" after our physical life. In other
words, that which is not personally integrated causes the return to
a lower level of reality because like interacts with like.

Are the person after death and this potential reinsertion within
the state of materiality the same? The person is *not* the same insofar
as a process of transformation has taken place in which corporal
and psychic characteristics have become immanently unrecogniz-
able. It *is* the same in that a continuity is recognizable in a spiritual
ground *sub specie Dei.*

In Figure 12-5 we schematize this suggestion of a holistic
teaching on continuous manifestation. The key to the diagram is as
follows:

Reality is a self-differentiated whole. The ground of the
wholeness is God, who manifests himself at various levels, each of
which forms a relative wholeness and reacts with the others. Since
this process implies creativity, insofar as new combinations and
substructures are produced, we can speak of creation.[55] An important point is that the relative wholeness of the substructures (e.g.,
the individual) are relatively stable, but only on the ground of the
overall whole. If the substructures are filled only with psychic,
unfulfilled longing, this leads anew to crystalization on the material level, i.e., in lower substructures. If they are filled with consciousness of God, they become transformed and remain in point ⊗
in communion with God. A karmic field is fashioned around personality, which is *essential* to the person, for its basic structures are
being imprinted at the personal level, which is above time. In death
a person encounters God. He/she is rejected if his/her karmic field
permanently resists God's power. He is sent back to the lesser,
material levels in order to complete the process of maturing. The
new embodiment is, of course, another individuality, who however
is determined by the psychic-mental field of personal encounter
with the first individual life. "Rebirth" would therefore be a lack
of receptivity to the creative power of the Spirit, who raises us
to God.

Another possible interpretation would be the following: In

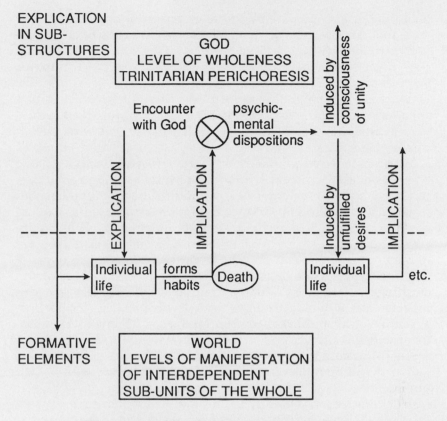

(The many sublevels are not represented here.)

Figure 12.5

death the person would be separated from its surrounding karmic field. Although the person enters into a more or less interior relationship with God, depending on his/her degree of maturity, the karmic field alone has a structuring function for other individuals. It shapes their "collective karman". The person's own "degree of maturity," in this case, would be final. Different persons would share in God's glory in more or less irrevocably different ways.

Both interpretations can be understood in such a way that they are implicit within the biblical message. While the first brings out the judgment aspect of biblical eschatology, the second solution emphasizes unconditional grace. Neither of the two must exclude the other, for we can argue that the person's purification is either by a kind of purgatory or by a kind of return to materiality. And thus this remains independent of the psychic field of the *samskaras*, which in either case has an effect on the material process. In both cases the various persons in God would be distinct from one another (since their historicity is essential) and yet one *in* him. The many persons in the eschaton are a network of differentiated personal spirit-continuums, whose spiritual quality (since they participate in God) is the same, although quantitatively they don't lose their own identity.

In our model there is no direct "leap" of soul monads from one body to another. Continuity is achieved through oneness in being in God, who continually explicates a multitude of individuals out of himself. God does not change, but *is* the movement of ex- and implication by means of the trinitarian *perichoresis.* He "experiences" himself by means of experiences which he has in his process of manifesting and incarnating (as in the second person of the trinity). This corresponds to Meister Eckhart's "God tastes himself in all things."[56] He is in all and yet transcendent; he gives a share of his reality in individuals, and yet is undivided oneness, as the Bhagavad Gita says.[57] He changes and yet does not change. The Absolute integrates and does not integrate individuality. God is beyond these distinctions and this unity beyond is what we can call transpersonal reality or non-duality in relationship to identity and non-identity.

The Absolute, beyond space and time, is therefore perfect interrelationality in which all conditioned elements, experiences, and individuals compenetrate one another mutually. This is the all-encompassing mystical body of Christ. Or, as Augustine says: *et erit unus Christus amans seipsum*—one Christ who loves himself.[58]

What is decisive in the Christian interpretation is this: individual life has meaning, since it is one with God. In this oneness it does not lose its consciousness of itself, but gains it in fulness. God does not change. Creation does not make him richer. Continuous manifestation, however, fulfills his Being. It is his self-explication.

13.

Christ's Salvific Work and the Unity of Reality

In chapter 10 we derived the unity of reality from trinitarian interrelationality. This unity was advaitic, i.e., it consisted in a polarity of unity and plurality. This was not an abstract postulate, but a specific experience, as was explained in chapter 11. In this insight reality reaches fulfillment, and this has consequences for the specific destiny of the human person, as was shown in chapter 12. This, then, leads to an all-important question for Christian theology: the meaning of Christ's salvific work.

The Scope of the Christ Event

The earliest Christian confession of faith proclaims: Jesus Christ is the Lord (Phil 2:11). The title, *kyrios*, has universal meaning at least in Paul's eyes, but also for the synoptics when they proclaim the irruption of God's kingdom (Mk 1:15). What does this sentence mean? Does it imply that no other is Lord? Or does it claim that in Jesus Christ *the* Lord is recognizable? In a more general sense, can the sentence be turned around to state: The Lord is Jesus Christ? Can the subject and the predicate be inverted without causing the subject to lose its characteristics as subject, or the predicate being limited to *this* subject?[1]

This inversion is not valid, as the exegetical context demonstrates. Aside from the fact that normally the inversion of subject and predicate is not logically permissible, since the areas defined by predicate and subject are not identical, it would also be a theological error to identify the human person, Jesus, with the Father. The Father maintains a priority over the Son, as clarified by the trinitarian relationships (*generatio*). Although the Logos is incarnate in Jesus, the Logos is ontologically prior to the incarnation. *The* Absolute must be distinguished from the manifestation (or incarnation) of the Absolute, which *per definitionem* is not Absolute, but concrete. *Within* a given area of concrete relationship, however, it has an *Absolute* character. Incarnation presupposes a subject who transcends historical appearances. A distinction must be made between the Father as absolute Absolute and the Son as relative Absolute. The second person of the trinity is "universal person," while Jesus, who is the historical concreteness of this person whom we encounter in faith, is known as *kyrios*. Jesus is the way (Jn 10:7; 16:6), but not the goal. Who sees him sees the goal, i.e., the Father (Jn 12:45; 14:9), for there is a non-dualistic unity between them. But the Father is nevertheless greater than the Son (Mk 3:32; Mt 19:17; Jn 14:28). Believers are brought into this relationship (Jn 6:57; 17:21,23), but they are not identical with the Father nor the Son, just as the Father is not identical with the Son. Thus the confession "Jesus is Lord" demands a clearer interpretation.

From the very beginning the church found itself in opposed dimensions within its self-understanding: the concreteness of Christ and the universality of Christ. Christ was a Jew, Jesus of Nazareth, and as such he had to be seen and understood in connection with Israel's history. His life was limited by spatio-temporal conditions and his salvific work was very much determined by the expectations that were part of Jewish culture. Needless to say, concepts such as "reign of God," "Messiah," "Son of God," etc., come out of specific theological traditions which have little to do with Egypt, Babylon, or other cultures. The relationships between promise and fulfillment, expectation and realization were interpreted in widely diverse ways. What interests us here is only the specific relationship to a context which, by definition, is limiting and particular. The incarnation took place in Bethlehem, not in Athens. The gospels give many limiting circumstances such as places, dates, etc., to establish the incontestable trueness of the events in and around Jesus. The fact that Jesus could be experienced as salvation acquired its certitude and justification within limiting circumstances. Pilate is an example of this functional use of circumstances. Even the resurrection acquires its credibility through the same pattern of argumentation (cf. Mk 16:9ff.).

But in Jesus' actions there is also the opposite tendency. He breaks out of all limitations or cultural patterns and interpretations (cf. for example, his attitude towards Law, Mk 7:1ff.). He was sent by God as a symbol of divine love for the world, the *cosmos* (Jn 3:16). He was crucified on Golgatha at a particular time, but this spatio-temporal event had theological interest only insofar as it revealed a dimension beyond space and time. The crucified Christ is Lord of Lords (1 Cor 2:8). This is the title of the universal Lord of creation (Jn 1:3; Col 1:16). He is the "first-born of all creatures." (Col 1:15–17), immortal (Acts 2:24), the only-begotten Son (Jn 1:14), the universal center of reality (Eph 1:10), the beginning and also the end (Rev 1:8; 21:6; 22:13). The conclusion from all this is that not only do humans stand beneath the saving work of Christ, but also all creatures, including animals, plants, and even so-called "inert matter" such as stones and water. They all await the transforming power of God's Spirit (Rm 8:17), which alone reveals the true nature of and destiny of reality.

The difficulty comes in joining together these two opposite experiences: the concreteness and the universality of Christ. The manner and kind of unification has far-reaching consequences, not only for Christian self-understanding, but for the praxis of the church in a pluralistic world, as we will explain later.

Gotthold Ephraim Lessing posed the question with exceptional clarity: How can we overcome the hideous chasm between contingent, historical truth and necessary, rational truth? This problem was urgent during the Enlightenment, for it was unthinkable that a historically conditioned event could have unconditional meaning. All of Western philosophy and most of its theology followed a Platonic model in accepting that truth must be an eternal essence or the *being* of beings. The original form, that which was considered to be the *principium*, must exist eternally in the realm of ideas so that the immutability of truth—or the reliability of God's truth—could be understood. Already this last part of the statement demonstrates that the Platonic notion of *idea* was not merely a heuristic principle or a hypothesis needed for the possibility of perception, but rather, reflected in it, is a soteriological necessity which could not easily be abandoned. Lessing, and after him the adherents of German Classicism, were intelligent enough to define this connection very exactly. But the problem remains: How can we understand a limited, historical event, which by definition is an historical accident, as having consequences far beyond the context of the event; namely beyond the space, time, and meaning of the historically defined event?

In later developments of Western Christian theology we note a gradual widening of the area of theological discussion. In every case it is a quantitative widening, yet in all probability this corresponds also to a qualitative widening. Presumably we have reached a stage at which quantitative and qualitative changes must be interpreted in mutual relationship to one another; i.e., through dialectical viewpoints. This becomes an important point for our theological understanding of the *oecumene*.

I would like to explain my argument by means of an example; namely, the biblical understanding of salvation. Christian faith is grounded in the event of Christ's life and death, which reveals the trinitarian God. The belief itself is an aspect or an existential expression of the mystery. This is an *eternal truth*. But what does "eternal" mean here? Is not the existential expression of faith embedded in and marked by the specific context?

We could extend this idea: The mystery itself has a history. And this is supposedly a—if not *the*—specific biblical insight, which is based on a particular experience.

1. Israel's confession of faith begins with the grateful memory of historical experiences. God's saving action was revealed in Egypt when he called his people and led them out of slavery. Then he appeared on Mt. Sinai and revealed his saving will in the form of laws. Only later were these experiences broadened to include a theological interpretation of the beginning of the world in the teaching on creation. This implies that the interpretive movement is from a particular to the whole, or from the historical to the transhistorical or universal. A similar tendency can be seen in the development of the idea of Messiah. The earlier prophets were concerned with the redemption of the people of Israel. Later it was added that the peoples of the world would all be called together under the throne of Yahweh (Is 2:2ff.; Mi 4, etc) or that the whole of creation would be redeemed (Is 33:31ff.) in the new Covenant which is an immediate presence of God in a transformed world (Jer 33:31ff.).

2. This tendency was continued in the New Testament and further extended by means of the Greek understanding of *cosmos*. It was observed that the cosmic powers were transformed and newly ordered by the same power which had appeared in Jesus Christ (Col 1; 1 Cor 15). More and more salvation was seen in its universal dimension; i.e., not as an extraordinary and particular act

of God to rescue a chosen "remnant" (as in Amos and Zephaniah), but as the fulfillment of creation. Salvation was now seen within the horizon and scope of the history of creation.

3. The developments in the Western church led to a further unfolding of the implicit universality of salvation—even though we now see the ambiguity of this process. It has been said that the church inherited the structures of the Roman Empire. The climax of the Constantinian era can be seen in its faith that a Christianized state is an anticipation of the future eschatological order.

4. Today we feel that the Constantinian era is coming to an end, and therefore the church is beginning to have a completely new understanding of itself. Our experience, as distinct from earlier eras, is global and intercultural. Shockingly, this implies the brokenness of *every* cultural and religious expression. Our experience is oriented towards wholeness. Yet it suffers from today's breakdown of wholeness, which is destructive and has universal consequences.

Thus, while our attempt to understand our trinitarian faith in God in the light of Vedantic tradition (or vice versa) can lead us out of the narrowness of Western modes of thinking, nevertheless it also remains partial and is conditioned by specific historical experiences. There can be no universal hermeneutics, because language and communication are historical. When we try to elevate the whole to the level of concepts (and *salvation* is the whole), we end up in contradictions. This was true during the time of the New Testament and has not changed today. The result is the permanent crisis of theological knowledge or of humankind overall *coram Deo*.

The crisis is one of perception. What is necessary historically is continually new reorientations of our fundamental ways of thinking. The presupposition for this is that we have overcome the limitations of Jewish, Greek and Roman paradigms of salvation, whose undoubted value was for a completely different context.

To achieve this freedom we must learn the lesson which history itself teaches us. At all of the levels which were summarized above in four points, there is the danger of demonizing reality, when that which as such is particular is mistaken for a universal archetype. In other words, when we leave out of our awareness the symbolic difference, God's healing touch becomes instead a destructive blow. Keeping in mind this viewpoint, therefore, the whole of church history can now be recapitulated.

This means that at the first level—the experience of God in a particular historical event—exclusivist pride throws a cloak over the correct attitude of thankfulness and humility. A great part of so called Christian apologetics unfortunately falls under this category.

At the second level—the integration of a *cosmic* dimension—the problem is that reality as such is sanctified without first undergoing the spiritual transformation of death and resurrection. This is the danger of pantheism. Our experience of brokenness is real and disturbing: brokenness as such, as well as the experience of brokenness, have a destructive and fragmenting effect. Only when all things and events are seen in their true perspective, or when their true nature is understood, can creation be a *cosmos.*

The danger is clearest at the third level—the socio-political structures of human existence. Today the church of believers is no longer mistaken for a state church or a Christian empire. However, equally dangerous is a subtle tendency to identify salvation with certain social theories, political movements, or theological confessions.

We could summarize our argument as follows: Incarnation does not sanctify history, but qualitatively transforms it. This argument supports the thesis that the scope of the Christ event is by no means quantitative. Instead it refers to another *quality* present in *every* quantitatively defined area.

This means that in attempting to express suitably the extent of Christ's salvific work we should not look at maps of the world or models of the solar system, and then attempt to extend the lines beyond what our forefathers, limited by geography, could imagine. Nor need we base our efforts on a new chronological map, which would enable us to extend Christ's saving work further back to the "big bang" that began the universe, or perhaps forward to possible future catastrophes. All of these are quantitative attempts, examples of a "bad infinity" (Hegel). Instead we have to realize that salvation is *the* basic ground which underlies every real or possible event. It is an unmanifested creative ground "in, with, and under" every conditioned event.

This is clear to Paul. Abraham is justified by faith (Rm 4). He glorified God and did not doubt the promise (Rm 4:20); i.e., he lived from the creative ground of divine, saving reality which was already effective *before* Jesus Christ and then appeared in a specific way in him, although basically it cannot be limited by spatial-temporal categories and is therefore present at *all times* and *in all places* (Rm 1:19ff.). According to trinitarian theology, it is meaningful to say that Abraham, through his faith in God, experienced salvation mediated by the *implicit Christ*.

The argument which we are bringing forward here is simply this: because God is one, reality is one. The mystery revealed in Christ points to a trinitarian *perichoresis*, which comes forth from itself as the whole and likewise implies it, i.e., it encompasses every possible dimension. The trinity is the essence of holistic experience and totalistic understanding. It is essentially inclusive.

The three hypostases, persons, or relations interpenetrate one another perfectly. Thus, creation and redemption are not to be divided. They are not dissolvable into historical temporality. The Father's work of creation *is* a saving work and vice versa, and yet it is *through* the Son *in* the power of the Spirit. Consequently it is not permissible to accept Abraham's salvation as *per fidem* and yet to exclude non-Christians *post Christum natum* (after Christ is born) as an *extra ecclesiam*. Abraham's faith already is mediated by the trinity.

We can view the problem of Christ's salvific work within the perspective of the unity of reality from a second perspective; namely, in relationship to the development of philosophy in Europe. European history could be divided into three periods or paradigms, with a fourth now beginning.

1. The Greco-Roman worldview held sway until about the fourth century A.D. It was essentially anthropocentric, and is best summarized by Protagoras' famous sentence: man is the measure of all things. This assumes the measurability of things, and this acceptance is, in fact, the basic presupposition of Western culture and of theology. This *metron* was an inherent structure, which enabled each thing to appear in its own form. It was an aesthetic quality, since correct measure implies beauty (*kalon*), harmony, and the well-being of things, thus *salus*. Later, measuring became an external undertaking. Things were now measured by standardized measures, and this was dependent on human interest, and paid little attention to the indwelling harmony of things. *Humankind* becomes the measure, and this was the beginning of the history of Western science.

Other cultures, e.g., Indian culture, have another attitude to-

wards the measurable. Reality, *brahman*, the Absolute or God are
experienced as *sat* in such an overpowering way that measure
breaks down. In the end, reality is not measurable. It is the explo-
sion of being or, symbolically, the ecstatic dance of the god *Siva*.
The Indo-European root *ma* found in both *metron* and *maya*
means, to measure. *Maya* is the measurable, and precisely for this
reason it has a lesser degree of reality and in the end cannot be
definitive as the indeterminable (*anirvacaniya*) *brahman*. In the
history of Greek religion the same problem is seen in the tension
between Dionysius and Apollo. But in Greece, at least for the history of philosophy, Apollo was the victor.

2. This paradigm gave way to Christian theism, which gained
control around the fourth century. Throughout the Middle Ages
and the time of the Reformation we have a *theocentric* view which
is centered on God and God alone. Culture became inebriated with
consciousness of God. It maintained a grasp on and determined
every level: the cosmological, the social and the psychological. Everything that happened was constantly being safeguarded by a personal God, who was basically friendly, and in his unlimited power
reigned completely over history, which was therefore sacred history. Life had meaning because God gave it meaning. Creation had
come about because God had spoken. Humans could not know
God's secrets, but God had revealed all that was necessary for
human happiness, and God had given each person his or her place
and duty.[2]

3. The modern worldview emerged in the 16th and 17th centuries and led to the expansion of European civilization into the entire world. It is the basis of science, technology, and social structures which later led to democracy. It depends on the acceptance of
reality as a knowable order. Reality as personal becomes less certain and in any case loses its significance. Human identity and
fulfillment are no longer to be awaited in a transhistorical realm,
but consist primarily in knowledge of the laws of nature and the
use of this knowledge for the improvement of the external conditions of life.

It is not necessary to go into the details, for it is this worldview
which has lead to secularization, under which we all live. It has also
led to the fragmentation of human life and the many disasters connected with this fragmentation. It is also the basis for all of our
successes in science and technology, which make possible our mod-

ern social well-being, and this worldview would not be possible without democracy. Here, of course, the ambiguity of *all* historical reality should not be overlooked.

4. A post-modern worldview is gradually becoming evident as more and more people lose faith in the presuppositions of modernity. There are several causes for this. We mention two. Our encounters with different cultures and religions allows us to see their relativity. What they confront us with is not just a different content and different values, but different ways of perceiving and thinking. For this reason interreligious dialogue implies mutual relationship, enlightenment, and even opening up mutually new paths other than those to which we had grown accustomed.

Secondly, the consequences of an absolutized rationality are becoming so oppressive that "New Age" scientists, ecologists, feminist movements, meditative groups, etc., are now seeking a holistic paradigm by means of which they can experience reality. One of the main sources of this revolution in consciousness is science itself, which is discovering its own methodical limitations and bringing this discovery to general awareness.

What Immanuel Kant knew two hundred years ago, is today becoming the basis of a new branch of physics: that we cannot describe reality "as it is," but rather project our own categories onto it. Knowing depends on the knowing subject. This is not new. What is newly dawning upon us, however, is not only that there can be no clear division between the knowing subject and the known object, but that this is an abstraction that cannot deal correctly with the facts of how we actually come to know. This can transform our whole culture. Transcending the subject-object duality is, however, the basic experience of the mystics of all ages and cultures. Thus the theme of "mystics and modern physics" is fascinating, as is witnessed in a rapidly growing number of publications.

The scope of the Christ event must be understood within this context; viz., of a search for a holistic model of the world. God's universal salvific will cannot be questioned, since it is a consequence of his universal, unconditional love. This love expresses itself concretely wherever it is effectively working; i.e., in Jesus Christ and in the history which begins in him. The fact that it is not expressed only then or only there was demonstrated by the example of Abraham. The symbol of this love is sacramental communion (in word and sacrament), through which the new creation is coming to light. The *ecclesia* is not a place, but essentially this communion, according to the New Testament witnesses.

The sentence *extra ecclesiam nulla salus est* ("outside the church, no salvation") needs interpretation. If *ecclesia* is reduced to its historically conditioned and conditioning dimension, it is false, for *salus* is rooted in the transhistorical dimension of God's salvific work. This salvific will can be grasped historically, but only as *kenosis* (Phil 2:5). In Jesus' name there is salvation, but he is the "name above all names" (Phil 2:9), the one who perfectly abandons all particular claims and therefore can be universal. In Jesus' name the individual dies a death in order to become resurrected in personal communion, culminating in trinitarian wholeness (Jn 16:7). We recall what was said in the section "Realization in the Son" (chapter 10).

Thus the sentence "Jesus is Lord" cannot be interpreted in an exclusive sense and cannot be used in conjunction with a triumphalist ecclesiology. This Lord is the crucified one (1 Cor 1:23), who went the path of self-emptying so that the universal power of the Spirit over all peoples might be revealed (Acts 2) and so that each person may experience this saving reality in his/her own cultural (including religious) context; i.e., in his/her language and thus with another concrete name. We will discuss later what this means concretely.

The problem of the universality and concreteness of salvation in Jesus Christ reaches its climax once we realize that there must be an *encounter* with Jesus Christ, not just a theoretical insight which could be abstract.[3] Encounter is a personal communication. Personality means interrelation between those communicating and includes an element that basically cannot be objectivized. The salvation event is *pro me*, for me. But this *pro me* is based on a transpersonal structure: the interrelational trinity as a universal event, as the process of God's love.

In fact, salvation is granted in *the name* (Acts 4:12) which is above all names (Phil 2:9) and nowhere else. The name beyond all names refers to the apophatic extension of the concrete historical event (Jn 16:7). It refers to the intra-trinitarian communion realized in *perichoresis*, in which we share *in* the Spirit *through* Jesus Christ along the way *to* the Father. "Through our Lord Jesus Christ, in the unity of the Holy Spirit" has been the liturgical formula since the earliest times. Prayer is not addressed to Jesus, but becomes effective *through* him, in the intra-trinitarian mystery.

At this point it is important to explain the *per Christum.* We have already touched upon the question of the difference between Christ and us in relationship to participation in trinitarian love. In Vedantic thinking this distinction would be completely eliminated, for it is not trinitarian. Christian mystics (*The Cloud of Unknowing, Theologia Germanica*) however, refer to the fact that Christ possesses by *nature* what we receive *through grace*, leading to the scholastic understanding of the relationship between nature and grace. Jesus is the prototype, directly grounded in the source. He possesses an original fullness; our fullness is received. He dwells perfectly in the Father, while we have a share in the Father through him.

But this answer is insufficient, since it can only ground the difference, not the *per Christum.* Therefore, our suggestion is that we describe Christ as the power of God through which all creatures exist and participate in God. This would be a trinitarian understanding of the *per Christum* which is in relationship to creation-redemption-sanctification simultaneously. This corresponds to scholastic tradition, for here the act by which the Father engenders the Son is the same as the act by which he creates the world: the being of creation is also *per Christum.*[4]

Through Christ we are able to enter the trinity because he does not remain transhistorical, but appears in history and mediates historical concreteness, leading it into the Absolute. The model for the relationship between God and humans should not be understood as hierarchical, but as inclusive and as concentric participation with ever greater degrees of intensity (see Figure 13.1).

The non-dualistic (advaitic) polarity of concreteness and universality is an application of the general polarity of the one and the many, which we presented while discussing the symbol of the trinity. This polarity is the horizon for our interpretation of the Christ event. Christ is the concrete name for God's universal action. Salvation is perfectly immanent wherever the depth dimension of reality breaks forth, causing perfect transcendence to be manifest. *Every authentic religious tradition reflects such a breakthrough in history.* Each breakthrough of this sort is a reflection of the eternal intra-trinitarian *perichoresis.* In this name all names which are authentic; i.e., communion of the personal, are called to salvation.

Hierarchical Model   Participation Model

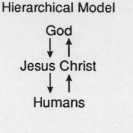

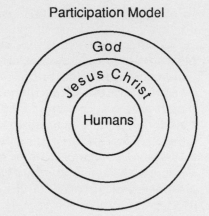

Figure 13.1

The concreteness of the Christ event implies its relativity. The Messiah (Christ) is understood as the fulfillment of Israel's history. Within this framework he not only announces, but embodies absolute truth. Outside this cultural-historical framework, however, the concrete symbol is meaningless. It is a *relative absolute:* absolute because it is grounded in the ground of wholeness, relative because it is historically conditioned. The notion of a *relative absolute* makes possible and requires the next step, absolute relativity. For the Absolute *is* not. Its *is* is in a form, i.e., concrete. In the trinitarian *perichoresis* the relative absolute and the absolute relative are constantly sublated into the Spirit, who creates unity in pluriformity. Reality participates in the Spirit through God's eternal power of love in the beginning. This movement is unity—the whole. Outside it there is nothing.

Absolute relativity qualifies the relative absolute, and conversely. Each empties itself of its substantiality in relationship to the other. Thus they pass over to the other. It follows, therefore, that God is perfectly in Christ and thus Christ is salvation and the *kyrios.* Outside this force-field (of the name, which describes personal relationship) there is no salvation because there is no outside. Therefore, humans have freedom to reject any participation in God. This is sin and the sin remains as long as there is no communion in, through and with God. As long as we continue to objectivify the name, i.e., misuse its absolute absoluteness, we are not *in* him. His call awakens us as persons. As long as we are persons, our sin is overcome.

Redemption by Another—Self-Redemption

The terminology of the last section involves an imprecision, which is typical of advaitic thinking. Who is the "I" or "we" who overcomes sin? Who is the subject in the event of grace?

In Vedanta only *brahman* can be understood as subject. The "I" (*jiva*) is not. It *is* only in recognizing its true identity which is *brahman*. The trinitarian notion of person implies that persons come to recognize their true identity not *in* themselves, but *in* God, i.e., in the perichoretic interrelation. Thus salvation is given in the name which is above all names, and is therefore potentially *in* all names. A call or calling-to is required to awaken personality. The Son and the Father are not-two. The Son is what he is in the Father. And this mutuality holds true for all three persons of the trinity. The perichoretic subject is the mystery of personality as such.

Our existence as persons who are redeemed from sin makes us one with God and yet not identical with him. We are not identical with him nor with other persons. This Advaita is reflected in the apparent contradiction of self-redemption and redemption by another. The contradiction is only apparent, and would only become real if the notion of God were objectivized; i.e., if the transcendent aspect of grace were to be overemphasized. In a conception of reality where grace is present as the unity of transcendent immanence and immanent transcendence, the contradiction between self-redemption and redemption by another is meaningless.

This is the case in Vedanta, in all Eastern paths of meditation (even Buddhistic ones), and also in the trinitarian experience of God. Superficially, Vedanta seems to accept "self-redemption." Thus Sankara says: "A father may command his son or someone else to wipe out his financial debt, but no one besides he himself can free him from his illusion" (i.e., his ensnarement in *samsara*).[5] In the same text, however, three things are needed for salvation (*moksa*): birth as a human (which makes possible decisions), longing for *moksa*, and the capacity to trust an experienced master. Only by the grace of God (*mahapurusa*), however, can all three of these conditions be fulfilled.[6] A famous text in India, obligatory for this context, and one which is found in two of the most important Upanishads (KU II.23; MU III,2,3), proclaims:

> That self (*atman*) cannot be gained by knowledge, nor by understanding, nor by much learning. He whom the self chooses, by him the self can be gained.

Only by devotion to God (*bhakti*), which is dependent on faith

(*sraddha*) can a person empty him/herself of all egotistic wishes
and attitudes so that God may take hold of him/her. In S. Radhakrishnan's words: "The obstacles to this God-possession are our
own virtues, pride, knowledge, our subtle demands and our unconscious assumptions and prejudices. We must empty ourselves of all
desires and wait in trust on the Supreme Being. To fit God's pattern, all our claims are to be surrendered."[7] This is not neo-Ve-
danta, but is exactly what Sankara means.[8]

Radhakrishnan's reference to the Pelagian controversy is, however, misleading,[9] for Augustine's concept of God is quite different
from Sankara's. The European categories of self-redemption and
redemption by another cannot be transposed to India. For in the
Upanishads and the Gita *atman* is the center of the person. The
goal is to free it from the illusion of egotism. To the extent that the
ego disappears, *atman* becomes known. It is the subject of this
process, and as such, immanent as well as remaining the transcendent ground of reality in general. "Self"-redemption is "*atman*"-
redemption; *atman* is likewise subject and object of the salvation
event. Subjectivity and objectivity disappear as opposed, and this is
Advaita. Consequently "self-redemption" and "redemption by
God" are identical.

It should not be difficult now to apply these ideas to the problem of who the subject of meditation is—who exactly "does" the
meditating. Each person who meditates experiences a process
which begins with his/her own efforts and gradually leads him further and further from egotistical willing; i.e., it leads to letting
oneself be led. If this exercise is forced, the result may be a certain
concentration (*dharana*), but it is not properly meditation
(*dhyana*). Such a person will not be ready for the detachment where
truly *it* meditates. The more there is detachment from the controlling and directing ego, the deeper the meditation. Thus the *subject*
of meditation is in no way the ego, but the meditated "object"—in
the end, God, who is beyond all objectivity. This is what lies at the
basis of Paul's experience when he says that he no longer lives, but
Christ lives in him (Gal 2:20). Who is properly the subject who
speaks this sentence? A meaningful answer can only be given in an
advaitic way, and this is confirmed by Christian mysticism.

Thus the mystical experience is always understood as the gift
of God's gratuitous grace. The human techniques of prayer or meditation serve only indirectly as preparations. They are a means of
opening up the human spirit.[10] Naturally the person is active. The

driving power, however, is not the ego (*sarx* in Paul), but the divine
Spirit (*pneuma*). This is the judgment of Suso, the *Cloud of Unknowing* (esp. chs. 24, 71) and *Theologia Germanica* (chs. 44, 49,
51). Nevertheless, a consciously willed decision, by which we open
ourselves to grace, is still required.

The *Cloud of Unknowing* considers *prayer* as the correct preparation for mystical union with God (ch. 35). Contemplation is a
pure gift of grace: from it comes an "enabling of the soul" to see
God (ch. 71). The same ideas are found in Teresa of Avila, for
whom the highest degree of prayer is a mystical state that depends
on "infused recollection."[11]

Whether they experience grace as coming from outside or from
within depends on the theological models at the basis of the expectation. Even "from within" does not mean something which comes
from the ego, but rather from God indwelling. He is more interior
to the soul than the soul is to itself, to use the language of both
Augustine and Luther.[12]

We see here an extensive parallel to the experience of *atman*,
the subject of all knowing. Thus Paul, too, claims that it is not the
"I" which experiences revelation (2 Cor 12:2ff.) and would therefore be the subject of faith, but rather the Spirit. If the experience of
faith were carried out by the ego, there would be no sublation of
duality in the one reality of Spirit, but only more, even stronger,
emprisonment within egocentricity (Rm 3:27; 4:2; 1 Cor 1:29,31; 2
Cor 12:5; Gal 6:14; Ja 4:16).

We have already discussed the parallel here between Pauline,
as well as Reformation theology and the Indian Advaita Vedanta;
viz, when we treated Luther's trinitarian theology. There we saw
that the opposite of being determined advaitically is being sinful.
For Paul as well as for Luther, and for the Bhagavad Gita as well as
for Sankara, sin is humankind's striving to make itself into God:
not by realizing the self, but by preoccupation with the ego. The
root of evil is in this egocentric separation, which Vedanta consigns
to the area of the cognitive, Christianity more to the area of the
affective.

The basic attitude of the mystic as well as the Advaitin is receptivity. The intensity of our receptivity is influenced by behavior or
habits, and these are karmically conditioned. Karmic conditioning
(*samsara*) can only be broken by the other dimension (*atman*). *Karman* is a condition, causal connectedness, which is overcome by the
unconditional—that is, by grace. If there were nothing but *kar-*

man, there could be no end to *samsara*, and *atman* would then be conditioned, which would be a contradiction. Within *samsara* we discover something over which we have no control. In India this inexorable reality was called *atman*; in Christianity, the Holy Spirit.

Grace and human will are the two poles of a single basic advaitic experience. Gregory of Nyssa formulates it as follows: Just as God's grace cannot come into the soul which flees from its salvation, so too the power of human virtue is not enough by itself to raise souls to perfection if grace is lacking.[13] Grace is neither a gift which is given on the basis of our merits, nor something quantitatively determinable, which is added to the ego. On the contrary, grace is "God's presence in us,"[14] which transforms, renews, and introduces our essential humanness into the divine *perichoresis*. The human and the divine wills do not converge in an identity, nor are they two different centers. This is precisely what is experienced in authentic meditation.

Therefore we can by no means speak of self-redemption. Instead, as we explained, the self is redeemed by the Self (*atman*): we prepare ourselves for the experience, which is precisely what the Christian does in prayer or in hearing the word of sacred scripture. Humans must open the door, as Karl Barth says, so that Christ can enter. But already the motivation and power for such preparation is the work of the Spirit, and it should not be overlooked that Christ can even come through closed doors (Jn 20:19f.).[15] The fully spontaneous enlightenment experience of Advaita, without any preparatory exercise, is both known and treasured in India also.

Clement of Alexandria uses a striking image. The person united in knowledge and love with God has become a flute which is played by the Spirit of God.[16] But the complete advaitic experience goes one step further: the person is so perfectly permeated by the Spirit that the Spirit-Human becomes the flute and likewise the one playing it.

Syncretism or Creative Integration

When the term "syncretism" is used, there is almost always a pointing of the finger. What are we being warned about? And what does the term mean?

It is very indicative that the World Council of Churches, in making recommendations on dialogue, devotes an entire section to the problem of syncretism.[17] It is a danger to be warned against, although in fact it is not completely unavoidable if the Christian message is to be related to given situations.

Every translation is an interpretation. Every act of understanding depends on unique circumstances, and therefore involves interpretation. It is not just a matter of finding equivalent terms to translate the original text of the New Testament. The hermeneutical problems is much more complex, as the theological debates of the last decades demonstrate.[18] The cultural context not only leaves its mark on certain concepts, but also forms ways of thinking which are not interchangeable. This can be illustrated by the example of the term for truth.[19]

The Greek concept of truth *aletheia* refers to an active mental operation of pulling back the veil which conceals the real, so that what *is* may *show* itself. What *is* comes under the light of knowledge. Since the veil can always return and knowledge become obscured, this notion of truth is historically determined.[20] The Latin term *veritas* points more to the permanence of things (and is thus in tension with the Buddhist *vidya*), while the English *truth* describes more forcefully the trustworthiness of a situation as do also its adjectival forms. The Hebrew word *emeth*, however, means ultimate dependability, and therefore refers directly to God. By contrast the Sanskrit *satya* has practically no epistemological or moral overtones. *Satya* is the direct manifestation of *sat*, being. In *satya*, being is as it is without having any need of the mind's mediative or knowing role.

The various expressions depict different forms of learning about truth. They cannot be reduced one to the other. However, they do not exclude one another. On the contrary, each concept brings to light a new aspect. We can therefore speak of a complementarity of thought-forms.

Another, even more rewarding hermeneutical study involves the translation of the word *God* into the Indian spiritual world. If we choose the lexically accurate term *deva* (Latin: *deus*), a serious theological error results. For *deva* is a finite being, which exists above the mundane level of the world. Thus it is more directly something angelic, rather than the Absolute or God. For this reason Christians in India usually translate the term "God" by *isvara*. But this term is problematic. As we saw above, in Vedantic thinking *isvara* is only a qualified self-manifestation of the Most High, the approximate equivalent of the Greek Logos. The only word which corresponds to *theos* is *brahman*. *Brahman*, however, is neutral;

i.e., impersonal, and thus we demonstrated above that the doctrine of the trinity is needed to actually bring together the notions of *God* and *brahman.*

In India the basic *structures of perception* are different from those in Europe. And they were already different in Jerusalem and in Athens or Rome. Naturally there is no question here of contradictory opposites, which would render any attempt at understanding the impossible. It would be better to speak of different "phases," but this term is ambiguous. For truth insofar as it is historical is concrete. Thus the gospel cannot claim any one thought structure or language as its own. In *all* languages, each as a specific expression, it never loses its identity as gospel. Its identity can only be based on an insight which is the unity of reality, and this is fulfilled in many forms. The gospel grew up with the cultures it first touched. Thus Christianity today is essentially "the complex Hebraic-Hellenistic-Greek-Latin-Celtic-Gothic-modern religion *converted* to Christ more or less successfully."[21] This is what the incarnation implies, and it is unavoidably syncretistic.

If we were to accept *a priori* that the gospel has been "diluted" or lost in the process, we would be accusing the Holy Spirit of being a liar. For the ongoing incarnation in the Holy Spirit, which recognizes neither spatio-temporal nor cultural nor religious border (Jn 3:8) is better expressed as a building up of the kingdom experience of the wisdom and depths of God. The Son must die so that the Spirit can be universally effective (Jn 16:7); but this always remains connected to the Son who has established a unique standard. It is this connection that the "enthusiasts" of all ages had difficulty with. In this same Spirit Jesus promises that we will do greater works than the Son (Jn 14:22). Thus we can conclude that the "Christian experience" develops as it penetrates and assimilates other cultures and thought forms—similar to salt or yeast.

Thus syncretism cannot be avoided. It is a sign of life in the Spirit. The Guidelines of the World Council of Churches warn against the danger that occurs when a religion is not interpreted "in its own terms," but in the symbols and language of another faith (Thesis 27). This should not be allowed on the basis of hermeneutical considerations as well as out of respect for the integrity of the partner in dialogue.

The thesis is correct in warning against superficiality, but in the end it is unhistorical and dodges the deeper problem of interreligious hermeneutics. What would Christianity's "own terms" be? If Aramaic (Jesus' language) were made the norm for Christian terms this already would involve killing the Spirit of the gospel, which involves the dialectic of incarnation (he has become present in every created situation—*pro me*) and resurrection (he is not here or there). If we withdraw to dogmatically defined terms such as creation in order to defend our position against the Hindu teaching of *karman*, creation must still be interpreted. This interpretation must match the context, and today this involves more than it did in the time of Darwin and the Europe-centered world of the 19th and early 20th centuries. The meaning of the gospel message concerning creation can perhaps be stated more effectively today in terms of the *karman*-theory and by showing how *karman* is overcome by *moksa*, rather than by classical Western categories.

The problem with syncretism is in other areas, and the WCC declarations also recognize this. We should guard against conscious and unconscious attempts to create a new religion, which would consist in eclectically chosen elements of various religions and ideologies (Thesis 26). This thesis can be understood in different ways. It is clear that syncretism should not serve other purposes. There may be hidden ideological, political, or other motives behind our attempts to bring the Indian gurus into Christianity without first facing up to the spiritual challenge this idea presents. Conversely, the rejection of syncretism may also be motivated by power politics; for example, when liberation theology is rejected as "unbiblical," even though it can be shown that it is the product of Marxist analysis integrated into Christianity. Both readiness for and rejection of syncretism must be examined by analyzing their motives. The syncretistic element *may* bring back to life an important and *latent* tendency present within one's own tradition, or it may have a deepening function as well as overall hermeneutical value—though not necessarily.

The original meaning of the term *syncretism* is a political one: different political parties in ancient Crete joined in one action in order to confront a common enemy. It is not by chance that the term *syncretism* has also been connected to the observation of organic life. It is related to wholeness and the interrelation of different life-processes, as this is described by the laws of *assimilation* and *dissimilation*. In a simplified way, whatever is assimilated must have been integratable, and what is dissimilated was not able to be integrated. Life is only possible when both processes are present. Things which can be integrated promote the growth of an organism and help it develop in the sense of favoring the latent powers and tendencies that produce fruit. Foreign bodies are repulsed, since they disturb the organism. What can be assimilated, and what will remain foreign, is continually being tested wherever there is contact between the organism and its environment.

In a similar way, human history can be understood as a field of interrelationships of various cultures and religions. In this process, the question of truth is not bracketed or methodically reduced to something relativistic. Rather, it encompasses the process and sees its concrete hermeneutics in historical relationships which can be characterized as assimilation and dissimilation.

But because the term syncretism has acquired (because of Christianity's own history) a negative connotation of eclecticism or opportunism, it is better to avoid it and replace it with the notion of *creative integration*. This term also better describes the historical relationship of Indian religions to one another—better than the vague (and frequently condescending) term, "tolerance," or the polemicized notion of syncretism. *Creative integration* could provide a key to understand the encounter of different religions in today's world. Also by bringing in the third person of the trinity to interpret the phenomenon of creativity we would be highlighting the transtemporal significance of this encounter. The result of such an event is not a super-religion which integrates all the others, but rather each religion realizing its own deeper identity, since it is assumed that each religion is the subject of its own history.

Understanding is not just a cognitive act. The truth question has many dimensions, and the use of a multidimensional methodology implies that we are able to pose the question over and over using new terms. Creative integration signifies the growth and maturation of the *whole* person and *whole* cultures. A superficial syncretism which "arises from enthusiasm or a rationalistic indifference, or as a self-proclaimed mixture of truths which have not truly been practiced,"[22] is to be rejected. It would not express the freedom of God's children, but rather the greatest lack of freedom and confusion stemming from poverty of insight. For integration there must be a center, the very heart of one's own faith. It requires that we have subjected ourselves to the problem at stake.

Dialogue—Mission—Conversion

Interreligious dialogue has become the most important instance of what we are calling *creative integration*. We cannot present here a complete theory of dialogue, but will discuss a few of the points that have been developed in the present study.

At the very beginning of any discussion about dialogue is the realization that we today are living, *nolens volens*, in a dialogical situation. I can know my individual self only in the tension of encountering a thou. This I-Thou tension is itself the dialogical situation. It is to be distinguished from the objectivized I-it relationship, which is secondary to the history of individuals or cultures. Here the "thou" is the source of or even the necessary presupposition for self-knowledge. This holds true for encounters between different, coexisting cultures and religions. Every religion formulates its own dogmas in mutual relationship to—in limiting or rejecting—other religions or other forms of thinking. Often one's own latent idea is brought to consciousness because of a challenge from another. This phenomenon can be observed in the history of Christianity as well as in Vedanta's history of thought.[23]

Our "own" consciousness is therefore like a light which is switched on in the meeting with another. However, what is new in today's interreligious situation could be described as a *worldwide* and *conscious* application of this principle to interreligious dialogue, with the goal of cooperation in all areas of life.

It is striking that Christians are foremost in seeking out interreligious dialogue. Practically all the initiatives in programs of interreligious dialogue until now have come from Christian groups. There are historical and political reasons for this, connected with the heritage of the Enlightenment, secularism and a growing de-Christianization of the West. This is due also to Christian self-understanding: they are leaven, light or salt for the world, and this is connected with the incarnation. Only when we can treat others in their otherness, as a thou and as a source for our self-understanding is true brotherhood/sisterhood possible between all peoples. When the dialogue partners recognize their relativity— and this means relationality—dialogue becomes fruitful. In such encounters Christians should be critical catalysts who stimulate faith, love, and hope. This means taking responsibility for the world and holding out for justice and peace in other religions.[24]

The central problem of dialogue is hermeneutical. In this area of hermeneutics two viewpoints emerge:

1. When the dialogue partner becomes for me a source of my own self-understanding, he/she is also a source of my understanding of God. In general we become free to open new horizons when we discover the relativity of our own culture, language, and theolo-

gies. On this basis Advaita Vedanta can become a source for a specifically Christian trinitarian understanding of God, as we have
tried to demonstrate here.

   2. It is not so much a question of finding in the partner's position analogous terms for one's own system. Rather, we try to clarify *equivalent functions* of our own practices, symbols and terms,
in order to recognize, adapt, and fulfill the existential *meaning* of
religious reality which comes to light in the encounter.

   In order to see more clearly the complex reality of "dialogue
with other religions," we will distinguish three levels and three
dimensions of dialogue. The three levels describe the various
aspects of the dialogical situation, while the dimensions allow us to
recognize the goals of dialogue. Levels and dimensions are not
identical, though interconnected.

Levels of the Dialogue

   We begin with a description of the dialogical situation on three
levels:

   1. The first and most basic level of dialogue is the whole area
of spiritual experience, which precedes the Logos and thus also
theological concepts. Paul's *anthropos pneumatikos* is not the
homo theologicus of religious traditions. This distinction opens up
a path for overcoming self-justifying conduct expressed as dogmatic rigidity. I refer back to what was presented in chapter 11 and
add that what is meant is neither a subjectivistic understanding of
experience nor an uncontrolled syncretism in the area of spirituality. Subjectivism in spiritual experience can be overcome by recognizing the experience as an *encounter* with the Absolute, mediated
historically in various ways as human experience. "Experience"
and "revelation" imply one another. Uncontrolled syncretism can
be overcome if the Spirit dimension enters into a dialogical relationship with the Logos. Thus when a Christian and a Vedantin
meditate together in silence, both experience something which enables them to go beyond the conceptual language of dogmatics.
This does not mean that their experiences are identical. This cannot be decided since each decision assumes a linguistic; i.e., a relative, expression of the spiritual. Both experiences can, however, be
analogous in referring those involved in the encounter to praxis,
which may enable them, acting in common, to overcome alienation
and the absolutizing of their own viewpoints.

The area of spiritual experience makes dialogue possible as a twofold introduction to praxis: as mutual help towards the practice of spiritual ways of living (*sadhana*) in prayer and meditation, and as common realization of spiritual experiences in the socio-political arena.

2. The second level of interreligious dialogue is the area of *theological reflection*, which necessarily involves the Logos. The agreements as well as the differences between different religions have to be precisely formulated so that there can be a theological learning process on both sides. Each partner is a light for the other and enables him/her to see better the depths of his/her own tradition. The religion of the partner is like a sounding board in which one's own terms and symbols acquire new over- or undertones. In this study Advaita Vedanta was such a sounding board that caused the symbol of the trinity to resonate in a new way.

The essential differences between Vedanta and Christian ideas of God have become clearer. This difference—to combat a common prejudice—is not that Vedanta claims God and humans are identical, while Christianity maintains a basic division. Advaita is not identity, but a form of polarity.

This difference can be seen especially in three problem areas:

a) Personal trinitarian experience is growth in a dynamic nonduality, whereas reality in Advaita Vedanta is essentially static; i.e., it consists in a return to what is essentially undivided and present in the silence of being (*sat*).

b) The experience of Christ as a personal, advaitic experience ("The Father and I are one") is historically mediated. It integrates temporality in the ways that were discussed above many times. It is concrete and therefore goes beyond the ideas of Advaita Vedanta. It could be said that Jesus' experience both contains advaitic experience and proceeds towards a goal. It reaches its climax in the union of a personal encounter: i.e., it is in a perpetual dynamic of becoming one. The New Testament's experience of a trinitarian dynamism, as a perichoretic movement mediated by the Spirit, came out of the Old Testament's encounter between God and humans. Humans are determined by their participation in this process. Therefore it is up to us to complete the path of non-duality of Advaita Vedanta in the dynamic non-duality of the trinity.

c) For the Christian the power of evil is overcome in Christ in principle, even though it does not disappear existentially. Humans remain *simul iustus et peccator*. There is indeed a growth involved in Christian identity or a divinization (*theopoiesis*), yet no one is

jivanmukta, viz., a perfect being who is not even potentially under
the power of sin or ignorance, as Vedanta teaches.

We may bring into relationship the concept of the Absolute in
Advaita Vedanta and the Christian trinitarian concept of God in
the following way. That which is beyond all qualities and therefore
to be understood as the source *nirguna brahman* corresponds to the
Father; the Absolute in its threefold, revealed form *saguna brahman* corresponds to the Son; and *atman* as the self of all beings is
the equivalent of the Spirit.

Figure 13.2 brings out the significant difference between the
Vedanta and the trinity. In Vedanta there can only be a *perichoresis*
between *nirguna brahman* and *atman.* The other relations have no
ultimately ontic qualities. Thus Advaita cannot integrate the areas
of the Son (history, the concrete).

The result of this is that in some of Indian spirituality there is a
tendency to neglect the concrete,[25] and the consequences of this are
negative with regard to human realities. The Indian social situation
is an eloquent example of this inherent danger.

This is not, however, consequent upon, but rather inconse-
quent with advaitic experience, which reformers such as Vivekananda, Gandhi, and others continue to emphasize. To reform Hinduism on this point means helping it discover its own profundity
so that it can reach complete advaitic integration in practice as well
as in theory.

Another danger, probably connected to this blindness to real
history, is: the belief that humans during this life can reach a point
of being immune from the potential power of evil—in other words,
the ideal of *jivanmukta.* The Yogi experiences the "kingdom of
God" interiorly, but this has no effect on his external relationship.
But this in itself demonstrates how much the human remains human. Trinitarian realism, which describes human life as simultaneous existence and takes seriously the power of sin, is therefore
ready to take a stance against it. In the light of the real history
situation of humankind, this would seem to be called for.

This, then, is an important theme for future dialogue. An integrated advaitic consciousness should not simply declare the real
alienations of history as unreal. They must be overcome by means
of an integration. Here the advaitic doctrine of the trinity offers
important help for dialogue with India, for it can make intelligible
the meaning of incarnation in connection with the Vedantic experience of Advaita. Conversely our theoretical knowledge does not
exempt us from the responsibility of really undertaking the advai-

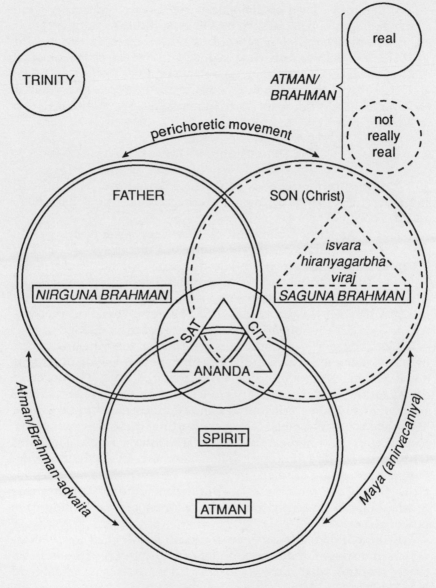

Figure 13.2

tic experience so that it might renew us spiritually. The fact that we have pointed out a certain lack of consequentiality in Indian advaitic thinking does not mean that we discount its truth!

3. The third level of dialogue is the area of communitarian living and common social activity. This is going on anyway, yet it requires reflection. If our reflections with regard to the lack of historicity in the Vedantic view of unity are correct, the theological dialogue will result in a social-ethical motivation for both partners, and in fact it is the common responsibility of Western as well as Oriental cultures for the future of humankind. We will go into this in chapter 14.

The Dimensions of Dialogue

Along with the three levels we can distinguish three *dimensions* of interreligious dialogue: the theological, the pedagogical, and the political.

The *theological dimension* is that the partners are basing themselves on and exercising themselves in their own faith as they learn humility and respect for the otherness of the partner. Dialogue is a form of *kenosis*. We learn that we cannot possess the Absolute. Rather, in common with brothers and sisters who are and remain other to us, we go towards the Absolute. This is the theological ground for the solidarity and love practiced in dialogue.

The *pedagogical dimension* is the mutual learning and teaching. The dialogue partners enlighten one another and open up new doors to their own traditions in very profound ways. The *political dimension* consists in solidarity with the oppressed. This corresponds to God's liberating reality and demonstrates it in concrete historical ways. The advaitic understanding of the unity of reality forbids us from either identifying our freedom in and through God with social freedom or keeping them separate. In dialogue we recognize that we are brothers and sisters because there is one God. However, at the same time it should not be forgotten that this brotherhood is presently hidden because of present exploitative power structures.

I would like to discuss some of the *ecclesiological* conclusions which come out of this chapter under three headings without, however, claiming that this is in any way already a *dialogical ecclesiology*.

1. Can the church lay exclusive claim to Christ, the second person of the trinity, since this claim would seem to be an attempt to confine him *intra muros*, more of a possessive than a devotional attitude?

My suggestion for finding an answer involves two steps. First, we must realize that many people are inspired by the person and teaching of Jesus Christ, people who do not (or do not wish to) belong to the institutionalized church. This is especially true in India and Eastern Asia, but also more frequently in Europe and America. Such people maintain the direct historical line with Jesus Christ by means of sacred scripture. Since they are developing a consciousness and a conscience based on Christ (naturally, in different degrees) and are trying to find their own way to be followers, it is phenomenologically clear that this must be called the salvific work of Christ. The theological interpretation of this phenomenon is another matter, but the fact itself cannot be ignored.

Secondly, there are people, whole movements, and traditions which do not reflect the light and life of the historical Jesus Christ, but are implicitly living in him, with him and under his rule. They are not in any historical relationship to Jesus Christ, but may have a transhistorical link to him in the Holy Spirit. They do not call upon his name, but "act" in it (Mt 25:31ff.; Mt 7:21). On the basis of what we have said concerning a trinitarian understanding of Christ's work of salvation, the *perichoresis* of reality, and the unity of creation and redemption, it is impossible to exclude such people from Christ's work of salvation.

In this context we would like to comment on the description of other believers as "anonymous Christians" (Rahner). When Christians in dialogue with others recognize that their dialogue partner is a sister or brother under one God, different yet within the scope of Christ's salvific work, it can be inconvenient to call them part of Christ's salvific work. While the term "anonymous Christians" is problematic, it cannot be given up without replacing it with something else, for it expresses a *necessary* theological fact.[26] The term is unfortunate because it applies the ecclesiastical term "Christian" to another context, which causes the dialogue partner to suspect ecclesiastical imperialism. Besides, this partner is not anonymous. Thus we suggest dropping the term and replacing it with the *implicit Christ* in different religions. This term is not oriented to the church, but to reality as universally trinitarian—within which Christ is one moment. It uses the ontological categories of implication and explication, which we have already discussed. Thus, too, we are not denying that the historical explication of the implicit Christ in Jesus of Nazareth is unique. Likewise, no justification is needed when we learn that this implicit can work in other ways. Of course the Christian must be prepared to accept, for instance, an implicit Buddha in Christianity.

This has consequences for our understanding of the church. No notion of church can be derived from one or other institutionalized, denominational form. Nor can there be an abstract "world church," which in fact does not exist. There can only be a *communio sanctorum*, which expresses the eschatological dimension of reality and is thus becoming. Since eschatological fulfillment refers to the true nature of creation and the divine will which is expressed in it, the significance of the *communio sanctorum* is universal. It is realized by the power of the Spirit, who cannot be contained by human ideas and institutional borders. It is a *communio* of "men and women of good will" (Lk 2:14). And this is manifested in various religions as well as in secular societies, and to an extent in every human heart.

2. Jesus Christ or Jesus as the Christ (Messiah) is undoubtedly to Christian experience the fulfillment of all the hopes and expectations of Israel's history or of Israelite religion. The historical phenomenon "Jesus the Christ" must be seen against this background, and this is what the church claimed against Marcion. However, the incarnation is not just an historically conditioned event, but rather history with universal meaning (Jn 3:16). Its universal dimension cannot be limited to the particular manifestation. Jesus is embedded in the history of Israel, but the history of Israel is not the universal model for history as such, or for the transhistorical dimension of reality.

This means that we can find other manifestations of the Christ event which are from God's grace as part of the trinitarian rhythm. They flow forth and are examples of other *forms* of fulfillment. This paradigm suggests that the universal Christ of the perichoretic process of the trinity, is not only seen as Messiah, but also as the *Tathagata*, who enters into truth, i.e., the Buddha. There is no historical link between the two, but a transhistorical interrelationality.

It should not be too difficult for Christian theology to relate these other manifestations to Jesus Christ and work out needed distinctions on the basis of one simple theological insight: God is One and therefore God does not contradict himself. Thus, we can accept that whatever does not contradict the experience of the historical Jesus Christ, could be regarded as the saving work of the trinitarian God.[27] Even the New Testament, within its extremely limited historical and geographical horizon, reflects such experiences: Who is not against us is for us (Mk 9:40). How much more should we, with our broadened intercultural context, follow the same advice!

The New Testament already applies the advaitic relationship between the Father and the Son to whoever is within the works or power of the Son (Mt 10:40; Lk 10:22). They are included as part of a trinitarian love. The consequence of the intimacy between Father and Son (Jn 5:19ff.; 17:10–21) is that the Father as source is only accessible through something realized in the Son (Jn 14:6f.). The realization of the eternal Father in the eternal Son is the universal event of trinitarian self-manifestation. The statement that no one comes to the Father except through the Son (Jn 14:6) is thus inclusive: it describes trinitarian unity where the Father is the ground, and the Son its realization. The trinity is a symbol for God's finality-oriented self-movement, which means that there is a way. This way is visible in Jesus Christ. By experiencing being as a way we come to the Father as source, who realizes everything that is real in the Son (Jn 14:10–24). In fact, no one experiences the Father except through the Son and no one experiences the source except through its realization. No one experiences the "whence" unless it is experienced in the "whither" of his/her life.

3. The question concerning Jesus Christ is not so much the problem of whether and where he is present, but of whether we recognize his presence. The continual process of finding an answer to this problem is itself a moment in God's salvation history. It is the process of *ecclesia.* Since it is said that we participate in the divine nature (2 Pet 1:4), we do share in the trinitarian process in all its dimensions. Since we have been freed in order to have a share in the freedom of children of God (Rm 8:14,17,21), we are no longer completely bound by historical conditions, but participate in the transhistorical power of the Spirit. This also means that our lives reflect divine creativity. Through our relationship to all other forms or manifestations of divine life we are continually expanding, concretizing, and realizing God's creativity. In this we *are* the body of the Christ of glory.

This knowledge frees theology from its over-rigid fixation on solving the dogmatic problems of the past regarding this question. We saw that theology has *always* learned about and carried out its hermeneutical and apologetic tasks in dialogue with peoples of other faiths. What we should not forget is that the witnessing (*martyrion*) on the part of early Christians was not directed against a certain *religion,* but against the *idolization of the finite* in every religion: for example, against Jewish law or the Roman cult of Caesar. This factual basis was the criterium which led Christians to become martyrs.

In interpreting this fact for today's more universal forum of religions and ideologies, the criterium cannot be some one religion or ideology, but the problem of idolizing the finite. Wherever such idolization is found, "law" is dominating. Wherever it is overcome, "gospel" has come to the light—throughout all religions and ideologies. Christians are called to be catalysts in this process of discernment and clarification.

In dialogue we do not give up our own identity, but achieve it anew in a more all-encompassing context. Thus, for example, there can be an implementarity between Advaita and the trinity, remembering however that the knowing process which recommends this relationship is also a path leading to God. In *this* sense dialogue has a missionary aspect. Mission, as I have suggested elsewhere,[28] should be taken as a *maieutic* process which makes the implicit Christ as explicit as possible. Christ is always already present, for he is the light that enlightens every person coming into the world (Jn 1:9). But this missionary "explication" implies a becoming aware of this fact, a continuation of the incarnation through the Spirit. The criterium is not Christianity as European, but the universal power of Christ's spirit as proclaimed in the New Testament —as historically conditioned and thus in need of interpretation.

Dialogue is conscious participation in Christ and his universal work of salvation. Mission is *maieutics.* Christ did not come to found a new religion, but to bring fullness and newness of life in *every* situation, including every religion and culture.

Conversion, therefore, is not primarily passage from one, conditioned system of beliefs to another, but an encounter with the unconditioned *in* every possible conditioned situation. Conversion is *metanoia:* the turning of the whole person towards fullness. The essence of mission is people mutually leading one another to this fullness—in a spiritual and theological, as well as a socio-political sense. Mission needs to be a *mutual* challenge, for if Christians have the right and duty to be missionaries, so do Hindus, Buddhists and others—and not just because the secular state tolerates this, but because of Christian-theological legitimation! This does not abandon the spirit of dialogue—unless, of course, we are thinking of ourselves, rather than living in the liberating power of Christ which we proclaim.

Dialogue is not an abandonment of the Christian's duty to be a missionary. Rather, it helps us to understand conversion as something more profound than a change in one's membership in a given church. Conversion refers not only to the advaitic experience of individuals as this is visible in Jesus Christ, but rather to the realization of the Advaita of God and humankind tending towards universal integration, which is what we described as the unity of reality. Wherever this advaitic power of the Spirit becomes real, the kingdom of God proclaimed by Jesus is also near. A conversion is taking place, and this need not be (yet it can involve) a conversion to a specific confessional church.[29]

Such a view makes possible a monergism in the strict Reformation sense, since it frees us from our compulsion to be successful—along with the accompanying frustrations—within the scope of a visible church. If the church's influence and greatness are dwindling, this does not mean that the reality of the kingdom of God is not being spread by the universal promise of Jesus (Mk 4:31, etc.) The renewing power of the Spirit alone is what is effective. The "how" and the "where" of this realization cannot be confined to our theological pronouncements and church walls.

Conversion is a process of death and resurrection in which new life is made possible—whether individually or politically or socially. The real Christian community is wherever new spiritual life is taking place by the freedom of the gospel, whether this happens within established Christianity or established Hinduism or any other religion or culture. All are in equal need of authentic *metanoia*. A genuine Christian community, as salt, light, and leaven penetrates all of society and all religion, and as such can never be confined *intra muros*.

14.

Return to Unity—Cosmic Solidarity

The advaitic experience can become part of the lives of individuals at appointed times, yet for the whole of human history it is not the driving force. Most of our life experiences are marked by egotism, fragmentation, and destructive antagonisms or power struggles. The unity of reality is a hope grounded in experience. Its universal realization as love, however, continues to escape us, although it is already there *sub specie Dei*—or, in *principle.* But since this is not a mere velleity, but something already experienced in meditation, which can be meaningfully interpreted as part of our trinitarian notion of God, the need to actually realize this is all the greater. The trinitarian *perichoresis* is a process. Unity is in becoming. What we have described as the second person of the trinity is not yet a perfection (*perfectum*). In other words, we could say that only in the first and third persons is the unity fully there explicitly. Incarnation, crucifixion, and resurrection are lived out anew in the daily life of those who are called.

Non-duality as an Ethical Principle

In the West ethics is generally grounded either in the twofold commandment of love (Christianity), in the Golden Rule or categorical imperative (humanism), or in class solidarity (Marxism). What is common to all these otherwise quite different conceptions, is that they are all based on an imperative. However, we already find in the New Testament (Rm 5:1; 8:9ff.; 1 Cor 2:15ff., etc) and also in later Christian mysticism, that another starting point makes its appearance, namely, the *indicative* of ongoing certainty about our reconciliation—the fact that humans are already what they should become. While the expression "Become what you are" goes back to classical Greece, in Christianity, with its message of reconciliation, it acquires a real historical framework.

Does the *paramarthika* standpoint of Vedanta offer a wide-reaching principle for an ethics, beyond the legalism of an interpretation of *dharma* (which ends up in the hopelessness of the caste system)?[1]

There can be no doubt that virtuous living is considered as unconditionally necessary as a preparatory discipline for *jnana*. Thus the Brhadaranyaka Upanishad, in connection with a discussion of the nature of *brahman*, describes the three great "*da*": self-control (*dama*), merciful giving (*dana*), and sharing in the destiny of all living beings (*daya*).[2] These three are a counterweight against lust, anger, and greed,[3] the direct preparation for meditation.[4] They exercise us in detachment, which is necessary in order to concentrate on the essentials.[5] The ideal is the natural attitude of a child (*balya*), who is free from conceit and self-justification.

The person who judges things from the *vyavaharika* standpoint cannot exhibit these virtues even if he/she accepts them as a moral imperative of *dharma*. Only one who has experienced the universal non-duality of all things in *atman/brahman*—in other words, judges *paramarthika*—can fulfill these virtues because on this level they are self-evident. Egocentrism, avarice, and hatred have of themselves been overcome, for in the advaitic view hatred returns to the one who is hating.[6] No imperative is needed, for there is really no alternative.[7] "Whoever sees all beings (*sarvani bhutani*) in the self (*atman*) and the self in all beings, feels no hatred because of this knowledge."[8]

The advaitic view, namely, seeing God and the many in the world non-dualistically, and grasping all that is as not-two in *atman*, is the principle of a *paramarthika* ethics in Advaita Vedanta.[9] The classical expression of this teaching is a dialogue in the Brhadaranyaka Upanishad[10] which the sage Yajnavalkya has with his wife, Maitreyi: A person is not loved because he is husband, wife, son or anything else, but because of *atman*, which is not-two in the lover and the loved one. *Atman* is what is most worthwhile and is worthy of love generally.[11]

The self is to be meditated on and experienced. Since the other person is not really another, the Advaitin can say: love for *atman* is the same as love for another as *atman*, not as an individual, temporal structure, but as that person's very essence. Because *atman* is identical with *brahman*, Advaita Vedanta includes "love of God" and "love of neighbor" in the one movement of devotion to *atman*, which is all-in-all because it is the outward form of the self.[12]

Such an ethics is not based on the distinction of good and bad, true and false. Recognizing a measure within these opposites

would imply blindness to a part of reality and an overpowering of
one to the exclusion of the other. But when we do this there can be
no equanimity, no harmony, and no peace. The advaitic ideal is
grounded in a principle which is beyond morality and virtue,
namely in the experience of non-duality where the drive towards
self-promotion, the root of all evil, is dissolved.[13]

Nevertheless, the Upanishads are very sensible with regard to
the fulfillment of everyday duties. *Dharma* should be carried out
unconditionally. Fulfilling one's duties in a spirit of detachment
without seeking personal gain (*naiskarmya*) is itself a spiritual exercise within everyday life, a meditative exercise in unity of
vision.[14]

In the *paramarthika* viewpoint, the greatest freedom from
dualist oppositions consists in overcoming *samsara.* This does not
mean that the one who has this experience has no further need to
continue acting and to despise the world. On the contrary, the dualism of self and other, of God and the world has been overcome so
that the world is seen in its absolute dimension and experienced as
in its true essence. The Advaitin should act on the basis of the
unity, but he should not wish to enjoy the fruits of his actions in an
egotistical manner. Thus every imperative, which would have to be
based on a dualistic attitude, disappears. There is only the indicative of the One for a person realized in Advaita.

Thus the doctrine of *karman* can be clarified in two different
ways, and an interpretation in one sense or the other will be most
heavy in consequences for the religions of India today, as well as
movements in the West, which are influenced by Indian spirituality. Indeed, it depends less on religious philosophical considerations than on social and political interests. Nowhere else is it
clearer that theological interpretations are ideologically motivated.
The two possible interpretations are:

1. The life of any individual can be regarded as the result of
past actions, as penance to satisfy *karman.* Naturally this attitude
accepts suffering and sees alienation as the natural consequence of
conditioned or causal connections. It is fatalistic, and a great number of believers in India, as well as in Western movements, tend
towards this attitude.

2. Life is seen as a possibility of determining future *karman.*
This can be an incentive to action and to activities that change the
world. The future determines what is to be changed in the present.
The doctrine of *karman* can thus provide a strong motivational
framework to legitimate social activity. All the reformers of Hin-

duism have used this argument, from Ram Mohan Roy and Vive-kananda to Aurobindo and Gandhi.

The second interpretation can likewise be supported by a broad textual basis. It is by no means an intrusive addition or a Neo-Hinduistic gloss: "The self is Brahman indeed: as a person acts, as he behaves, so does he become; whoever does good, becomes good: whoever does evil, becomes evil."[15] Sankara remarks in his commentary that the pursuit of good always remains under the law of *samsara* because pursuing presupposes a dualism between wish and reality. Yet a relative (because temporally bound) forward movement within *samsara* is not only unmistakable, but is something to be pursued and actively to be strived for, as this text of the Upanishads recommends.

Vedanta teaches a balanced attitude, one which includes both active behavior (*karman*) and exercises in detached meditation (*sannyasa*). Often however, following Sankara's lead, it recommends that the detachment of the *sannyasin* is a presupposition for the advaitic experience.[16] *Sannyasa*, the life of the wandering monk, would be in danger of remaining no longer merely one proven means to develop spiritual abilities—just as Yoga and meditation are—but could become an end in itself. But this would be the seed of a renewed disintegration of the non-duality of God and world, eternity and history, contemplation and action, the monastic life and the householder. In trying to achieve ontological non-duality we would fall into *existential dualism.*

If it is correct to see the basic tension of Indian spirituality as a continual hovering between fatalism and the will to be personally active in a physical or spiritual sense,[17] this tension culminates here as the problem of either detachment from the world or integration of the world in Advaita. The foundation laid down here of a loving regard for all beings on the basis of and in relation to the *paramarthika* standpoint could resolve this tension insofar as the Advaitin has knowledge of release (*moksa*) as something spontaneous and beyond all dualistic norms, as something to be exercised on the basis of an experience of the all-encompassing fulness of love.

This leads to the question of the *Advaita of the concrete*, after the moment when the historical has been integrated into the One. The concept of trinitarian *perichoresis* can perhaps help overcome the suspicion of existential dualism in Vedanta. For it sees reality as an energetic event that is happening, and not a unity abstracted from history.

Ethics is rooted in the dynamism of love which, as we have

demonstrated, is participation. Insofar as humans become aware of
being and recognize *atman* they realize not only their own identity—"loving the other because of *atman*"—but they also integrate the polarity of difference and identity in the participatory act
of lovingly becoming one. Thus the particular and the individual
acquire infinite worth.

In Advaita Vedanta solidarity with all of life is only grounded
"vertically." By negating the differences of concrete things it
grounds the unity of *atman* and *brahman* as well as the unity of all
beings, reducing them to an identity in *atman*.

The trinitarian experience of God, too, leads to a solidarity of
all beings by the "vertical" participation of all humans in God's
trinitarian dynamism. At the same time, however, the "horizontal" differentiation is not an obstacle in the path of this realization,
but rather the place where the spiritual event becomes concrete.

This different way of arguing is clearly seen in Matthew 25:45.
To the Indian Advaitin, helping others would be recommended *not*
because they see another concrete person, but because they see
their own *atman*. There would remain a difference between the
vyavaharika and the *paramarthika* levels. It could be meaningful
and in accordance with *dharma* to be for the other on the basis of a
vyavaharika argument. But this would have no ultimate meaning
and would not be considered in order for the *jivanmukta.*

In Christian ethical arguments, on the other hand, this opposition does not exist, since, because of the influence of trinitarian
perichoresis, paramarthika and *vyavaharika* appear as moments in
the *one* trinitarian process. What we do to our neighbor, we do to
Jesus and vice versa. The good deed is directed not only towards
Jesus, but to the neighbor in his/her particularity. Love of God and
love of neighbor are two poles of one event, and the one does not
dissolve the other. We might add that this attitude *also* exists in
India, although it is not typical of strict Advaitins.

There is a story that once an Advaitin was asked whether he
would allow his energies to be placed at the disposition of a hospital. The Advaitin refused, for health care is useful and concerned
only with the temporal and limited well-being of the body. It would
be better to work in an ashram, which leads people to the temporally unlimited and spiritual good, for here people learn the way to
moksa. This opposition sheds light on the unclarified relationship
between *brahman* and *maya.* It indicates an existential dualism.

An ethics grounded in the trinity considers this opposition as
invalid, for the eternal is *in* the temporal and the temporal *in* the

eternal. Hospital and ashram must merge to provide holistic care for the one human person, who in his/her wholeness shares in the trinitarian event of the one God. In other words: *paramarthika* and *vyavaharika* constitute one another in the one, encompassing event of trinitarian *perichoresis.*

Action, Love, and Contemplation

All Indian systems recognize the significance of three spiritual ways (*marga*), which open us to more perfect life patterns: *karma marga* (the way of action), *bhakti marga* (the way of worship and love), and *jnana marga* (the way of knowledge and contemplation). In Vedanta *jnana marga* plays the decisive role, whereas popular piety usually revolves around *bhakti* or *karman.* Basically, the three ways belong together, but their unity is difficult to establish and especially to live. It has not been different in Christian history where the polarization of "contemplatives" and "activists" has always led to mutual suspicion, each accusing the other of diminishing Jesus' ideal.

The unity of the three ways can be established by means of the trinitarian *perichoresis.* The three ways are expressions of the structure of human consciousness and therefore of reality itself. Action corresponds to the aspect of the Father, love corresponds to the aspect of the Son, and contemplation can be ordered in the aspect of the Spirit.

1. *Action* is connected with the aspect of the Father because it is the immediate and initially still external answer to the primordial source. Action (*karman*) is at first the cultic sacrifice, i.e., an expression through an action which wants to correspond to the divine source of reality by renewing and strengthening it. The one who sacrifices places him/herself within the efficacious space of the source and gains a share in the freedom of divine creative power. The sacrifice, however, remains abstract, for it is related to a source that is beyond.

Classical Indian *karma marga* represents a step towards immanent transcendence. Because all events are interdependent, *each* human action has infinite meaning (each action is sacrifice) since it realizes this interdependence. Action is therefore a way of preserving the whole. Human activity is the achievement of creative freedom, which appears in the trinity under the aspect of the Father.

The double commandment of love is really, therefore, one

commandment: what a person does to his/her neighbor is direct service to God, on the basis of its connectedness in *karman,* for God is continuously realizing himself in the whole of creation.

2. *Love* is connected with the aspect of the Son because it represents a personal relationship to God who has become concrete. It is devotion (*bhakti*) and a becoming-available, and is not to be taken in a merely emotional sense, but a personal sense. Here the basic interrelationality of being grows into the intimacy of an I-Thou relation. God manifests himself in the Son as an "I" who calls humans into partnership and thus reveals the human "thou," the personality. (Is 43:1) This is not a love which merely intensifies the human "I" in the pathos of being grasped—which is the danger of an emotional love mysticism, for Christianity as well as for Indian *bhakti.* On the contrary, this love has its theo-ontological basis in the trinitarian aspect of the Son. Love is devotion and this makes receptivity possible.

3. *Contemplation* is connected with the aspect of the Spirit, because here we experience the perfect immanence of transcendent-trinitarian reality. The Spirit is the true self (*atman*) of humans, perfectly immanent and yet remaining transcendent with regard to any grasping or "having." This is the realization of nonduality, the very essence of contemplative experience and transformation. In the Spirit the concrete form is sublated into the whole. Through contemplation love achieves its universal meaning, and the unity we try to achieve through action is seen comprehensively. Thus action reaches its finality and its power in contemplation, whereas the contemplative vision is historically realized by action and continues by means of love.

Most importantly, we can now recognize and live the unity of these three spiritual paths. Just as the unity of the trinity is a *perichoresis* of three persons so, too, are the moments of action, love and contemplation all parts of one transformation and maturation process in human life. In the advaitic experience, contemplation and action do not interfere with one another, but are moments in a *return to unity.*

We can also use the classical Christian triad of faith-love-hope (1 Cor 13:13) to argue for the perichoretic unity of action, love, and contemplation. These three human forms of consciousness correspond to the moments of Father, Son, and Spirit. Thus Paul can claim that love is the greatest of these because by love we are granted *entrance* into the unity of the three dimensions, just as our entrance to participation in the trinity was possible through the

Son. The three forms of consciousness can be seen as subjective aspects of unity, whereas the objective aspects are in the immanent trinitarian relationships. We note, however, that these are modes of seeing, and should not be separated from one another. Subject and object are not-two, a point that was explained by the notion of participation. If we now relate the types of spirituality to Figure 13.2 that demonstrated our interpretation of the trinity, the following picture emerges (see Figure 14.1).

All these aspects are nothing by themselves, but are partial aspects of the whole. They all serve one purpose, to make humans ready to open themselves to the mystery of God's immediate present, which transforms human existence/consciousness, so they may act in and for participation with the whole. Thus ethics has its basis not in a forever grounded ought, but in a real transformation, which includes being aware of the interdependence of all being, and this, in turn, has consequences for their behavior towards the whole of nature.

At present Christian piety always wishes to say something, to know something, to do something, or learn something. All of this striving is directed outwards. The danger here is that humans will fall prey to following the way of law and will depend on what is visible. Even what we call faith frequently falls into such "spiritual materialism."

The spiritual paths of the East take the opposite path, and this may also be found in our own tradition, although it is generally forgotten. The person goes away from whatever is external—this would only confine him/her—and towards nothingness, where HE/SHE truly appears. According to a famous word of Zen Buddhism that echoes the opinion of the Upanishads (neti, neti), even the Buddha must be put to death once he becomes an object; i.e., when a person begins clinging to his/her idea of him, for this, too, is a subtle, egocentric act of grasping instead of a radical being-determined by the One.

Thus, both of these ways can be fruitful for one another when they meet in the human heart. For in Asia as well as in Christianity they want to experience the presence of the One, or God. In an image from the German mystics, human life is like a flower, which willingly unfolds in order to receive the rays of the sun (G. Tersteegen).

The advaitic attitude, as we saw above, frees us from fear, because we now know ourselves as given over into the One. Fearlessness and safety carry us forward to overcome aggression, which is

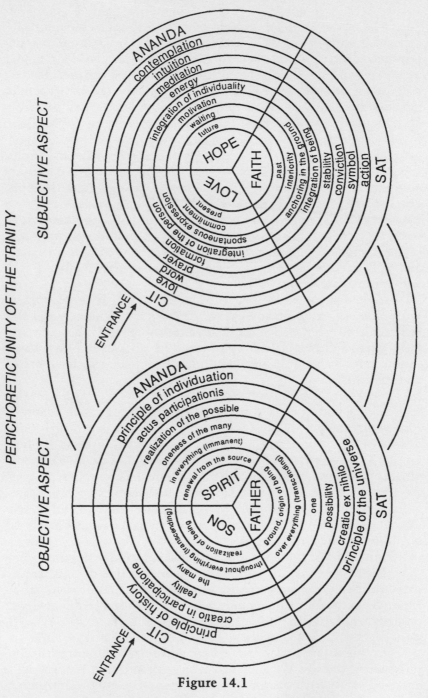

Figure 14.1

rooted in egocentrism. Freedom from aggression is the precondition of unconditional love, which knows no boundaries: viz., as *cosmic solidarity.*

In summary: All aspects of spirituality are praxis in its twofold dimension, vertical and horizontal. "Vertical praxis" is meditation, fulfilled silence, which establishes the mystery of the One. Not theories, but this praxis has a transforming power. Critical reflection must accompany this way and prevent us from ending in impasses. But it is not an end in itself. Thus there are three steps: *sravana* (hearing the scriptures), *manana* (intellectual testing and acceptance of what was heard), *nididhyasana* (meditation on the basis of what was heard and reflected on).

"Horizontal praxis" means realizing in daily life what was experienced in meditation, action through the power of love. Just as in the Benedictine rule, *ora* is accompanied by *labora*, not as a second step, but as the necessary unfolding of the first. This type of action does not just complement contemplation, but is rather a kind of dealing with the everyday, which itself is contemplation. Work becomes a method which incorporates contemplative silence and recollection. From silence comes the power of the word, which creates reality. The consequence of contemplation is action oriented towards participation in the whole. The consequence of thinking, on the other hand, is only intelligible concepts.

Cosmic Solidarity

As humankind struggles today with its doubts over its future because of all its ecological, political, and social conflicts, the responsibility correctly falls upon religion to discover a new interpretation of the relationship between humans and nature. An ethics that does this will, however, be insufficient if it is based only on imperatives, which in turn come from what has been experienced and done up until now. Since we need a radical transformation of behavior, we must find a radically new orientation within the foundations of ethics: The only possibility of a solution is not a quantitatively refined imperative, but rather a qualitatively changed indicative.

Two aspects which such a new experience has to include are the "autonomous worth of creatures" and the "interdependence of all beings."[18] If the West represents especially the "autonomous worth of creatures," Eastern thinking takes place in the context of the experience of interdependence. The dialogical community of the two could thus be important in working out our destiny.

In the Western-Christian view the unity of reality tends to remain only a theological postulate. It lacks a truly transformative experience that could orient human identity and action towards cosmic solidarity. The ontonomous roots of ethics in the experience of the One are not widely acknowledged. Yet we could discover a sufficient number of starting points in the early church's notion of the trinity, in the mystics, in Luther, and in Hegel. But these have little effect on our consciousness. Luther's experience of temptation and his overcoming it through *conformitas Christi* point towards a radical conversion, which breaks the whole chain of humankind's narrow egotism. But the meaning of this experience was all too quickly rationalized, made part of a system, and thus deprived of its effectiveness.

C.F. von Weizsäcker has pointed out that the weakening and decentralizing of the "I" in European thought is also being accomplished in other ways: namely by a disillusionment caused by overcoming the geocentric worldview as well as by Darwinism and Freud's theories of unconscious control mechanisms in the human psyche: "That this growing disillusionment signifies a growing conflict with religion only follows if we see religion as representing a self-glorification of the human ego. But we could reverse this by seeing the disillusionment with self as a return to the heart of religious experience."[19] This points to a religious experience which can at least be related to the advaitic experience of the unity of reality.

The intuition of the unity of reality, on the basis of advaitic experience, can be a decisive impetus for the needed reinterpretation of relationships among persons as well as between humans and nature. It is not merely a theoretical postulate, but indicates a life orientation, realized by meditation and by action which actively influences social events, as seen in their cosmic solidarity in *atman*.

As in our critical remarks above, the *jivanmukta* in Advaita Vedanta is elevated beyond the alienation of duality, yet is still faced with an alienated historical environment. Thus a harmony is reached which, in Feuerbach's sense, is not projected onto heaven, but onto the *jivanmukta*. It continues in crass opposition to the very real disintegration of social life.[20] Harmony, powerlessness, and the enjoyment of peaceful unity (*santi*) remain the privilege of a few.

Within this ideal we could, however, see an anticipation of real cosmic harmony which can be realized in active achievement of cosmic solidarity. Cosmic solidarity then would not be a heteronomous duty, but an onto-theonomous unfolding of the real. It would be knowledge of the self in knowledge of God and vice versa.[21] Because *atman* as spirit describes the reality of the trinitarian God, and also because the reality of God and the realization of true human existence can be thought of in the universal connectedness of the unity of reality, cosmic solidarity is thus the deepest expression of integral advaitic consciousness, which unfolds the human personality.

Letting oneself enter into cosmic solidarity means that humans make themselves a meditative achievement of the unity of reality, that they become completely determined by the Spirit of God. It also means that in the universal realization of love, cosmic solidarity of concrete persons becomes structured in such a way that the Advaitin actively enters into the work of integration and the overcoming of dualistic alienation in ecological, psychological, social, and political problem areas. Contemplation and action are a polar unity.

Action begins when we open ourselves to a new kind of perception: a letting be.[22] At the same time the reality of new being breaks in. This means that we participate in the reality of the Spirit, that we are drawn into the event of God's self-realization, and thus have a share in the original creative reality of the one Subject. The field of realization of this creativity is the dimension of the Son, the *mode* is cosmic solidarity, which binds together the universal network of love, i.e., it forms the mystical body of Christ.

Therefore, we are determined by the unity of reality and at the same time are an active moment in its realization. We are both receivers and makers of cosmic solidarity. For we experience our identity in *atman*, in God as Spirit, who leads us into the movement of the trinitarian God. This trinitarian God is the very essence of the unity of reality. This is the kairos of the advaitic trinitarian experience: cosmic solidarity—"So that they may all be one" (Jn 17:21).

ABBREVIATIONS

AU	Aitareya Upanishad
AmU	Amrtabindu Upanishad
AV	Atharvaveda
BG	Bhagavad Gita
BS	Brahma-Sutra
BSB	Sankara's Brahma-Sutra-Bhasya (Commentary)
BU	Brhadaranyaka Upanishad
CU	Chandogya Upanishad
GK	Mandukya-Karika of Gaudapata
HYP	Hatha Yoga Pradipika
IU	Isa Upanishad
KaivU	Kaivalya Upanishad
KU	Katha Upanishad
KausU	Kausitaki Upanishad
KeU	Kena Upanishad
MB	Mahabharata
MaitriU	Maitri Upanishad
MandU	Mandukya Upanishad
MU	Mundaka Upanishad
MW	Monier-Williams, *A Sanskrit-English Dictionary*, Oxford, 1964.
PU	Prasna Upanishad
RV	Rgveda
SB	Satapatha Brahmana
SU	Svetasvatara Upanishad
TA	Taittiriya Aranyaka
TU	Taittiriya Upanishad
VPS	Vivarana-prameya-sangraha
YS	Yoga-Sutra of Patanjali

SANSKRIT GLOSSARY

Adhyaropa	false transference
Advaita	non-duality
Akasa	space, ether
Ananda	bliss
Anirvacaniya	undeterminable
Antaryamin	internal ruler
Atman	the self (which transcends the empirical) which is immanent in every creature
Anubhava	experience, immediate vision
Avidya	ignorance
Bhakti	devotion
Bhedabheda	differentiation in the non-differentiated, identity in difference
Brahman	the Absolute, the ultimate ground of reality
Buddha	the awakened one
Cit	the mind, spirit, consciousness
Dharma	nature, cosmic order, law
Dhyana	meditation
Duhkha	suffering
Ekagrata	concentration of consciousness on one point
Ekam	the One
Guru	teacher, spiritual master
Isvara	lord, personal God
Jiva	the individual or ego
Jivanmukta	he who is free while still alive, a "living-redeemed," highest form of fulfillment
Jnana	knowledge, wisdom
Karman	action, link between past causes and present works in the material and the moral-spiritual realm
Karuna	healing attitude, compassion, solidarity

Laksyartha	metaphorical sense
Manas	the understanding, thinking
Mantra	a formula used in meditation and prayer
Maya	creative, but also obscuring power, illusion
Moksa (mukti)	release, liberation
Mukhyartha	the true, proper meaning
Nama-rupa	name and form
Nididhyasana	meditation
Nirguna	without qualities
Nirvana	dissolution of self-delusion
Paramarthika	absolute standpoint of knowledge, transrational knowing
Pradhana	non-spiritual, fundamental matter
Pramana	means of knowing
Prana	vital energy, primal energy, breath
Purna	fullness
Purusa	person (not to be confused with the empirical ego), personal primal God, the spiritual principle
Rsi	seer
Rta	eternal order, law of the world
Sadhana	spiritual path, methodical exercise
Saguna	determined by qualities
Sakti	power
Samadhi	fulfilled union, contemplative immersion
Samsara	the empirical world, the cycle of death and rebirth
Samskara	impressions which remain in the continuum of the conscious self from physical-psychic-mental activity
Sannyasa	renunciation
Santi	peace
Sarira	body, level of reality
Sat	being
Satya	truth

Sraddha	faith, trust
Sruti	what has been heard, the Vedic revelation, the revealed and therefore absolutely valid scriptures
Suksma	the fine or refined, subtle levels of reality
Sunyata	emptiness
Sutra	condensed sentence, a compendium of aphorisms
Turiya	the fourth, transrational state of consciousness
Upadhi	limiting determinations
Upasana	objective or thematic meditation
Vac	word, primal sound
Vyavaharika	the relative standpoint of knowledge, empirical knowing

Notes

Introduction

1. C.F. von Weizsäcker, *Der Garten des Menschlichen. Beiträge zur geschichtlichen Anthropologie* (Munich, 1977) 434.

2. Th. Kuhn, *The Structure of Scientific Revolutions* (Chicago, 1970).

3. "Witnessing in a Divided World" (WCC, 6th Assembly), in: *Current Dialogue* 6 (Spring, 1984) WCC Geneva, 15.

4. M. Mildenberger, "Dialog in Deutschland?" in: *Denkpause im Dialog. Perspektiven der Begegnung mit anderen Religionen und Ideologien* (Frankfurt, 1978) 141.

5. Ibid, 145.

6. H. Ott. "The Beginning Dialogue between Christianity and Buddhism, the Concept of a Dialogical Theology and the Possible Contribution of Heideggerian Thought," in: *Japanese Religions*, Vol. 11, 2–3: Sept. 1980, 81; *idem*, "Der Dialog zwischen den Religionen als theologische Aufgabe unserer Zeit," in: *Unterwegs zur Einheit*. Festschr. für H. Stirnimann, eds.: J. Brantsche & P. Selvalico (Fribourg, 1980) 884ff.

7. H. Ott, "The Beginning Dialogue," 88.

8. Mildenberger, op. cit., 156.

9. Cf. P.K. Sundaram, *Advaita Epistemology* (Madras, 1968) 189.

10. M.K.V. Iyer, *Advaita Vedanta. According to Sankara* (Bombay, 1964) 136.

11. R.V. DeSmet, "Questioning Vedanta," in: *Indian Philosophical Annual* VII, (Madras, 1971) 99.

12. Cf. esp. R. Panikkar, *The Unknown Christ of Hinduism* (London, 1964); *idem, The Trinity and World Religions* (Bangalore, 1970); *idem, Myth, Faith and Hermeneutics* (New York, 1979); *idem, Rückkehr zum Mythos* (Frankfurt, 1985); Abhishiktananda, *Saccidananda. A Christian Approach to Advaitic Experience* (New Delhi, 1974); B. Griffiths, *Vedanta and Christian Faith*

(Los Angeles, 1973); idem, *The Marriage of East and West* (Spring-field/Ill, 1982); M. Sunder Rao, *Ananyatva. Realization of Christian Non-Duality* (Bangalore, 1964). Dated, yet still significant is the study by R. Otto which compares Sankara and Meister Eckhart: *West-Östliche Mystik* (Gotha, 1926).

13. Ott, op. cit., 92.

14. Ch. Birth "Schöpfung, Technik and Überleben der Menschheit: . . . und füllet die Erde," in: *Jesus Christus befreit und eint.* Vorträge von Nairobi. Ed.: H. Krüger. *Ökumenische Rundschau Beiheft* 30 (Frankfurt, 1976) 110f.

Chapter 1

1. T.M.P. Mahadevan, *Invitation to Indian Philosophy* (New Delhi, 1974) 367f.

2. Sankara's commentary on TU II,VII,1; cf. his commentary on TU II,I,1.

3. At the end of the commentary on Mandukya Karika (IV,100), Sankara recognizes that *brahman*, "though unborn, appears to be associated with birth through its unscrutable power, which though ever at rest, appears to be moving, and which though non-dual appears to have assumed multifarious forms to those whose vision is deluded by the perception of endless objects and their attributes." It "destroys all fear for those who take shelter under it."

4. BU II,V,1ff.

5. Sankara's commentary on TU II,VIII,5.

6. TU III,X,3–4; cf. Sankara's commentary on TU II,VI,1.

7. H. Zimmer, *Philosophie und Religion Indiens* (Frankfurt, 1976) 366.

8. T.M.P. Mahadevan *The Philosophy of Advaita* (New Delhi, 1976) 277.

9. Mahadevan, *Invitation*, 367f.

10. BS I,I,2.

11. Zimmer, 368.

12. B.K.S. Iyengar compares the teaching of five *kosa* to modern anthropological notions: "Man is made up of five sheaths . . . In modern terminology they are known as the anatomical, physiological, psychological, intellectual and blissful states. Body has various systems such as the circulatory, respiratory, digestive, nervous systems, glandular, etc. There is a large organization with various subdivisions as in society, and the presiding officer is the Self."

13. BU III,VII,4–23.

14. *adrsto drsta asrutah, srotra, amanto manta, avijnato vijnata,* BU III,VII,20.

15. Another example of this argument is found in BU III,VII,5: God is the inner power abiding in fire, but is other than fire, and therefore fire does not know him.

16. BG VI,30: *yo mam pasyati sarvatra sarvam ca mayi pasyati.*

17. BG VI,32.

18. R. Panikkar, *The Vedic Experience* (Mantramanjari, London, 1977) 649.

19. The Vedanta thus describes the same basic experience as Mahayana-Buddhism.

20. BU II,IV,14; T.M.P. Mahadevan, *Gaudapada. A Study in Early Advaita* (Madras, 1975) 108.

21. BU V,I,1; cf. BSB II,I,27.

22. Sankara's commentary on BU IV,IV,9.

23. Sankara's commentary on BU IV,V,15.

24. B.K.S. Iyengar, *Light on Yoga* (London, 1977) 42.

25. M. Eliade, *Yoga. Immortality and Freedom* (Princeton, 1973) 9.

26. "The final aim of Vedanta is not to negate the world through its doctrine of *maya* . . . , but to establish the sole reality of *brahman*. . . . To the enlightened, *maya* is also *brahman.*" Swami Nikhilananda "A Few Stray Thoughts on Non-Dualistic Vedanta," in: *Essays in Philosophy.* Mahadevan Festschrift. (Madras, 1962) 1.

27. Cf. Eliade, *op. cit.* 268–273.

28. BG XIII,27f. *The Bhagavad Gita.* A New Translation. Kees W. Bolle (Berkeley: Univ. of Calif. Press, 1979).

29. RV X,129.

30. RV X,129,2–3; cf. AV X,7; II,1,1.

31. RV VIII,58,2.

32. AV XIV,4,12–27.

33. AV XIII,4,12–21.

34. TA III,2,1.

35. Panikkar, 656.

36. RV VIII,58,2.

37. H. Nakamura, *Ways of Thinking of Eastern Peoples* (Honolulu, 1964) 73–78. Nakamura points out that the Indian mind favors nouns because of the Sanskrit language. There are certainly connections. However, we would exercise the same caution here

because the style of preferring nouns could also be explained by a substratum-theory.

38. MW,737.
39. Mahadevan, *Invitation*, 386.
40. BS I,I,2.
41. BU II,I,20.
42. BU IV,IV,22.
43. BU IV,IV,25.
44. BU IV,IV,22.
45. BSB I,III,22.
46. MU II,II,10.
47. BG XIII,12b-17.
48. TU II,7.
49. CU VI,II,1.
50. MU I,I,5-6.
51. R. DeSmet, "Does Christianity Profess Non-Dualism?" in: *The Clergy Monthly* 37,9 (New Delhi, 1973) 354.
52. TU II,I,1.
53. Sankara's commentary on TU II,I,1. Advaita Vedanta identifies immutability with eternity. An eternal being which changes in itself is unthinkable. Cf. W.M. Indich, *Consciousness in Advaita Vedanta* (Varanasi, 1980) 33.
54. MU II,II,2.
55. The Agamas are Tantric scriptures. Cf. *The Cultural Heritage of India*, Bd. 2 (Calcutta, 1953) 585.
56. Maitrayani Samkita III,70,76.
57. *The Cultural Heritage of India*, Bd. 3, 586f. Cf. the essay of R. Panikkar "Vac in the Sruti," in: *God's Word among Men*. Ed.: G. Gispert-Sauch (Delhi, 1973) 3ff; and R.C. Pandeya, *The Problem of Meaning in Indian Philosophy* (Delhi, 1963) 262.
58. Sankara's commentary on CU VIII,1.
59. BSB II,III,7.
60. BS II,II,38; cf. P.K. Sundaram, *Advaita Epistemology* (Madras, 1968) 185–189.
61. Sankara's commentary on TU II,VI,1.
62. H. Nahamura, *Parallel Developments. A Comparative History of Ideas* (Tokyo/New York, 1975) 455ff.
63. P. Deussen, *Das System des Vedanta* (Leipzig, 1883).
64. BSB II,II,1. We translate the whole text which develops this argument in detail in: M. v. Brück, *Advaita und Trinität. Indische*

und *Christliche Gotteserfahrung im Dialog der Religionen* (Doctoral Dissertation: Univ. Rostock, 1980).

65. This is already the case in SU. But here *pradhana* is a miraculous power dependent on a personal God (*purusa*). Cf. H. v. Glasenapp, *Die Philosophie der Inder* (Stuttgart, 1958) 157.

66. Glasenapp, op. cit., 211.

67. BSB II,III,8. Similarly Sankara in his commentary on TU II,VI,1.

68. Deussen, op. cit., 234: n.69 claims that the close relationship of the European and the Indian arguments is obvious. Both also share the same weakness of not taking into account an empirically apparent *regressus ad infinitum.*

69. BSB II,III,7; Deussen, 135ff.

70. BSB II,III,7. Descartes' *res cogitans* and Sankara's *atman* are, however, different in that Descartes' *cogito* is grounded in the thinking subject and thus cannot be doubted, while Sankara as well as all of Buddhist philosophy transcend thinking because of its duality.

71. TU II,I,1.

72. CU VII,XXIII,1. The term *bhuman* originally described the earth as neuter. As masculine it is fullness and manifold, undoubtedly the fullness which the earth brings forth, i.e., the whole of reality. In the later Upanishads the term *purna* (related to the Latin *plenus*) assumed the fullness of *bhuman.*

73. Mahadevan, *Philosophy of Advaita*, 119.

74. BG II,16: *na 'sato vidyate bhavo na 'bhavo vidyate satah.* Cf. Mahadevan, 114f.

75. Mahadevan, 116.

76. Mahadevan, 117.

77. BU IV,V,13; BSB III,II,16.

78. Panikkar, op. cit., 669f.

79. Mahadevan, *Invitation*, 368; MU II,II,11.

80. TU II,I,1; cf. Kaiv U 19.

81. Pandeya, op. cit., 254f.; "The pure existence is Absolute, without a second. It is of the nature of consciousness, because only conscious existence can manifest itself in the world. A table cannot manifest itself in various forms because it is dead matter. Only conscious being has power to appear in various forms . . . The Absolute is not dead. He is dynamic. He is endowed with power. The power is not separate and distinct from him. It is His very existence. He is the powerful conscious Absolute."

82. AU III,I,1-4.
83. TU III,VI,1.
84. BU III,IX,28.7.
85. R.K. Tripathi, "Advaita Vedanta and Western Thought," in: *Indian Philosophical Annual* Vol. VII (Madras, 1971) 42.

Chapter 2

1. BU II,IV,12.
2. IU 5; cf. BG XIII,15, etc.
3. H. Zimmer, *Philosophie und Religion Indiens*, 317; H. Nakamura: in *Parallel Developments*. 92 ff, notes that the history of the word *brahman* has parallels with the Greek concept, Logos.
4. Cf. H.v. Glasenapp, *Die Philosophie der Inder*, 156. The self is thus different from all sense or spiritual appearances on the empirical level, just as it is different from material appearances. Cf. BU IV,III,6 and Sankara's commentary on BU IV,III,7 & TU II,VII,1.
5. BU I,II,4; CU VIII,VIII,1; TU II,I,1.
6. BU I,V,20; CU V,I,6.
7. BU II,I,17; Kaus U III,8.
8. BU I,IV,7; Kaus U III,8.
9. BU III,VII,16ff.
10. BU II,IV,5f.
11. BU III,IV,2; CU VIII,XII,4ff.
12. BU II,V,1ff.; CU III,XIV,2ff.
13. BU III,VII,23.
14. KeU II,4; KU I,II,18.
15. BU II,V,15.
16. KU I,III,3-9.
17. BU IV,III,7.
18. T.M.P. Mahadevan, *The Philosophy of Advaita*, 235.
19. Ibid., 239.
20. BU IV,IV,20.
21. GK IV,45.
22. However, *atman* can be compared with Plato's seldom-used *seauton*. (F. Brunner, "A Comparison between Proclus' Philosophy and Advaita," in: *Spiritual Perspectives*. Ed.: Mahadevan: New Delhi, 1975; 107). Since even in Neoplatonism the soul is considered as an entity of a special kind and different from God, the

Indian idea cannot be compared with the notion of soul in Neoplatonism.

23. Cf. also Zimmer, op. cit., 81 & 88. This corresponds much more with *ruah* in Hebrew or with *pneuma* in the N.T.

24. IU 5; BU IV,IV,19.

25. BU IV,III,23; I,IV,2.

26. CU III,XIII,1ff.

27. P. Deussen, *Das System des Vedanta*, 503.

28. Mahadevan, 102.

29. In the question of the universals the logicians of Advaita Vedanta should rather be considered realists, and they express the modus of the *universalia in re* by the notion of *tadatmya*.

30. BSB II,I,9 and Sankara's commentary on TU II,VI,1.

31. Cf. R. DeSmet, "Does Christianity Profess Non-Dualism?," in: *The Clergy Monthly* 37,9 (New Delhi, 1973) 356.

32. Cf. the instructive essay by S. Grant, "Reflections on the Mystery of Christ Suggested by a Study of Sankara's Concept of Relation," in: *God's Word among Men*, ed. G. Gispert-Sauch, 105ff.

33. The question of whether the self is a kind of substratum and the uninvolved observer (*saksin*) of changes in the world, or the inner ruler (*antaryamin*) which actively determines the course of the world without itself changing, has never been clearly decided. The viewpoint of the Upanishads favors self's activity.

34. CU VI,VIII,7 and parallels.

35. BG XI,41-42.

36. BG VII,24-26.

37. Sankara's commentary on BU I,IV,7.

38. Cf. R.H. Jones, "A Philosophical Analysis of Mystical Utterances," in: *Philosophy East and West* XXIX,3 (July, 1979) 255–274.

39. Cf. Mand U 7 and GK on this, which represent a radical apophatism.

40. The meaning is determined in two ways: by what the word expresses in the context (*sakya*) and by what the same word in other contexts would implicitly mean. Cf. Sundaram, op. cit., 96–106.

41. Swami Vimalananda, *Introduction. Chandogya Upanishad.* Edited by Sri Ramakrishna Math (Madras, 1956) XLIII.

42. BU III,VIII,8. In the early hymns of the Rigveda the negative expressions are not yet as predominant as in later texts. Possibly this development refers back to pre-Aryan, Dravidic influences.

43. BU III,IX,26; IV,II,4 etc. Sankara defines *neti, neti* in BSB III,II,22.

44. Nakamura, 57.

45. Nakamura, *Parallel Developments*, 119.

46. H. Nakamura, *Ways of Thinking*, 90ff. has also recently proposed that the Vedantic concept of *atman* need not contradict the Buddhistic theory of *anatta*. The same is maintained by Lama Anagarika Govinda, "The World View of a Mahayana Buddhist," in *ReVision* Vol. 2, No. 2 (Cambridge/Mass., 1979) 36.

47. Nakamura, *Ways of Thinking*, 15f.

48. Idem, *Parallel Developments*, 410f.

49. For the concept of *nirvana*, cf. Zimmer, 172, 423ff. and M. v. Brück, "Sunyata in Madhyamika Philosophy and the Christian Concept of God," in: *Jeevadhara* (Nov, 1983) 385–402. For the discussion in Japan, cf. H.Sh. Hisamatsu, *Die Fülle des Nichts. Vom Wesen des Zen* (Pfullingen o.J); K. Nishitani, *Was ist Religion?* (Frankfurt, 1982) 201ff. A wide range of literature can be found in H. Waldenfels, *Absolutes Nichts. Zur Grundlegung des Dialogs zwischen Buddhismus und Christentum* (Freiburg, 1976).

50. H. Oldenberg *Buddha* (Stuttgart, 1923) 40. Something similar is found in Christianity in Dennis the Areopagite and his followers. Oldenberg cites W. James, who compares India's *neti, neti* with the word of Scotus Eriugena: *Deus propter excellentiam non immerito Nihil vocatur.*

51. GK I,26.

52. GK III,36.

53. GK III,33.

54. GK I,12; IV,81.

55. GK I,29; IV,93.

56. Zimmer, 408f.

Chapter 3

1. MW, 811.

2. K.B. Ramakrishna Rao, "Relativity and Spiritual Experience," in: *Indian Philosophical Annual* VII (Madras, 1971) 51f.

3. BSB I,III,19.

4. R.V. DeSmet, "Maya or Ajnana?" in: *Indian Ecclesiastical Studies* 9 (1970) 80ff.

5. T.R.V. Murti, Foreword to L.N. Sharma, *Kasmir Saivism* (*Varanasi*, 1972) III.

6. T.M.P. Mahadevan, *Gaudapada*, 155.

7. GK I,26; II,13.

8. Cf. H. Zimmer, *Philosophie und Religion Indiens*, 31f.

9. Mahadevan, 158. It is typical for the philosophy of Advaita Vedanta that it makes the category of indeterminability or ineffability (*anirvacaniya*) one of its basic concepts without considering this a deficiency.

10. SU IV,10; Sankara's commentary on IU 13 & MU II,I,2 where *purusa* is described as transcendental, divine essence and thus pure, immutable and without limiting attributes. Cf. BG XV,16-18. R.C. Pandeya, *The Problem of Meaning in Indian Philosophy* (Delhi, 1963), 3 describes *maya* as blind potentiality, which works in connection with and under the ordering power of absolute consciousness.

11. The aspect of creative power in the notion of *maya* is especially emphasized by R. Reyna, *The Concept of Maya* (London, 1962) 20 and M.K.V. Iyer, *Advaita Vedanta*, 5.

12. P.K. Sundaram, *Advaita Epistemology*, 196.

13. MW, 826.

14. BSB I,IV,3 & I,IV,9.

15. M. Eliade, *Yoga, Immortality and Freedom*, XVIIIf and Reyna, op. cit., 34f.

16. Mahadevan, 17.

17. BG VII,25.

18. Cf. the context of BG VII,25.

19. Sankara's commentary on GK III,19.

20. Iyer, op.cit., 161ff; P. Deussen, *Das System des Vedanta*, 55ff; Sundaram, 240ff.

21. Sundaram, 241ff.

22. This corresponds throughout to Christian ideas about sin. Cf. S. Grant, "Reflections on the Mystery of Christ," in: *God's Word among Men*, 113.

23. Sankara's commentary on BU I,IV,10.

24. This play on words is used often in Advaita Vedanta. However it has absolutely no etymological value. Cf. T.M.P. Mahadevan, *Invitation to Indian Philosophy*, 390.

25. Ibid., 390.

26. AmU 11f.

27. BU,I,IV,17.

28. BU III,IX,1ff.

29. Sankara's commentary on BU I,III,1.

30. Eliade, op. cit., 76.

31. BU IV,IV,5.

32. A.G. Aranjaniyil, *The Absolute of the Upanishads, Personal or Impersonal?* (Bangalore, 1975) 18f.

33. Sankara's commentary on BU V,II,3.

34. Sankara's commentary on BU I,IV,10: "While the one who does not know *brahman*, who prays to God as an other, a God different from himself, who approaches him with a humble attitude, bringing him praise, honor, sacrifice, gifts, devotion, meditation etc. and thinks 'He is a non-self, different from me, and I am another, determined to carry out rites, I must serve him as a debtor'—while he prays with such ideas, he does not know the truth . . . he is like a beast in relationship to the gods. Just as a cow or other animal is used for its services . . . so too this man will be useful for the gods on the basis of his many services, such as, for example, his offering sacrifices." True faith and devotion, which lead to *brahman*-knowledge, are distinguished by Sankara from this "servile" piety.

35. C. Ramalingam, "How Far is it Correct to Say that God is a Projection of the Human Mind?" in: *Indian Philosophical Annual* VII, (Madras, 1971) 161.

36. RV X, 129,1-2.

37. SU VI,9. Sankara favors these ideas in BSB I,I,11.

38. SU IV,1ff.

39. SU VI,6.

40. SU VI,10.

41. BSB I,II,28 & 31.

42. BSB I,I,21.

43. BG XV, 16–18.

44. This contradiction can be clarified on the basis of ancient mythological ideas. The "position" or function of the highest being, which is considered as empirical truth, always remains intact. Various carriers fulfill this function corresponding to their *karman*.

45. The concept of *mayasaktih* can be understood equally as a composite of either *bahuvrihi* or *tatpurusa* type.

46. BSB II,I,30.

47. This is taught by both the BG and the Upanishads. The tradition is continued in the Tantras. The Mayahana joins Buddhism. Cf. Zimmer, 364,380,505.

48. Cf. R.K. Tripathi, "Advaita Vedanta and Western Thought," in: *Indian Philosophical Annual* VII, 37.

49. Cf. especially the hymans to *Daksinamurti* and *Bhajagovindam* in: *The Hymns of Sankara.* Ed. T.M.P. Mahadevan (Madras, 1970) Ananda K. Coomaraswamy calls Sankara "a devoted worshipper before images of God, a visitor of temples, and a singer of respectful hymns" (A.K. Coomaraswamy), *The Transformation of Nature in Art:* New York. 1934, 160). Cf. also Reyna, op. cit. and R. Otto, *West-Östliche Mystik,* 143f.

50. Especially impressive are the five hymns to Arunachala, in: *The Collected Works of Ramana Maharshi.* Edited by A. Osborne (Tiruvannamalai, 1974), 79ff.

51. MU II,I,2. Cf. O. Lacombe, *L'Absolu selon le Védanta* (Paris, 1966) 270f.

52. SB X,VI,1.11 & BSB I,II,26.

53. BU I,IV,10.

54. BSB I,III,11.

55. Aranjaniyil, op. cit., 7f. with special regard to the text BU III,VIII,10. The text calls the saved *brahmanah,* not *brahman.* Grammatically this can be interpreted as a genitive neuter, and a genitive of place. *Brahmanah* would thus mean a belonging to, or it would refer to the origin of *brahman.* But it can also be construed as adjectival, and would then be translated as "a brahmanic" and have a meaning similar to the genitive. Here, however, in this expression, the difference is clearly maintained. Analogously BU III,VII,3f. is to be read: God is fully immanent, but he is likewise infinitely more or is fully transcendent and is not known by the world; *yam sarvani na viduh* (15). In the commentary on BU IV,III. (intro.) and BU II,I,20, however, Sankara more strongly emphasizes the identity.

56. R. Panikkar, *The Vedic Experience,* 749.

57. CU VI,I,1ff.; Kaiv U 16.

58. Deussen, op. cit., 127.

59. K.C. Pandey, *Abhinavagupta* (Varanasi, 1963) 317.

60. T.M.P. Mahadevan, *The Philosophy of Advaita,* 203.

61. A central text for Sankara's notion of causality is BSB III,I,6f.

62. Mahadevan, 201.

63. BSB II,I,18ff.

64. SU I,14.
65. GK IV,73.
66. Mahadevan, *Gaudapada*, 115ff.
67. CU VI,II,1.
68. BU II,IV,14; cf. Mahadevan, *Invitation*, 358f.
69. S.M.S. Chari, *Advaita and Visistadvaita* (London, 1961) 112f.
70. This relationship is developed in the Mand U, also in GK. We cannot discuss the theory in detail here, but only cite one text which summarizes the doctrine well: "In the state of waking, the self consorts with the objects of sense which are external, and its enjoyments are gross. In dreams it revels in a world of images, and its experience is subtle. In sleep there are no desires, nor dreams; the self becomes one, without the distinction of seer and seen object; it remains as bliss enjoying bliss. . . . The fourth *caturtha* (or *turiya*), which is the real self, is beyond the changing modes of existence. It is not caught in the triple stream of waking, dream, and sleep, though it is the underlying substrate of these states." (Mahadevan, *Invitation*, 39f.)
71. RV X,121. On the development of the concept of *isvara*, cf. R. Panikkar, *The Unknown Christ of Hinduism* (London, 1964) 119ff.
72. Mahadevan, *The Philosophy of Advaita*, 206.
73. BSB I,III,27; cf. also BSB IV,III,10 & 14, where it is said that *hiranyagarbha* stands above becoming and passing.
74. BU III,IX,9 and Sankara's commentary.
75. Sankara's commentary on PU VI,4.
76. BSB I,II,23. Sankara invokes RV X,121, where it says "*Hiranyagarbha* was first born, and when it was born it became the Lord of all being." Sankara makes no distinction between "was born" (*samavartata*) and "was created" (*asrjyata*: imperf. passive).
77. GK III,25.
78. BSB I,IV,3 w. ref. to KU I,III,11.
79. IU 12 and Sankara's commentary, cf. Mahadevan, *Gaudapada*, 135.
80. Mahadevan, *The Philosophy of Advaita*, 206.
81. BU IV,II,3.
82. RV X,90,5.
83. BU I,IV,1 and Sankara's commentary.
84. Sankara's commentary on BU II,V,19.
85. Eliade, op. cit., 337f.

86. MW,705.

87. MW,701.

88. Zimmer, 338 & 477; Swami Sivananda, *The Science of Pranayama* (Sivanandanagar, 1971) 27ff. It would be false to understand *prana* primarily as emotional-sexual energy. Sexuality is only one possible form of expression of *prana*, Cf. B.K.S. Iyengar, *Light on Yoga*, 12.

89. Nakamura, *Parallel Developments*, 413.

90. Zimmer, 309.

91. BU VI,I,1; BU I,V,21 and Sankara's commentary on Kaus U III,8 clarifies: "Just as the rim is closely joined to the spokes of a wheel and the spokes to the hub, so too the objects of the senses are closely linked to the sense organs and the sense organs to *prana*. This *prana* has the consciousness of the self (*atman*), it is happiness, it does not age or die. Through a good work it does not become greater and through a bad one not less, but it enables the doing of the good work, which it lifts up from this world and the evil work which it pulls down. It is the guardian of the world, the highest Lord and giver of the world. Humans must recognize: 'it (he) is my self.' "

92. BU I,III,19.

93. CU VI,XII,2.

94. BSB II,IV,1ff., esp. Sankara's introduction to section II,IV.

95. Sankara's commentary on BU V,I,1.

96. BU III,IX,9ff. and Sankara's commentary.

97. CU VII,XV,1.

98. Sankara's commentary on BU I,VI,3. If *prana* describes the individual organs of life and energy, there is naturally no identity with the Absolute. Here we must be attentive to the double use of the concept *prana*, in order to verify whether the original energy itself or its transformation is meant in particular areas of its operation. On the theory of *prana's* individual ways of working, cf. Deussen, 191ff & 217f.

99. BU IV,I,3.

100. BU IV,I,4ff.

101. BSB II,IV,2.

102. Mand U I,6 and Sankara's commentary.

103. Mand U I,6.

104. Iyer, 96.

105. BG XIII,1ff. The similarity to Samkhya-philosophy cannot

be denied. There too, especially in connection with Yoga practice, material (*prakrti*) and spirit (*purusa*) are seen not only as two principles in opposition, but sometimes also as steps in an evolving process. The intellect is a "highly developed form of matter" (Eliade, op. cit., 30). However, Advaita Vedanta is vehemently against this.

106. BG XIII,19.

107. Nakamura, *Ways of Thinking*, 124f.

108. H.v. Glasenapp, *Die Philosophie der Inder*, 160.

109. Nakamura, *Parallel Developments*, 64f.

110. On the various kinds of *karman* and their meaning in the functioning of the elements of destiny, cf. Zimmer, 395ff.

111. BU III,VII,23.

112. BSB I,I,5. Cf. the commentary of A.K. Coomaraswamy on this: "On the One and Only Transmigrant," in *Selected Papers*, Vol. II. (Bollingen Series LXXXIX: Princeton Univ. Press, 1977) 66–87.

113. The relationship between *karman* and creation is not without contradictions in Advaita Vedanta. If God is the only cause of the world, *karman* cannot be a necessary condition which binds God. Although the world has an end, it must be without beginning, because the karmic factors reach back indefinitely. Cf. R.V. DeSmet, "The Law of Karma: A Critical Examination," in *Indian Ecclesiastical Studies* VIII,3 (Bangalore, 1969) 181ff.

114. Panikkar, "The Law of Karman and the Historical Dimension of Man," in: *Philosophy East and West* XXII,1 (Honolulu, 1972) 40.

115. BSB II,II,37; Cf. DeSmet, 181ff.

116. Sankara's commentary on BU III,I,6.

117. Panikkar, *The Vedic Experience*, 216ff; cf. Kaiv U 8.

118. BG XI,39.

119. Eliade, 195.

120. T.M.P. Mahadevan, *Time and the Timeless* (Madras, 1953).

121. Nakamura, *Ways of Thinking*, 64, 80f., 146.

122. R. Panikkar, "Le Temps circulaire: Temporisation et Temporalité," in: *Temporalité et Aliénation* (Paris, 1975), 225.

123. Panikkar, 234.

124. Nakamura, 111.

125. God continually returns in other forms as *avatara*. This

teaching characterizes Visnuism and only stands on the periphery in Advaita Vedanta.

126. MB XIV,39,21; Panikkar, *The Vedic Experience*, 645.

127. BU I,II,3.

128. BU I,VI,1.

129. CU III,XVII,6.

130. Panikkar, 645.

131. SU I,12.

132. We cannot follow up this interesting parallel. Cf. S.B. Dasgupta, *An Introduction to Tantric Buddhism* (Berkeley/London, 1974), 10ff.; Zimmer, 471f.

133. Reyna, *The Concept of Maya*, 35. In India there is the image of the three-headed God (*trimurti*), which means the trinity of the gods Brahma, Visnu and Siva. This expresses three functions or characteristics of the divine, and these are thought of as three persons. They should not be confused with the steps of manifestation in Advaita Vedanta and are not properly a trinity.

Chapter 4

1. T.M.P. Mahadevan, *The Philosophy of Advaita* (New Delhi, 1976) 110. For a comprehensive introduction to Advaita epistemology, cf. P.K. Sundaram, *Advaita Epistemology* (Madras, 1968).

2. P. Deussen, *Das System des Vedanta* (Leipzig, 1883) 153f.

3. T.M.P. Mahadevan, *Gaudapada* (Madras, 1975) 116f.

4. GK III,15 and Sankara's commentary.

5. Mahadevan, op. cit., 159.

6. H. Nakamura, *Parallel Developments* (Tokyo/New York, 1975) 431.

7. Sankara's commentary on BU III,VI,1; Mahadevan, *The Philosophy of Advaita*, 562, 201f.

8. R. DeSmet, "Questioning Vedanta," in: *Indian Philosophical Annual* VII (Madras, 1977) 104f.

9. BU IV,III,22; Mahadevan, *Gaudapada*, 84, 93.

10. BG X,10–11; XI,47–53.

11. BU IV,IV,20.

12. Mahadevan, *The Philosophy of Advaita*, 255, 275.

13. Sankara's commentary on BU IV,IV,20.

14. TU III,I,1.

15. Swami Vimalananda, *Introduction, Chandogya Upanishad.* Edited by Sri Ramakrishna Math (Madras, 1956) XLIII.

16. CU VII,VII,1; Sankara's commentary on BU I,IV,7.

17. Mahadevan, op. cit., 264ff.; Sankara's commentary on BU I,IV,7.

18. BG V,4f.: *ekam samkhyam ca yogam* (5b) The way of knowledge is described here as *samkhya*. This does not refer only to the philosophical school of the same name.

19. BU III,V,1; III,IV,47.

20. O. Lacombe, *L'Absolu selon le Védanta* (Paris, 1966) 352f.

21. Sankara's commentary on BU IV,IV,21.

22. H. Zimmer, *Philosophie und Religion Indiens* (Frankfurt, 1976) 385ff.

23. T.M.P. Mahadevan, *Invitation to Indian Philosophy* (New Delhi, 1974) 398f.

24. Sankara's commentary on BU IV,IV,12.

25. AV XIII,IV,14–16; TU II,I,1 and elsewhere.

26. Sankara's commentary on BU I,IV,7 and IV,IV,17.

27. KeU II,1 and Sankara's commentary.

28. BG II,55. Cf. Nakamura, *Parallel Developments*, 116 establishes a parallel with the concept of *noesis noeseos*.

29. KeU II,3; BSB I,I,4.

30. Mahadevan, *The Philosophy of Advaita*, 261, 277.

31. MU III,II,3.

32. MU III,I,8.

33. M. Eliade, *Yoga. Immortality and Freedom*, 80.

34. KU II,20 and 23; SU III,20.

35. SU VI,21. Cf. Deussen, op. cit., 90ff., who collects and interprets the corresponding texts from Sankara's BSB.

36. BG XI,47: *maya prasatnena tavarjunedam rupam param darsitamatmayogat.*

37. BG X,11.

38. Sankara's commentary on Mu III,II,3. The concept for revelation used in the Upanishads is derived from the root *vivr* (uncover, reveal). The desire for release is expressed by a form of the root *vr* (wish, ask, accept.)

39. KU I,II,23. The verse is almost identical to MU III, II, 3. However in the two cases Sankara gives a somewhat different interpretation.

40. KU II,I,2 and Sankara's commentary on KU I,III,23.

41. Cf. the collection of prayers: *Endlos ist die Zeit in Deinen Händen.* Eds.: I. Puthiadam/M. Kampchen (Kevalaer, 1978).

42. Kaus U II,7.

43. TU I,I,1: *tvam eva pratyaksam brahma vadisyami, rtam va-*

disyami, satyam vadisyami, tat mam avatu . . . tat vaktaram avatu, OM, santih, santih, santih.

44. Swami Bhajanananda, "Ramakrishna Mission," in an interview on 9/1/1976 in Bangalore.

45. Zimmer, op. cit., 56f.

46. B.K.S. Iyengar, *Light on Yoga* (London, 1977) 39f. This attitude is presupposed for the practice of Yoga.

47. BG IX,29.

48. Ibid.

49. BG XVII,3.

50. BG IX,28b; Cf. M.K.V. Iyer, *Advaita Vedanta* (Bombay, 1964), 175ff. where other texts are discussed as well.

51. BG IX,30.

52. H. Nakamura, *Ways of Thinking of Eastern Peoples* (Honolulu, 1971) 116.

53. Sankara's commentary on BU II,I: Introduction, where he refers to BG IV,39.

54. BG VI,47.

55. Ibid.

56. BG VIII,5; IX,3. The fact that these ideas on *sola fide* are structurally similar has already been pointed out by Deussen, op. cit., 433f.

57. BG XII,8.

58. BG XII,5.

59. Cf. R. Otto, *Die Gnadenreligion Indiens und das Christentum* (Munich, 1930); Zimmer, 339ff.

60. H.v. Glasenapp, *Die Philosophie der Inder*, 177f.

Chapter 5

1. HYP I,64f.

2. Sankara's commentary on BU V,I,1.

3. Swami Vimalananda, *Introduction. Chandogya Upanishad*, Sri Ramakrishna Math (Madras, 1975) XLIII and LVI.

4. SU II,6; Cf. M.K.V. Iyer, *Advaita Vedanta* (Bombay, 1964) 136ff.

5. There are parallels between the individual elements of temple cult and the practice of yoga even in details. Cf. Tara Michaëlle, *Religion and Yoga* (French Institute of Indology, Pondicherry, 1977).

6. M. Eliade, *Immortality and Freedom*, 227ff.

7. Ramana Maharshi, *Spiritual Instruction* (Tiruvannamalai, 1969) 6f.

8. Ibid.

9. Sankara's commentary on BU I,IV,7.

10. MU III,II,9; Sankara's commentary on BU IV,IV,25.

11. KeU II,4f.

12. H. Nakamura, "Weisheit und Erlösung durch Meditation. Ihr Sinn in der Philosophie Sankaras," in: *Munen muso. Ungegenständliche Meditation* Festschrift für P. Lassalle. Ed., G. Stachel (Mainz, 1978) 55f.

13. However these kinds of eschatological discussions are not infrequent in popular Hinduism. Thus there is a Brahma-world (*brahma-loka*) which is a paradise beyond this world, e.g., CU VIII,V,4. But this sort of dualism is foreign to Advaita.

14. Sankara's commentary on BU I,IV,7; I,IV,15; III,III,1; IV,IV,20.

15. Sankara's commentary on BU IV,IV,6. The similarity to Buddhist *tathata* (thusness) is obvious.

16. BG X,4f.

17. BSB I,IV,19.

18. BSB II,III,46.

19. BG XIV,7.

20. BG XIII,7.

21. BG XVI,4.

22. TU II,VII,1.

23. Sankara defines *santi* in his commentary on BG XIII, 7 as the immutability of the heart when this or that has been killed (*paraparaghapraptau avikriya*).

24. For a description of the ideal of *jivanmukta* and its clarification by means of the theory of *karman*, cf. BU IV,IV,7; KU VI,14; H. Zimmer, *Philosophie und Religion Indiens*, 394.; Ch. Valiaveetil, *Liberated Life. Ideal of Jivanmukti in Indian Religions* (Madurai, 1980).

25. Iyer, op. cit., 191f. Death is also a major philosophical theme in India where it is seen as the door to true life. The quest for immortality was expressed in the meditation on death, and in Yoga death is anticipated in meditation, and this is borne out by the initiation experiences of many great Yogins, such as Mataji Krishnabai, Ramana Maharsi and others. Cf. Eliade, op. cit., 362ff.; H. Nakamura, *Ways of Thinking of Eastern Peoples*, 165.

26. T.M.P. Mahadevan, *Invitation to Indian Philosophy*, 402.

27. Zimmer, op. cit., 21f.

28. Zimmer, 53f.

29. MU III,II,8; PU VI,5; Cf. Iyer, op. cit., 53f.

30. BG XIII,24ff.

31. BU I,IV,10; IV,IV,12; Kaiv U 19.

32. W. Indich, *Consciousness in Advaita Vedanta* (Varanasi, 1980) 111f.

33. Valiaveetil, op. cit., 50,59.

34. T.M.P. Mahadevan, *Gaudapada*, 23.

35. KU II,III,10f.: *yada pancavatistthante jnanani manasa saha, buddhiscana vicestate tamahuh paramam gatim*—When the five senses of knowledge and the mind have come together and become silent, and the intellect is not active, this is called the highest state. Cf. also SU II, 8ff.

36. BSB I,III,18; BSB II,III,48, where this basic attitude is also related to the whole of moral casuistry.

37. BSB II,I,3: *etena yogah pratyuktah*—This disapproves of Yoga. Cf. Sankara's commentary on GK III,39; T.R. Kalkarni, *Upanishads and Yoga. An Empirical Approach to the Understanding* (Bombay, 1972).

38. B.K.S. Iyengar, *Light on Yoga*, 19.

39. Zimmer, op. cit., 152ff.

40. Sankara's commentary on BU I,IV,7.

41. BU I,III,19; Cf. B.K.S. Iyengar, *Light on Pranayama* (London, 1981).

42. Eliade, op. cit., 362ff.

43. Sankara's commentary on BU I,III,11.

44. Sankara's commentary on BU I,IV,1.

45. BSB I,II,7.

46. MU III,I,8.

47. Ananda Giri's commentary on KU I,III,12.

48. BSB IV,III,15.

49. Sankara's commentary on CU I,I,1.

50. Seen already by Gaudapada, Cf. *Gaudapada*, op. cit., 185.

51. GK III,1; III,16.

52. Mahadevan, op. cit., 174.

53. Zimmer, op. cit., 338f. OM is formed by the three letters a - u - m. The diphthong *au* in Sanskrit changes into o.

54. MU III,II,6.

55. BSB IV,IV,2.

56. BSB IV,IV,5.

57. Sankara's commentary on TU I (introduction).

Chapter 6

1. P. Schoonenberg, "Gods tegenwoordigheid in Christus: voortzetting van een gedachtenwisseling," in: *Tijdschrift voor Theologie* 9 (Nijmegen, 1969) 384ff.

2. R. Seeberg, *Lehrbuch der Dogmengeschichte*, Bd. II (Erlangen/Leipzig, 1923) 163ff.

3. P. Tillich, *Systematic Theology*, vol. III (Univ. of Chicago Press, 1963) p. 283ff.

4. H. Küng, *Existiert Gott?* (Munich/Zurich, 1978) 765.

5. R. Seeberg, *Zum dogmatischen Verständnis der Trinitätslehre* (Leipzig, 1908) 10.

6. Küng, op. cit., 765f.

7. Thomas of Aquinas, *Summa contra gentiles* I,25,233.

8. Anselm of Canterbury, *Proslogion* cap. 2 & 3.

9. R. Otto, *Aufsätze das Numinose betreffend* (Gotha, 1929) 1ff.

10. Cf. "Problemanzeige," in: E. Jungel, *Gott als Geheimnis der Welt*, Tübingen 1977, 7f. (English: *God as the Mystery of the World*, Eerdmans Publishing Co., Grand Rapids, 1983; 3 "Definition of the Problem.")

11. Seeberg, *Dogmengeschichte* II, 53.

12. Hilarius, *De Trinitate* 3,13; 2,24f.; 9,5 etc.

13. Jungel, op. cit., 206; Cf. G. Ebeling, *Dogmatik des christlichen Glaubens* Bd. III (Tübingen, 1979) 529.

14. C.F. v. Weizsäcker, *Der Garten des Menschlichen*. Beiträge zur geschichtlichen Anthropologie (Munich/Vienna, 1977) 529f. He shows that "becoming-aware," as distinguished from "thinking," is linked with every meditative, spiritual experience. The one who becomes aware is changed and elevated. He/she participates in a spiritually higher stage of integration.

15. A. Adam, *Dogmengeschichte* Bd. I (Berlin, 1970) 119.

16. Philo, *De Abr.* 121, cited by Adam, op. cit., 119f.

17. Philo, *De fug.* 109f. cited by ibid.

18. Adam, op. cit., 122.

19. Much material has been collected along these lines, esp. ideas coming from anthropology. Cf. A Schütze, *Vom Wesen der Trinität* (Stuttgart, 1954).

20. Cf. E. Pagels, *The Gnostic Gospels* (New York, 1981). It cannot yet be convincingly demonstrated how far gnosis—and, along with it, trinitarian thinking—was influenced by India. That there are relationships seems probable.

21. F.H. Kettler, in: RGG VI, 1025ff.

22. Adam, ibid., 130.

23. F. Chr. Baur, *Die christliche Lehre von der Dreieinigkeit und Mensch-werdung Gottes in ihrer geschichtlichen Entwicklung*, Bd. I (Tübingen, 1841) 171ff.

24. Irenaeus, *Adv. haer.*, 5,28,3.

25. Ibid., 4,7,4; 4,20,4; 3,24,2.

26. Ibid., 4,20,1: *Adest enim ei semper verbum et sapientia, filius et spiritus, per quos et in quibus omnia libere et sponte fecit.*

27. Irenaeus, *Epideixis* 1,1,7.

28. Irenaeus, *Adv. haer.*, 2,10,4.

29. R. Seeberg, *Dogmengeschichte* Bd. I, 396.

30. Ibid., 394f.

31. Tertullian, *Adv. Marc.* 2,27.

32. Idem, *Adv. Prax* 2,3,8f.; 11,12,24f.

33. Adam, op. cit., 164f.

34. F.H. Kettler, op. cit., 1025ff.

35. Tertullian, *Adv. Hermog. 3: fuit tempus, cum ei filius non fuit.*

36. A.V. Harnack, *Lehrbuch der Dogmengeschichte* Bd. I (Freiburg im Br., 1888) 489.

37. Ibid., 489.

38. Tertullian, *Adv. Prax.* 14.

39. Ibid., 29.

40. Tertullian, *Adv. Marc* 3,6.

41. RGG VI, 1023ff.

42. Tertullian, *Adv. Prax.* 8.

43. Baur, op. cit., 171ff.

44. Irenaeus, *Adv. haer.* 2,28.

45. Harnack, 492. Of course this demonstration does not cover the same matter as *paramarthika* and *vyavharika*. Yet the similarity of the starting point is obvious.

46. K. Ruth, "Die Trinitarische Spekulation in Deutscher Mystik und Scholastik," in: *Zeitschrift fur Deutsche Philologie* 72,1 (Stuttgart, 1951) 50ff.; Cf. also G. Kretschmar, *Studien zur Frühchristlichen Trinitätstheologie* (Tübingen, 1956). The judgment of Harnack, (op. cit., 583) that the teaching on the Logos is related less to the aspect of redemption than to creation, is problematic because it divides what in Origen's eyes was indivisible.

47. Origen, *De princ.* 1,1,1.

48. Ibid., 1,1,6.

49. Origen, *C. Cels.* 7,38.

50. Adam, op. cit., 180.

51. Origen, *In Joh.* 2,10,72.

52. Baur, op. cit., 208f.

53. Adam, op. cit., 184.

54. Origen, *C. Cels.* 5,39.

55. Origen, *In Joh.* 13,36,234; *De princ.* i,2,6 etc.

56. Origen, *De princ.* 1,24; 1,2,9.

57. Seeberg calls attention to the fact (op. cit., 510, note 1) that on the one hand the same idea is found in Plotinus; on the other hand, eternal generation holds true for Christians insofar as they are in Christ.

58. Origen, *De princ.* 4,28; 1,2,4.

59. Origen, *De orat.* 15,1.

60. Origen, *De princ.* 1,3,5.

61. Origen, Ibid., 1,3,5ff.

62. Harnack, 583.

63. This way of picturing things comes from Seeberg, op. cit., 515. It is not found in Origen himself, but is used by Irenaeus, *Adv. Haer.* 2,13,6.

64. Adam, op. cit., 190.

65. Origen, *In Ezech. Hom.* 3,3.

66. Here we cannot discuss the details of the doctrine of *theopoiesis* and *apokatastasis*, although it is extremely important for the theological dialogue with the Orthodox Church and also in dialogues with India. Cf. M. von Brück, "Sanctification, Glorification, Theosis," in: *A Dialogue Begins. Lutheran-Orthodox Dialogue in India.* Eds. K.M. George, H. Hoefer (Kottayam 1983), 268–282.

67. Origen, *De princ.*, 1,2,13.

68. We have not presented Clement here because Origen is more significant for the development of the trinity. But it remains important that Clement strongly emphasized apophatic language about God and thus influenced the Areopagite.

69. Adam, op. cit., 228.

70. Athanasius, *C. Ar. or.* 1,27f.

71. Seeberg, *Dogmengeschichte*, Bd. II, 62f.

72. Athanasius, *C. Ar. or.* 1,58.

73. For Athanasius' position on the term, *hypostasis*, cf. C. Andresen, "*Zur Entstehung und Geschichte des Trinitarischen Personbegriffs*," in: ZNW 52, 1961, 36ff.

74. Seeberg, op. cit., 71.

75. Athanasius, *C. Ar. or.* i,16 with ref. to 2 P 1:4.

76. Seeberg, op. cit., 78 gives a complete list of the pertinent texts from Athanasius.

77. Athanasius, *C. Ar. or.* 3,19; 4,20.

78. Harnack, 291f; Seeberg, 86.

79. Adam, op. cit., 238f.

80. Ibid., 235. Harnack points out (op. cit., 286ff.) the similarity between the Cappadocians' and Tertullian's doctrine of the trinity.

81. Harnack, 256f. For a good introduction to the theology of the Cappadocians, cf. K. Holl, *Amphilochius von Ikonium* (Tübingen, 1904) 130ff.; M. Gomes de Castro, *Die Trinitätslehre des hl. Gregor von Nyssa* (Freiburg, 1938); F. Diekamp, *Die Gotteslehre des hl. Gregor von Nyssa* (Münster, 1896).

82. Gregory of Nyssa, *De trin.* (Öhl. II,176f.) cited by Seeberg, op. cit., 128.

83. Harnack, 257, note 1.

84. Gregory of Nazianzus, *Or.* 42,15; 20,6f; Gregory of Nyssa, *Ad gentil.* (Öhl. II,226); Basil, *C. Eunom.* 1,20.

85. Gregory of Nyssa, *C. Eunom.* 2 Mi. 45,564; Gregory of Nazianzus, *Or.* 23,11.

86. Seeberg, op. cit., 128.

87. John Damascene, *De Fide Orthodoxa* MPG 789–1228.

88. Baur, op. cit., Bd. II,180.

89. Adam, op. cit., 278f.

90. Augustine, *De trin.* 5,1,2.

91. Augustine, *De trin.* 5,2,3; 5,1,2; 7,5,10. According to Basil's presentation of the trinity the *ousia* is related to the *hypostaseis* as *koinon* is to *idion* (exemplar), and this leads to the suspicion of tritheism. But Augustine clearly defines the indivisible unity of God. He translates *ousia* as *essentia* and *hypostasis* as either *substantia* or *persona* (without any consistent pattern). The difficulty is that Tertullian had already used *substantia* to describe the unity of God's essence. Cf. Schmaus, Introduction to the German edition of *De Trinitate*, BdK II. Reihe Bd. XIII (Munich, 1935) XXX.

92. Augustinus, *De trin.* 2,5,9; 5,14,15; etc.

93. Ibid., 2,5,9: *Cum eum pater verbo misit, a patre et verbo eius factum est, ut mitteretur. Ergo a patre et filio missus est idem filius, quia verbum patris est ipse filius.*

94. Ibid.

95. Ibid., 2,5,10.

96. Ibid., 6,9,10.

97. Ibid., 5,11,12.

98. Ibid., 7,6,11.

99. Ibid., 6,7,8.

100. Ibid., 6,7,8.

101. Ibid., 5,5,6: *relativum non est accidens, quia non est mutabile.*

102. Seeberg, op. cit., 158, gives the reason why Augustine hesitated over this idea; in *De trin.* 5,6, however, it becomes a necessary and unavoidable conclusion.

103. Augustine, *De trin.* 5,11,12.

104. Ibid.

105. Ibid., 4,20,27.

106. Ibid., 5,9,10.

107. Augustine, *Conf.* 13.11.12.

108. Augustine, *De trin.* 4, prol. 1.

109. Ibid., 10,11,18.

110. Ibid., 9,4,7; 9,5,8.

111. Ibid., 8,10,14.

112. In principle, what Augustine describes here is what the later Eastern Christian teaching called *perichoresis* (John Damascene).

113. Seeberg, op. cit., 162.

114. Augustine, *De trin.* 7,6,11; 15,28,51.

115. Ibid., 15,17,31.

116. Ibid., 6,5,7; 5,11,12.

117. Ibid., 2,17,28; 7,3,4.

Chapter 7

1. R. Otto, *West-Östliche Mystik* (Gotha, 1926).

2. Sh. Ueda, *Die Gottesgeburt der Seele und der Durchbruch zur Gottheit. Die Mystische Anthropologie Meister Eckarts und ihre Konfrontation mit der Mystik des Zen-Buddhismus* (Gütersloh, 1965).

3. Ph. Hodgson, *Three 14th Century Mystics* (London, 1967) 21.

4. W. Johnston, *The Mysticism of the Cloud of Unknowing* (Wheathamstead, 1980) 11.

5. Th. Merton, Foreword to Johnston (note 4) IX.

6. Hodgson, op. cit., 25.

7. Johnston, op. cit., 68ff.

8. Cited in Johnston, ibid.

9. The humanity of Christ is the way to God, not something on which we should dwell as an end in itself, but what leads us to God. (Thomas Aquinas, cited in Johnston, 72.)

10. Ruysbroeck, *Die Zierde der Geistlichen Hochzeit*, 66.

11. Johnston, op. cit., 40.

12. Johnston gives all the citations on this theme from the *Cloud.* op. cit. 182ff.

13. Johnston, 193.

14. *Privy Counsel* 136,9.15; cited in Johnston, 218f.

15. *Privy Counsel* 137; 141,20; 142,17 etc.; Johnston, 234ff.

16. *Privy Counsel* 169,27.

17. Johnston, 253.

18. Theresa von Avila (Seelenburg), *Seventh Mansion* 2,4.

19. H. Dumoulin, *Östliche Meditation und Christliche Mystik* (Freiburg/Munich, 1966) 118.

20. J.B. Chethimattam, "The Greek Religious Apophatism," in: *Journal of Dharma* VI,1 (Bangalore, 1981) 79f.

21. E. Cousins, "Fulness and Emptiness in Bonaventure and Eckhart," in: *Journal of Dharma* VI,1 (Bangalore, 1981) 66f.

22. Dumoulin, op. cit., 118.

23. *Des Mystikers Heinrich Seuse deutsche Schriften*, ed.; Nikolaus Heller (Heidelberg, 1926) 155; cited in Dumoulin, op. cit., 67.

24. *Heinrich Seuse, Büchlein von der Wahrheit*, in: *Deutsche Mystische Schriften.* Ed.: G. Hofmann (Düsseldorf, 1966) 331–362. Our citations refer to this edition.

25. *"Die Trinität ist nur die Manifestation der Gottheit"* (The trinity is only the manifestation of the divinity). *Meister Eckhart*, Pfeiffer (Göttingen, 1924), Sermon 76: "Expedit vobis." Even if this sermon is not authentic—as Quint admits in his commentary on it—it presents a clear summary of Eckhart's position.

26. The editor refers to Dennis the Areopagite, *On the Holy Names* I,1,5; idem, Mystical Theology V; idem, *The Celestial Hierarchy* II,3, and also to Thomas Aquinas, *Summa theol.* I,9,13 ad 3.

27. Cf. esp. Suso's *Büchlein der Ewigen Weisheit.*

28. E. Jungclaussen, *Der Meister in Dir. Entdeckung der Inneren Welt nach Johannes Tauler* (Freiburg, 1975) 20f.

29. Ibid., 25.

30. Ibid., 26.

31. J. Tauler, *Predigten* Bd. I & II. G. Hofmann (Einsiedeln, 1979) Bd. II, 611ff.

32. Tauler, Bd. I,84.

33. Tauler, Bd. II,621ff.

34. Tauler, Bd. I,80.

35. Tauler, Bd. I,14f.

36. Tauler, Bd. I,202f.

37. Tauler, Bd. I,201.

38. Tauler, Bd. II,583.

39. Tauler, Bd. II,537f.

40. Tauler, Bd. II,539.

41. Luther, WA 1,153.

42. Luther, WA 1,378f.

43. "Der Franckforter," *Theologia Deutsch*, A.M. Haas (Einsiedeln, 1980).

44. WA 1,20,1ff.

45. WA 12,585ff. (probably 1523).

46. WA 54,28ff.

47. WA 39/2 esp. 1ff., 92ff., 122ff., 284ff.

48. R. Seeberg, *Dogmengeschichte* IV, I. "Die Lehre Luthers" (Leipzig, 1933) 173.

49. R. Jansen, *Studien zur Trinitätslehre Luthers* (Frankfurt, 1975) 218.

50. E. Jungel points this out in: *Gottes Sein ist im Werden* (Tübingen, 1965) 16 (note 12); cf. R. Prenter, *Spiritus Creator. Studien zur Theologie Luthers* (Munich, 1954) 178.

51. Seeberg, op. cit., 235.

52. WA 42,17,2f.; 167,7ff.

53. Jansen, op. cit., 215ff. Nevertheless we cannot conclude that Luther was a subordinationist in his thinking.

54. WA 56,177,9f.

55. Seebert, op. cit., 179ff., where many examples are provided. Cf. also Prenter, op. cit., 179.

56. WA 18,684f.

57. WA 10/1,1.182–187; WA 42,27,1ff.

58. Jansen, op. cit., 208f.

59. Prenter, op. cit., 197.

60. WA 14,101,24: *id est spiritus sanctus, qui omnia vivificat, tenet, conservat;* Cf. also WA 24,30,20–29.

61. WA 12,450,7ff.; Cf. R. Weier. *Das Thema vom verborgenen Gott von Nikolaus von Kues zu Martin Luther*, Doctoral dissertation (Mainz, 1965) 85ff.

62. Seeberg, op. cit., 223f.; WA 34/1,147.

63. WA 57,99.

64. WA 5,129,9ff.

65. WA 5,128f.

66. WA 2,138,15ff.; Cf. F. Gogarten, *Luthers Theologie* (Tübingen, 1967) 91.

67. WA 5,176,32f.

68. WA 39/1,455; Cf. Th. Harnack, *Luthers Theologie* Bd. I (Munich, 1927) 70ff.; 444ff.

69. WA 3,246,19f.; 4,87,22ff.; 4,331,16. Luther here couples *opus alienum* with *opus suum.*

70. Seeberg, op. cit., 174.

71. Seeberg, 178; WA 18,633,15ff. Cf. also the excellent study of H.J. McSorley, *Luthers Lehre vom unfreien Willen* (Munich, 1967) 317ff.

72. WA 18,661,28; Cf. H. Bandt, *Luthers Lehre vom Verborgenen Gott* (Berlin, 1958) 117.

73. WA 18,753,36ff.

74. McSorley, op. cit., 278ff.

75. WA 42,11,11ff., Cf. Weier, op. cit., 176ff.

76. H. Bornkamm, *Luthers geistige Welt* (Gütersloh, 1953) 86.

77. WA 5,144,19ff.; *qua deus iustus est, ut eadem iustitia Deus et nos iusti simus, sicut eodem verbo deus facit et nos sumus, quod ipse est, ut in ipse simus, et suum esse nostrum esse sit.*

78. Gogarten, op. cit., 127.

79. Concerning the following presentation, cf. H. Junghans, "Das Wort Gottes bei Luther während seiner ersten Psalmenvorlesung," in: ThLZ 1975,3, cols 161–174.

80. WA 3,561,1ff.; 1,28,2ff.

81. Junghans, op. cit., 164f.

82. WA 1,23,21–24; Junghans, col 166.

83. Junghans, op. cit., cols 166f. claims that for Luther there is also an interior word of Satan, and for this reason humankind is especially tempted. Thus the teaching on an *interior* word should not be reduced to something rationalistic, but describes a transrational event. Cf. B. Hoffman, *Luther and the Mystics* (Minneapolis, 1976) 133.

84. Cf. note 83. The rationalization of the notion of word is a development of later Lutheran theology.

85. Junghans, col 171 in ref. to WA 1,28,35.

86. In my opinion this idea cannot be found in Luther *verbis expressis.* It is, however, meaningful in systematizing his thought. It is interesting that Luther, at least in his early writings, speaks of an interior word which is not necessarily mediated by the external word.

87. WA 30/1,191,17ff.

88. H. Beintker, *Die Überwindung der Anfechtung bei Luther* (Berlin, 1954) 170.

89. Prenter, op. cit., 220f.

90. WA 56,300,11.

91. WA 40/2,582,5.

92. WA 5,111,35; 207,7ff.; 387,9f.: *tamen in media tentatione non apparet inimicus, sed solus deus omnia facere.*

93. Prenter, op. cit., 39ff.

94. WA 5,411,40f.; 5,297,30ff; WA 10/3,11ff.

95. WA 3,283,5.

96. WA 5,604,8; 5,176,24.

97. WA 56,388,11; 391,10.

98. WA 5,168,1.

99. WA 5,168,1–4: *Quo enim perveniat, qui sperat in deum, nisi in sui nihilum? Quo autem abeat, qui abit in nihilum, nisi eo, unde venit? Venit autem ex deo et suo nihilo, quare in deux redit, qui redit in nihilum.*

100. WA 40/3,154,11f.; Cf. Gogarten, 145f.

101. Cf. Prenter, op. cit., 207ff. The fact that Luther's understanding of faith must be considered in conjunction with such mystical expressions as *raptus* and *translatio* is pointed out by Hoffman, op. cit., 141, 156ff., 174ff., etc.

102. WA 40/3,738,6ff.; WA 57/3,144,10.

103. Thus, in the mystics, *mortificatio* is not understood simply as an exercise of abandonment which humans could do. John of the Cross, for example, considers that the experiences of temptation come from God alone. Luther's understanding is within the mainstream of the mystical tradition (against Beintker, op. cit., 88).

104. WA 4,87,22f.

105. Gogarten, op. cit., 167f.

106. McSorley, op. cit., 278ff. The true free will according to Luther is the theonomous will, WA 2,104,1f.

107. WA 40/1,488,1ff. (Roerer 1531): *ad hoc iusta humiliatio, contritio, contusio per ferreum malleum servit, ut gratia ad te veniat. Sic lex est praeparator ad gratiam.* Cf. Prenter, op. cit., 222f., also WA 5,179,31; 183,21; 7,556,30.

108. WA 18,782,30ff.

109. Gogarten, 61ff.; Beintker, op. cit., 41f.

110. WA 40/3,517.

111. Gogarten, op. cit., 39, with regard to the problem of *communicatio idiomatum*; cf. Hoffman, op. cit., 174ff. The person

living in faith can say: "I am Christ" (WA 40/1,285,5). Cf. the Vedantic *aham brahmasmi*, "I am Brahman."

112. WA 1,125,24.

113. Prenter, 41.

114. Prenter, 44, who presents many passages showing this realism, e.g., WA 1,593,1ff.: *per fidem Christi efficitur Christianus unus spiritus et unum cum Christo;* WA 2,146,14f.; *qui credit in Christo, haeret in Christo estque unum cum Christo;* WA 2,535,24; *Credere enim in Christum est eum induere, unum cum eo fieri.*

115. WA 56,250,18ff.; 359,27ff.

116. WA 56,450,2ff.

117. Cf. Harnack, op. cit., Bd. I 76ff.

118. Prenter, op. cit., 41; 185ff.

119. WA 30/1,183,8ff.

120. WA 54,64,4.

121. WA 26,505f.

122. Seeberg, 234.

123. WA 10/1,16,14f.

124. WA 52,344,11.

125. Seeberg, 233.

126. WA 50,274; 46,536.

127. Prenter, 188.

128. Seeberg, 112f.

129. WA 45,175,1ff. (Roerer 1537): *Qui baptisatus, est renatus coram deo nach seiner rechnung, er hats angefangen, Ideo coram eius oculis schon geschehen, der jungst tag sthet in fur oculis und in der thur. Coram oculis nostris nondum sic. Sed sua misericordia schon gerechnet, quando plenus, quasi effusus opulente etc. modo halten fest an dem anfang.* Cf. also Prenter 230f. Other passages are, e.g., WA 24,258; 18,203 & 205.

130. WA 56,234,7ff.; Seeberg, 173ff.

131. WA 23,133,21f.

132. WA 26,339,39ff.

133. WA 23,135,3ff.

134. WA 23,137,33ff.

135. WA 23,135,35ff.

136. G. Ebeling, *Luther. Einführung in sein Denken* (Tübingen, 1964), 305.

137. WA 23,133,26; 151,4. The hidden presence concerns not

only the realm of nature, but also human history, which is expressed by the teaching concerning "the larva of God." Cf. Seeberg op. cit., 192f. On the problem of determinism and contingence in Luther's notion of God, cf. McSorley, op. cit., 242ff.

138. Bandt, op. cit., 109f.

Chapter 8

1. G.W.F. Hegel, *Science of Logic*, Vol. 1, tr. by A.V. Miller. (N.Y. Humanities Press, 1976) 47f.

2. Ibid., p. 50: ". . . but a matter which is not external to the form, since this matter is rather pure thought and hence the absolute form itself. Accordingly, logic is to be understood as the system of pure reason, truth as it is without veil and in its own absolute nature. It can therefore be said that this content is the exposition of God as he is in his eternal essence before the creation of nature and a finite mind."

3. Hegel, ibid., 74.

4. Hegel, ibid., 82f.

5. Hegel, ibid., 92.

6. Hegel, ibid., 105.

7. Hegel, ibid., 94.

8. Hegel, ibid., 106.

9. Hegel, ibid., 121, 138ff.

10. Hegel, ibid., 139.

11. Qu. Lauer, "Hegel's Negative Theology," in: *Journal of Dharma* VI, 1 (Bangalore, 1981) 46.

12. Hegel, ibid., 144.

13. Hegel, ibid., 142.

14. L. Oeing-Hanhoff, "Hegel's Trinitätslehre," in: *Theologie und Philosophie* 52,3 (Freiburg, 1977) 384.

15. Hegel, ibid., 146: "The finite is not sublated by the infinite as by a power existing outside it; on the contrary, its infinity consists in sublating its own self."

16. Hegel, ibid., 149. 153. To demonstrate this starting point Hegel can appeal to church tradition. Especially Scotus Eriugena thinks God as the infinite who mediates the finite within himself in a trinitarian process.

17. On the following ideas of Hegel, cf. Vorlesungen über die

Philosophie der Religion (Lasson) Bd. II. *Die Absolute Religion* (Hamburg, 1966) 30f.

18. E. Jüngel, *Gott als Geheimnis der Welt* (Tübingen, 1977) 123f., notes that Hegel's special achievement is to have thought through philosophically the theology of the cross *as* the doctrine of the triune God.

19. Hegel, op. cit., 35.

20. G.W.F. Hegel, *Phenomenology of Spirit*, trans. A.V. Miller, Oxford University Press, 1977, 477.

21. Hegel, *Science of Logic* I, op. cit., 158. Hegel here grasps being-for-self as the spirit mediated in itself in relationship to the determinations of the infinite and the finite—in the finite the infinite appears to itself.

22. Hegel, *Philosophie der Religion*, 57.

23. Ibid.

24. Ibid., 61: "Personality (is) freedom, (and) even in its infinite being-for-self it is truly itself in its concept, it is thereby the determination of identity with self, the general."

25. Ibid., 65f.

26. Hegel, *Phenomenology*, 476.

27. Hegel, *Philosophie der Religion*, 173f. The last sentence demonstrates once again that faith in Christ requires the trinitarian view of God on soteriological grounds. Cf. Jüngel, op. cit., 124.

28. Ibid., 73.

29. Hegel, *Phenomenology*, 464.

30. Ibid., 19f.

31. Oeing-Hanhoff, op. cit., 391f.

32. Thomas Aquinas, 1 Sent 14,1,1; Cf. Oeing-Hanhoff, 388–395.

33. Oeing-Hanhoff, 394f.

34. Oeing-Hanhoff, 380.

35. K. Wilber, *Up from Eden. A Transpersonal View of Human Evolution* (New York, 1981); idem, *The Atman Project* (Wheaton/Ill., 1980) 183.

36. P. Cornehl, *Die Zukunft der Versöhnung. Eschatologie und Emanzipation in der Aufklärung, bei Hegel und der Hegelschen Schule* (Göttingen, 1971) 356f.

37. C.F. v. Weizsaecker, "Zu Hegels Dialektik," in: *Der Garten des Menschlichen*, 393f.

38. M. Heidegger, "Nietzsches Wort 'Gott ist tot,' " in: *Holzwege* (Frankfurt, 1963) 200.

Chapter 9

1. W. Pannenberg, "Die Aufnahme des philosophischen Gottes-begriffs als dogmatisches Problem der frühchristlichen Theologie," in: *Grundfragen Systematischer Theologie* I (Göttingen, 1967) 302.

2. J. Moltmann, *Trinität und Reich Gottes* (Munich, 1980) 144ff.

3. Plato, *Parmenides*, 137c.

4. Ibid., 142a.

5. Ibid., 142b. Plato makes the difference clear, insofar as the *hén estin* in the first case has no accent and thus describes the copula, whereas in the second case *hèn éstin* with the accent is a statement of being.

6. Other places (e.g., the Diotima discourse) point clearly to a completely different kind of mediation. Cf. A. Speiser, *Ein Parmenideskommentar* (Leipzig, 1937) 26.

7. K. Barth, *Church Dogmatics*, I,1: Edinburgh, T & T. Clark, 1936, 552. We can only treat a few of the problems in Barth's treatment of the trinity. For an overview of Barth, cf. E. Jüngel, *Gottes Sein ist im Werden* (Tübingen, 1965) 12–53.

8. Cf. V. Lossky, *The Mystical Theology of the Eastern Church* (London, 1957) 44ff.

9. Moltmann, op. cit., 159.

10. Barth, op. cit., 311f.

11. For a critique of Barth, cf. L. Oeing-Hanhoff, "Hegels Trinitätslehre," in: KuD 23,1977, 25–40, now in: *Grundfragen Systematischer Theologie* II (Göttingen, 1980), 96–111, used by Moltmann, op. cit., 154ff.

12. Barth, op. cit., 371.

13. Ibid., 383ff.

14. Ibid., 390.

15. Ibid., 279.

16. Ibid., 278.

17. Ibid., 424. We understand the concept in the same sense as E. Jüngel, viz., his formulation, God's being *in* becoming, op. cit., 110f.

18. Ibid., 555.

19. Ibid., 277. The philosophy of identity in this sense is therefore *pantheism*. The expression *deus sive natura* (Spinoza) must be fundamentally distinguished from the non-duality of reality based

on God as trinity, insofar as the determinations *deus* and *natura* are understood on the same ontological level and with the same attitude towards reality.

20. On the meaning of the notion of person in constructing a trinitarian understanding, cf. Andresen, "Zur Entstehung und Geschichte des Trinitarischen Personbegriffs," in: ZNW 52, 1961,1ff. and Harnack, *Lehrbuch der Dogmengeschichte*, Bd. II,287ff., where he presents an interesting comparison between Tertullian and the Cappadocians.

21. Lossky, op. cit., 50ff.

22. It is true that the concept of person in the early church must be clearly distinguished from the modern concept. Yet for the church fathers the meaning of individuality (Cappadocians) and self-consciousness (Augustine) is also connected with it.

23. Adam, *Lehrbuch der Dogmengeschichte* Bd. I (Berlin, 1970) 282.

24. Augustine, *De trin.* 15,17,31; 5,11,12; 6,5,7; 5,9,10.

25. Cf. K. Ruth, "Die Trinitarische Spekulation in Deutscher Mystik und Scholastik," in *Zeitschrift für Deutsche Philologie* 72,1 (Stuttgart, 1951) 24ff.; F. Chr. Baur, *Die Christliche Lehre von der Dreieinigkeit und Menschwerdung Gottes.* Bd. II, 537 & 892, n. 13.

26. F. Gogarten, *Luthers Theologie* (Tübingen, 1967) 167f.

27. H. Küng, *Existiert Gott?* (Munich, 1978) 691.

28. Barth, op. cit., 379.

29. Barth, 380f.

30. Barth, 382.

31. Thomas Aquinas, *Summa theol.* 1,50,1c.

32. R. Panikkar, "Words and Terms," in: *Archivio di Filosofia* (Instituto di Studi Filosofici, Roma, 1980) 127.

33. Jüngel, *Gottes Sein ist im Werden*, 114f.

34. Barth, KD III,1,52.

35. W. Pannenberg, "Die Subjektivität Gottes und die Trinitätslehre," op. cit., 96ff.

36. Pannenberg, 97.

37. Pannenberg, 110.

38. Pannenberg, 105ff. The Orthodox criticism of the Western notion of person touches precisely on this point. Cf. Lossky, op. cit., 48ff. and P. Bilaniuk, *Theology and Economy of the Holy Spirit: An Eastern Approach*, (Bangalore, 1980) 24ff.

39. P. Tillich, *The Courage to Be* (Yale Univ. Press, Yale, 1952) 87.

40. Ibid., 88.

41. Ibid., 89.

42. Ibid., 186.

43. Ibid., 157.

44. Ibid., 180.

45. P. Tillich, *Love, Power, and Justice* (Oxford Univ. Press, London, 1954) 25.

46. Ibid., 108.

47. Ibid., 27.

48. It is not necessary to repeat what was said about the concept of person. Cf. also Panikkar, *Myth, Faith and Hermeneutics* (New York, 1979) 376ff.

49. Tillich, op. cit., 64.

50. J. Moltmann, *Trinität und Reich Gottes* (Munich, 1980).

51. J. Moltmann, "Die Gemeinschaft des heiligen Geistes. Zur trinitarischen Pneumatologie," in: ThLZ 10, 1982, col. 707.

52. Moltmann, *Trinität und Reich Gottes*, 111.

53. Ibid., 119.

54. Ibid.; cf. also *idem, Gott in der Schöpfung. Ökologische Schöpfungslehre* (Munich, 1985) 109.

55. Moltmann, *Trinität und Reich Gottes*, 168,174,191f.; cf. above p. 136f. (German).

56. Ibid., 174.

57. Moltmann, *Gott in der Schöpfung*, 309.

58. Moltmann, *Trinität und Reich Gottes*, 155.

59. Ibid., 162.

60. Moltmann, *Gott in der Schöpfung*, 109.

61. Moltmann, *Trinität und Reich Gottes*, 167.

62. Ibid., 191.

63. Ibid.

64. Ibid., 165.

Chapter 10

1. BS I,I,2. Cf. on this esp. R. Panikkar, "Isvara and Christ as a Philosophical Problem," in: *Religion and Society* VI,3 (Bangalore, 1959) 8–16.

2. Panikkar, op. cit., p. 13 notes that for Sankara the *saguna brahman* or *isvara*—in other words, God as in relationship—is in either case included in the world side of the relationship, whereas for Ramanuja, *isvara* is purely and simply God. The important

task, which is also recognized and carried out in BS I,I,2, is to maintain the advaitic middle position.

3. R. Otto, *West-östliche Mystik,* 41 f. The use of the term "mysticism" is imprecise. We tolerate this imprecision here because the meaning of this term for Advaita Vedanta becomes self-evident from our presentation in part I.

4. The concept of the Absolute tends to be dualistic and should therefore be avoided. *Paramarthika,* God is not cut off from the world. It is a holistic standpoint which tries to think the ontological totality. *Vyavaharika* is a relational standpoint which takes into account the interdependence of all partial systems of reality.

5. F. Chr. Baur, *Die Christliche Lehre von der Dreieinigkeit und Menschwerdung Gottes . . . , Bd. II, 180.*

6. *P. Tillich, Systematic Theology,* vol. III, (Chicago: Univ. of Chicago Press, 1963) 422.

7. Cf. E. Jungel, *Gott als Geheimnis der Welt* (Tübingen, 1977,472ff.) English translation, *God as the Mystery of the World.* Grand Rapids, Eerdmans, 1983; 387ff.

8. This problem has been genially presented by E. Jungel, op. cit., (German), 289f.

9. Clement of Alexandria, *Strom.* 5,11.

10. Abhishiktananda, *Saccidananda. A Christian Approach to Advaitic Experience* (Delhi, 1974) 3ff.

11. Dennis the Areopagite, *Myst. Theol.* 5, Migne PG 1048A,15; Sankara, BSB, introduction to I,1,8; cf. also B. Griffiths, *Vedanta and Christian Faith* (Los Angeles, 1973) 16ff.

12. J. Monchanin, "The Quest for the Absolute," in: *Indian Culture and the Fulness of Christ* (Madras, 1957) cited by J. Mattam, *Land of the Trinity. A Study of Modern Christian Approaches to Hinduism* (Bangalore, 1975) 160.

13. Jüngel, op. cit., 334.

14. Richard of St. Victor, *De trin.* 4,22; Migne 196, 945c, cited by A. Peters, "Die Trinitätslehre in der Reformatorischen Christenheit," in: ThLZ 94 (1969) 8: col. 568.

15. Cf. H. Junghans, "Das Word Gottes bei Luther während seiner ersten Psalmenvorlesung," in ThLZ 100 (1975) 3: cols. 161–174, and I. Hirudayam, "Theology as Vag-Vidya or Word-Wisdom," in: *Unique and Universal: An Introduction to Indian Theology.* Ed.: J.B. Chethimattam (Bangalore, 1972); also R. Panikkar, "Vac in the Sruti," in: *God's Word among Men.* Ed.: G. Gispert-Sauch, 3ff.

16. BS I,I,2.

17. Luther, WA 54,64,4; Cf. Barth KD I,1,414.

18. Irenaeus, *Adv. haer.* 2,13,4ff; Clement, *Strom.* 5,11. Cf. W. Pannenberg, "Die Aufnahme des philosophischen Gottesbegriffs als dogmatisches Problem der frühchristlichen Theologie," in *Grundfragen systematischer Theologie* I, 320ff.

19. This contradicts R. Otto, *West-östliche Mystik*, 10, who understands Sankara's *sat* in relationship to *nirguna brahman* as an identity between the subject and the function of being.

20. Barth, op. cit., 415.

21. Pannenberg, op. cit., 341; on Christ as mediator of creation. Cf. Barth, op. cit., 464ff.

22. Jüngel, op. cit., 526.

23. For the exegetical connections of some of the texts used here, and especially the particularity of this problem in relationship to the synoptic parallels, cf. Schoonenberg, "Gods tegenwoordigheid in Christus," in: *Tijdschrift voor Theologie* 1969,9 (Nijmegen, 1969) 378ff.

24. R. Panikkar, "Isvara and Christ as a Philosophical Problem," 8ff.

25. On Tatian cf. Baur, Bd. I,166; cf. Schoonenberg, op. cit., 386f.

26. Tertullian, *Adv. Prax.*, 5.

27. Baur, 168ff.

28. Tertullian, *Adv. Prax* 8. Irenaeus objects to this (*Adv. Haer.* 2,8) because he saw *prolatio* as a form of emanation. In this he was in fact further from gnosticism than, for example, Tertullian, and the main reason for this was that Irenaeus wanted to avoid all anthropomorphisms.

29. Baur, Bd. I, 684ff.

30. Baur, 676f.

31. E. Kaesemann, *An die Römer. Kommentar zum Paulusbrief* (Berlin, 1974) 236.

32. We understand this interpretation in the sense of the dialectical logic of Hegel. Cf. ch. 8.

33. On this concept and on the experience of unity of time, cf. C.S. Weizsäcker, "Die Zeit und das Eine," in: *Der Garten des Menschlichen*, 432ff.

34. This notion of time would not be far from what Barth, using the doctrine of the trinity, said concerning God's becoming, or what Jüngel has stated clearly in *Gottes Sein ist im Werden*, 112 (n. 149): "Since God's being is in becoming, eternity is constituted by temporality in the sense of a being-in and a being-with of the three

modes of time. Not that becoming in temporality is the proper being of God, but rather the latter constitutes the former."

35. Barth interprets this in such a way that he grasps the Spirit as the wonder of real humankind in the presence of revelation. (KD I,1 350). The term we suggest, *actus participationis*, brings out more strongly the act of being seized by the self-revealing God.

36. R. Panikkar, *The Trinity and World Religions*, 56, describes the danger of basing a spirituality only on the historically conditioned figure of Jesus Christ.

37. Barth, 474.

38. G. Ebeling, *Dogmatik des christlichen Glaubens*, Bd. III, 157ff.

39. "Spirit of God, Spirit of Christ. Ecumenical Reflections on the filioque-Controversy." Ed.: Lukas Vischer. (WCC Geneva, 1981); J. Moltmann, *Trinität und Reich Gottes*, 198ff.

40. Cf. Moltmann, op. cit., 199ff. Undoubtedly the *filioque* does not imply *eo ipso* a restrictive interpretation of the Spirit as *per filium* in the instrumental sense. If there is an archetypal meaning at the basis of the presentation, perhaps in the sense of the Indian *hiranyagarbha* or of a *spiritus creator* who produces the newness of creativity through Christ as the universal mediator of creation, then both aspects can be taken into account.

41. D. Staniloae, "The Procession of the Holy Spirit from the Father and His Relation to the Son, on the Basis of our Deification and Adoption," in *Spirit of God, Spirit of Christ*, 178. Cf. M. v. Brück, "Sanctification, Glorification, Theosis," in: *A Dialogue Begins. Lutheran-Orthodox Dialogue in India*. Eds.: K.M. George/H. Hoefer. (Kottayam/Madras, 1983) 268ff. A significant Eastern Christian judgment on this is: ". . . it is the Holy Spirit who *restores* the *imago Dei*, not by instrumental grace but *participation in the Divine Nature*." (P. Bilaniuk, *Theology and Economy of the Holy Spirit. An Eastern Approach*, 163.)

42. The parallel between the Christian experience of Spirit and the corresponding Indian spiritual experience has been impressively presented by Swami Abhishiktananda (H. LeSaux). Cf. Abhishiktananda, "Communication in the Spirit," in: *Religion and Society* 18,3 (Bangalore, 1970), esp. 39f.

43. We need not take into account here Luke's peculiarity of distinguishing *pneuma* and *dynamis* in the sense that the latter is the powerful deed and the former is understood in a spiritual sense. Cf. E. Schweizer, *Heiliger Geist* (Stuttgart, 1978) 84.

44. Unfortunately Schweizer is guilty of this generalization, op. cit., 24.

45. E. Schweizer, 163f.

46. Hegel, *Phenomenology:* "Thus the life of God and divine cognition may well be spoken of as a disporting of Love with itself; but this idea sinks into mere edification, and even insipidity, if it lacks the seriousness, the suffering, the patience, and the labour of the negative." By this remark, Hegel himself points to the connection noted above between love and the cross.

47. Jüngel, *Gott als Geheimnis der Welt,* 513.

48. Thus it is understandable that the dove came to symbolize the Spirit, since it brings the message of God's reunifying love.

49. Paulos Mar Gregorios, "God's Becoming a Human Being and Human Beings Becoming God." A brief introduction to the Christian Doctrine of Theosis, in: *A Dialogue Begins.* Lutheran-Orthodox Dialogue in India, 283ff.; esp. 294.

50. V.V. Lossky, *The Mystical Theology of the Eastern Church* (London, 1957) 196.

51. "Jesus Christ—the Life of the Word." Contribution by an Orthodox Working Group on the Main Theme of the Sixth Assembly of the WCC, in: *The Ecumenical Review,* vol. 34,3 (July, 1982) 291.

52. Lossky, 198.

53. Lossky, 198f.: "Eastern tradition has always asserted simultaneity in the synergy of divine grace and human freedom."

Chapter 11

1. C. Colpe, "Drängt die Religionsgeschichte nach einer Summe," in: EvTh 39 (1979) 211–233.

2. E. Fromm, *Psychoanalyse und Religion* (Munich, 1980) 31.

3. Ibid., 33ff.

4. Ibid., 111f.

5. H. Dumoulin, *Östliche Meditation und christliche Mystik* (Freiburg/Munich, 1966) 82.

6. Ibid., 79.

7. K. Rahner/H. Vorgrimmler, *Kleines Theologisches Wörterbuch* (Freiburg, 1961), cited in Dumoulin, op. cit., 85.

8. When H. Ott, with reference to Heidegger's analysis of *Dasein* (*Das Reden vom Unsagbaren:* Stuttgart, 1978, 47f.), speaks of

320 THE UNITY OF REALITY

the primary experience of being grasped and links it to intuition, which comes forth from "creative emptiness" (86ff.), he is pointing in the same direction.

320 THE UNITY OF REALITY

the primary experience of being grasped and links it to intuition, which comes forth from "creative emptiness" (86ff.), he is pointing in the same direction.

9. R. Panikkar, *Words and Terms* (Instituto dei Studi Filosofici: Roma, 1980) 133.

10. T.R.V. Murti, *The Central Philosophy of Buddhism* (London, 1980) 112f.

11. For Ninian Smart *anubhava* is "immediate consciousness of the existence of the self in a non-dualistic teaching." (*Doctrine and Argument in Indian Philosophy*. London, 1964; 226).

12. Cf. K.C. Pandey, *Abhinavagupta. An Historical and Philosophical Study* (Varanasi, 1963) 286,305.

13. BSB I,I,2.

14. R.P. Singh, *The Vedanta of Sankara: A Metaphysics of Value*, Vol. I (Bharat Publ., 1949) 186f.

15. A.K. Coomaraswamy, "On the One and Only Transmigrant," in: *Selected Papers*, Vol. II. Ed.: R. Lipsey. Bollingen Series LXXXIX (Princeton Univ. Press, 1977) 66ff.

16. Meister Eckhart, *Deutsche Schriften*. Ed.: Pfeiffer (Göttingen, 1924) 180,261. The classical Vedantic texts are MU IV,4; BU IV,IV,6 etc.; cf. Coomaraswamy, op. cit.

17. R. Bultmann, *Das Evangelium des Johannes* (Göttingen, 1957) 378.

18. B. Griffiths, *Vedanta and Christian Faith* (Los Angeles, 1973) 12.

19. BU II,IV,14 & IV,V,15.

20. J. Kattackal, *Religion and Ethics in Advaita* (Kottayam, 1982) 10f.

21. R. Panikkar, *Kultmysterium im Hinduismus und Christentum* (Freiburg/Munich, 1964) 39.

22. F. Staal, *Exploring Mysticism* (Berkeley, 1975) 31. Thus also Erich Fromm takes exception to the extended meaning of mysticism as the irrational and emphasizes "that in Hindu and Buddhist thinking, as well as in Spinoza, mysticism is rather a most highly developed form of rationalism in religious thought." And he cites Albert Schweitzer: "thinking carried out to the end leads . . . somewhere and somehow to a living mysticism, which is logically necessary for all thinking." (*Verfall und Wiederaufbau der Kultur, Kulturphilosophie*. Erster Teil Munich, 1951; 57) cf. Fromm, op. cit., 111.

23. Here we should include esp. the connections between dreams, their interpretation, and the application to meditation. Cf. Naropa's dream-Yoga as one of the six ways of Tibetan Yoga.

24. R. Panikkar, "Rtatattva: A Preface to a Hindu-Christian Theology," in: *Jeevadhara* 49 (Jan/Feb, 1979) 60f.

25. J. Hick, *Philosophy of Religion* (New Delhi, 1981) 78.

26. W.T. Stace, *Mysticism and Philosophy* (London, 1961) 140.

27. D.S. Lopez, "Approaching the Numinous: Rudolf Otto and Tibetan Tantra" in: *Philosophy East and West* 29/4 (1979) 467ff.

28. *Tibetan Toga and Secret Doctrines*, ed.: W.Y. Evans-Wentz (London, 1958) 75f.

29. W. Pannenberg, *Wahrheit, Gewissheit und Glaube*, 263f.

30. H. Chaudhuri, "Yoga-Psychologie," in *Transpersonale Psychologie*. Ed.: Ch.T. Tart (Olten, 1978) 332.

31. H. Ott, *Das Reden vom Unsagbaren*, 131ff.

32. Ken Wilber, *The Spectrum of Consciousness* (Wheaton, Ill., 1979); idem., *The Atman Project. A Transpersonal View of Human Development* (Wheaton, 1980); idem., *Eye to Eye: The Quest for the New Paradigm* (New York, 1983).

33. K. Wilber, "Reflections on the New-Age Paradigm," in: *The Holographic Paradigm and Other Paradoxes* (Boulder/London, 1982) 254ff.

34. Cf. B. Bruteau on the essence of the contemplative way: "Insight and Manifestation: A Way of Prayer in a Christian Context—I," in: *Prabuddha Bharata* (July, 1983) 309.

35. B. Bruteau, 308. Creativity is seen here as *the* characteristic of the personal, which thus fully meets God or the underlying reality on the problem. On the problem of creativity in relationship to a holistic conception of reality, cf. M. v. Brück, "Sunyata in Madhyamika Philosophy and the Christian Concept of God," in: *Jeevadhara* 78 (Nov. 1983) 385–402.

36. Teresa of Avila, *Way of Perfection*, ch. 24.

37. J. Aumann, "The Practice of Prayer According to St. Teresa of Avila," in: *Asian Religious Traditions and Christianity*, Thomasian Forum 2 (Manila, 1983) 204.

38. Ibid., 213f.

39. Church tradition distinguishes *meditatio* and *contemplatio*. Meditation is concentration on an object, a more reflective consideration of a word of scripture, the sufferings of Christ, etc., while contemplation is the transobjective union of consciousness in God.

Both are steps along a way. This is how we understand them here. When we speak of meditation we thus mean all the exercises which lead to the non-dualistic experience of unity with and in God.

40. C. Albrecht, *Psychologie des Mystischen Bewusstseins* (Mainz, 1976) 142.

41. M. v. Brück, "Holistic Vision in Eastern Religions—Reality as Consciousness," in *Indian Theological Studies* XXII/1 (Bangalore, 1985) 28–61; K.C. Pandey, *Abhinavagupta*; L.N. Sharma, *Kasimir Saivism:* Bharatiya Vidya Prakashan. (Varanasi, 1972); Motilal Pandit, "Abhinavagupta's Contribution to Kasmira Saivism," in: *Indian Theological Studies* XX/2–3 (1983) 137 ff.

42. Albrecht, op. cit., 140 ff.

43. The otherwise highly recommendable writing of the "Frankfurter," the *Theologica Germanica*, which is also praised by Luther, unfortunately also fails in its denial of the concrete—vehemently, apparently (ch. 25). It argues the same way as many Indian philosophers. Thus spiritual fronts do not proceed along confessional lines, but rather within the praxis of *each* religion. It would be worthwhile to study pietistic, evangelical, pentecostal, and charismatic movements on the basis of this viewpoint.

44. *The Way of a Pilgrim* (Ballantine Books: New York, 1974).

Chapter 12

1. R. Panikkar, "The Law of Karman and the Historical Dimension of Man," in: *Philosophy East and West* XXII,1 (Honolulu, 1972) 37; (reprinted in *Myth, Faith and Hermeneutics.* New York, 1979. 362 ff.)

2. The term "centering" describes the coming to a middle point of all possible categorial determinations. It transcends the categorial although it manifests itself in the categorial.

3. Ch. Birch, "Shöpfung Technik und Überleben der Menschheit: . . . und füllet die Erde," in: *Jesus Christus befreit und eint. Vorträge von Nairobi.* Ed. H. Krueger, Oekumen. Rundschau, Beiheft n. 30 (Frankfurt, 1976) 110.

4. *Ramdas Speaks*, Bd. 3. Edited by K.M. Munshi, R.R. Diwakar (Bombay, 1971) 132. Deceptively similar is the formulation of H. Ott, who speaks of the "super-personality of the personal God" (H. Ott, *Wirklichkeit und Glaube*, Bd. II. Der Persönliche Gott. Goettingen, 1969: 165).

5. KU I,III,11 and Sankara's commentary.

6. BG XV, 16–18.

7. Cf. W. Pannenberg, "Der Gott der Geschichte. Der trinitarische Gott und die Wahrheit der Geschichte," in: *Grundfragen Systematischer Theologie*, Bd. II, 117.

8. H. Ott, op. cit., 380.

9. Barth, KD III,2,433.

10. In any case this is not Sankara's position.

11. R. Otto, *West-östliche Mystik*, 284f.

12. W. Pannenberg, "Wie kann heute glaubwürdig von Gott geredet werden?" Materials for the 14th Evangelical Kirchentag (Stuttgart, 1969) 11. Describing God as one who loves freely is a trend in recent Evangelical theology which goes back to Barth.

13. Cf. supra, 53–56 & below 215–220; Panikkar, op. cit., 25ff.

14. I have borrowed this, to my mind, fortunate formulation from W. Pannenberg, "Die Aufnahme des philosophischen Gottesbegriffs." op. cit., 344.

15. We cannot pursue the problem in detail here. Cf. M. v. Brück, "Gemeinschaft oder Kollektivismus? Bemerkungen zur Transformation menschlicher Beziehungen," in: *Rechtstaat und Christentum*, Bd. II. Ed.: E. Behrendt. (Munich, 1982) 173–195.

16. E. Pagels, *The Gnostic Gospels* (New York, 1981) 40ff.

17. Ibid., XXXVIIIff.

18. Moltmann, *Trinität und Reich Gottes*, esp., 215ff.

19. Idem., *Kirche in der Kraft des Geistes* (Munich, 1975) 342.

20. J. Hick, *Death and Eternal Life* (London, 1976) 297ff.

21. A. Koeberle, *Das Geheimnisvolle Reich der Seele* (Freiburg, 1984) 89ff. This also holds true for A. Rosenberg, *Die Seelenreise* (Olten, 1952).

22. H. Torwesten, *Sind wir nur einmal auf Erden? Die Idee der Reinkarnation angesichts des Auferstehungsglaubens* (Freiburg, 1983). This interesting book does not sufficiently differentiate among the Indian (and also Christian) ideas and does not at all grasp the uniqueness of Advaita Vedanta versus the popular ideas (133ff.). In particular, it does not distinguish precisely the "I," "soul," and *atman*. Thus it is not clear *what* is reincarnated. In a systematical-theological appendix, N. Klaes complains that the "Hindu opposition of unity and plurality is never included in the absolute freedom of God's love" (199). This is precisely what we are attempting by means of the advaitic teaching of the trinity, to be described in the following discussion on rebirth.

23. Hick, op. cit., 366ff.

24. Ibid., 393.

25. Köberle, op. cit., 90ff. It is true that joy and bodily suffering have only relative value and thus bring no ultimate happiness. *Kama* (enjoyment), *artha* (goals and duty), and *moksa* (release) are on a gradual scale of values.

26. Ingeborg Y. Wendt, *Japanische Dynamik und Indische Stagnation? Eine Antwort auf Theoretische Entwicklungsmodelle* (Darmstadt, 1978) 144ff.

27. R. Sheldrake, *A New Science of Life: The Hypothesis of Formative Causation* (Los Angeles, 1981); A.P. Smith, "Mutiny of the Beagle," in *ReVision* VII/1 (Spring, 1984) 18ff.

28. Thus, unconvincingly, Köberle, op. cit., 90.

29. BU IV,IV,5.

30. Sheldrake, op. cit., 92ff.; 170ff.; cf. also D. Bohm, *Wholeness and Implicate Order* (London, 1981), esp. 210ff. I have taken the diagram from Sheldrake.

31. "The doer of the acts . . . he is the enjoyer!" (SU II,6); Panikkar, op. cit., 366ff.

32. Panikkar, 370.

33. Swami Chinmayananda, *Vedanta the Science of Life* (Bombay, 1979) 220. The Indian threefold path of salvation (*jnana-bhakti-karma-Yoga*) would be absurd if this were not so. It is unfortunate that Christian theology—for apologetic reasons—is often imprecise on this particular point or argues falsely. For example O.V. Jathanna, *The Decisiveness of the Christ-Event and the Universality of Christianity in a World of Religious Plurality* (Bern, 1981), 475ff.; regrettably Köberle, too, 96ff. (It is absurd to ground the prohibition against the slaughter of cows in *karman*-theory, for in this case no flies should be killed either, which would be correct for Jainism and Buddhism, but by no means for Hindus.)

34. R. Panikkar, "Rtatattva. A Preface to a Hindu-Christian Theology," in: *Jeevadhara* 49 (Jan/Feb., 1979) 39f.

35. For a detailed presentation of the various teachings on rebirth, cf. the excellent studies of A.L. Herman, *The Problem of Evil and Indian Thought* (Delhi/Varansi, 1976) 143–230.

36. Hick, op. cit., 297f.

37. Koeberle, op. cit., 108ff.

38. J. Hick, *Philosophy of Religion* (New Delhi, 1981) 107ff.

39. Panikkar, *The Law of Karman*, 305f.

40. Hick, *Death and Eternal Life*, 305f.

41. Japji, 4, cited in Panikkar, op. cit., n. 3.

42. Sankara's commentary on BS I,I,5.

43. This theory is presented in detail by A.K. Coomaraswamy, "On the One and Only Transmigrant," in: *Selected Papers* Vol. II, Bollingen Series LXXXIX, 66ff.; cf. also Hick, op. cit., 311ff.; Panikkar, op. cit.

44. Hick, op. cit., 315.

45. BS XV,8.

46. BS VIII,6.

47. Coomaraswamy, op. cit., 82.

48. This is true not only in Buddhism. Also in Vedanta no "substance" is reborn (MU III,2, etc.). Not life, but the fire of life is handed on, i.e., an energy of a subtle order. *Atman* is something completely different. (Coomaraswamy, op. cit., 76.)

49. Hick, op. cit., 378.

50. Koeberle, op. cit., 107ff.; cf. esp. the study by J. Stevens, Reinkarnation. *Der Mensch im Wandel von Tod und Wiedergeburt* (Freiburg im Bresgau, 1979).

51. Cf. n. 27 and the book by Bohm (n. 30). This is not the place to comment on these models in detail.

52. Hick, op. cit., 383ff.

53. Thus Koeberle, who cites Jung-Stilling, op. cit., 111.

54. Against Hick, 364.

55. Cf. our study on creativity above (p. 157ff.).

56. Cited according to Coomaraswamy, op. cit., 70, n. 16.

57. BG XIII, 16: *caavibhaktam ca sthitam vibhaktam iva bhutesu.* (It is undivided and yet seems to be divided in all beings.)

58. Augustine, *Ep. ad Parthos* P.L.35,2055.

Chapter 13

1. R. Panikkar, *Salvation in Christ: Concreteness and Universality; The Supername* (Santa Barbara, 1972) 52.

2. H. Smith, *Beyond the Post-Modern Mind* (New York, 1982) 6.

3. Panikkar, op. cit., 37f.

4. Thomas Aquinas, *Summa Theol.* I,34,3: *Deus enim cognoscendo se congnoscit omnem creaturam. Verbum igitur in mente conceptum, est repraesentativum omnis eius quod actu intelligitur ... Sed quia Deus uno actu et se et omnia intelligit, unicum Verbum eius est expressivum non solum Patris, sed etiam creaturarum.* Cited by Panikkar, ibid., 43, A2.

5. Sankara, *Vivekacudamani*, 51.

6. Sankara, ibid., 3.

7. S. Radhakrishnan, *The Bhagavad Gita* (New Delhi, 1971) 62 with reference to BG XVIII,66.

8. Sankara's commentary on BG XVI,4.

9. Radhakrishnan, op. cit., 63.

10. W. McNamara, "Die Mystische Tradition des Christentums und die Psychologie," in: *Transpersonale Psychologie* (ed. Ch. T. Tart); Oltem/Freiburg, 1978, 528.

11. J. Aumann, "The Practice of Prayer according to St. Teresa of Avila," in: *Asian Religious Traditions and Christianity*, 211ff.

12. Augustine, *Conf.* III,6,11: *tu autem eras interior intimo meo;* Luther, WA 23,137,33ff.: God is to the creature "tieffer, ynnerlicher, gegenwertiger denn die creatur yhr selbs ist" (deeper, more interior, more present than the creature is to itself).

13. Gregory of Nyssa, *De Inst. Christ.* P.G. XLVI, 289c.

14. V. Lossky, *The Mystical Theology of the Eastern Church*, 198.

15. Barth, KD I,1,260f.

16. Clement of Alexandria, *Protr.* I,5,3.

17. *Guidelines on Dialogue* (WCC Geneva, 1979), Part II E Synkretism, 14f.

18. Cf. R. Panikkar, *Myth, Faith and Hermeneutics* (New York, 1979); H. Ott, "The Beginning Dialogue between Christianity and Buddhism, the Concept of a 'Dialogical Theology' and the Possible Contribution of Heideggerian Thought," in: *Japanese Religions*, Vol. II,2–3 (Sept. 1980) 74ff. H. Ott tries to apply Heidegger's concept of "being neighbor" to the relationships between religions.

19. R. Panikkar, "Ratatatta," in: *Jeevadhata*, 49, 1979, p. 60f.

20. H. Ott, "Einander Verstehen. Thesen und Bemerkungen zum Dialog," in: *Denkpause im Dialog.* Ed. Mildenberger (Frankfurt, 1978), 38.

21. R. Panikkar, "Christians and the So-called 'Non-Christians,' " in: *Cross Currents* 22,3 (1972) 298.

22. D. Fisher-Barnicol, Introduction to: K. Nishitani, *Was ist Religion?* (Frankfurt, 1982) 16.

23. R. Panikkar, "The Dialogical Dialogue," in: *The World's Religious Traditions*, ed. F. Whaling, 216f.

24. J. Moltmann, *Kirche in der Kraft des Geistes* (Munich, 1975) 180ff.

25. H. Zimmer, *Philosophie und Religion Indiens*, 368.

26. Ott, *The Beginning Dialogue*, 96.

27. We have presented elsewhere the fact that even the late Barth hesitantly began to use similar expressions, although not on the basis of his trinitarian theology, cf. M. v. Brück, *Möglichkeiten und Grenzen einer Theologie der Religionen* (Berlin, 1979).

28. Cf. M. v. Brück, 142 ff. The concept means that ontologically all persons are on the same level, yet noetically they all live in their own different situations. It is inferred from the method of Socrates. For him truth is found in dialogue and brought to the light by a *maieusis*—the art of the midwife.

29. R. Panikkar, "Prolegomena to the Problem of Universality of the Church," in: *Unique and Universal.* Ed.: J.B. Chethimattam (Bangalore, 1972) 155 ff.

Chapter 14

1. Cf. M. v. Brück, "Die Vedantische Erfahrung des Einen als Basis für Prinzipien der Ethik," in: ZMR 67 (1983) 163–190.

2. BU V,II,3. The third concept is ordinarily translated "compassion." But since this word connotes not so much active participation as passive "suffering-with," it is inadequate. What is meant is expressed well by Albert Schweitzer's "reverence towards life."

3. Sankara's commentary on BU V,II,3.

4. Sankara's introductory commentary on BU V,III.

5. BG II,12–15; II,48f.

6. BS XIII,27.

7. IU 6–8.

8. IU 6; BS VI,29.

9. M.K.V. Iyer, *Advaita Vedanta. According to Sankara* (Bombay, 1964) 61.

10. BU II,IV,5.

11. BU I,IV,8.

12. Cf. Sankara's commentary on BU II,IV,5. The fact that this position was never put into practice in a consequent way is also Gandhi's criticism of orthodox Hinduism: the caste-less are excluded from unity since they have no access to the holy scriptures. Nor is this striking contradiction removed by Advaita Vedanta.

13. H. Zimmer, *Philosophie und Religion Indiens*, 214.

14. TU XI,2–4 and Sankara's commentary. In Sankara, however, the tendency is to exempt the *jivanmukta* from all duties, i.e., to detach the *paramarthika* levels from *dharma*.

15. BU IV,IV,5.

16. Swami Vimalananda, Introduction to *Chandogya Upanishad.* edited by Sri Ramakrishna Math, XXXIIf.

17. Zimmer, 99f.

18. Ch. Birch, "Schöpfung, Technik und Überleben der Menschheit . . . und füllet die Erde," in: *Jesus Christus befreit und eint.,* 108.

19. C.F. v. Weizsäcker, "Notizen zum Gespräch uber Physik und Religion," in *Der Garten des Menschlichen,* 441.

20. R. Lannoy, *The Speaking Tree. A Study of Indian Culture and Society* (Oxford, 1971) 20f.

21. Cf. BG III,35; XVIII,47.

22. C.F. v. Weizsäcker, "Selbstdarstellung," in: *Der Garten des Menschlichen,* 597.

Index of Names

329

General Index